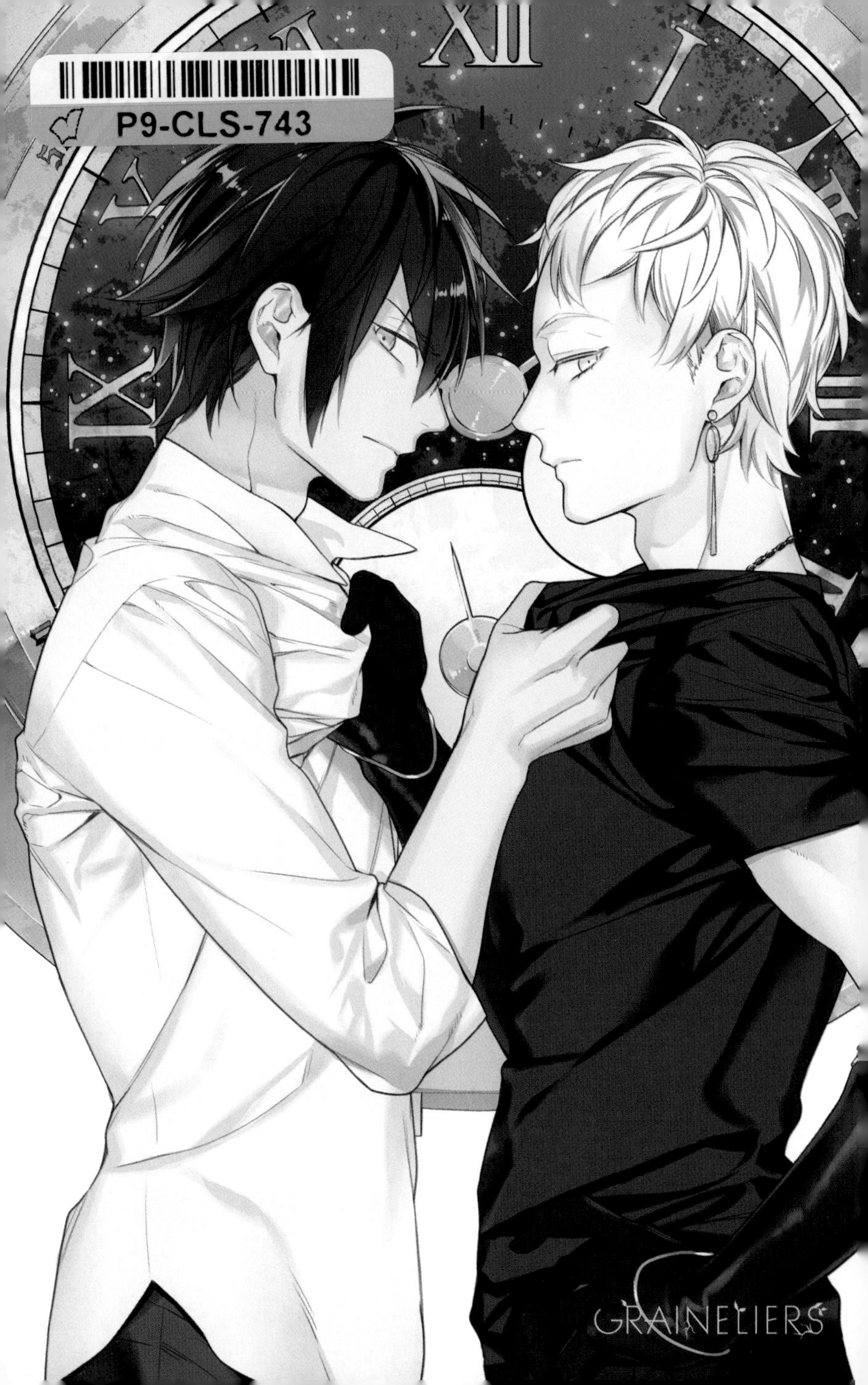
GRAINELIERS

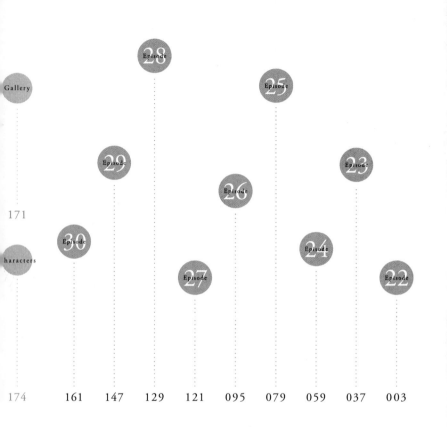

GRAINELIERS
3

Episode 《 22 》 —— 《 30 》

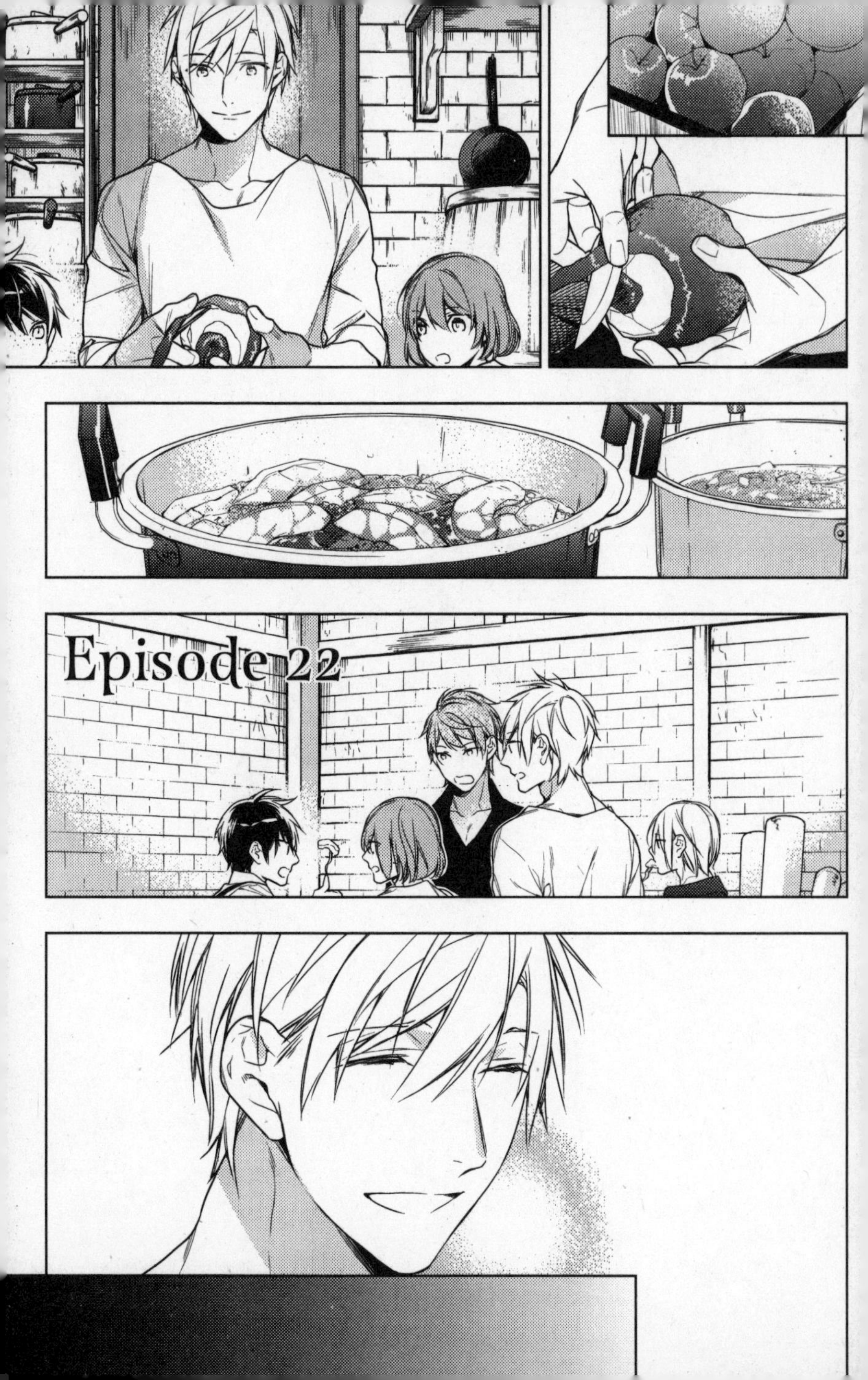
Episode 22

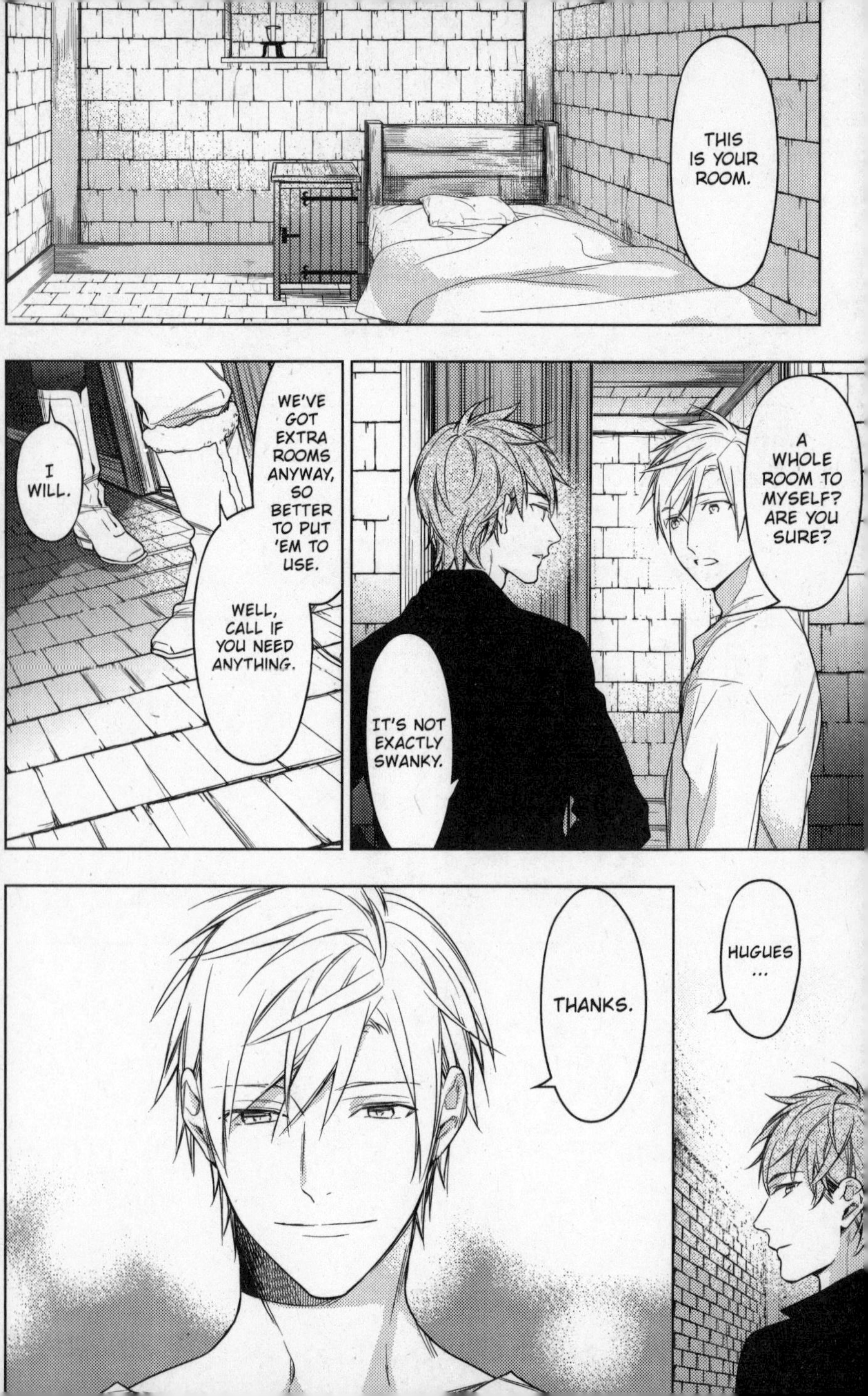
THIS IS YOUR ROOM.
A WHOLE ROOM TO MYSELF? ARE YOU SURE?
IT'S NOT EXACTLY SWANKY.
WE'VE GOT EXTRA ROOMS ANYWAY, SO BETTER TO PUT 'EM TO USE.
WELL, CALL IF YOU NEED ANYTHING.
I WILL.
HUGUES...
THANKS.

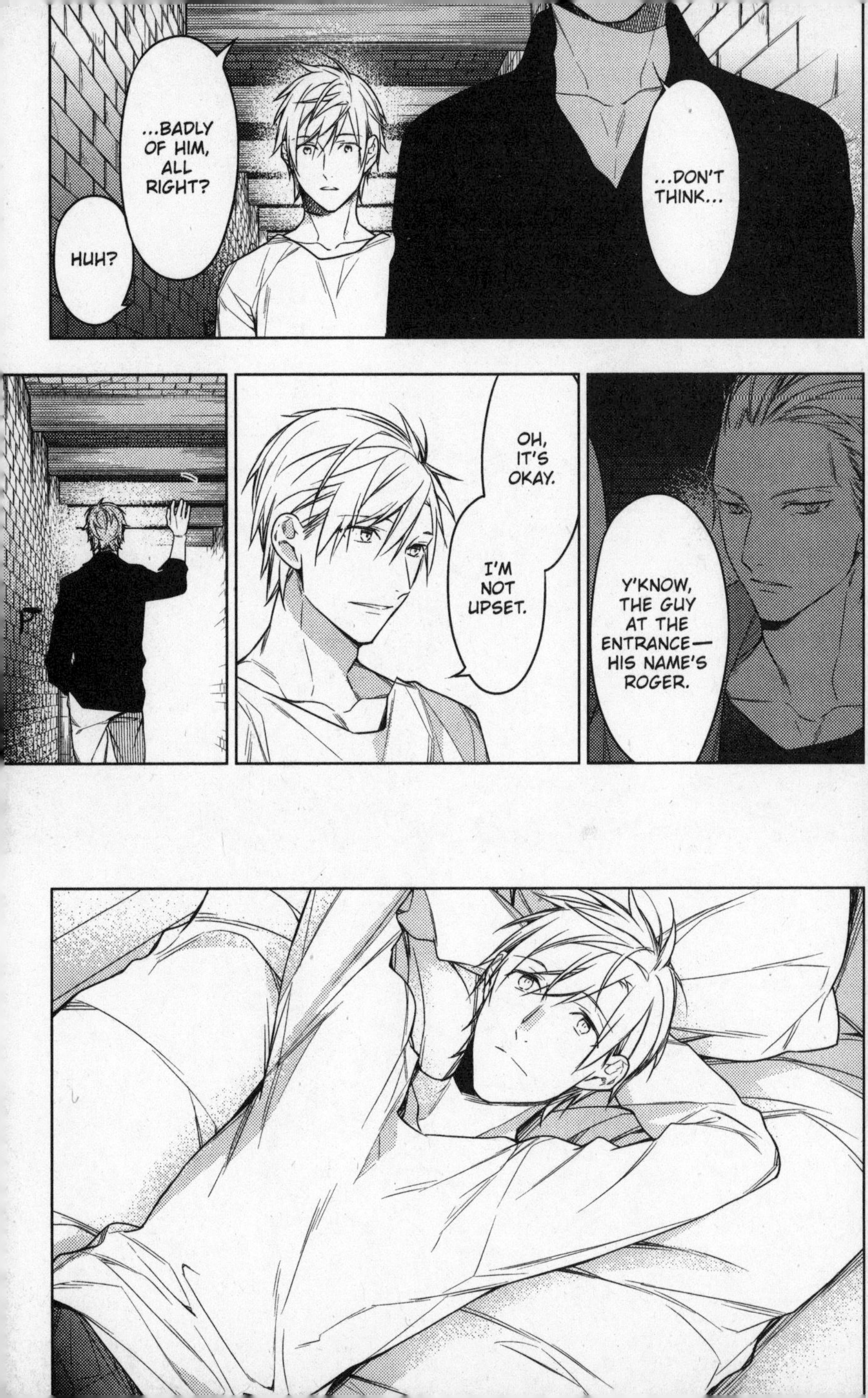
...DON'T THINK...
...BADLY OF HIM, ALL RIGHT?
HUH?
Y'KNOW, THE GUY AT THE ENTRANCE—HIS NAME'S ROGER.
OH, IT'S OKAY.
I'M NOT UPSET.

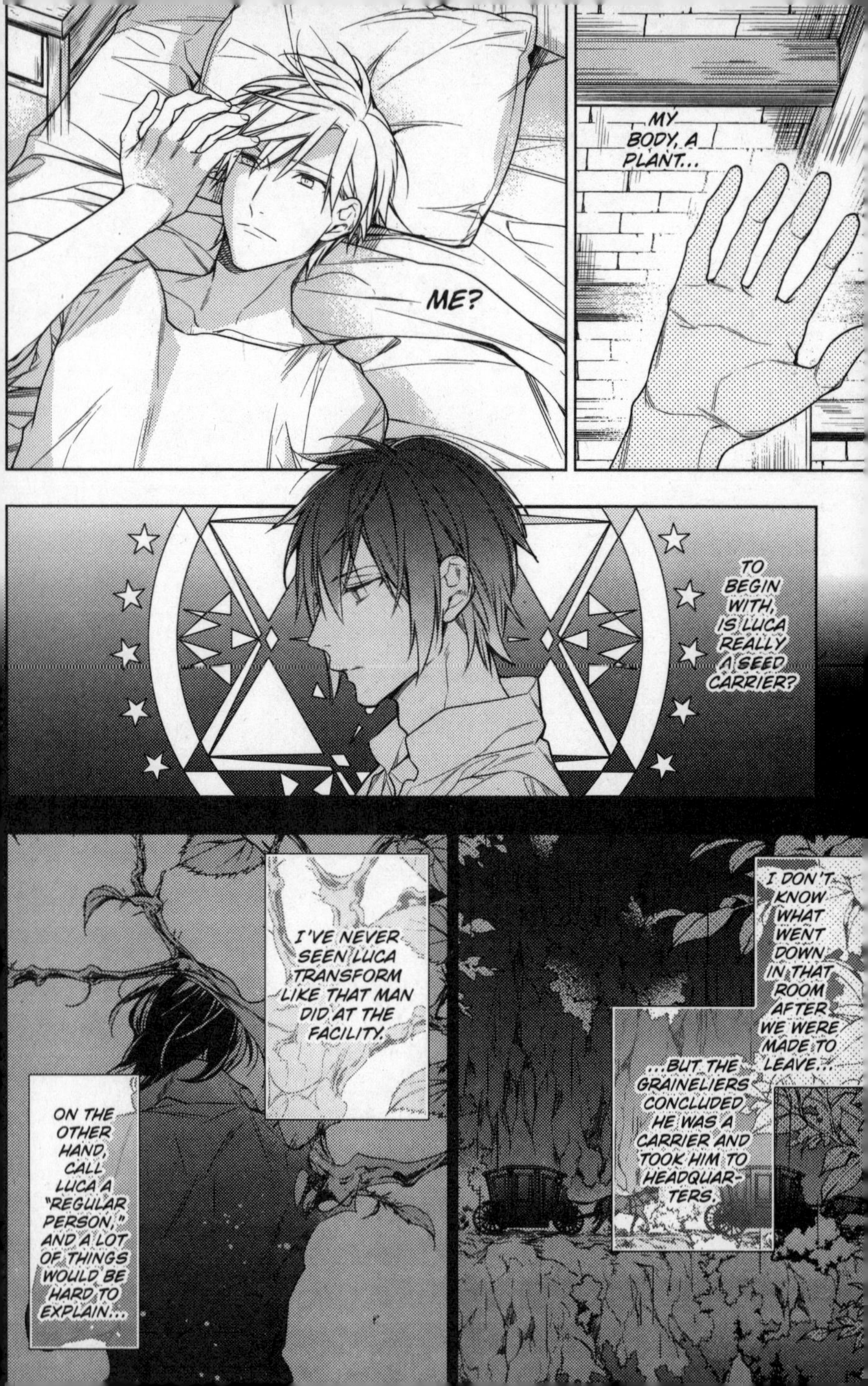
MY BODY, A PLANT...
ME?
TO BEGIN WITH, IS LUCA REALLY A SEED CARRIER?
I DON'T KNOW WHAT WENT DOWN IN THAT ROOM AFTER WE WERE MADE TO LEAVE...
...BUT THE GRAINELIERS CONCLUDED HE WAS A CARRIER AND TOOK HIM TO HEADQUARTERS.
I'VE NEVER SEEN LUCA TRANSFORM LIKE THAT MAN DID AT THE FACILITY.
ON THE OTHER HAND, CALL LUCA A "REGULAR PERSON," AND A LOT OF THINGS WOULD BE HARD TO EXPLAIN...

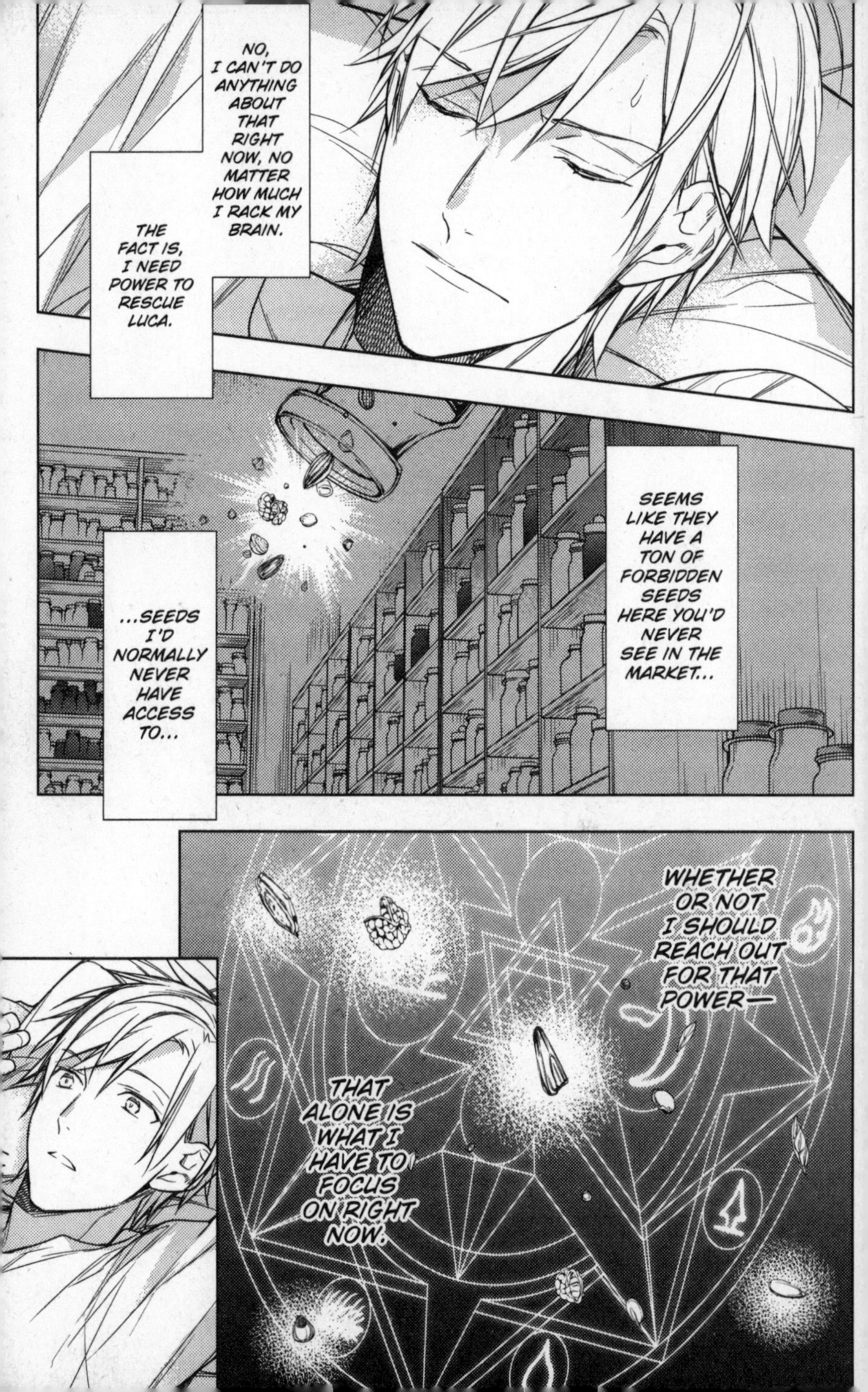
NO, I CAN'T DO ANYTHING ABOUT THAT RIGHT NOW, NO MATTER HOW MUCH I RACK MY BRAIN.
THE FACT IS, I NEED POWER TO RESCUE LUCA.
SEEMS LIKE THEY HAVE A TON OF FORBIDDEN SEEDS HERE YOU'D NEVER SEE IN THE MARKET...
...SEEDS I'D NORMALLY NEVER HAVE ACCESS TO...
WHETHER OR NOT I SHOULD REACH OUT FOR THAT POWER—
THAT ALONE IS WHAT I HAVE TO FOCUS ON RIGHT NOW.

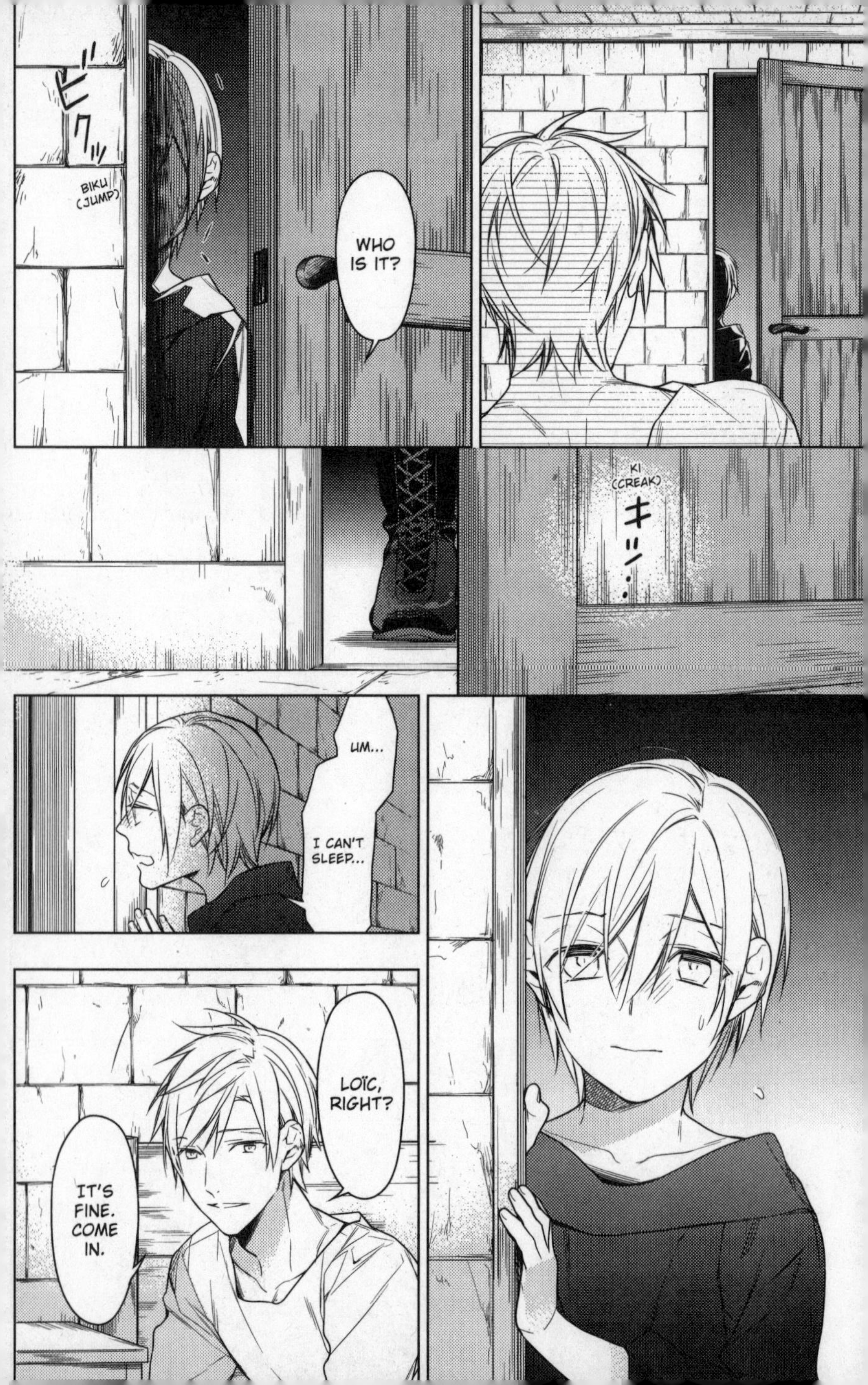
WHO IS IT?
ビクッ
BIKU (JUMP)
KI (CREAK)
キッ‥
UM...
I CAN'T SLEEP...
LOÏC, RIGHT?
IT'S FINE. COME IN.

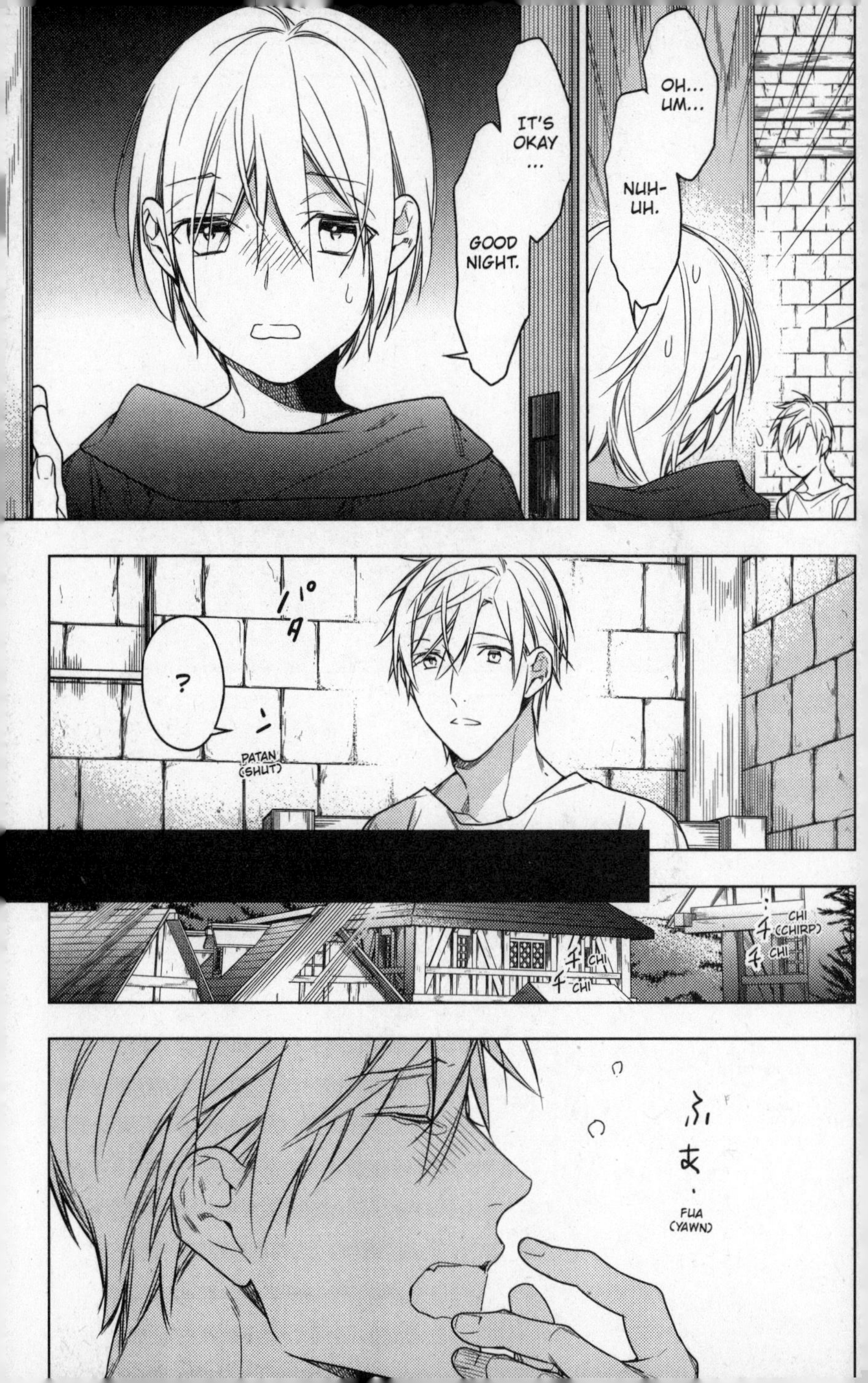
OH... UM...
NUH-UH.
IT'S OKAY ...
GOOD NIGHT.
パ
?
PATAN (SHUT)
[redacted]
CHI (CHIRP)
CHI
チ CHI
チ CHI
ふぁ
FUA (YAWN)

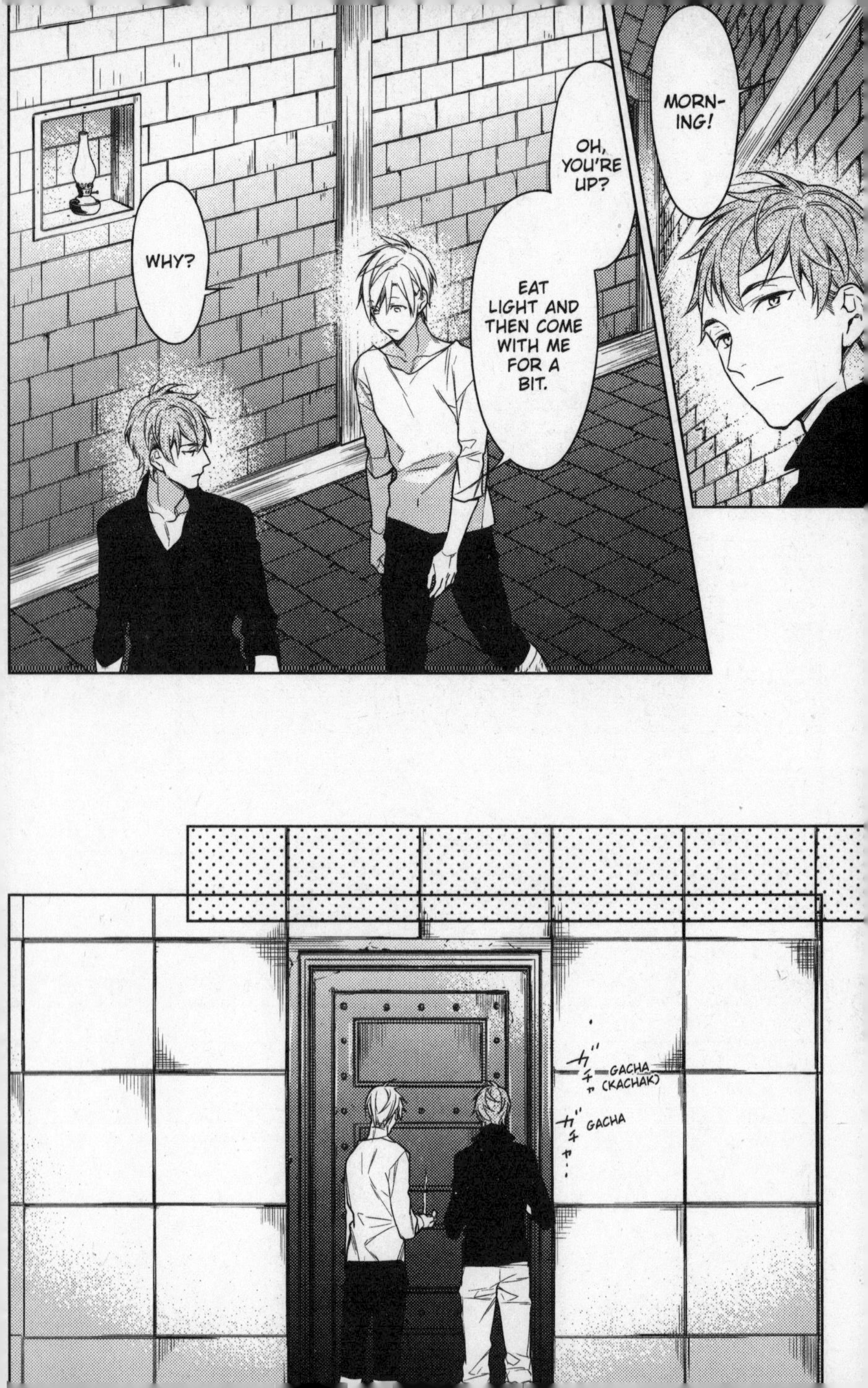
MORNING!
OH, YOU'RE UP?
EAT LIGHT AND THEN COME WITH ME FOR A BIT.
WHY?
ガチャ GACHA (KACHAK)
ガチャ… GACHA

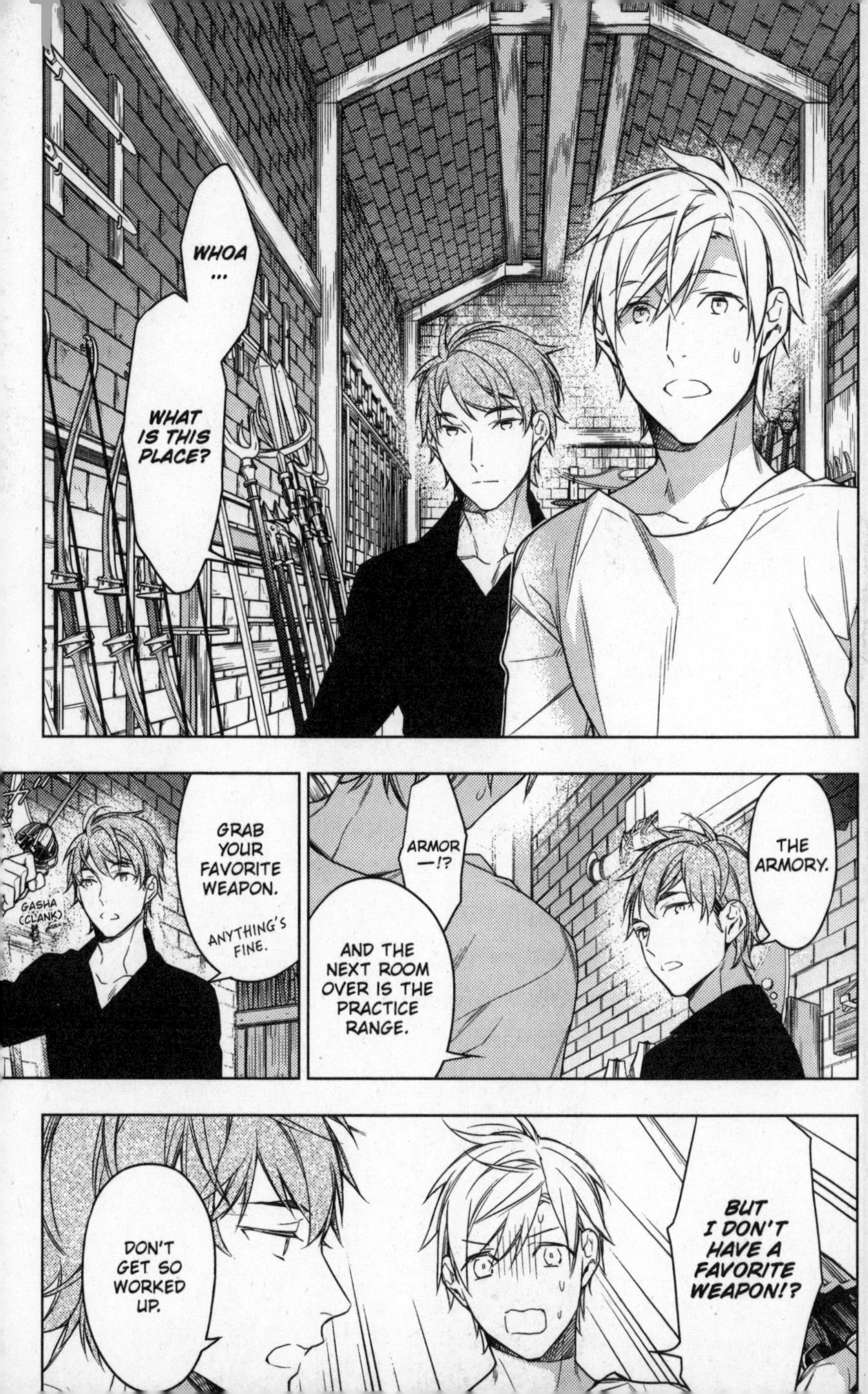
WHOA ...
WHAT IS THIS PLACE?
THE ARMORY.
ARMOR—!?
AND THE NEXT ROOM OVER IS THE PRACTICE RANGE.
GRAB YOUR FAVORITE WEAPON.
ANYTHING'S FINE.
GASHA (CLANK)
BUT I DON'T HAVE A FAVORITE WEAPON!?
DON'T GET SO WORKED UP.

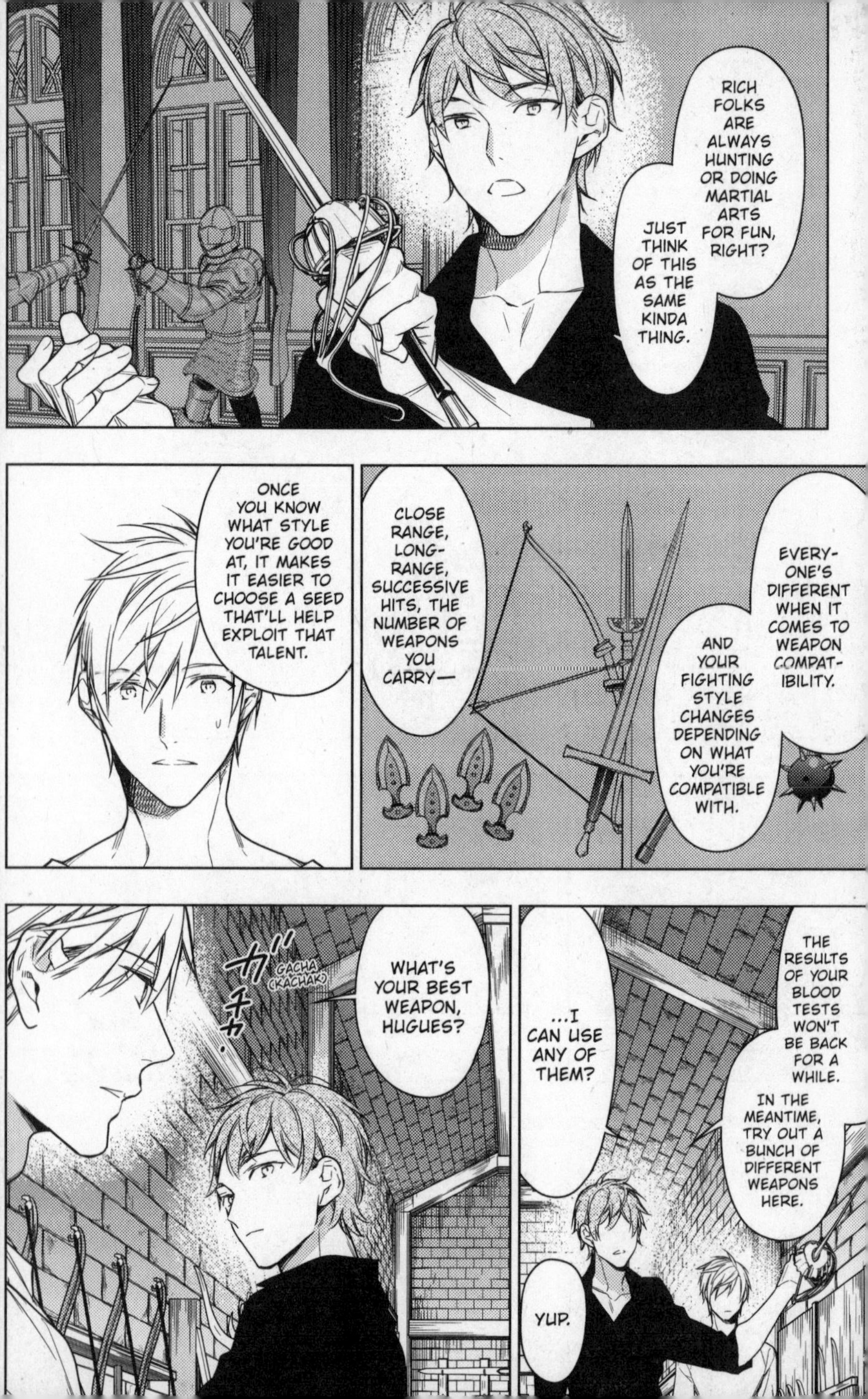
RICH FOLKS ARE ALWAYS HUNTING OR DOING MARTIAL ARTS FOR FUN, RIGHT?
JUST THINK OF THIS AS THE SAME KINDA THING.
EVERY-ONE'S DIFFERENT WHEN IT COMES TO WEAPON COMPAT-IBILITY.
AND YOUR FIGHTING STYLE CHANGES DEPENDING ON WHAT YOU'RE COMPATIBLE WITH.
CLOSE RANGE, LONG-RANGE, SUCCESSIVE HITS, THE NUMBER OF WEAPONS YOU CARRY—
ONCE YOU KNOW WHAT STYLE YOU'RE GOOD AT, IT MAKES IT EASIER TO CHOOSE A SEED THAT'LL HELP EXPLOIT THAT TALENT.
THE RESULTS OF YOUR BLOOD TESTS WON'T BE BACK FOR A WHILE.
IN THE MEANTIME, TRY OUT A BUNCH OF DIFFERENT WEAPONS HERE.
...I CAN USE ANY OF THEM?
YUP.
WHAT'S YOUR BEST WEAPON, HUGUES?
GACHA (KACHAK)

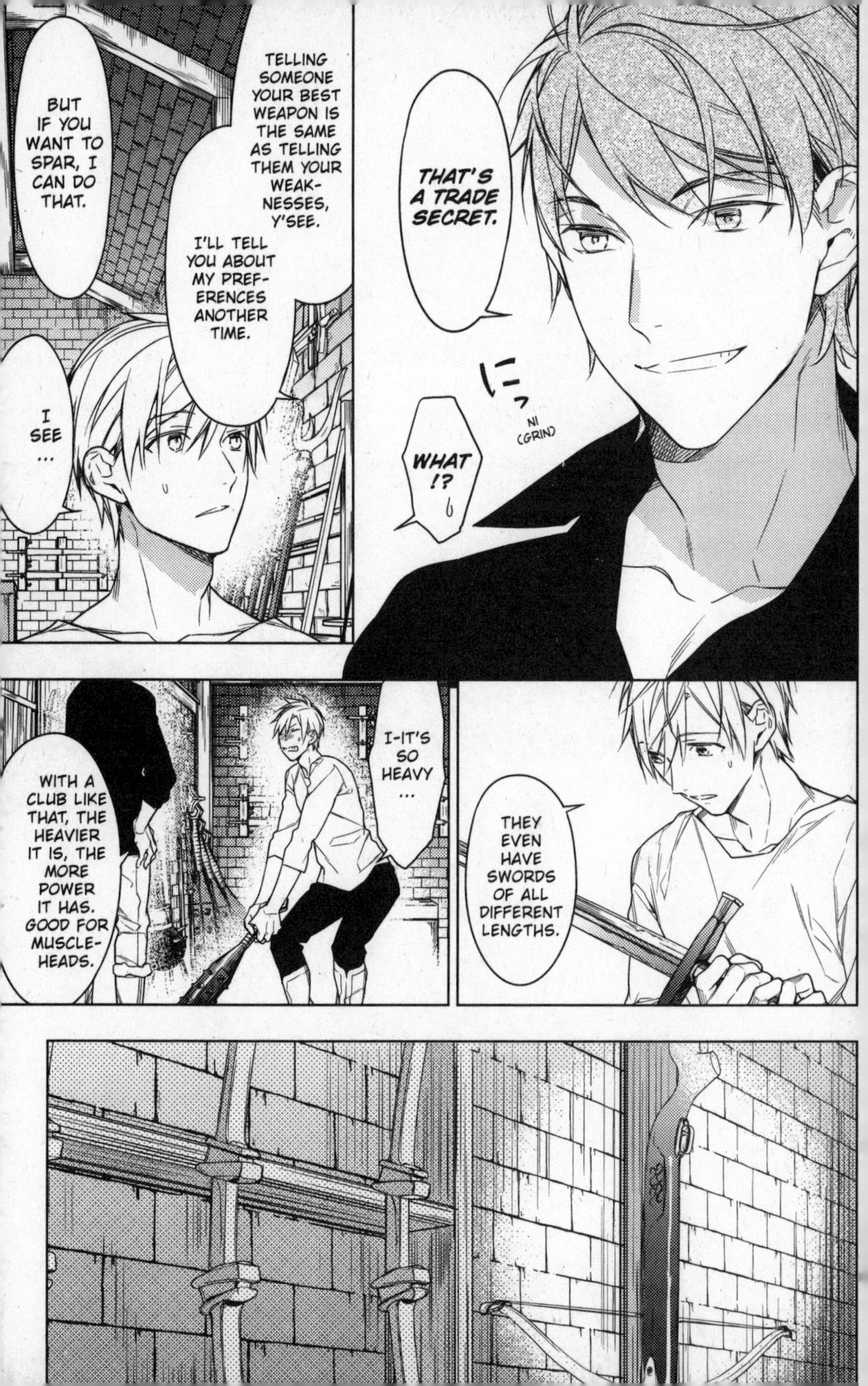
THAT'S A TRADE SECRET.
にっ
NI (GRIN)
WHAT!?
TELLING SOMEONE YOUR BEST WEAPON IS THE SAME AS TELLING THEM YOUR WEAKNESSES, Y'SEE.
BUT IF YOU WANT TO SPAR, I CAN DO THAT.
I'LL TELL YOU ABOUT MY PREFERENCES ANOTHER TIME.
I SEE...
THEY EVEN HAVE SWORDS OF ALL DIFFERENT LENGTHS.
I-IT'S SO HEAVY...
WITH A CLUB LIKE THAT, THE HEAVIER IT IS, THE MORE POWER IT HAS. GOOD FOR MUSCLEHEADS.

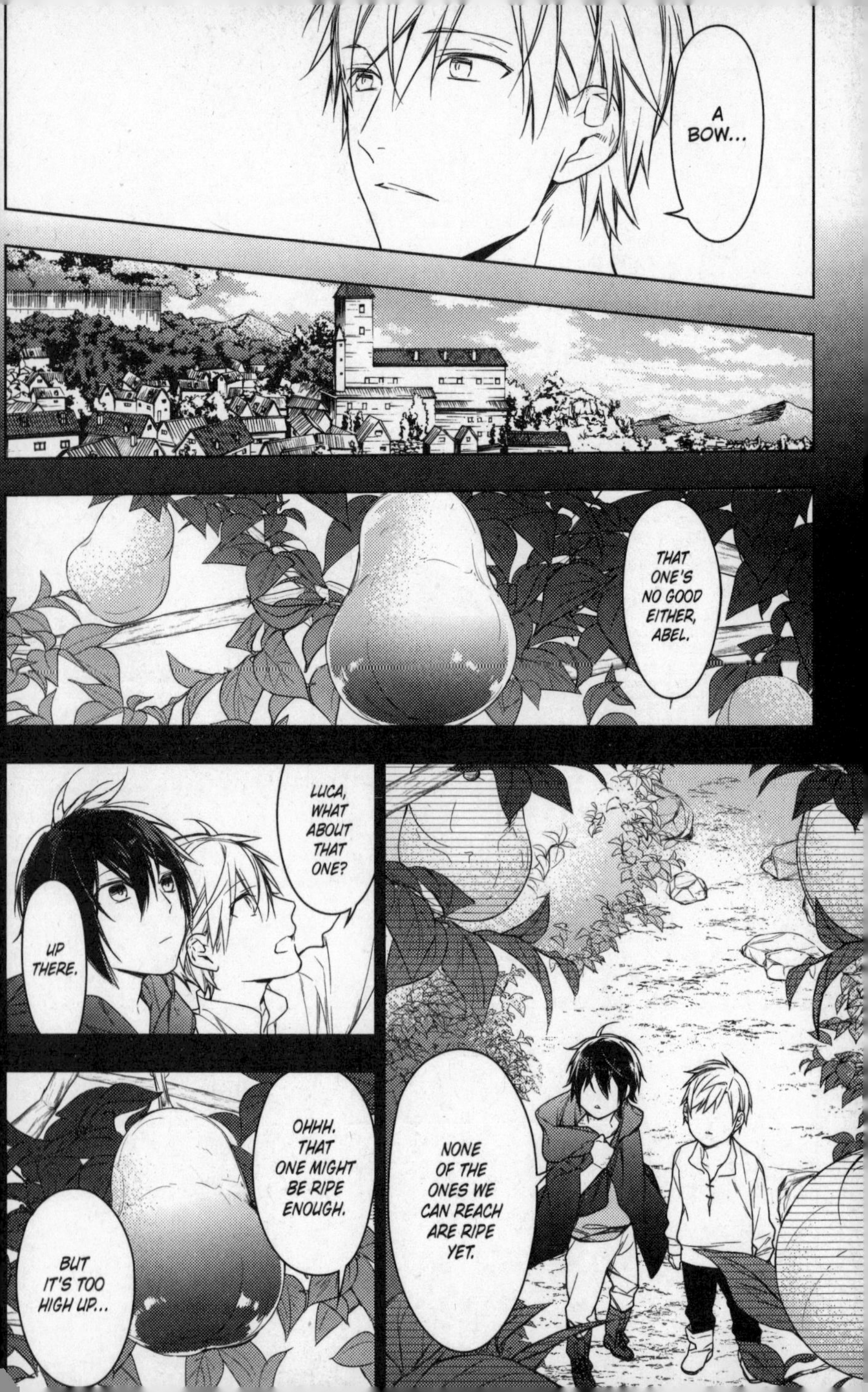
A BOW...
THAT ONE'S NO GOOD EITHER, ABEL.
NONE OF THE ONES WE CAN REACH ARE RIPE YET.
LUCA, WHAT ABOUT THAT ONE?
UP THERE.
OHHH. THAT ONE MIGHT BE RIPE ENOUGH.
BUT IT'S TOO HIGH UP...

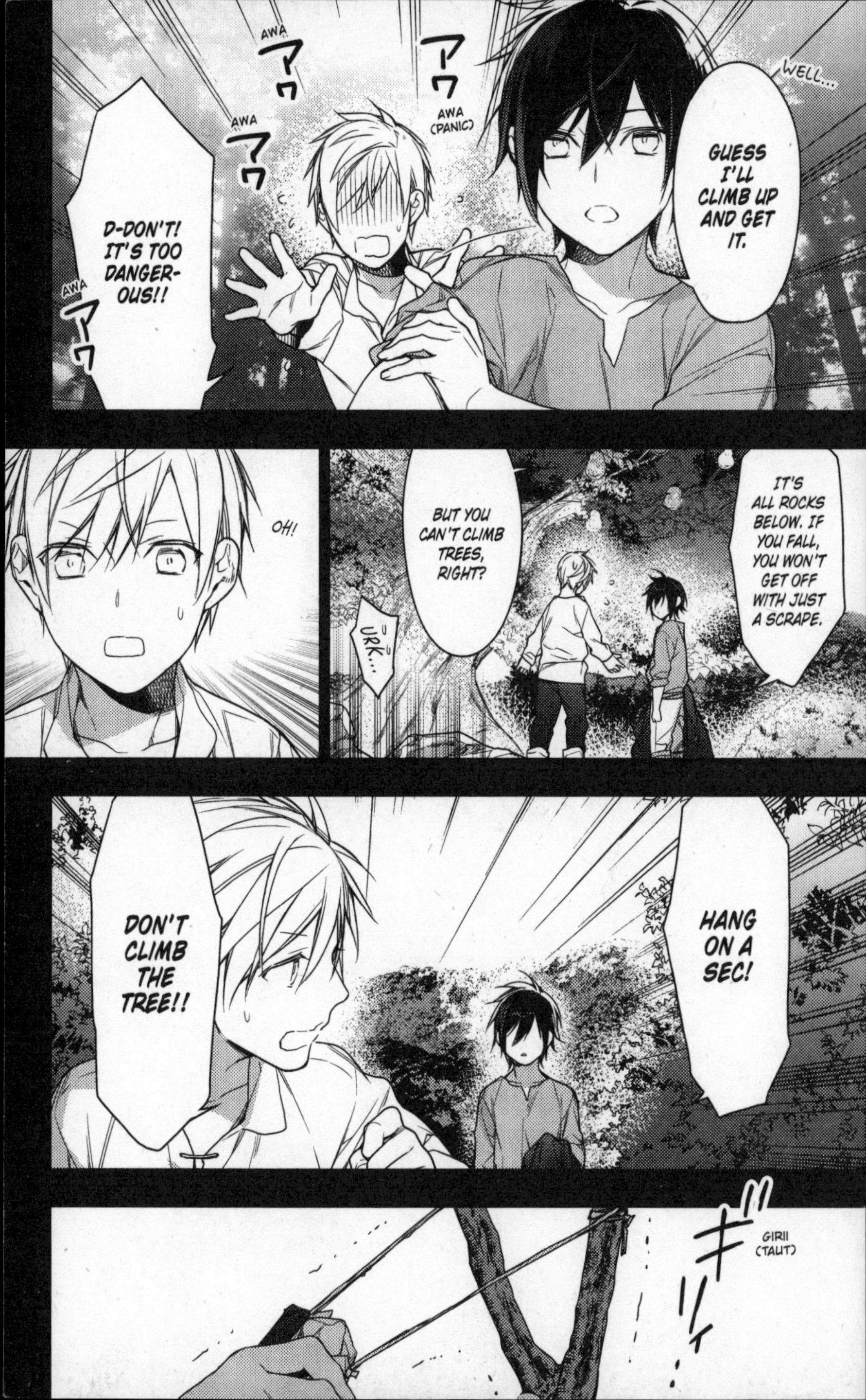
WELL...
GUESS I'LL CLIMB UP AND GET IT.
アワ
AWA (PANIC)
アワ
AWA
アワ
AWA
D-DON'T! IT'S TOO DANGER-OUS!!
アワ
AWA
IT'S ALL ROCKS BELOW. IF YOU FALL, YOU WON'T GET OFF WITH JUST A SCRAPE.
BUT YOU CAN'T CLIMB TREES, RIGHT?
URK...
OH!
HANG ON A SEC!
DON'T CLIMB THE TREE!!
ギリィ
GIRII (TAUT)

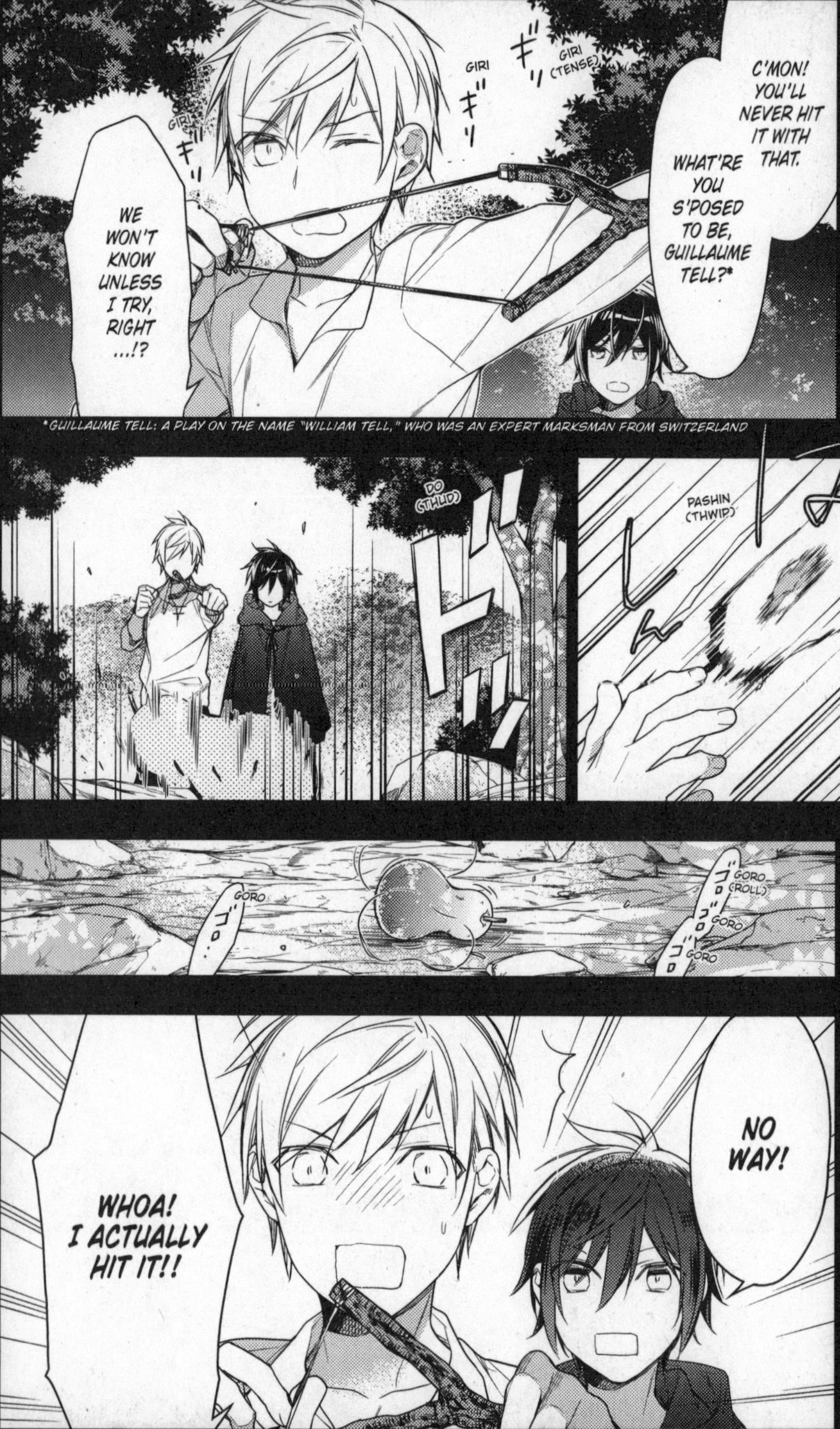
C'MON! YOU'LL NEVER HIT IT WITH THAT.
WHAT'RE YOU S'POSED TO BE, GUILLAUME TELL?*
GIRI (TENSE)
GIRI
GIRI
WE WON'T KNOW UNLESS I TRY, RIGHT ...!?
*GUILLAUME TELL: A PLAY ON THE NAME "WILLIAM TELL," WHO WAS AN EXPERT MARKSMAN FROM SWITZERLAND
PASHIN (THWIP)
DO (THUD)
GORO (ROLL)
GORO
GORO
GORO
NO WAY!
WHOA! I ACTUALLY HIT IT!!

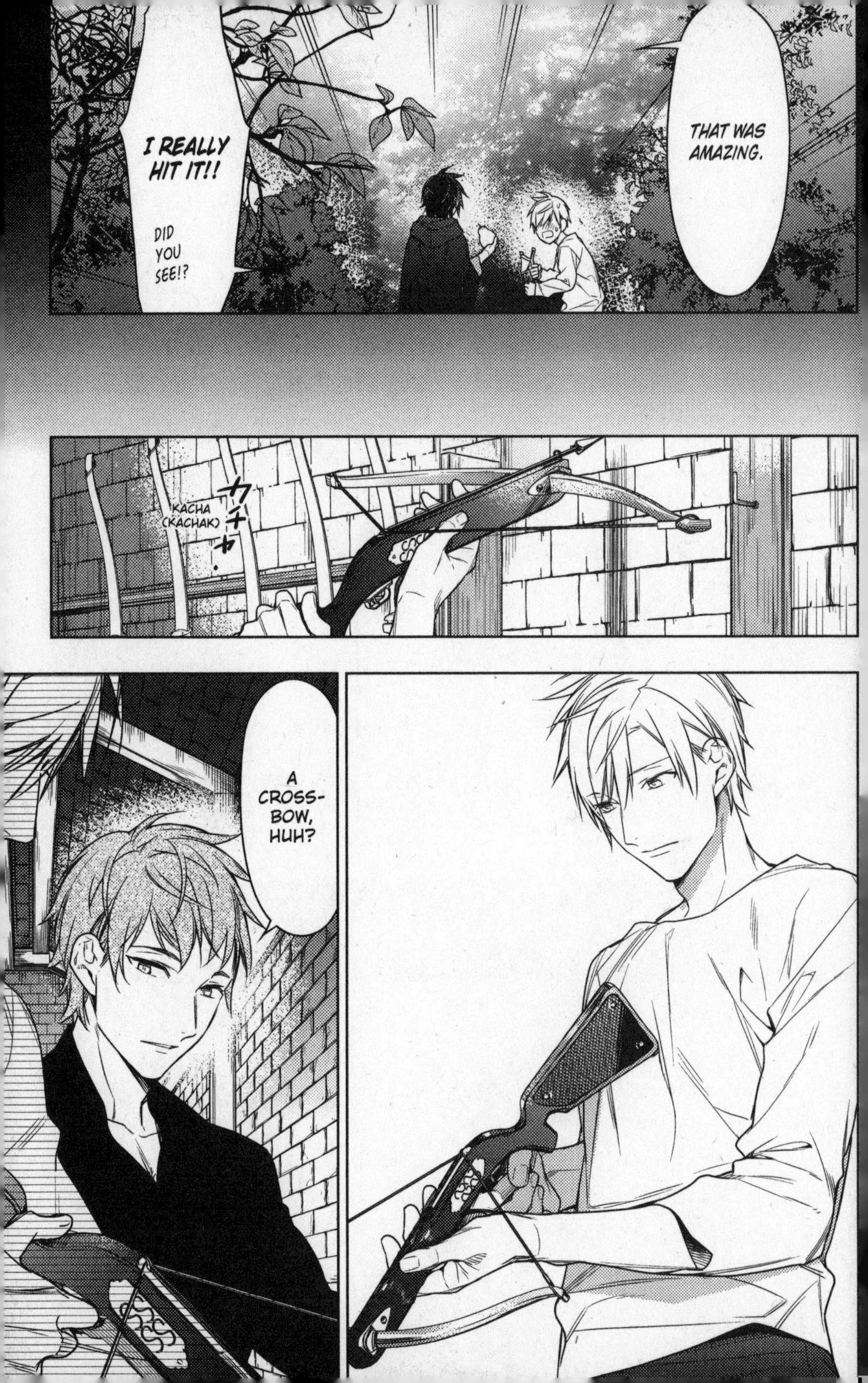
THAT WAS AMAZING.
I REALLY HIT IT!!
DID YOU SEE!?
カチャ
KACHA (KACHAK)
A CROSS-BOW, HUH?

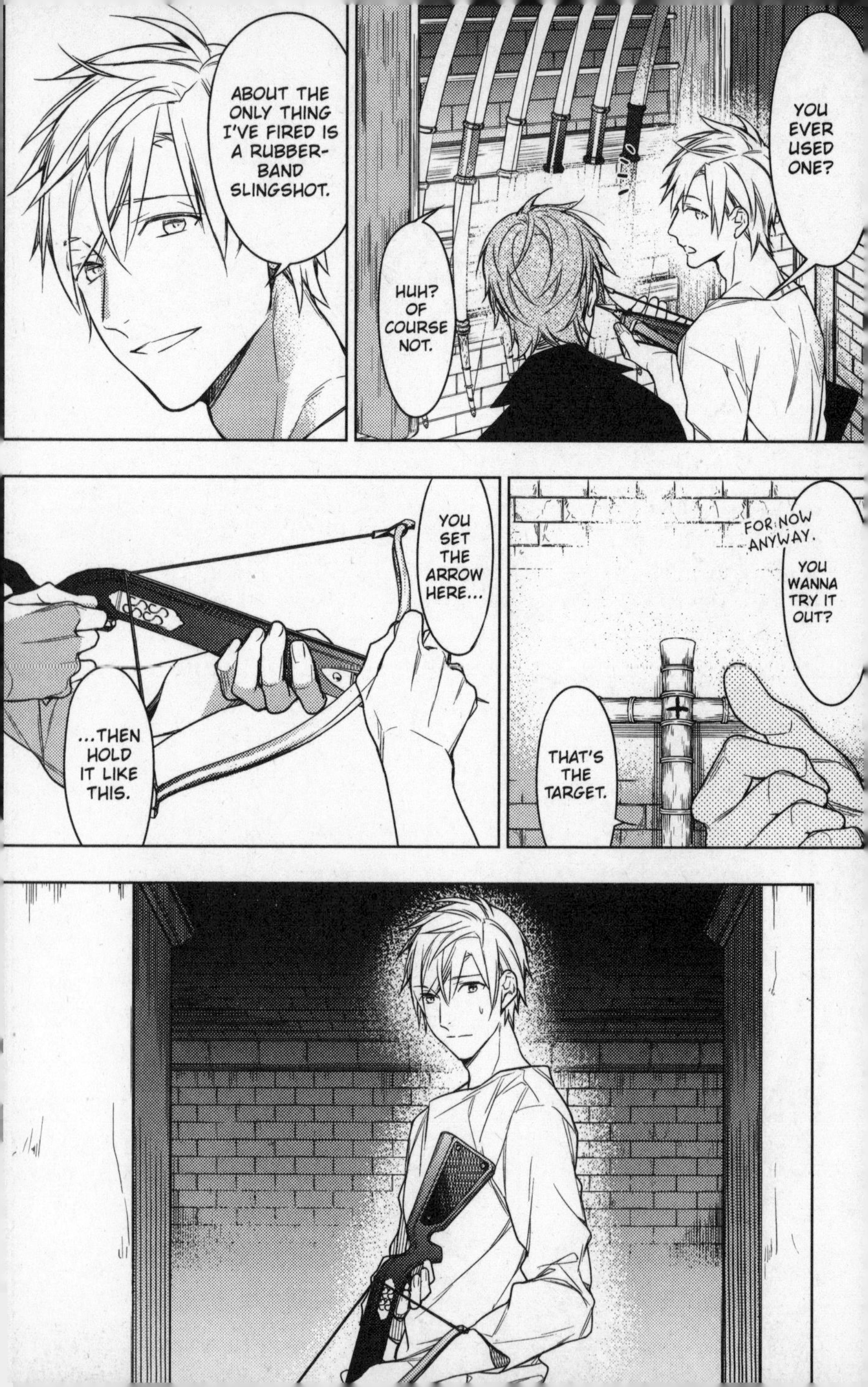
YOU EVER USED ONE?
HUH? OF COURSE NOT.
ABOUT THE ONLY THING I'VE FIRED IS A RUBBER-BAND SLINGSHOT.
YOU WANNA TRY IT OUT?
FOR NOW ANYWAY.
THAT'S THE TARGET.
YOU SET THE ARROW HERE...
...THEN HOLD IT LIKE THIS.

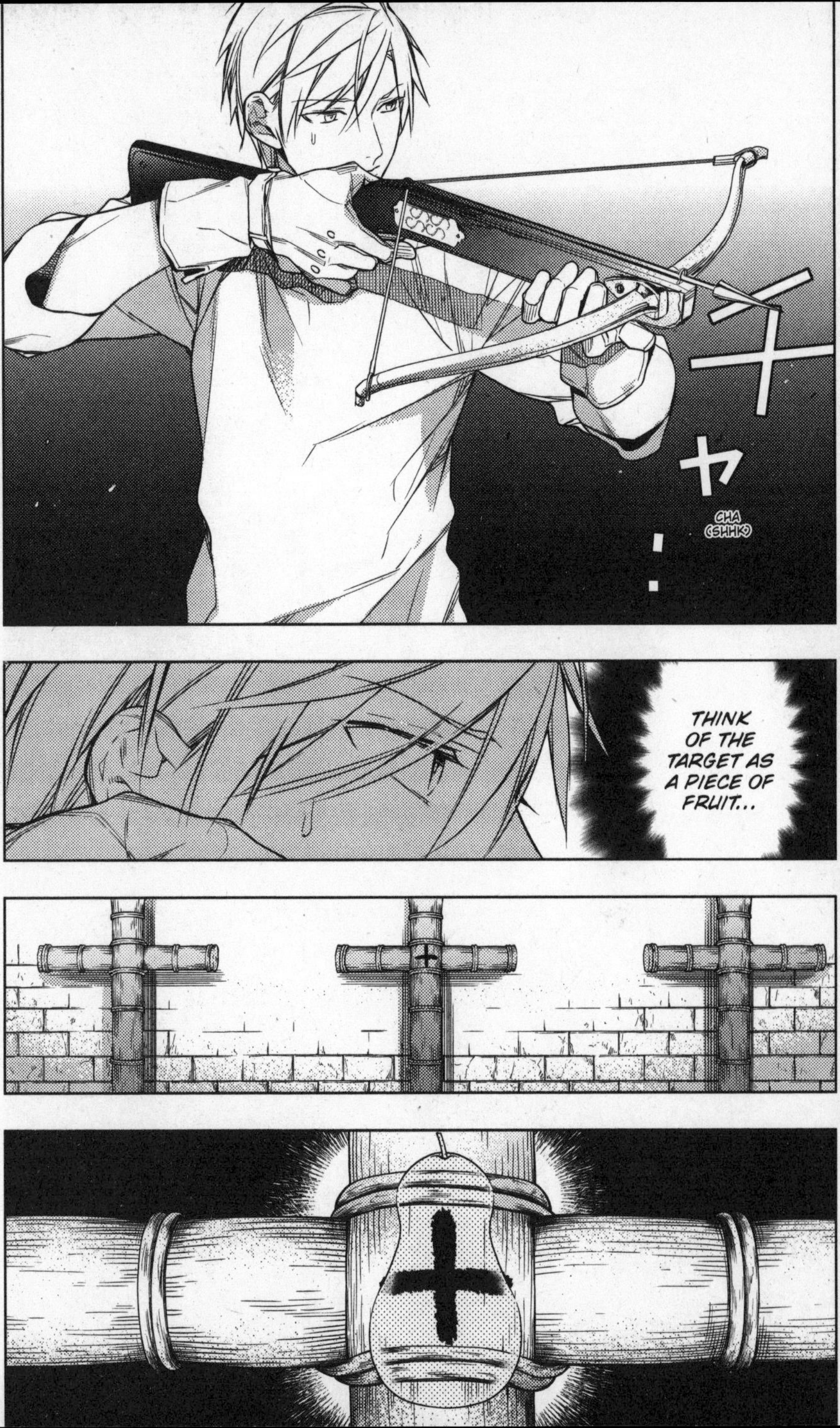
ャ
CHA (SHHK)
THINK OF THE TARGET AS A PIECE OF FRUIT...

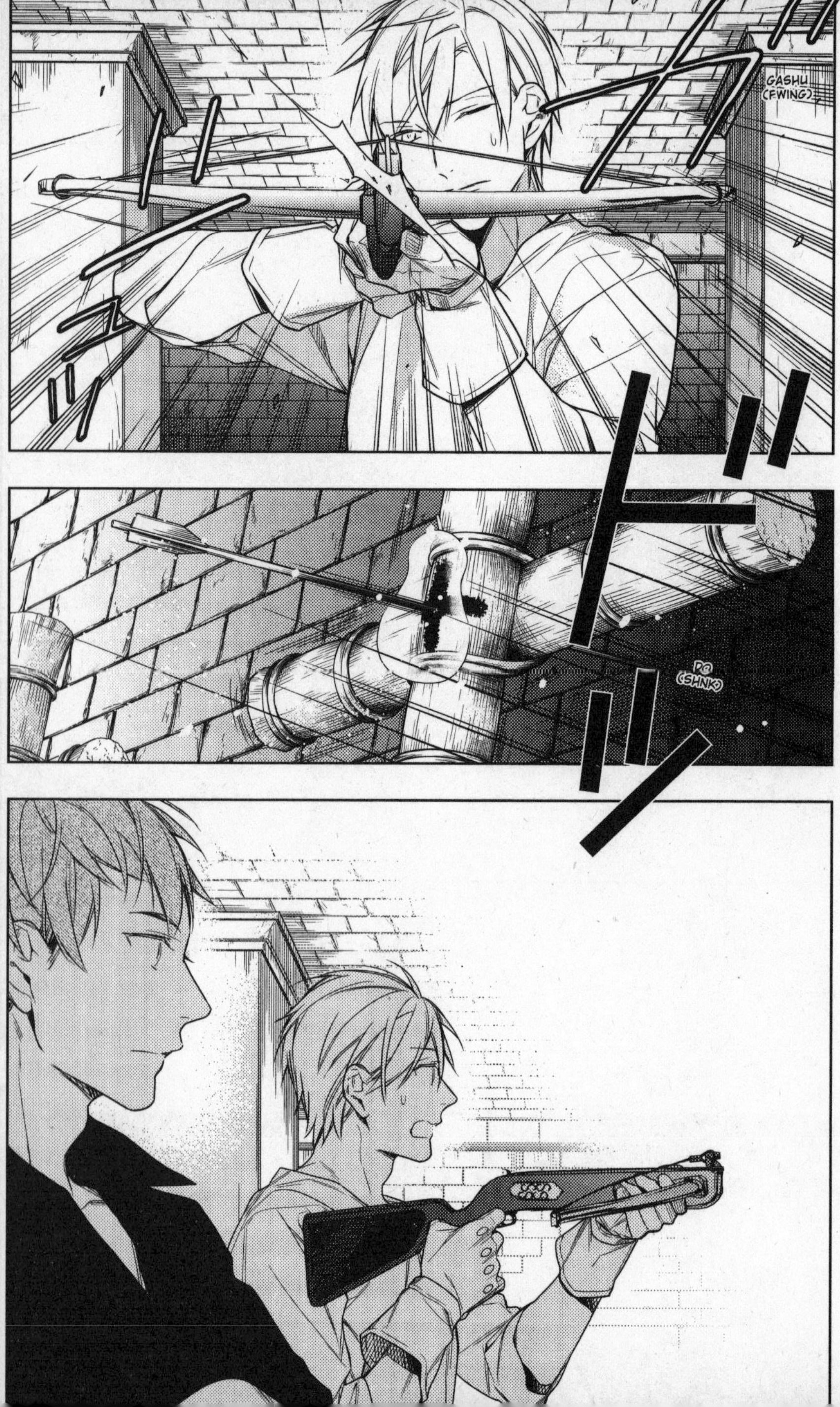
GASHU
(FWING)
DO
(SHNK)

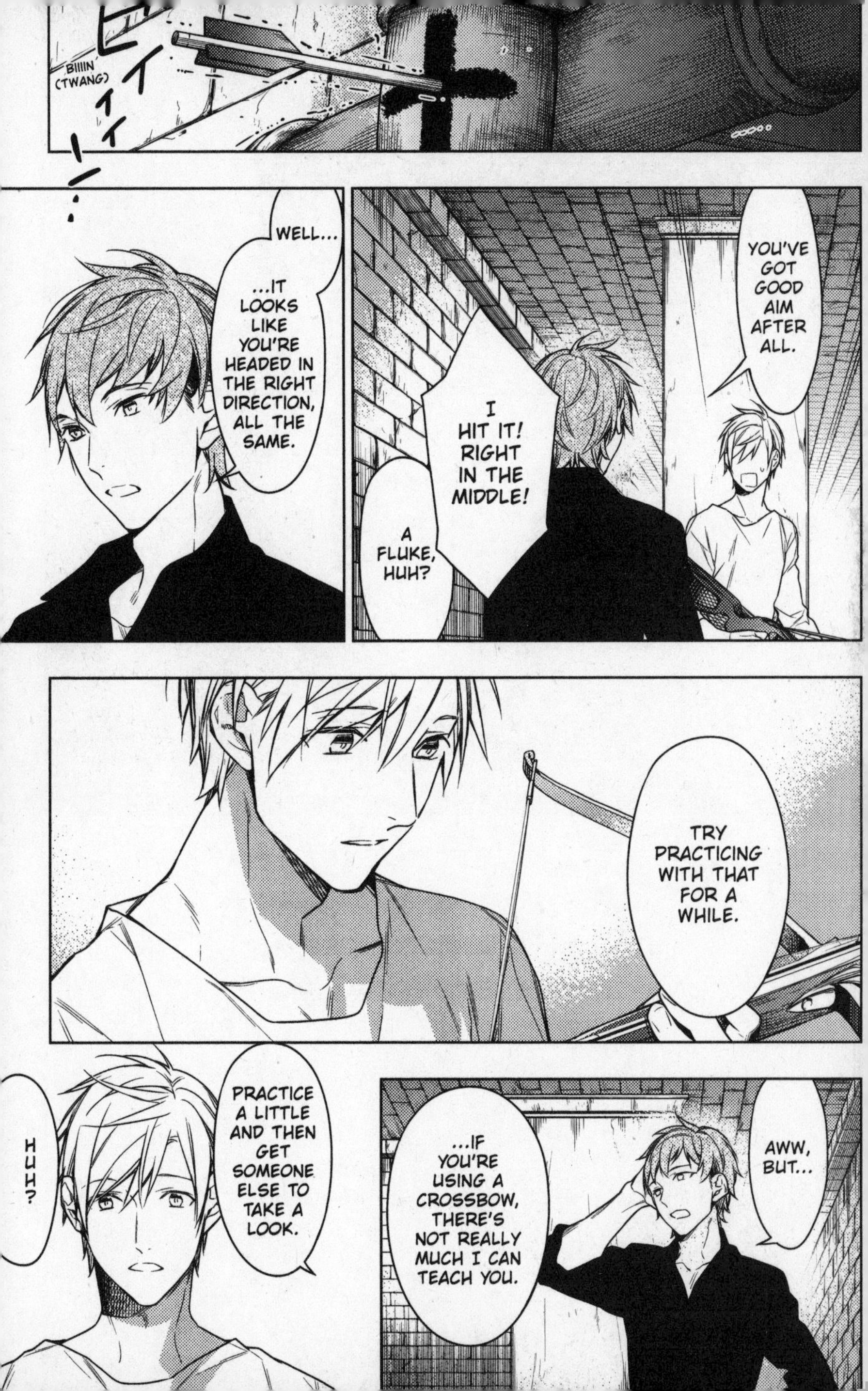
BIIIIN (TWANG)
YOU'VE GOT GOOD AIM AFTER ALL.
I HIT IT! RIGHT IN THE MIDDLE!
A FLUKE, HUH?
WELL...
...IT LOOKS LIKE YOU'RE HEADED IN THE RIGHT DIRECTION, ALL THE SAME.
TRY PRACTICING WITH THAT FOR A WHILE.
AWW, BUT...
...IF YOU'RE USING A CROSSBOW, THERE'S NOT REALLY MUCH I CAN TEACH YOU.
PRACTICE A LITTLE AND THEN GET SOMEONE ELSE TO TAKE A LOOK.
HUH?

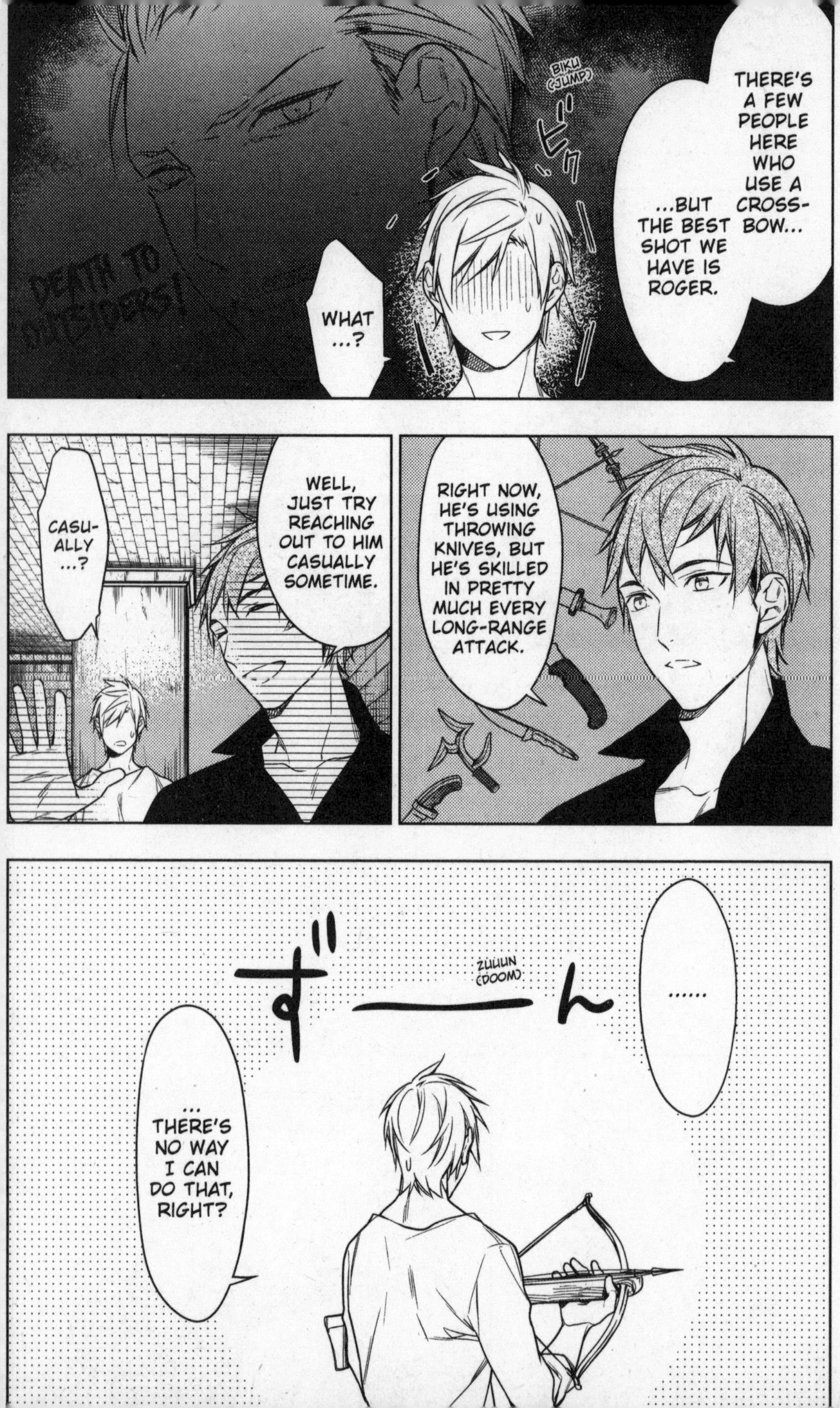
THERE'S A FEW PEOPLE HERE WHO USE A CROSS-BOW...
...BUT THE BEST SHOT WE HAVE IS ROGER.
BIKU (JUMP)
DEATH TO OUTSIDERS!
WHAT ...?
RIGHT NOW, HE'S USING THROWING KNIVES, BUT HE'S SKILLED IN PRETTY MUCH EVERY LONG-RANGE ATTACK.
WELL, JUST TRY REACHING OUT TO HIM CASUALLY SOMETIME.
CASU-ALLY ...?
......
ZUUUN (DOOM)
... THERE'S NO WAY I CAN DO THAT, RIGHT?

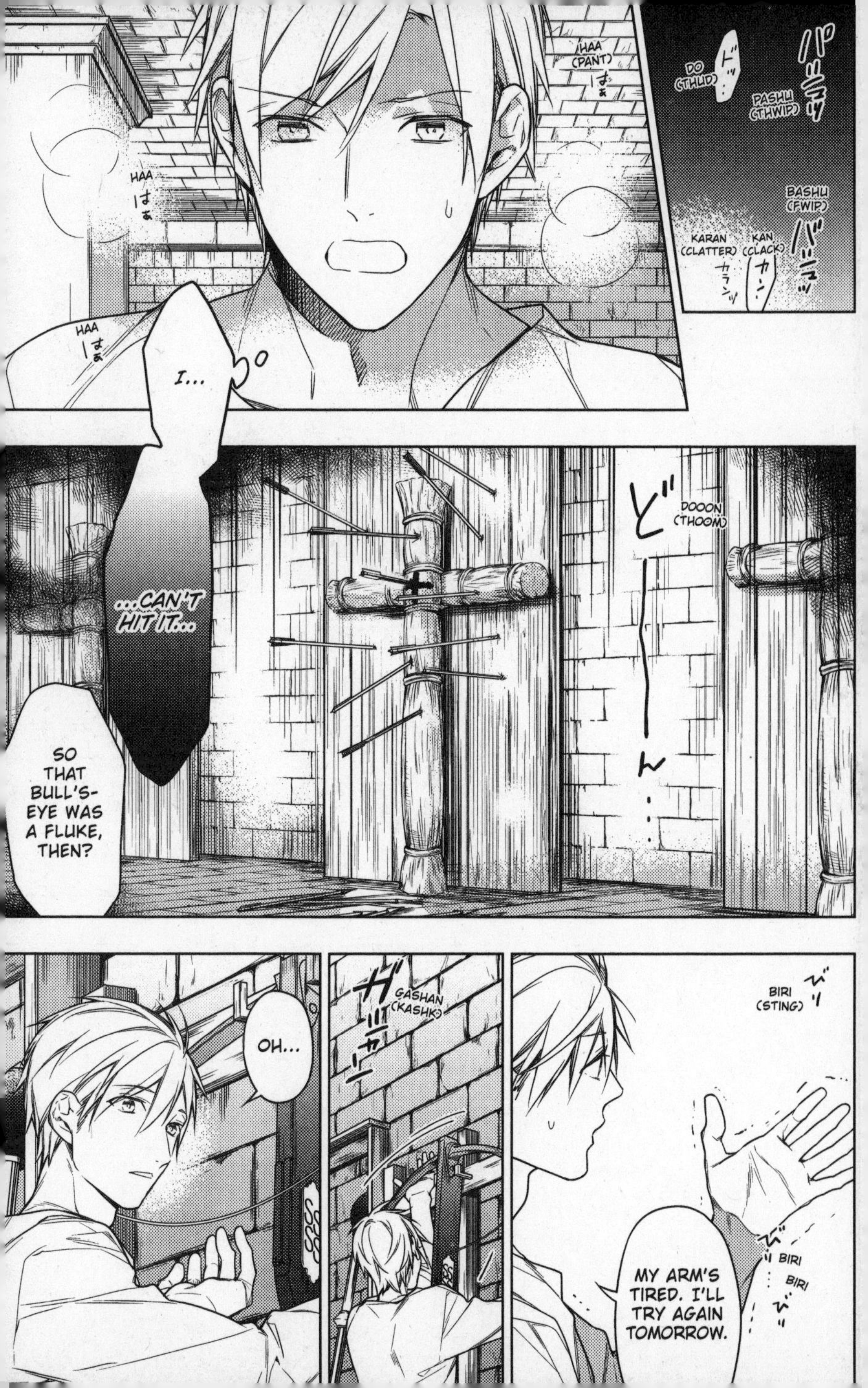
PASHU (THWIP)
DO (THUD)
BASHU (FWIP)
KAN (CLACK)
KARAN (CLATTER)
HAA (PANT)
I...
HAA
HAA
DOOON (THOOM)
...CAN'T HIT IT...
SO THAT BULL'S-EYE WAS A FLUKE, THEN?
BIRI (STING)
MY ARM'S TIRED. I'LL TRY AGAIN TOMORROW.
BIRI
BIRI
GASHAN (KASHK)
OH...

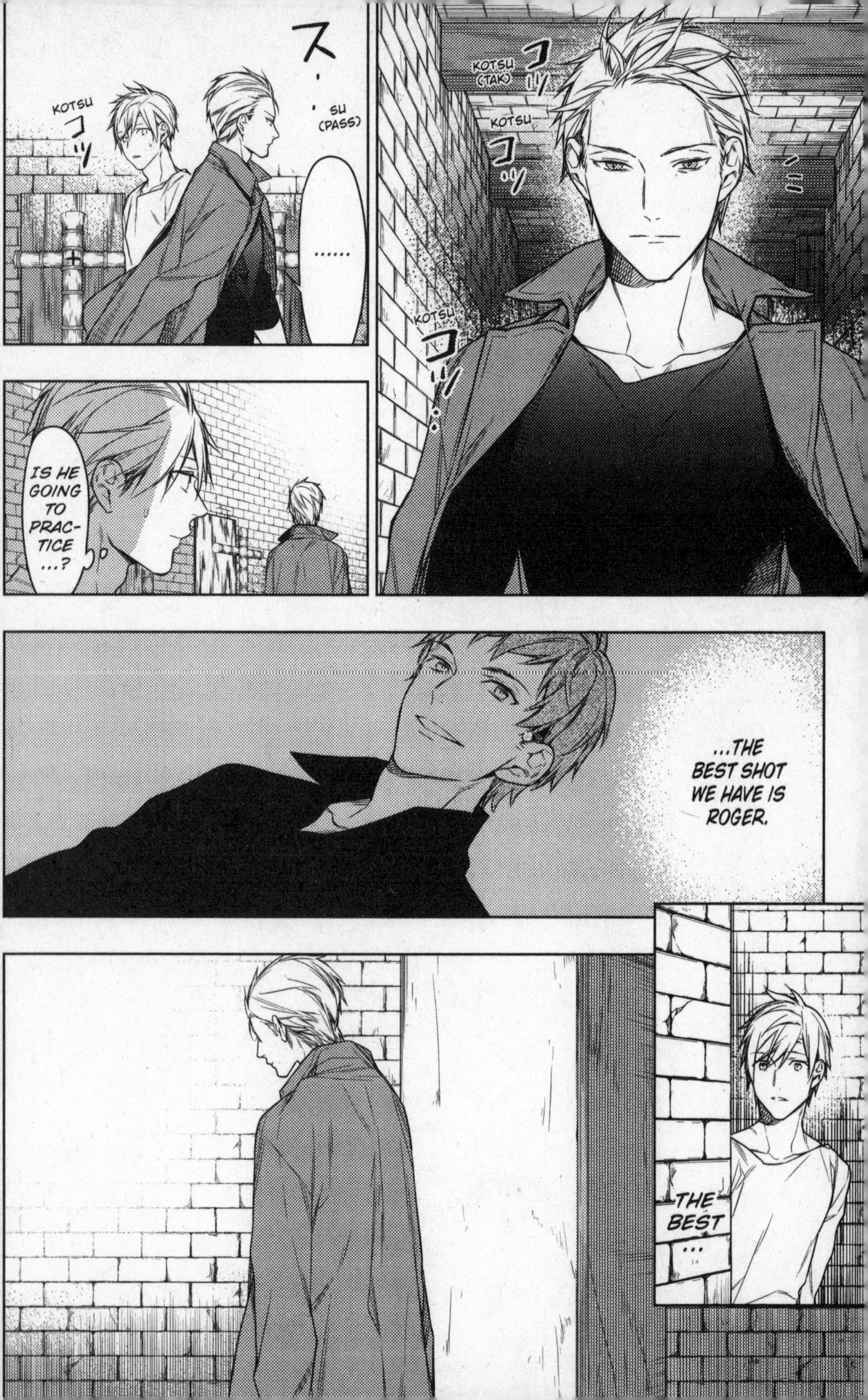
KOTSU (TAK)
KOTSU
KOTSU
SU (PASS)
......
KOTSU
IS HE GOING TO PRACTICE ...?
...THE BEST SHOT WE HAVE IS ROGER.
THE BEST ...

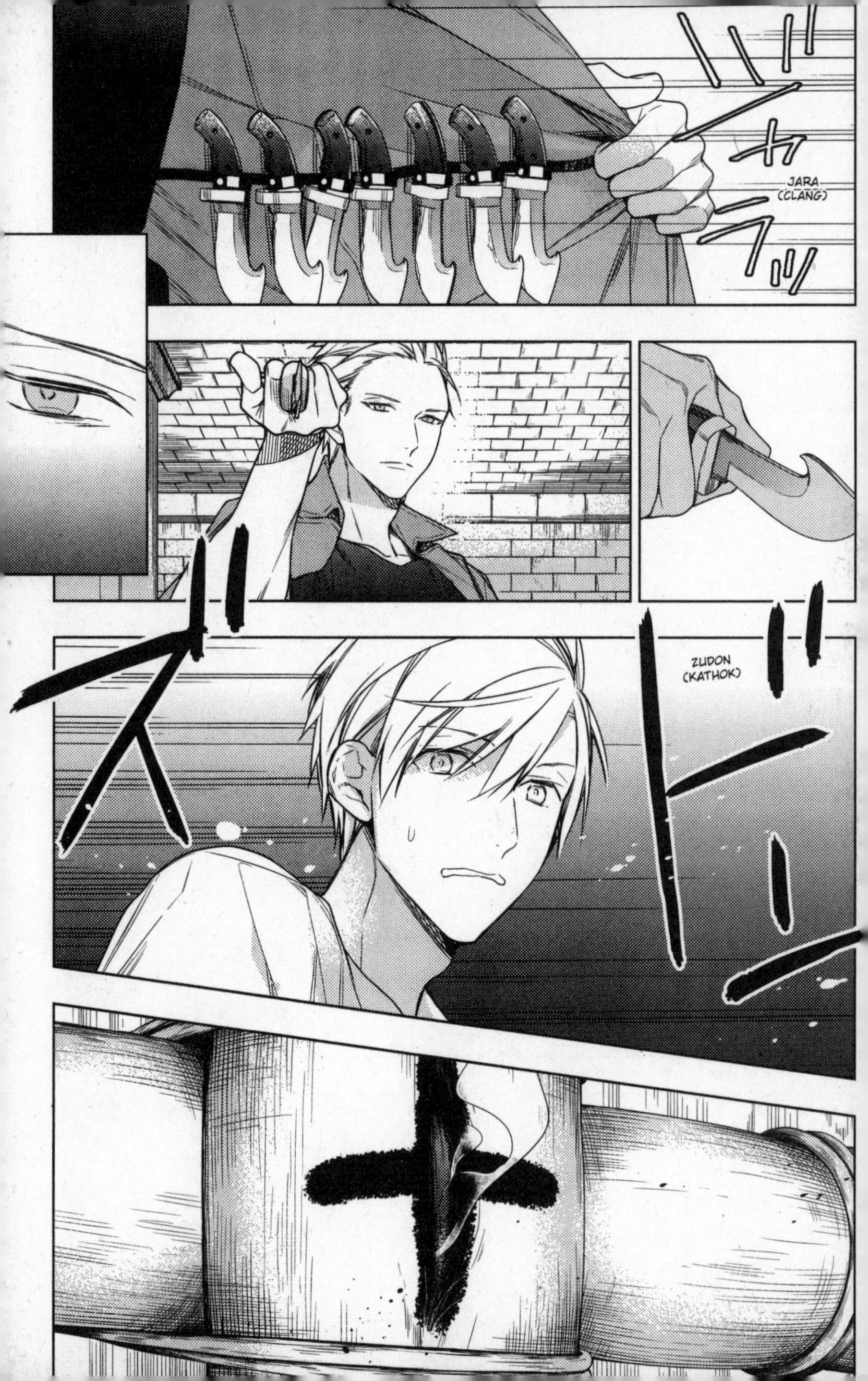
JARA
(CLANG)
ZUDON
(KATHOK)

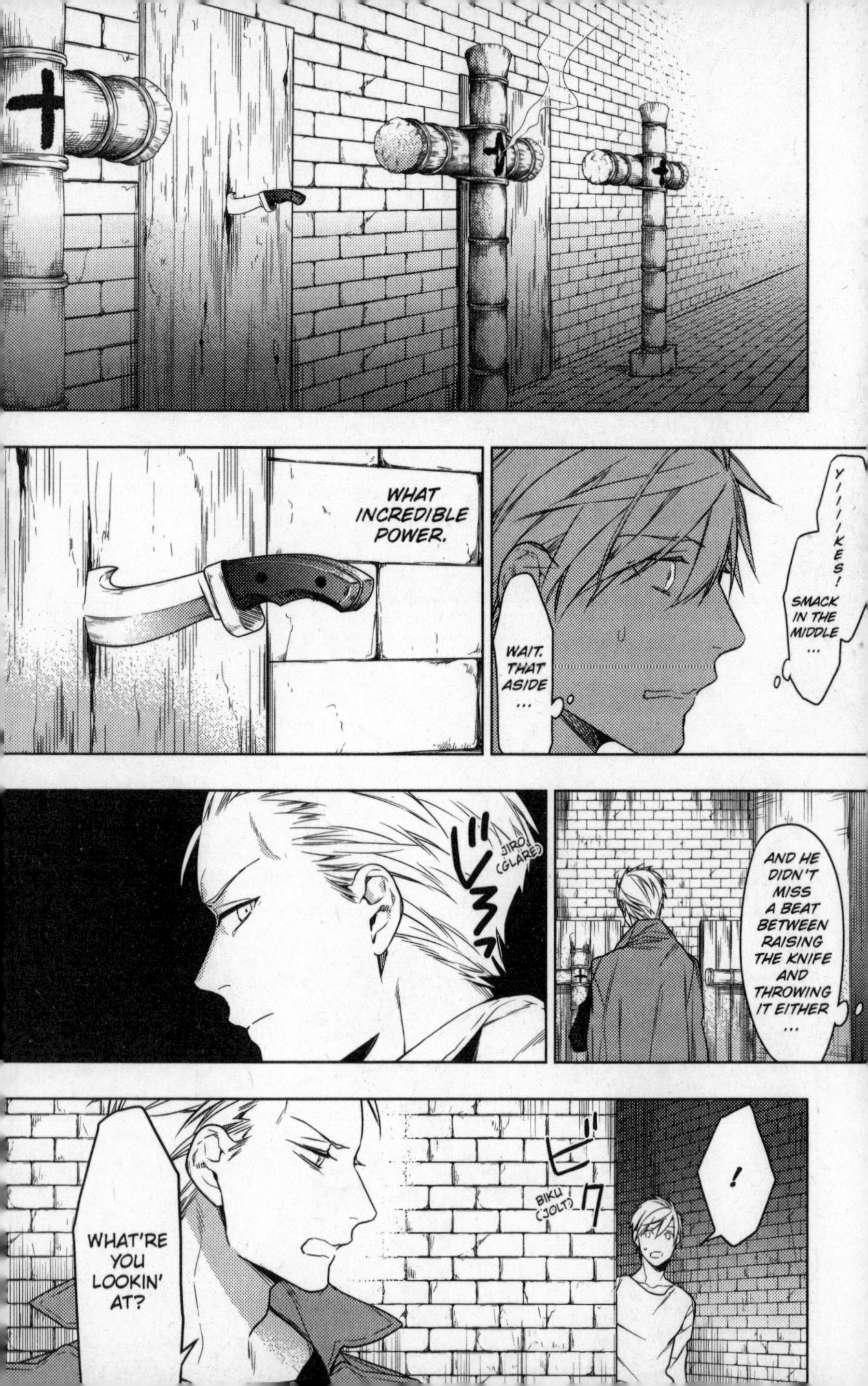
YIIIIKES! SMACK IN THE MIDDLE...
WAIT. THAT ASIDE...
WHAT INCREDIBLE POWER.
AND HE DIDN'T MISS A BEAT BETWEEN RAISING THE KNIFE AND THROWING IT EITHER...
JIRO (GLARE)
!
BIKU (JOLT)
WHAT'RE YOU LOOKIN' AT?

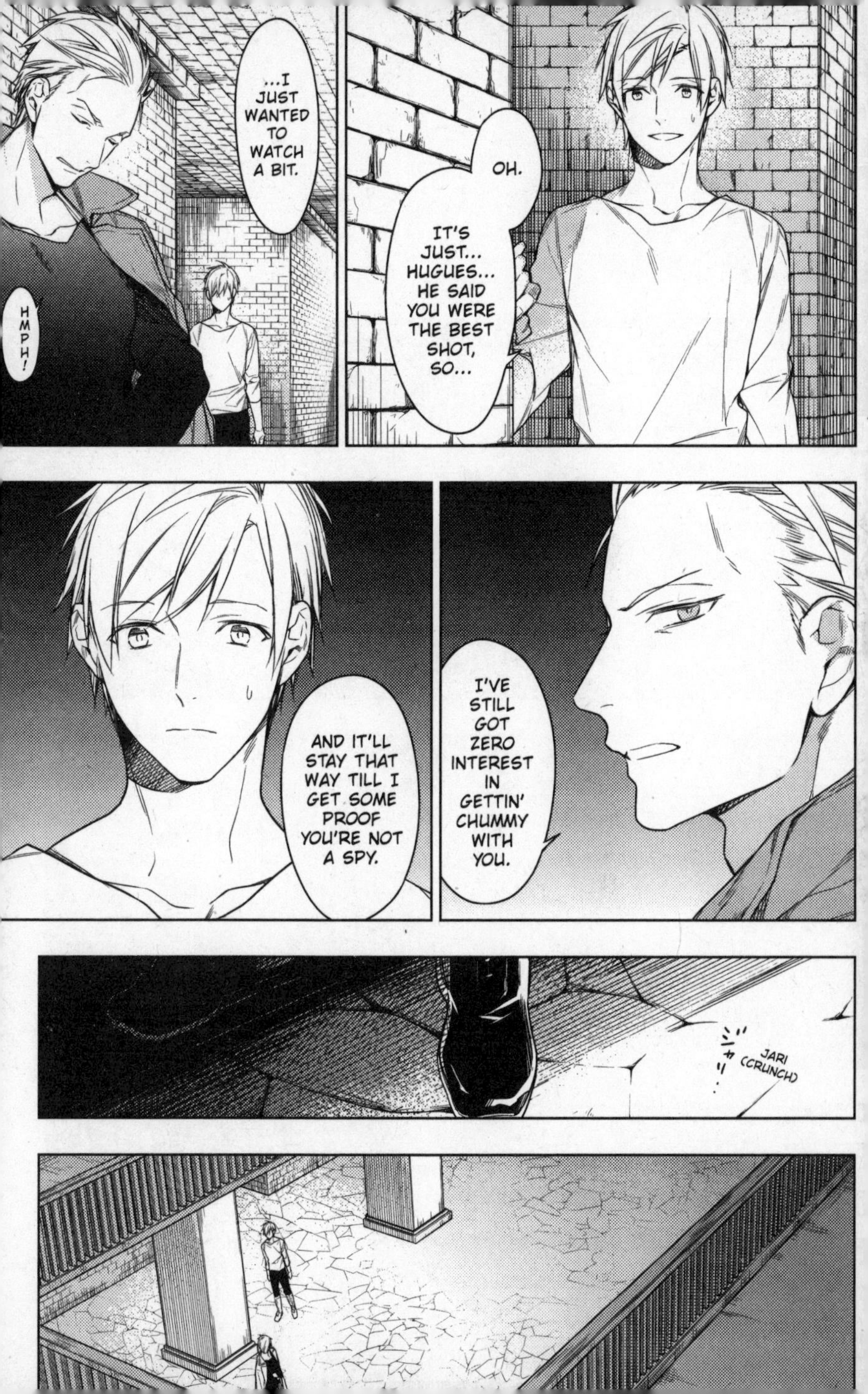
OH.
IT'S JUST... HUGUES... HE SAID YOU WERE THE BEST SHOT, SO...
...I JUST WANTED TO WATCH A BIT.
HMPH!
I'VE STILL GOT ZERO INTEREST IN GETTIN' CHUMMY WITH YOU.
AND IT'LL STAY THAT WAY TILL I GET SOME PROOF YOU'RE NOT A SPY.
ジャリ
JARI (CRUNCH)

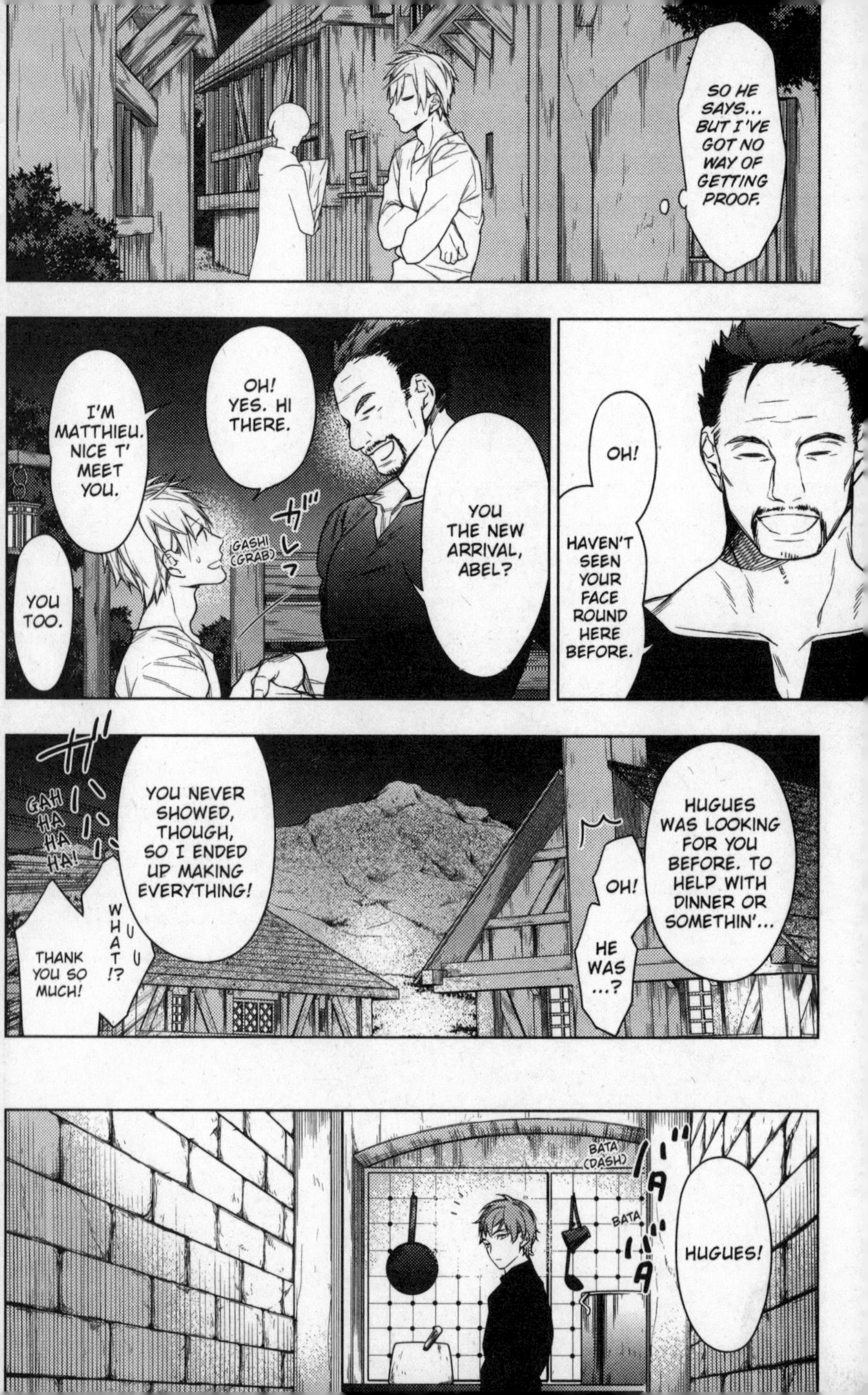
SO HE SAYS... BUT I'VE GOT NO WAY OF GETTING PROOF.
OH!
HAVEN'T SEEN YOUR FACE ROUND HERE BEFORE.
YOU THE NEW ARRIVAL, ABEL?
OH! YES. HI THERE.
GASHI (GRAB)
I'M MATTHIEU. NICE T' MEET YOU.
YOU TOO.
HUGUES WAS LOOKING FOR YOU BEFORE. TO HELP WITH DINNER OR SOMETHIN'...
OH!
HE WAS ...?
YOU NEVER SHOWED, THOUGH, SO I ENDED UP MAKING EVERYTHING!
WHAT!?
GAH HA HA HA!
THANK YOU SO MUCH!
BATA (DASH)
BATA
HUGUES!

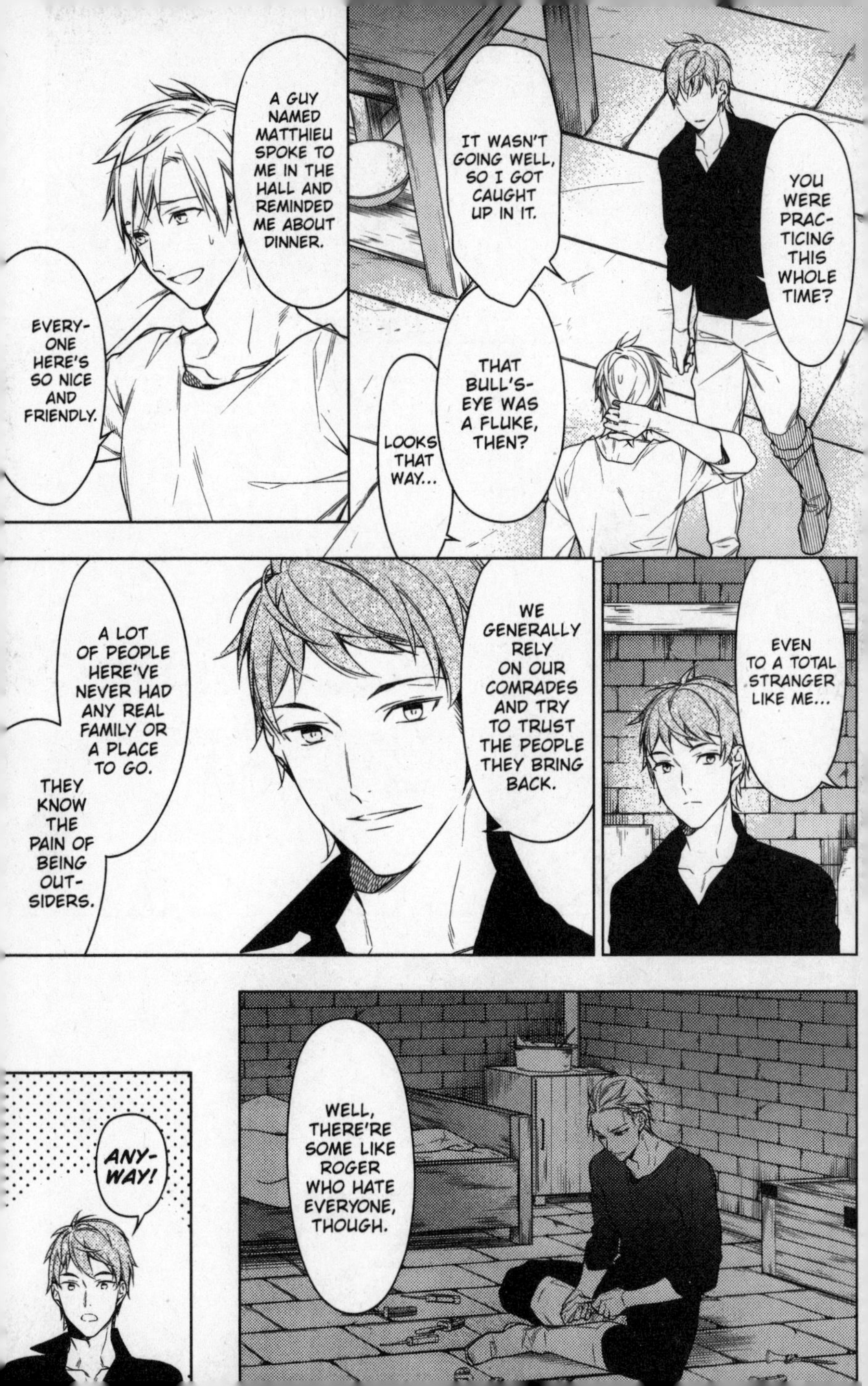
YOU WERE PRACTICING THIS WHOLE TIME?
IT WASN'T GOING WELL, SO I GOT CAUGHT UP IN IT.
THAT BULL'S-EYE WAS A FLUKE, THEN?
LOOKS THAT WAY...
A GUY NAMED MATTHIEU SPOKE TO ME IN THE HALL AND REMINDED ME ABOUT DINNER.
EVERYONE HERE'S SO NICE AND FRIENDLY.
EVEN TO A TOTAL STRANGER LIKE ME...
WE GENERALLY RELY ON OUR COMRADES AND TRY TO TRUST THE PEOPLE THEY BRING BACK.
A LOT OF PEOPLE HERE'VE NEVER HAD ANY REAL FAMILY OR A PLACE TO GO.
THEY KNOW THE PAIN OF BEING OUTSIDERS.
WELL, THERE'RE SOME LIKE ROGER WHO HATE EVERYONE, THOUGH.
ANYWAY!

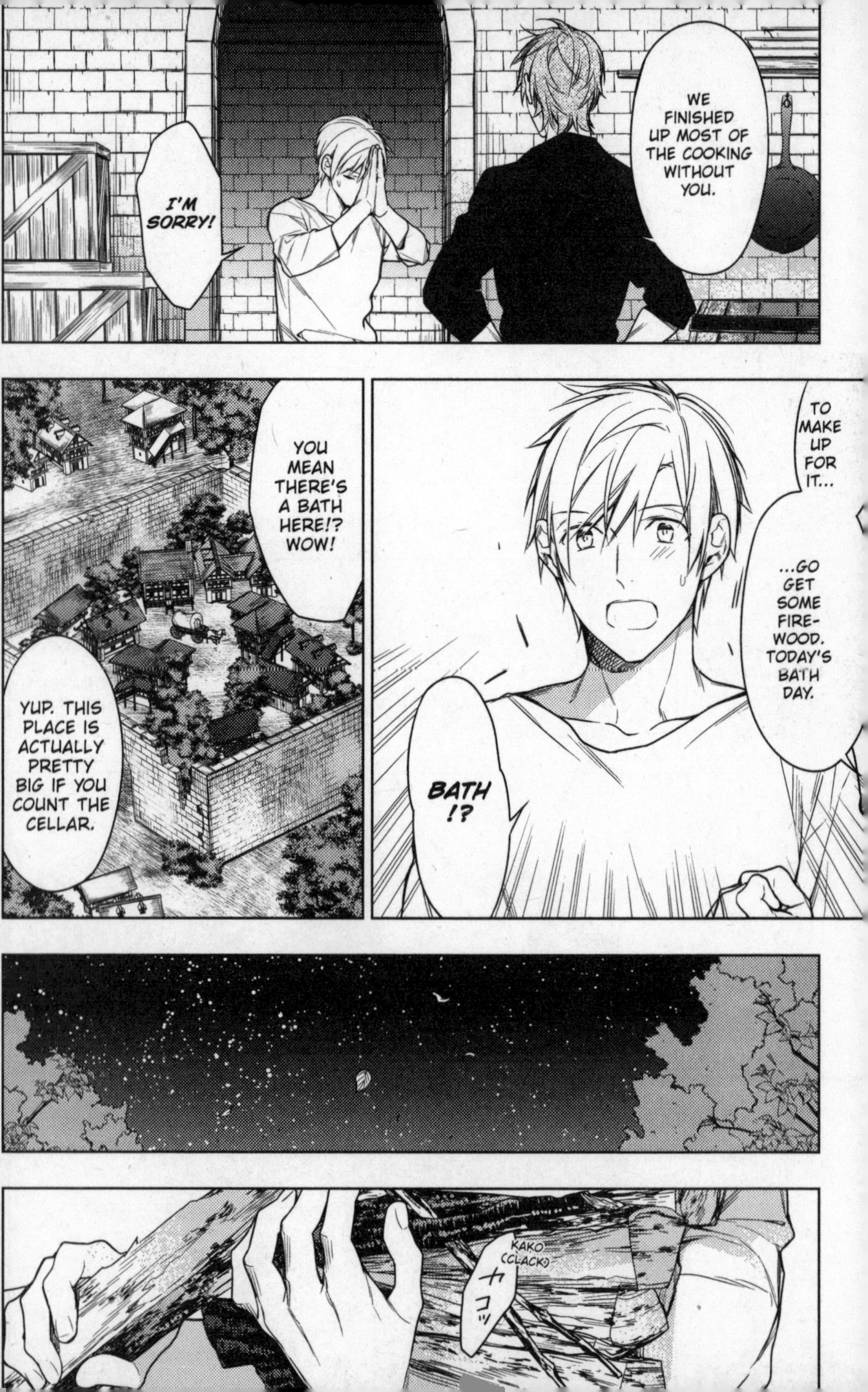
WE FINISHED UP MOST OF THE COOKING WITHOUT YOU.
I'M SORRY!
TO MAKE UP FOR IT...
...GO GET SOME FIRE-WOOD. TODAY'S BATH DAY.
BATH!?
YOU MEAN THERE'S A BATH HERE!? WOW!
YUP. THIS PLACE IS ACTUALLY PRETTY BIG IF YOU COUNT THE CELLAR.
KAKO (CLACK)
カコッ

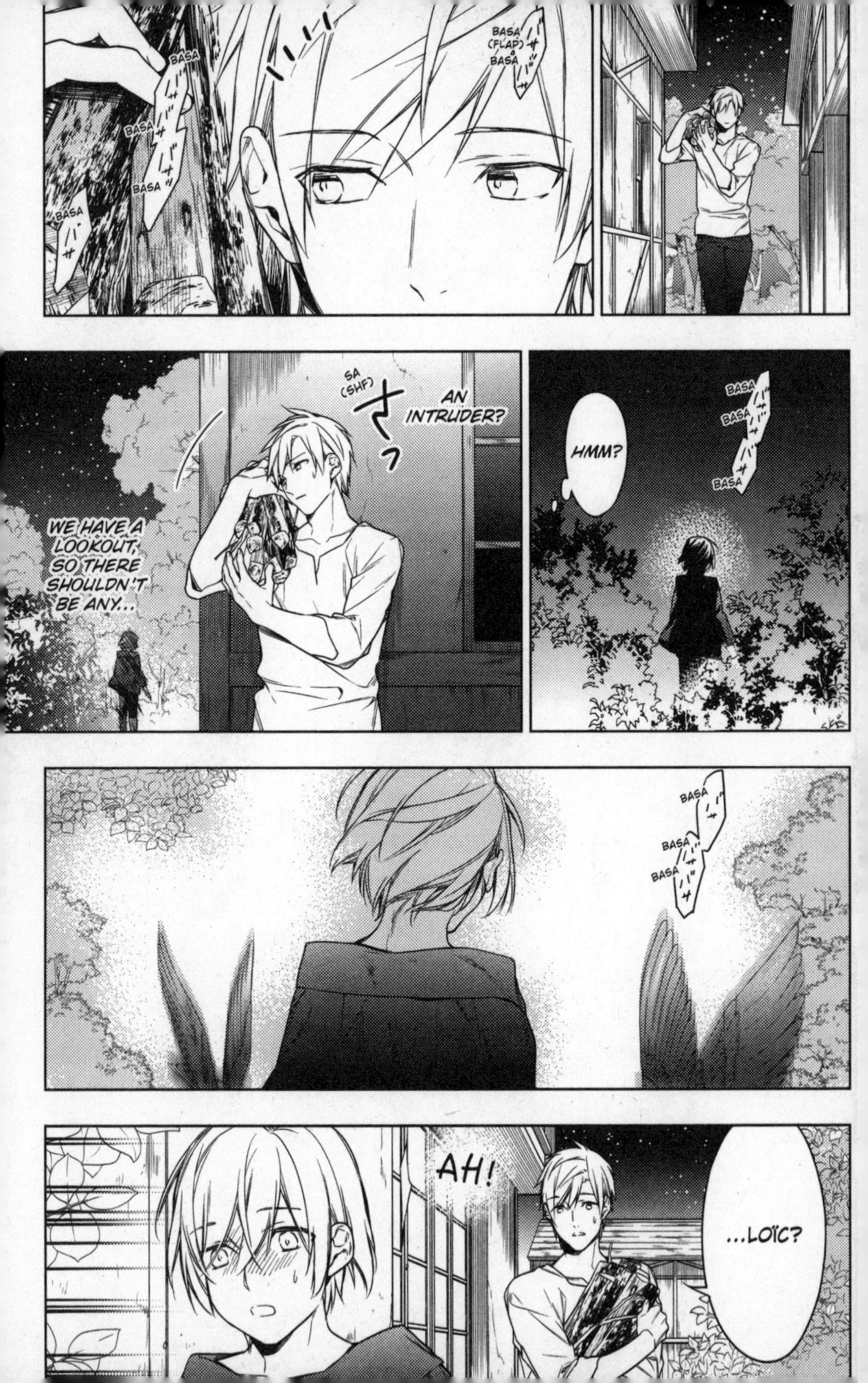
BASA (FLAP) BASA
BASA
BASA
BASA
BASA
HMM?
BASA
BASA
BASA
SA (SHF)
AN INTRUDER?
WE HAVE A LOOKOUT, SO THERE SHOULDN'T BE ANY...
BASA
BASA
BASA
...LOÏC?
AH!

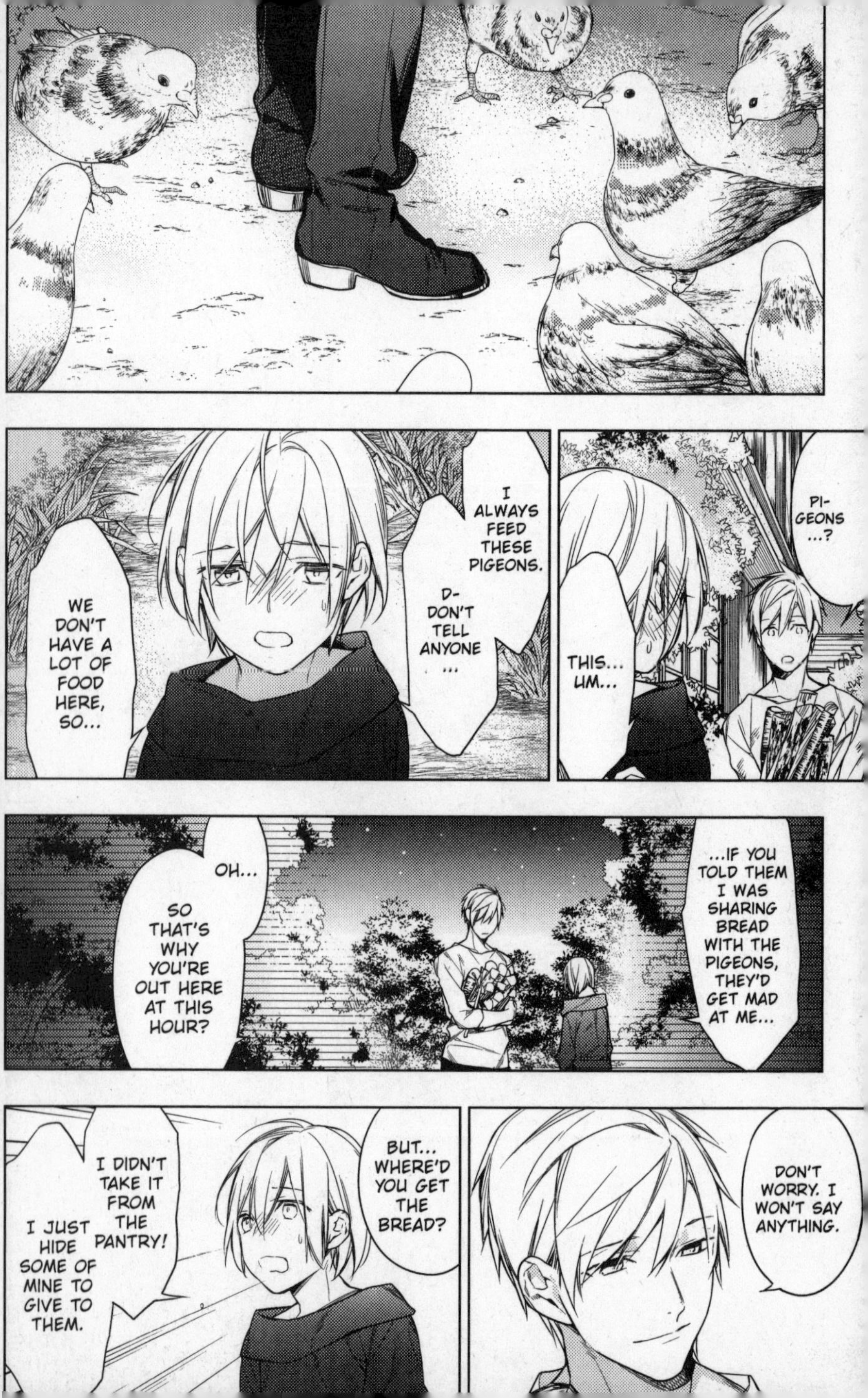
PI-GEONS ...?
THIS... UM...
I ALWAYS FEED THESE PIGEONS.
D-DON'T TELL ANYONE ...
WE DON'T HAVE A LOT OF FOOD HERE, SO...
...IF YOU TOLD THEM I WAS SHARING BREAD WITH THE PIGEONS, THEY'D GET MAD AT ME...
OH...
SO THAT'S WHY YOU'RE OUT HERE AT THIS HOUR?
DON'T WORRY. I WON'T SAY ANYTHING.
BUT... WHERE'D YOU GET THE BREAD?
I DIDN'T TAKE IT FROM THE PANTRY!
I JUST HIDE SOME OF MINE TO GIVE TO THEM.

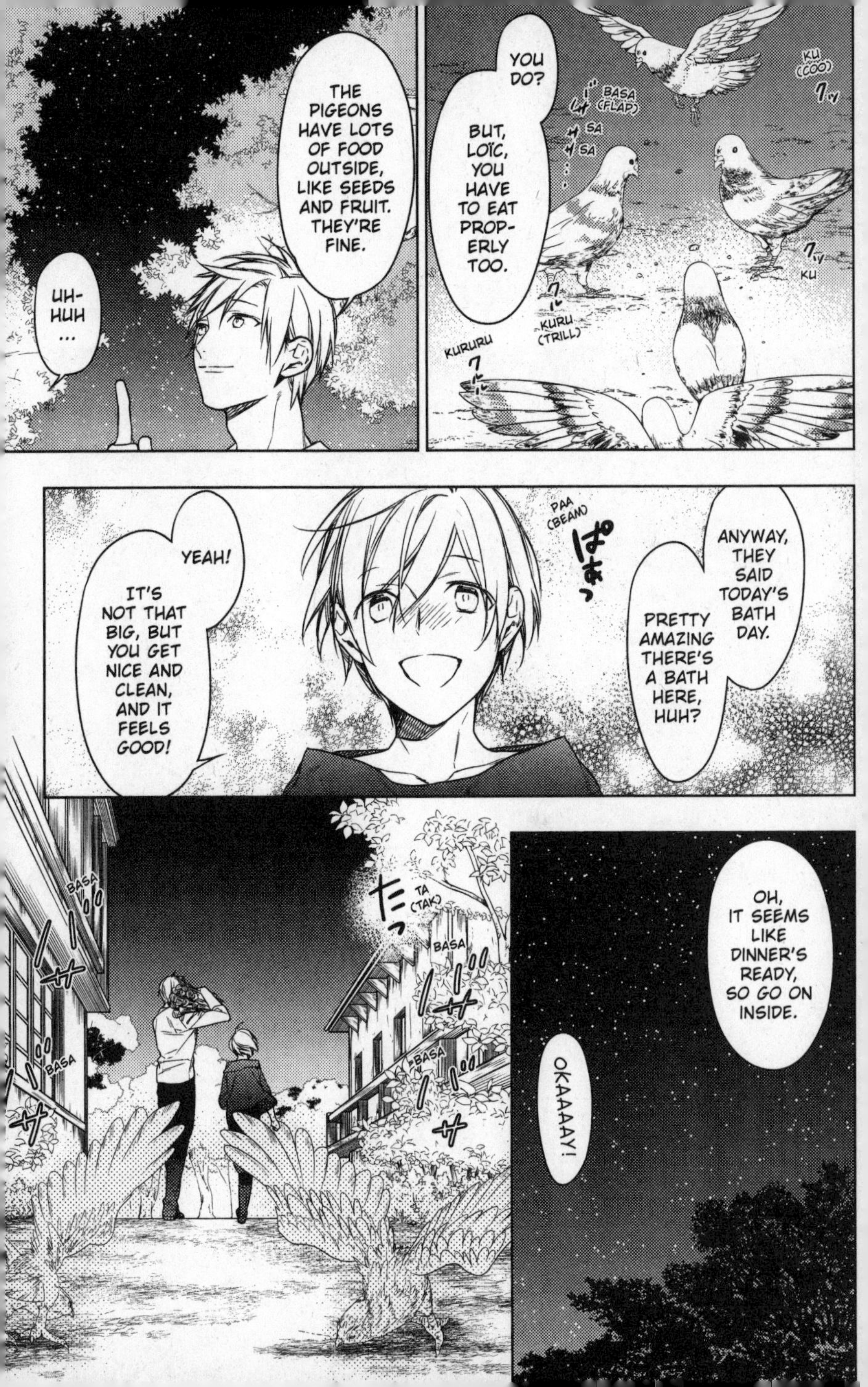
YOU DO?
BUT, LOÏC, YOU HAVE TO EAT PROPERLY TOO.
BASA (FLAP)
SA SA
KU (COO)
KU
KURU (TRILL)
KURURU
THE PIGEONS HAVE LOTS OF FOOD OUTSIDE, LIKE SEEDS AND FRUIT. THEY'RE FINE.
UH-HUH...
ANYWAY, THEY SAID TODAY'S BATH DAY.
PRETTY AMAZING THERE'S A BATH HERE, HUH?
PAA (BEAM)
YEAH!
IT'S NOT THAT BIG, BUT YOU GET NICE AND CLEAN, AND IT FEELS GOOD!
OH, IT SEEMS LIKE DINNER'S READY, SO GO ON INSIDE.
OKAAAAY!
TA (TAK)
BASA
BASA
BASA
BASA

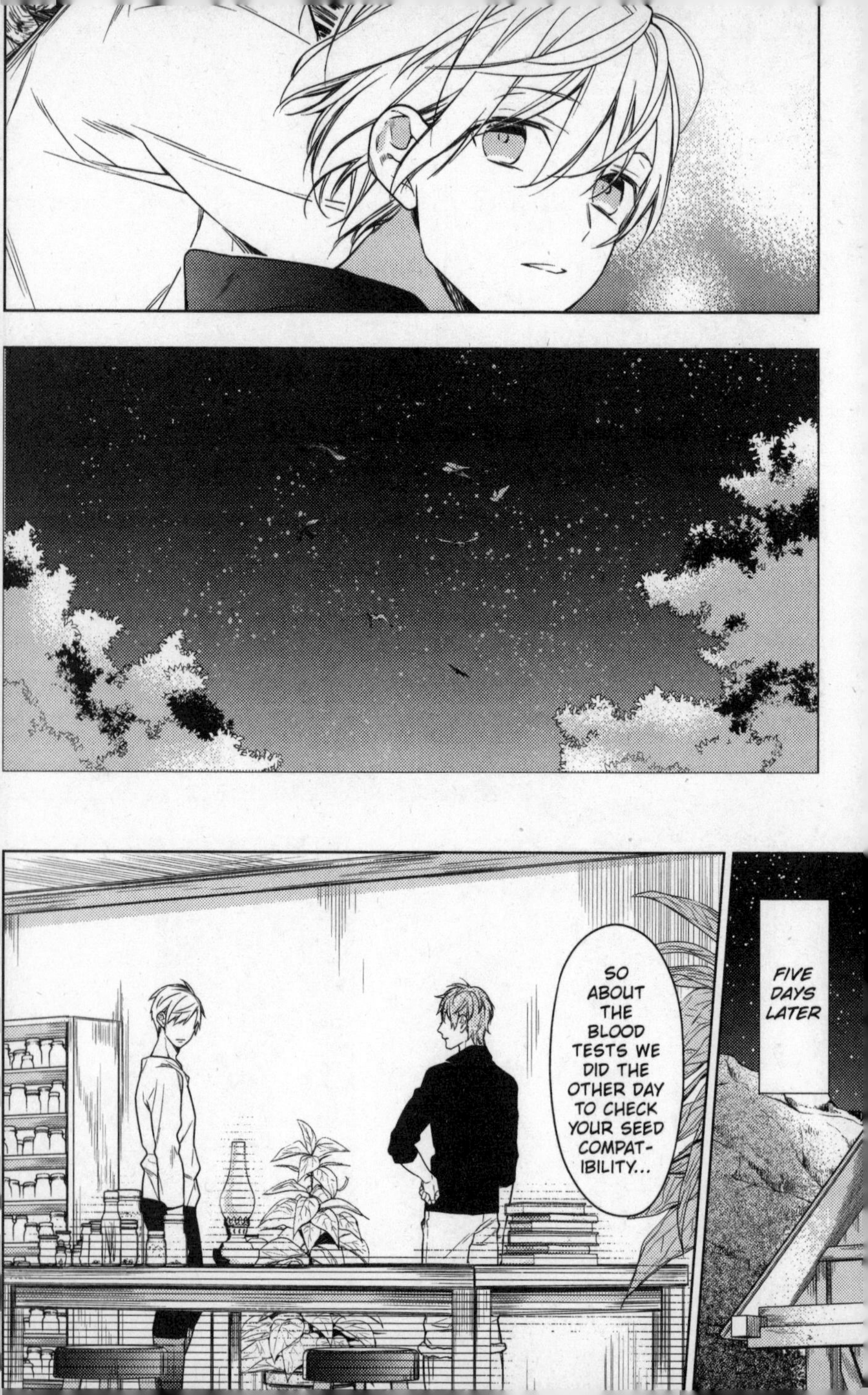
FIVE DAYS LATER
SO ABOUT THE BLOOD TESTS WE DID THE OTHER DAY TO CHECK YOUR SEED COMPAT-IBILITY...

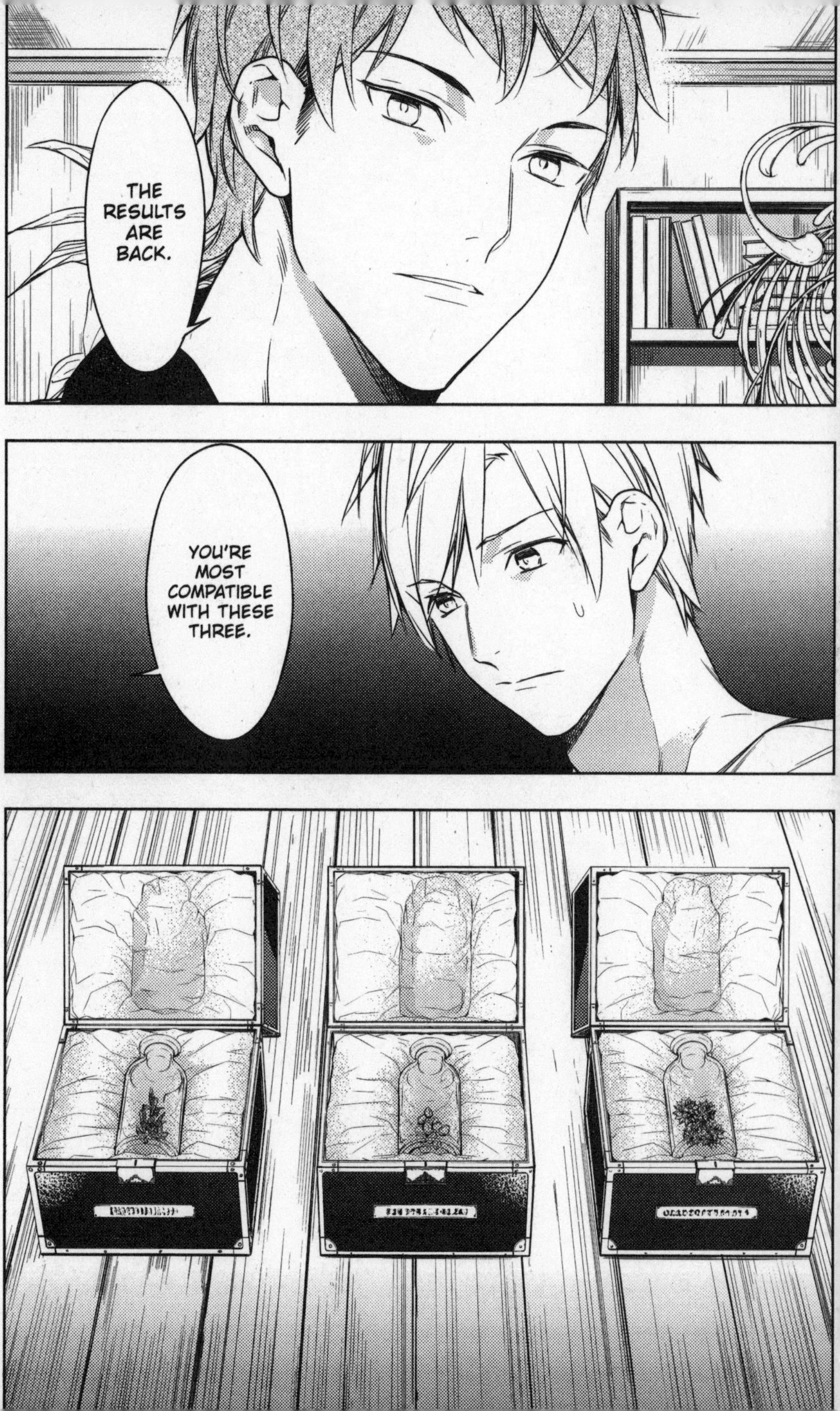
THE RESULTS ARE BACK.
YOU'RE MOST COMPATIBLE WITH THESE THREE.

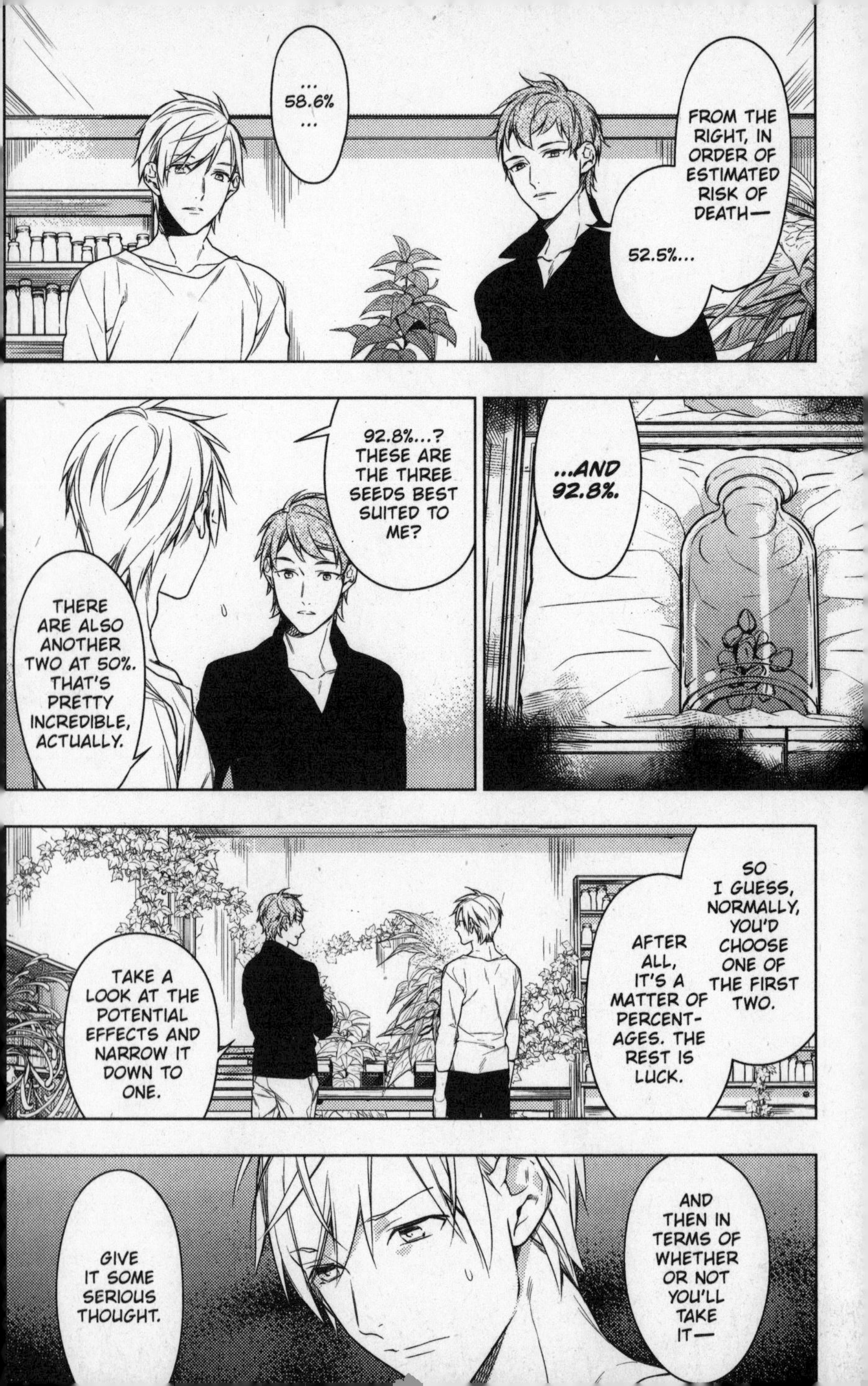
FROM THE RIGHT, IN ORDER OF ESTIMATED RISK OF DEATH—
52.5%...
...58.6%...
...AND 92.8%.
92.8%...? THESE ARE THE THREE SEEDS BEST SUITED TO ME?
THERE ARE ALSO ANOTHER TWO AT 50%. THAT'S PRETTY INCREDIBLE, ACTUALLY.
SO I GUESS, NORMALLY, YOU'D CHOOSE ONE OF THE FIRST TWO.
AFTER ALL, IT'S A MATTER OF PERCENT-AGES. THE REST IS LUCK.
TAKE A LOOK AT THE POTENTIAL EFFECTS AND NARROW IT DOWN TO ONE.
AND THEN IN TERMS OF WHETHER OR NOT YOU'LL TAKE IT—
GIVE IT SOME SERIOUS THOUGHT.

Episode 23

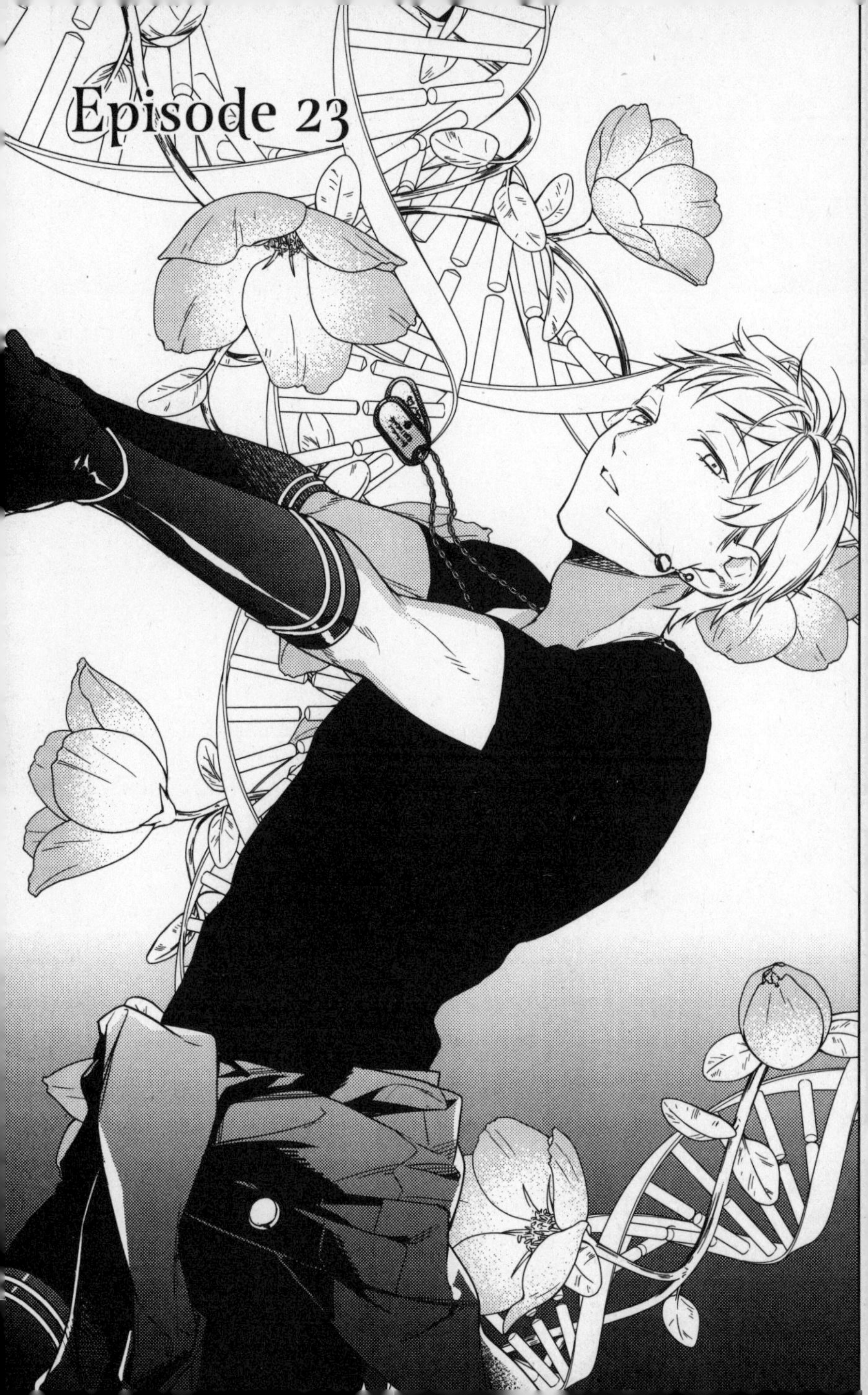

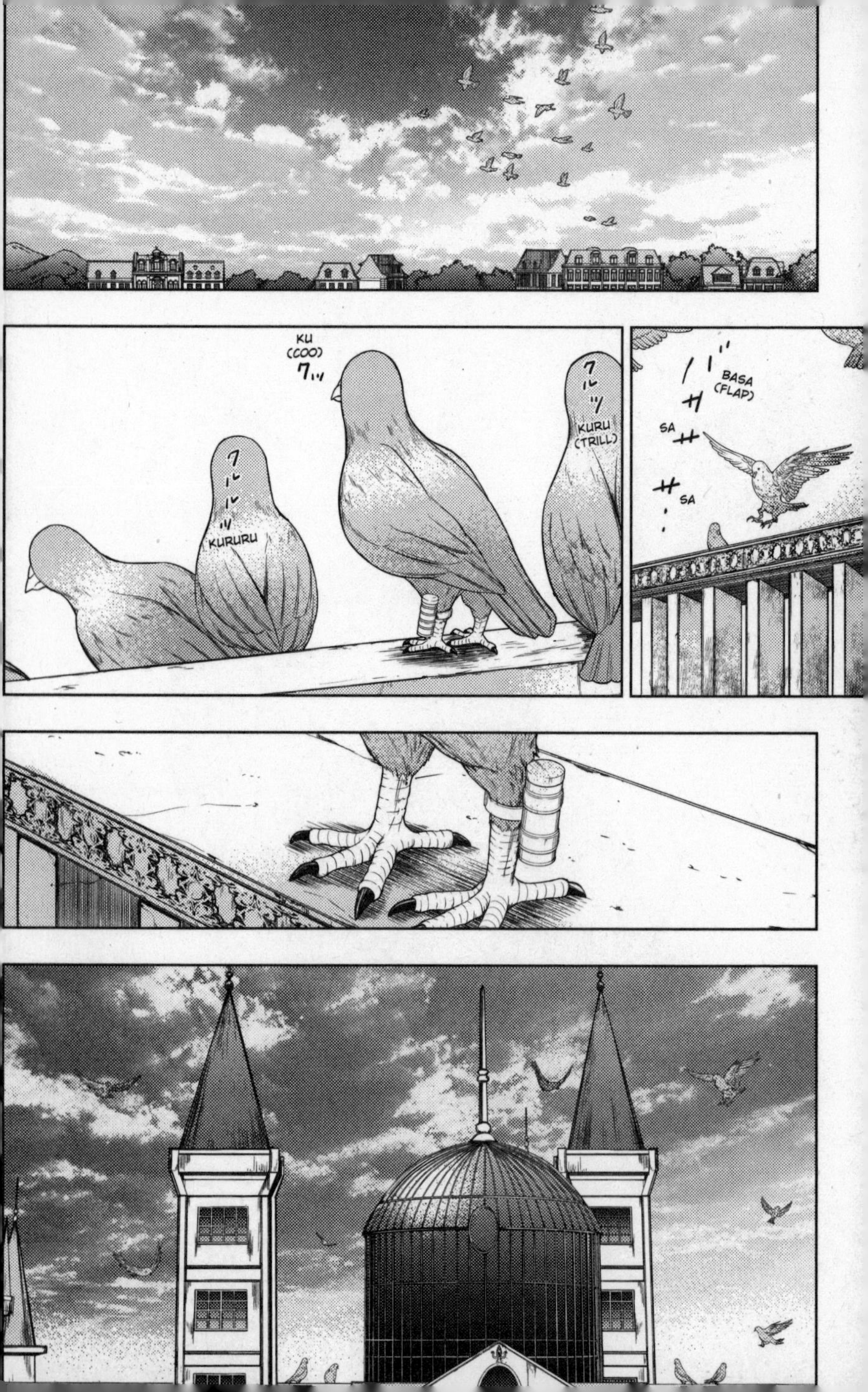
BASA (FLAP)
SA
SA
KURU (TRILL)
KU (COO)
KURURU

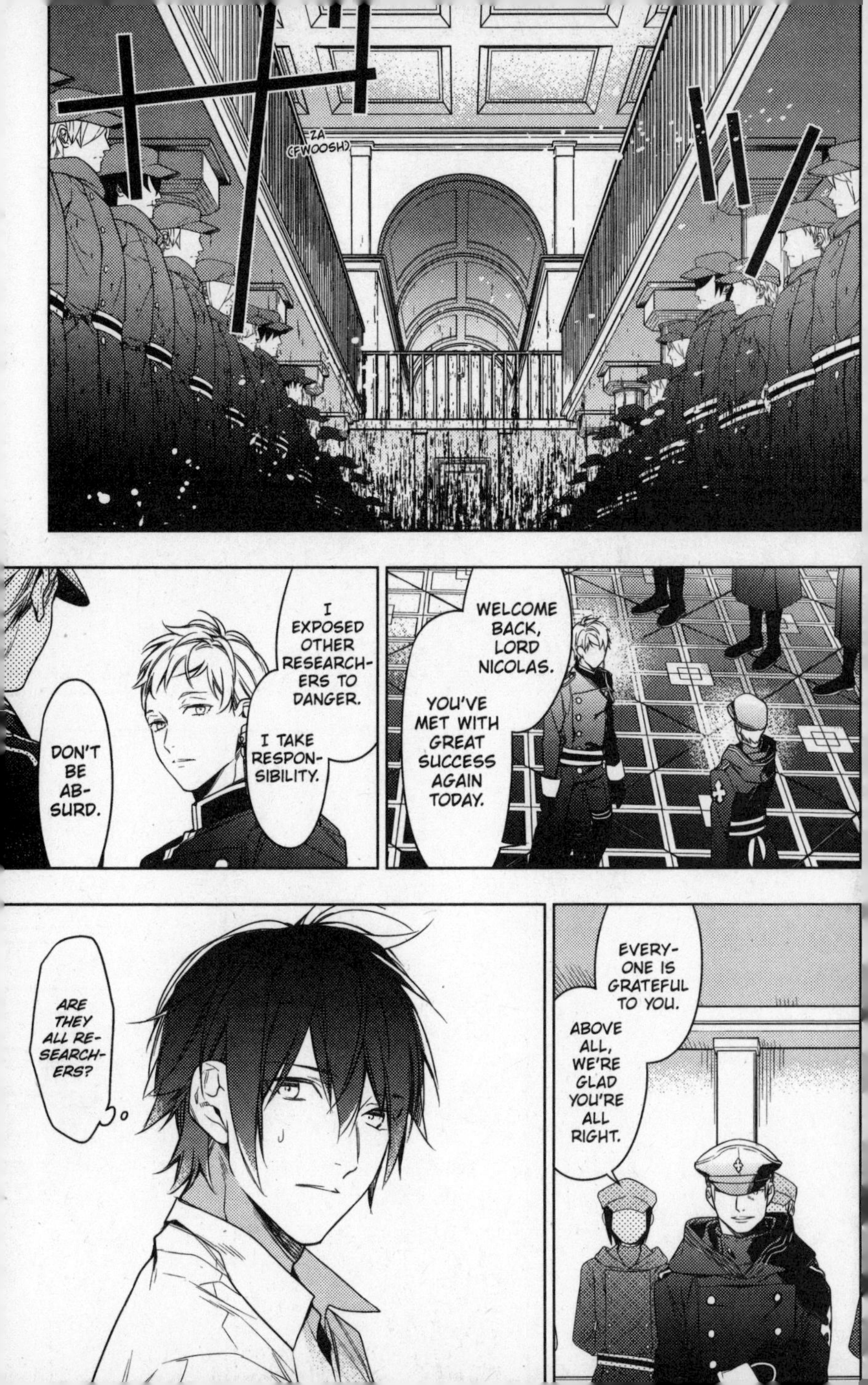
ZA (FWOOSH)
WELCOME BACK, LORD NICOLAS.
YOU'VE MET WITH GREAT SUCCESS AGAIN TODAY.
I EXPOSED OTHER RESEARCHERS TO DANGER.
I TAKE RESPONSIBILITY.
DON'T BE ABSURD.
EVERYONE IS GRATEFUL TO YOU.
ABOVE ALL, WE'RE GLAD YOU'RE ALL RIGHT.
ARE THEY ALL RESEARCHERS?

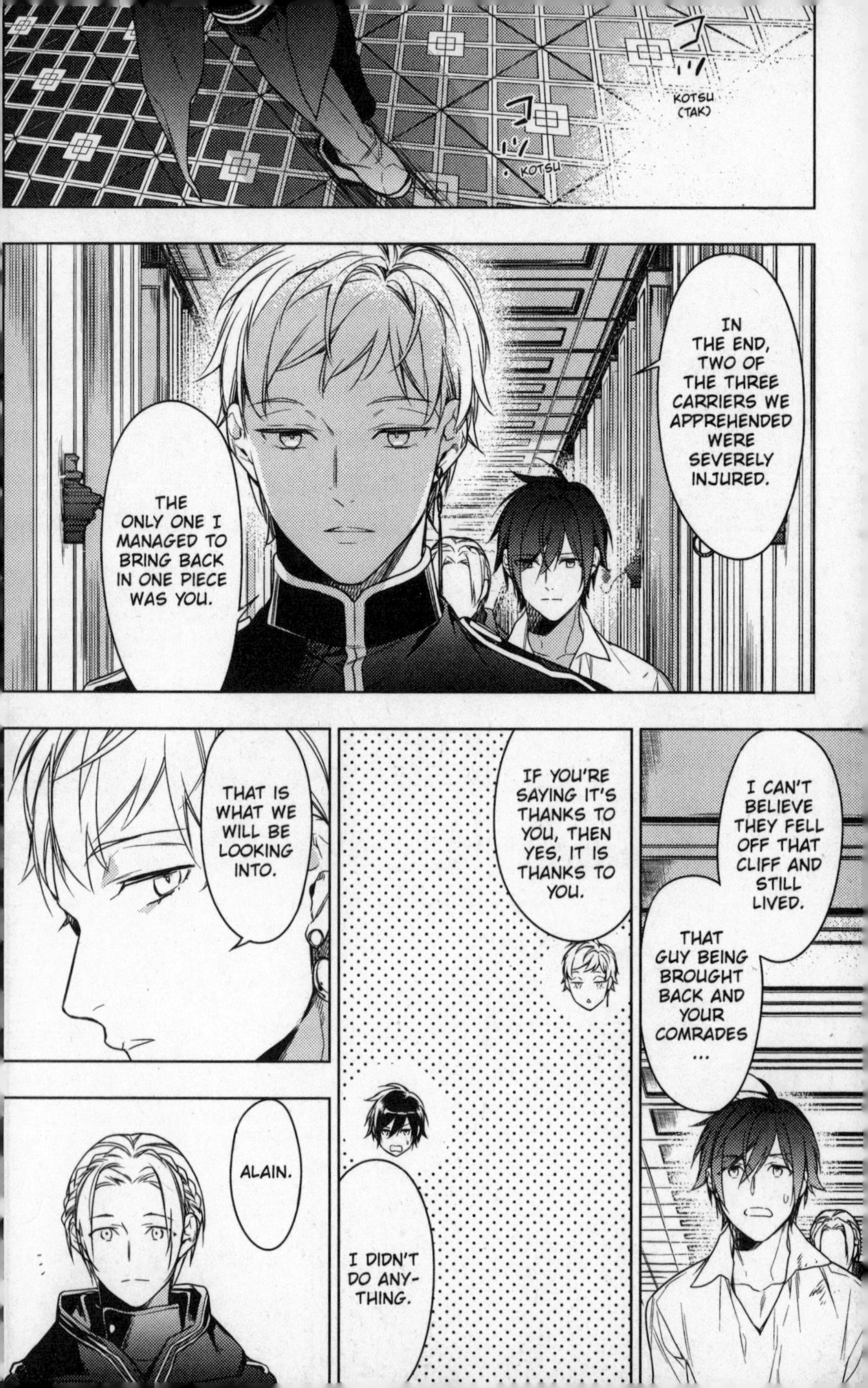
KOTSU (TAK)
KOTSU
IN THE END, TWO OF THE THREE CARRIERS WE APPREHENDED WERE SEVERELY INJURED.
THE ONLY ONE I MANAGED TO BRING BACK IN ONE PIECE WAS YOU.
I CAN'T BELIEVE THEY FELL OFF THAT CLIFF AND STILL LIVED.
THAT GUY BEING BROUGHT BACK AND YOUR COMRADES...
IF YOU'RE SAYING IT'S THANKS TO YOU, THEN YES, IT IS THANKS TO YOU.
I DIDN'T DO ANY-THING.
THAT IS WHAT WE WILL BE LOOKING INTO.
ALAIN.

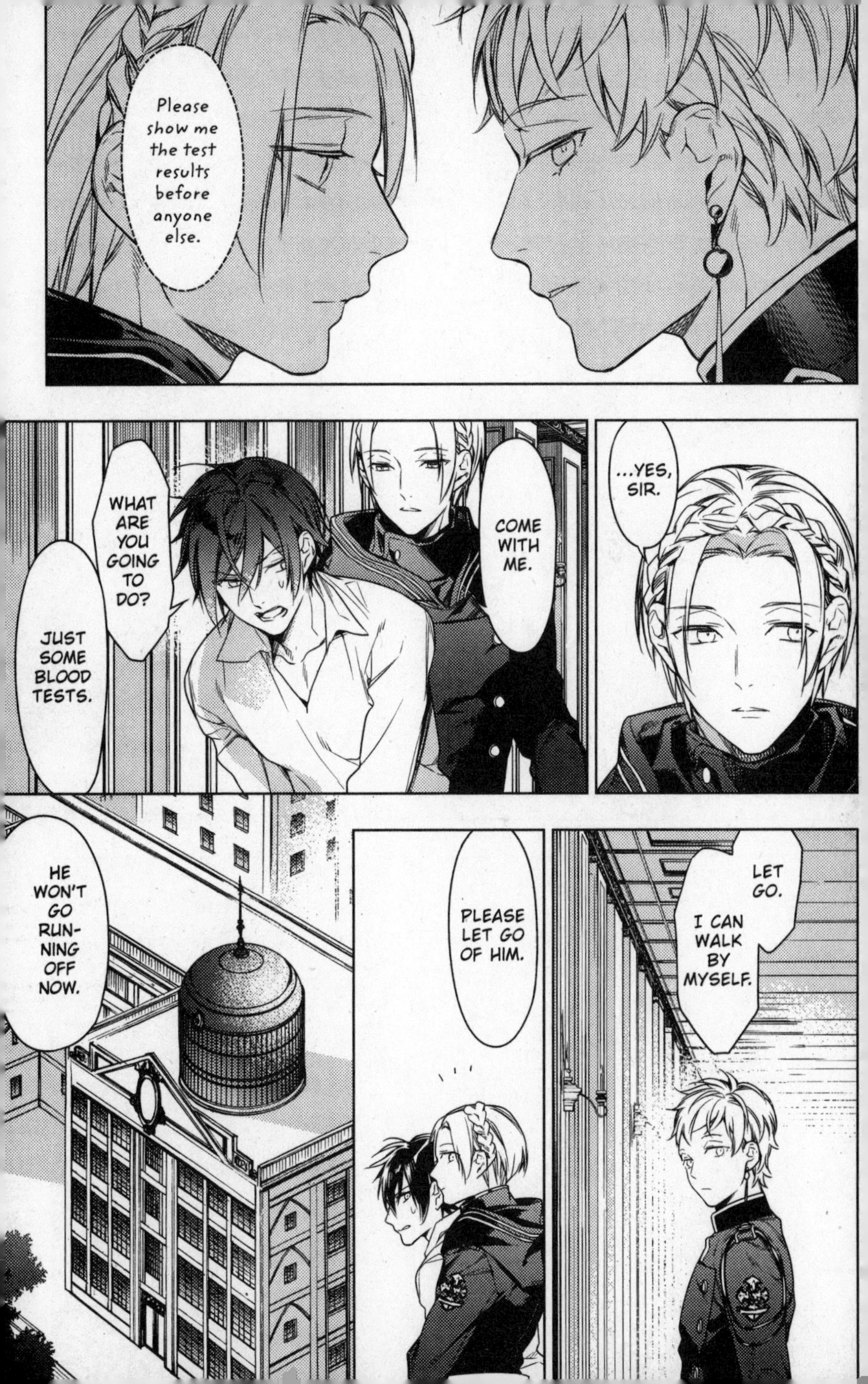
Please show me the test results before anyone else.
...YES, SIR.
COME WITH ME.
WHAT ARE YOU GOING TO DO?
JUST SOME BLOOD TESTS.
LET GO.
I CAN WALK BY MYSELF.
PLEASE LET GO OF HIM.
HE WON'T GO RUN-NING OFF NOW.

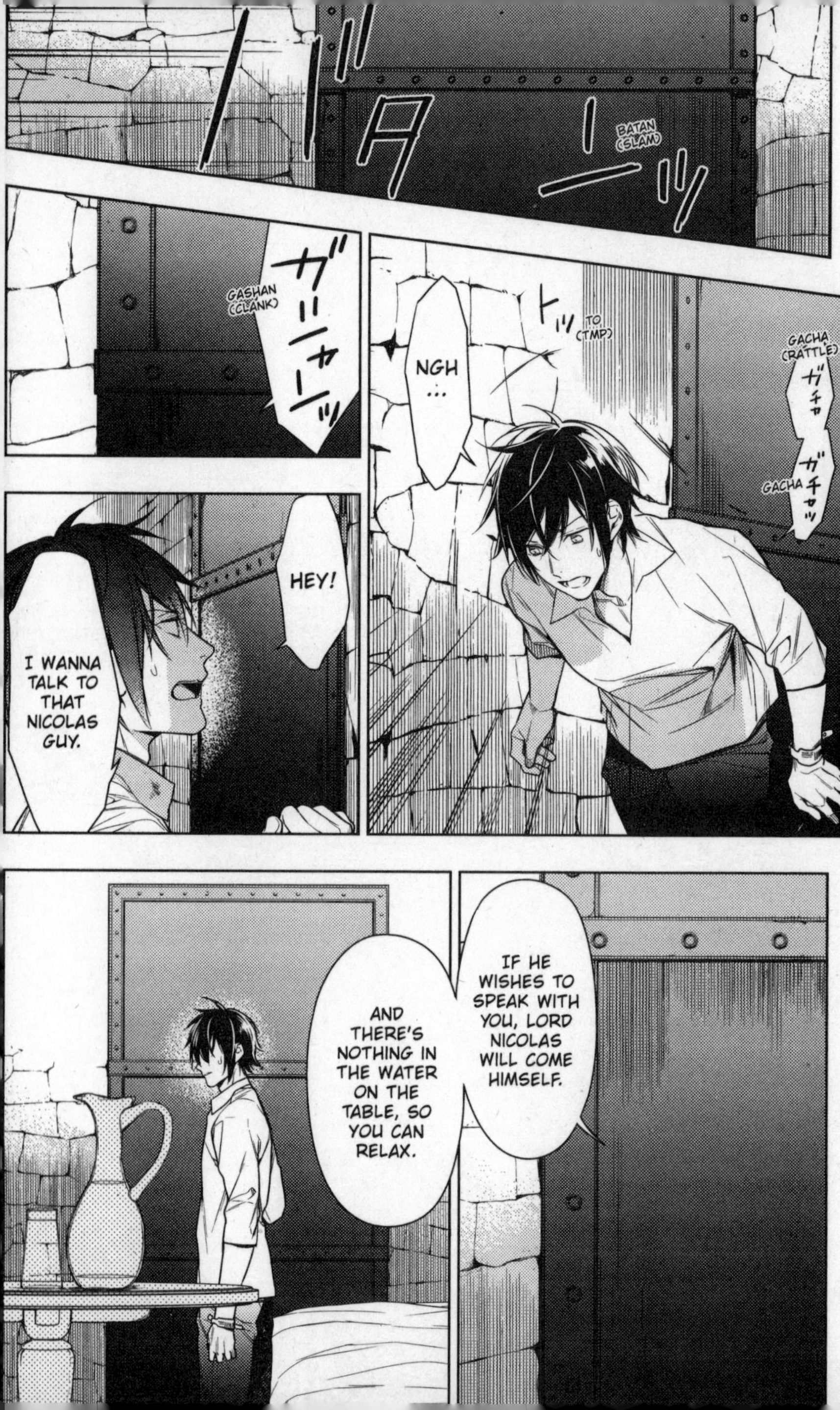
BATAN (SLAM)
GACHA (RATTLE)
GACHA
TO (TMP)
NGH...
GASHAN (CLANK)
HEY!
I WANNA TALK TO THAT NICOLAS GUY.
IF HE WISHES TO SPEAK WITH YOU, LORD NICOLAS WILL COME HIMSELF.
AND THERE'S NOTHING IN THE WATER ON THE TABLE, SO YOU CAN RELAX.

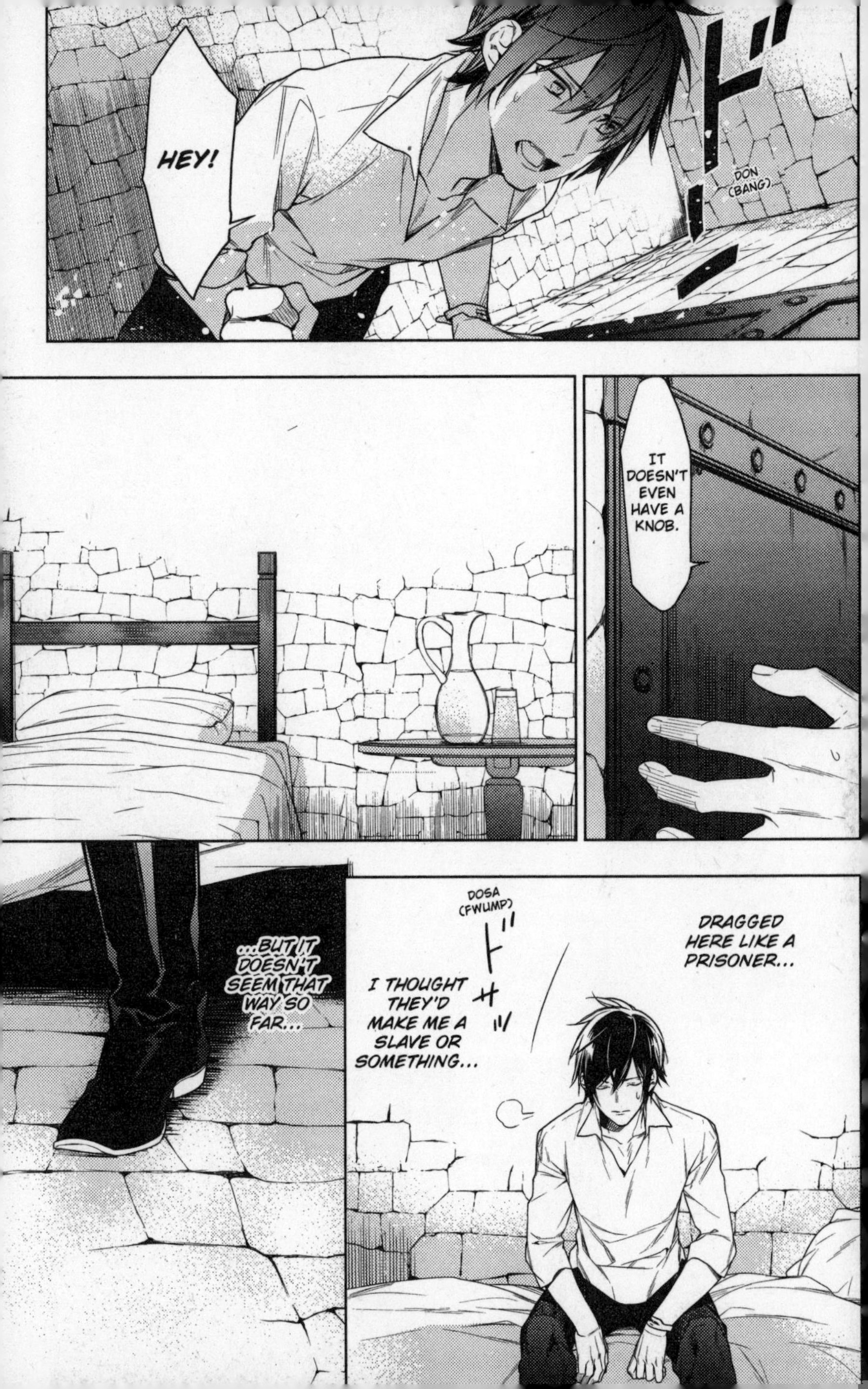
DON (BANG)
HEY!
IT DOESN'T EVEN HAVE A KNOB.
DRAGGED HERE LIKE A PRISONER...
DOSA (FWUMP)
I THOUGHT THEY'D MAKE ME A SLAVE OR SOMETHING...
...BUT IT DOESN'T SEEM THAT WAY SO FAR...

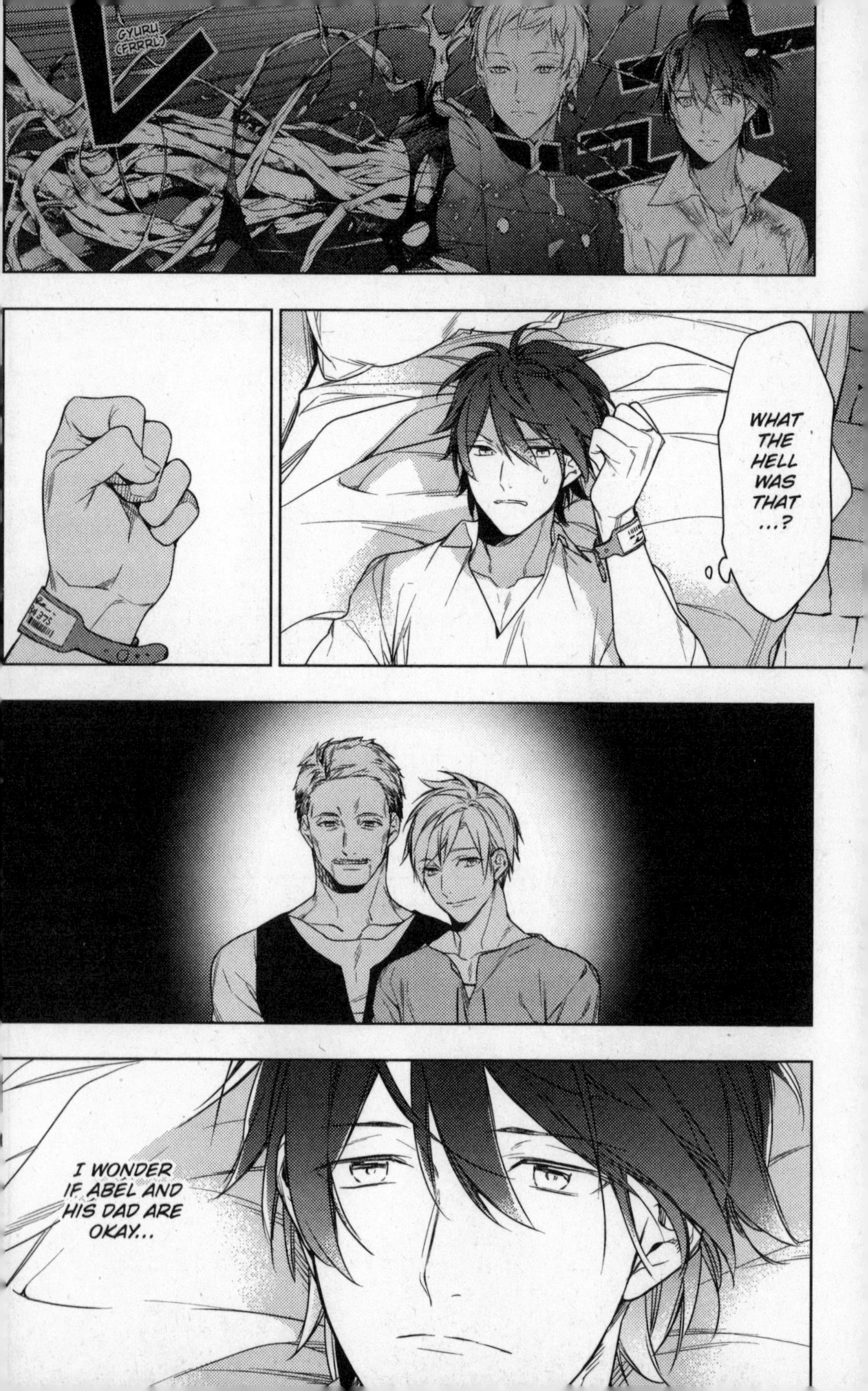
GYURU
(FRRRL)
WHAT THE HELL WAS THAT ...?
I WONDER IF ABEL AND HIS DAD ARE OKAY...

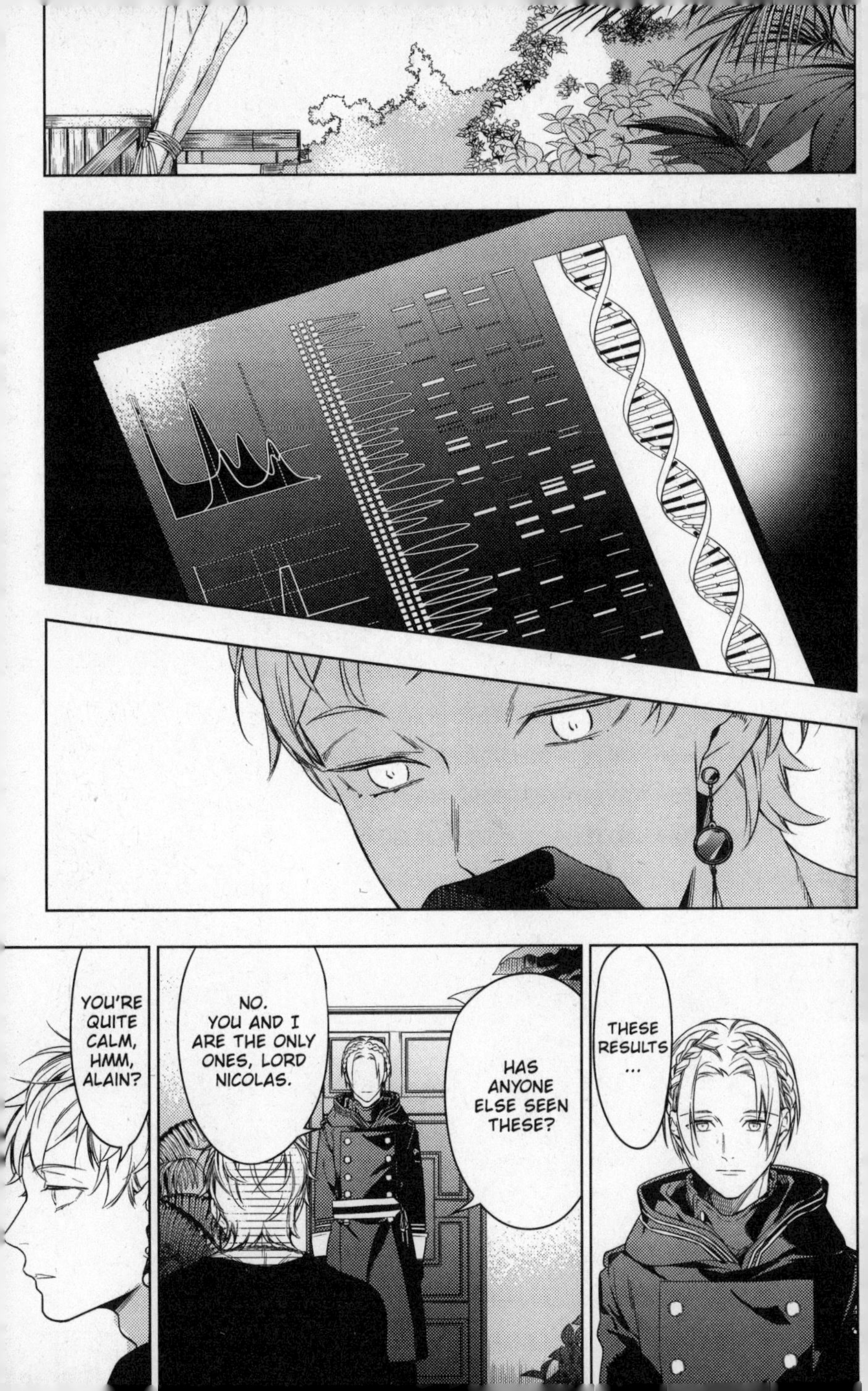
THESE RESULTS...
HAS ANYONE ELSE SEEN THESE?
NO. YOU AND I ARE THE ONLY ONES, LORD NICOLAS.
YOU'RE QUITE CALM, HMM, ALAIN?

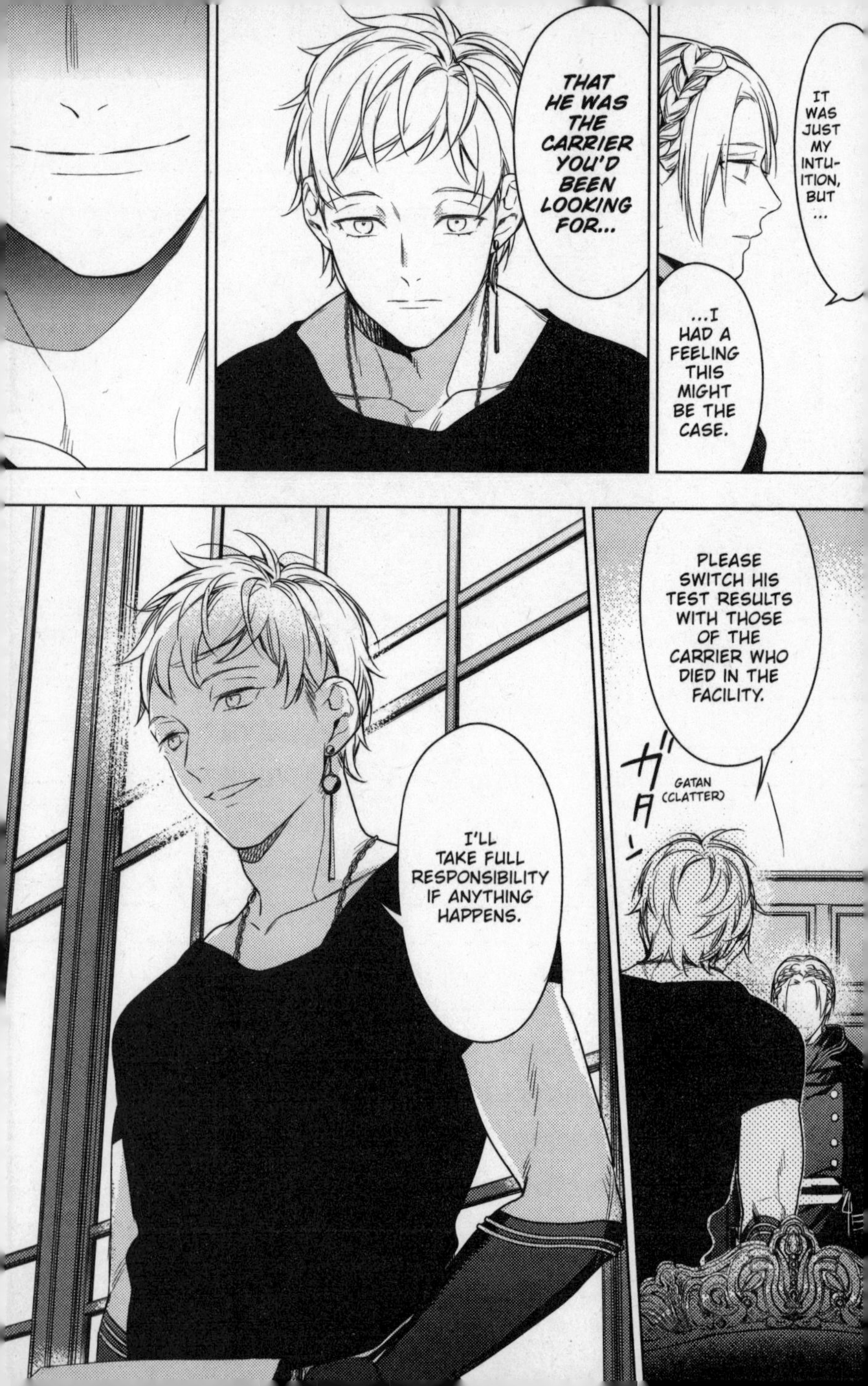
IT WAS JUST MY INTU-ITION, BUT ...
...I HAD A FEELING THIS MIGHT BE THE CASE.
THAT HE WAS THE CARRIER YOU'D BEEN LOOKING FOR...
PLEASE SWITCH HIS TEST RESULTS WITH THOSE OF THE CARRIER WHO DIED IN THE FACILITY.
GATAN (CLATTER)
I'LL TAKE FULL RESPONSIBILITY IF ANYTHING HAPPENS.

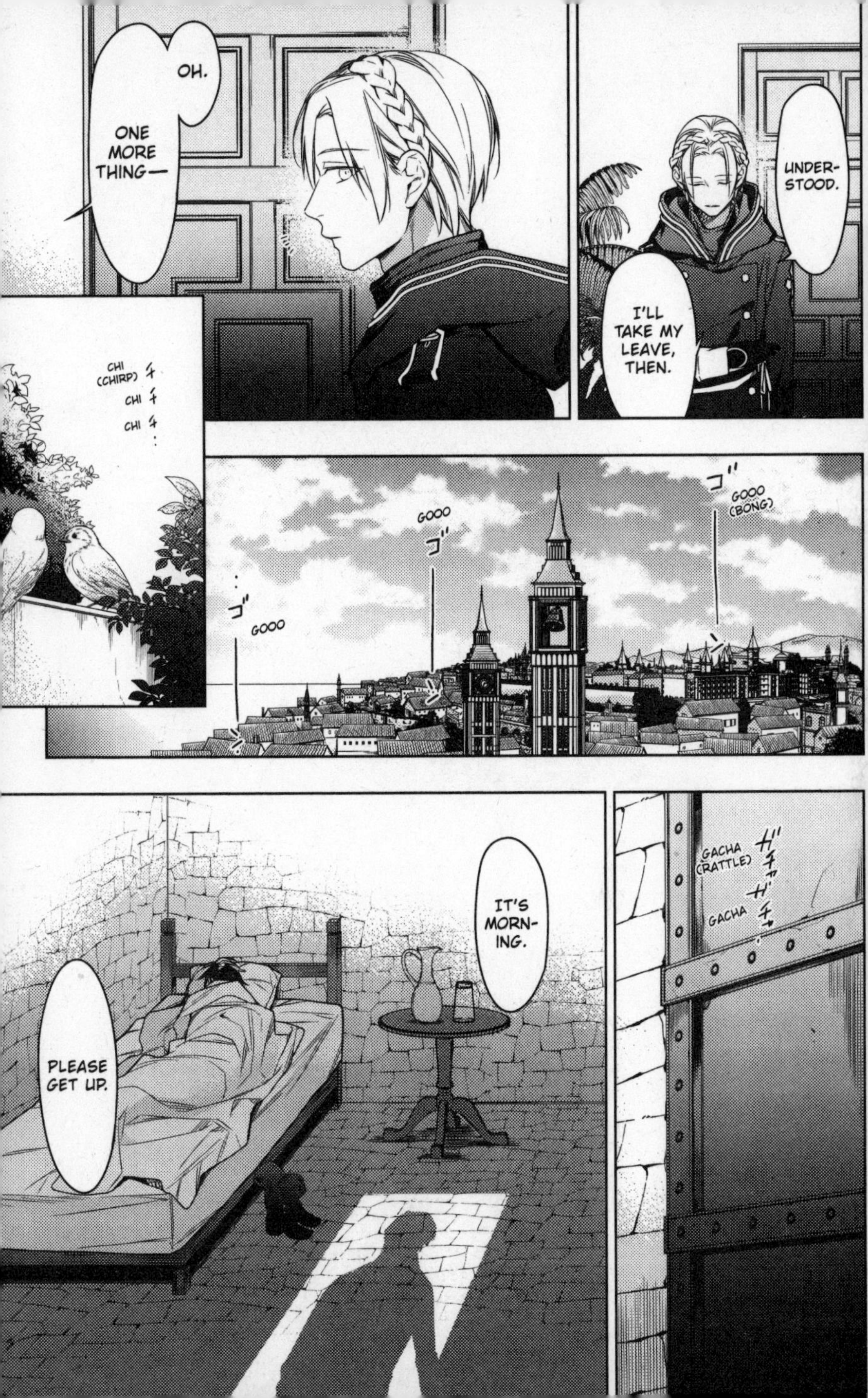
UNDER-STOOD.
I'LL TAKE MY LEAVE, THEN.
OH.
ONE MORE THING—
GOOO (BONG)
GOOO
GOOO
CHI (CHIRP)
CHI
CHI
GACHA (RATTLE)
GACHA
IT'S MORN-ING.
PLEASE GET UP.

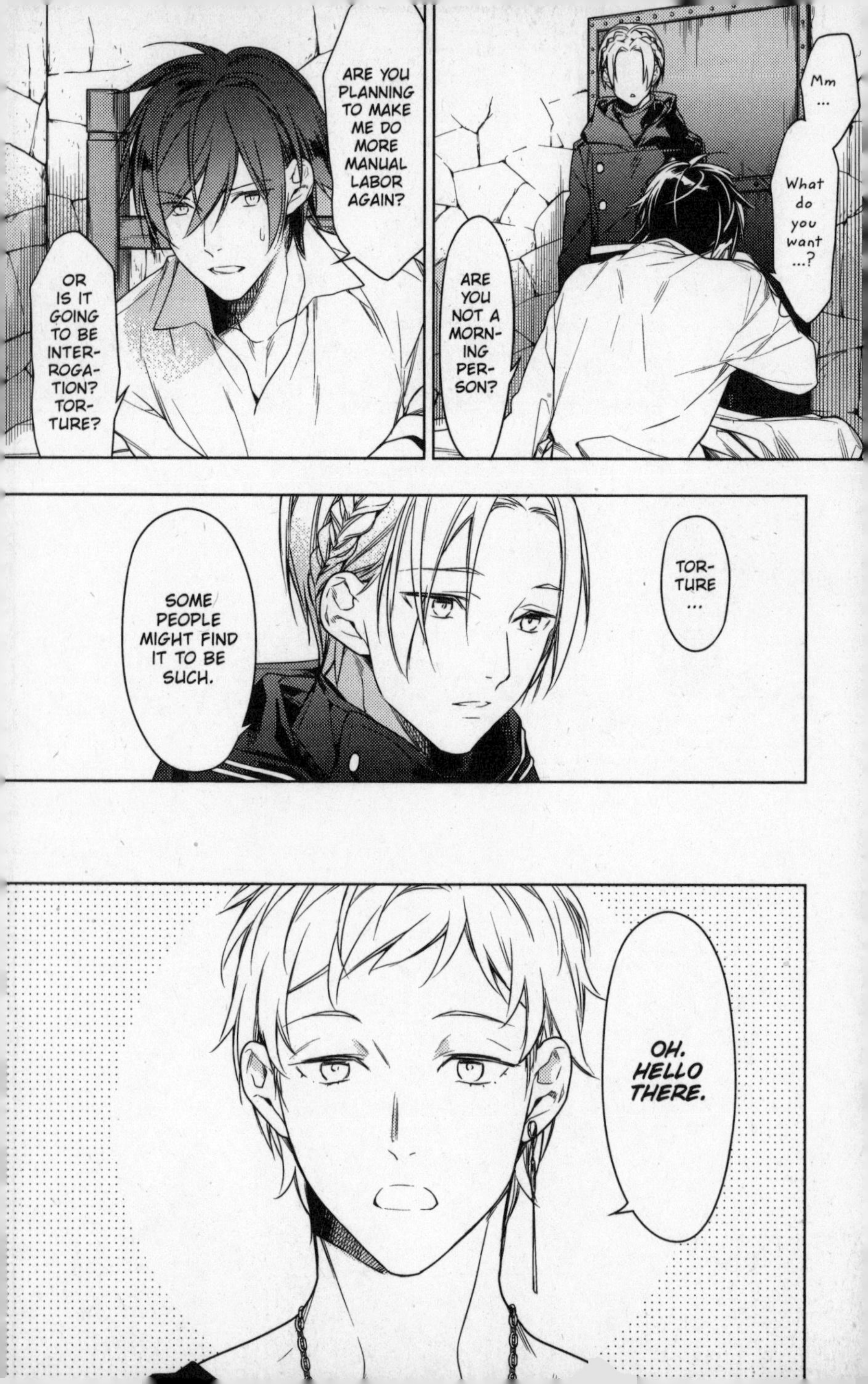
Mm... What do you want...?
ARE YOU NOT A MORNING-PERSON?
ARE YOU PLANNING TO MAKE ME DO MORE MANUAL LABOR AGAIN?
OR IS IT GOING TO BE INTERROGATION? TORTURE?
TORTURE...
SOME PEOPLE MIGHT FIND IT TO BE SUCH.
OH. HELLO THERE.

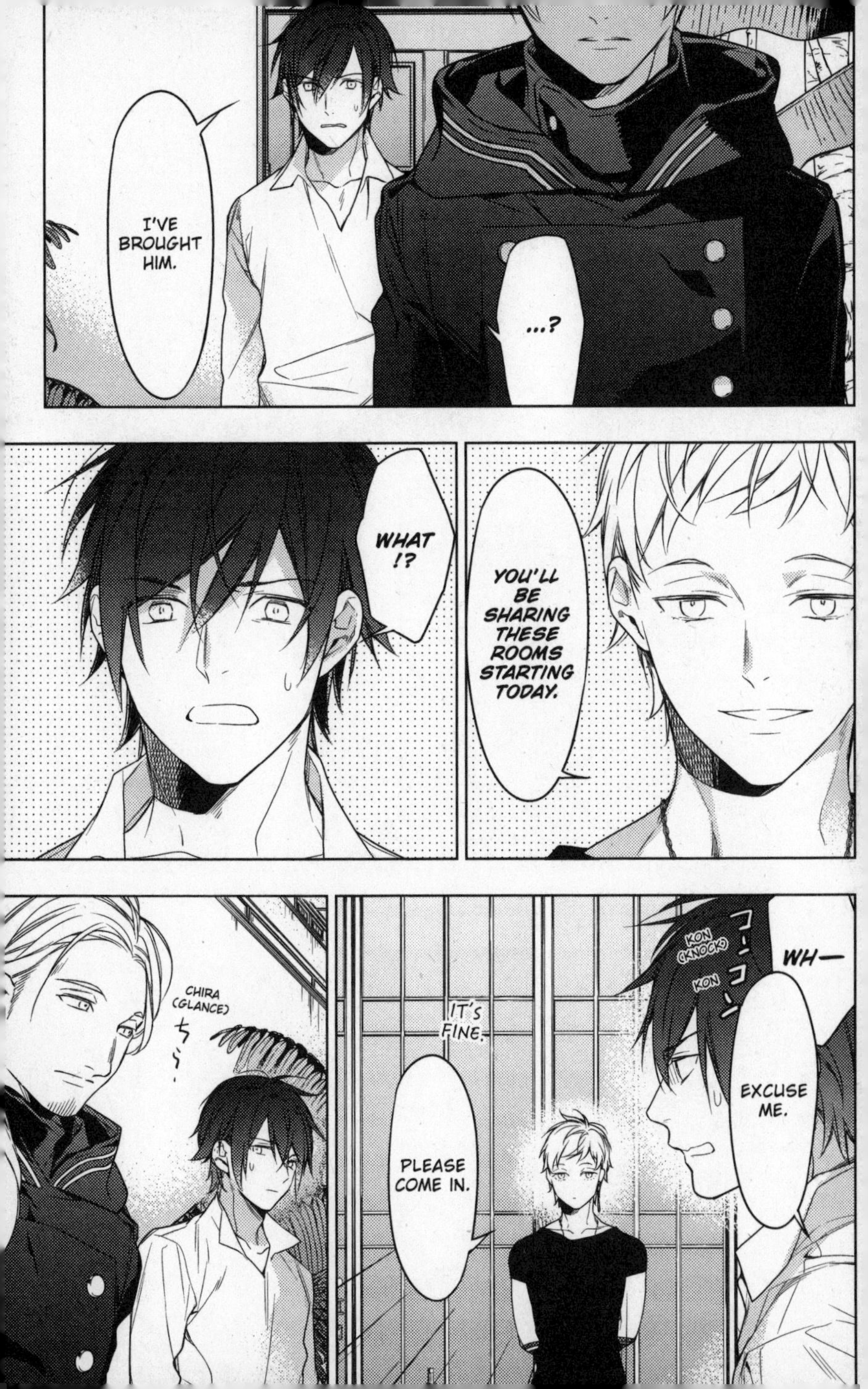
I'VE BROUGHT HIM.
...?
YOU'LL BE SHARING THESE ROOMS STARTING TODAY.
WHAT!?
KON (KNOCK) KON
WH—
EXCUSE ME.
IT'S FINE.
PLEASE COME IN.
CHIRA (GLANCE)
ちら

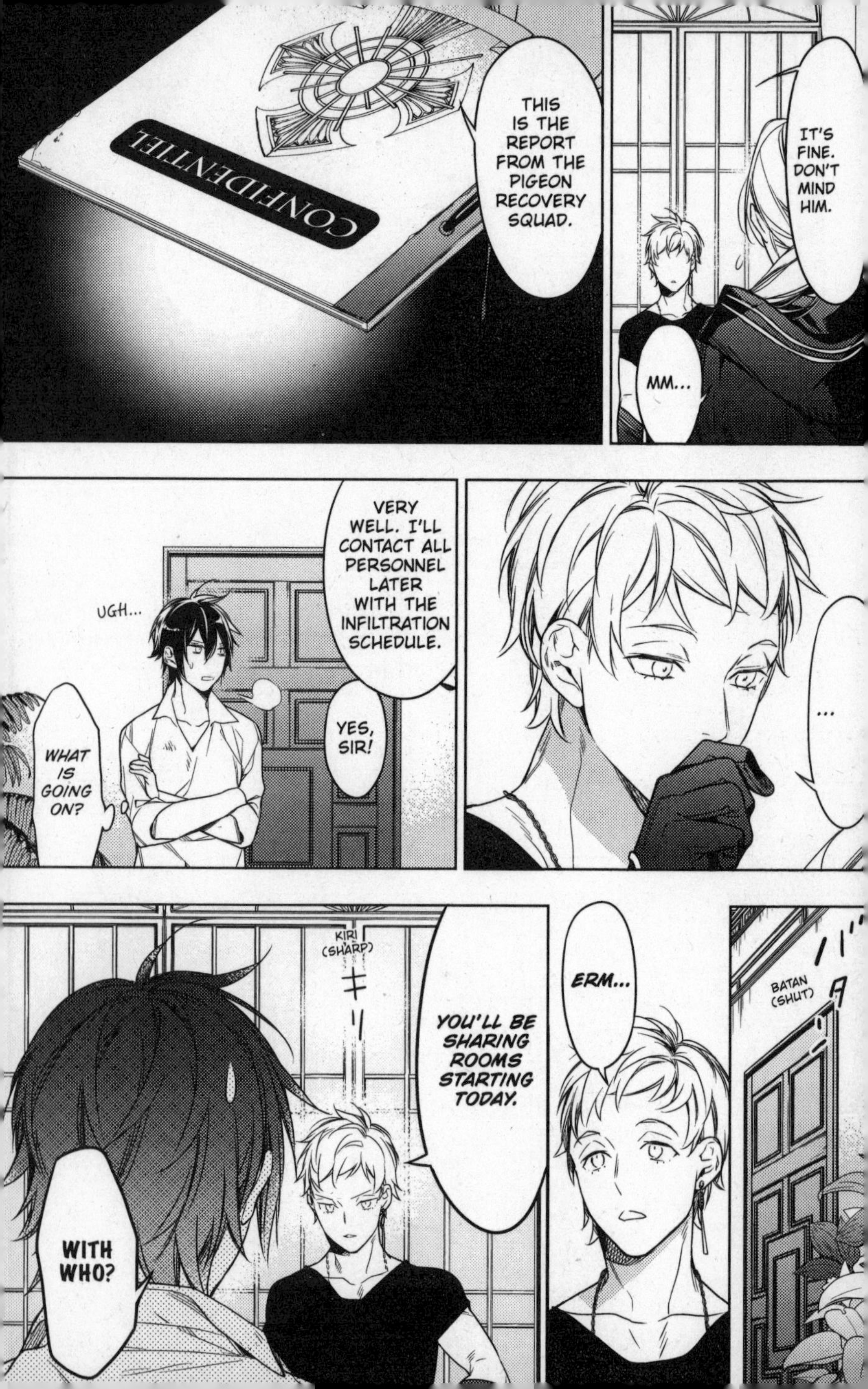
IT'S FINE. DON'T MIND HIM.
MM...
THIS IS THE REPORT FROM THE PIGEON RECOVERY SQUAD.
CONFIDENTIEL
...
VERY WELL. I'LL CONTACT ALL PERSONNEL LATER WITH THE INFILTRATION SCHEDULE.
YES, SIR!
UGH...
WHAT IS GOING ON?
BATAN (SHUT)
ERM...
YOU'LL BE SHARING ROOMS STARTING TODAY.
KIRI (SHARP)
WITH WHO?

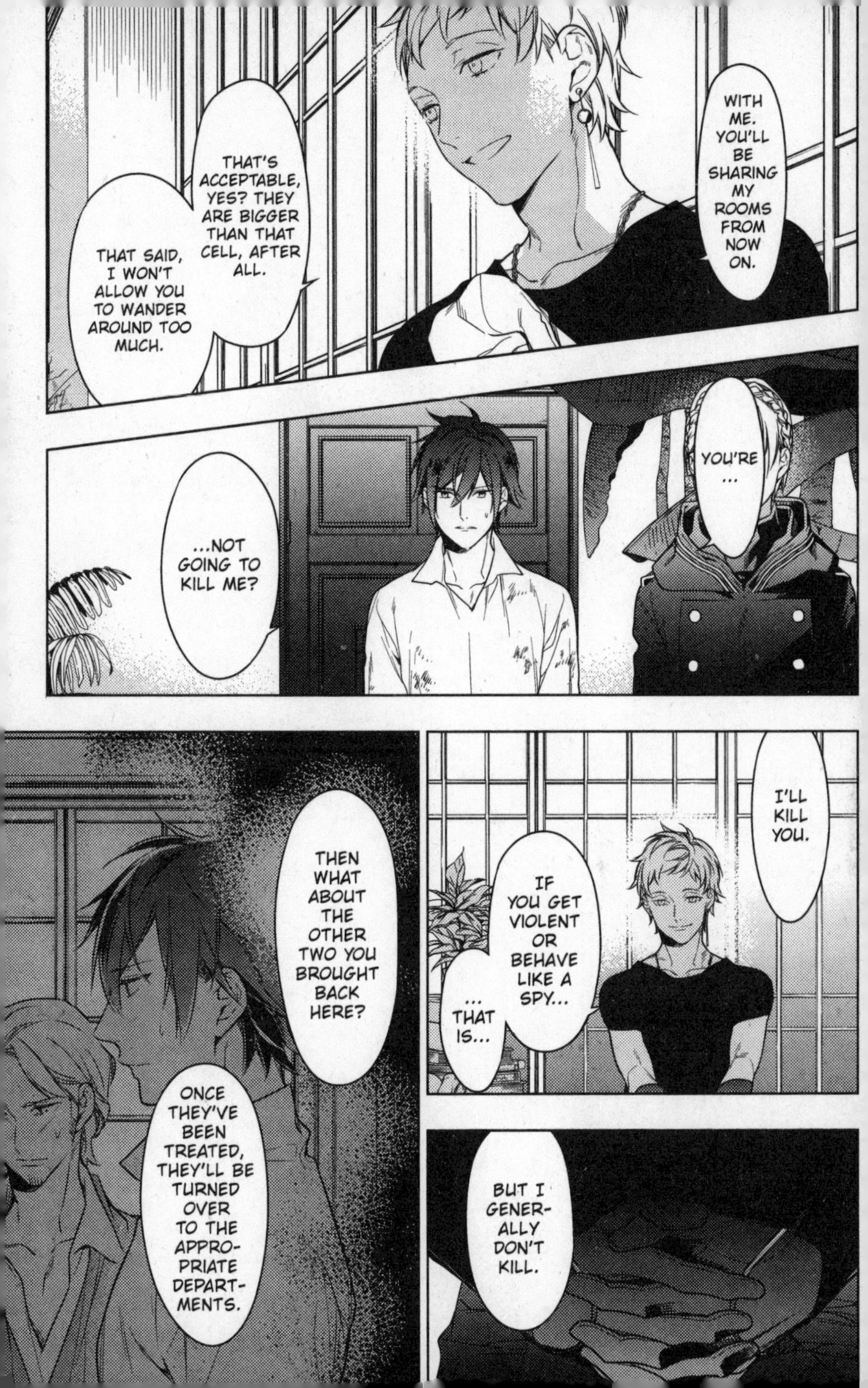
WITH ME. YOU'LL BE SHARING MY ROOMS FROM NOW ON.
THAT'S ACCEPTABLE, YES? THEY ARE BIGGER THAN THAT CELL, AFTER ALL.
THAT SAID, I WON'T ALLOW YOU TO WANDER AROUND TOO MUCH.
YOU'RE ...
...NOT GOING TO KILL ME?
I'LL KILL YOU.
IF YOU GET VIOLENT OR BEHAVE LIKE A SPY...
...THAT IS...
BUT I GENER-ALLY DON'T KILL.
THEN WHAT ABOUT THE OTHER TWO YOU BROUGHT BACK HERE?
ONCE THEY'VE BEEN TREATED, THEY'LL BE TURNED OVER TO THE APPRO-PRIATE DEPART-MENTS.

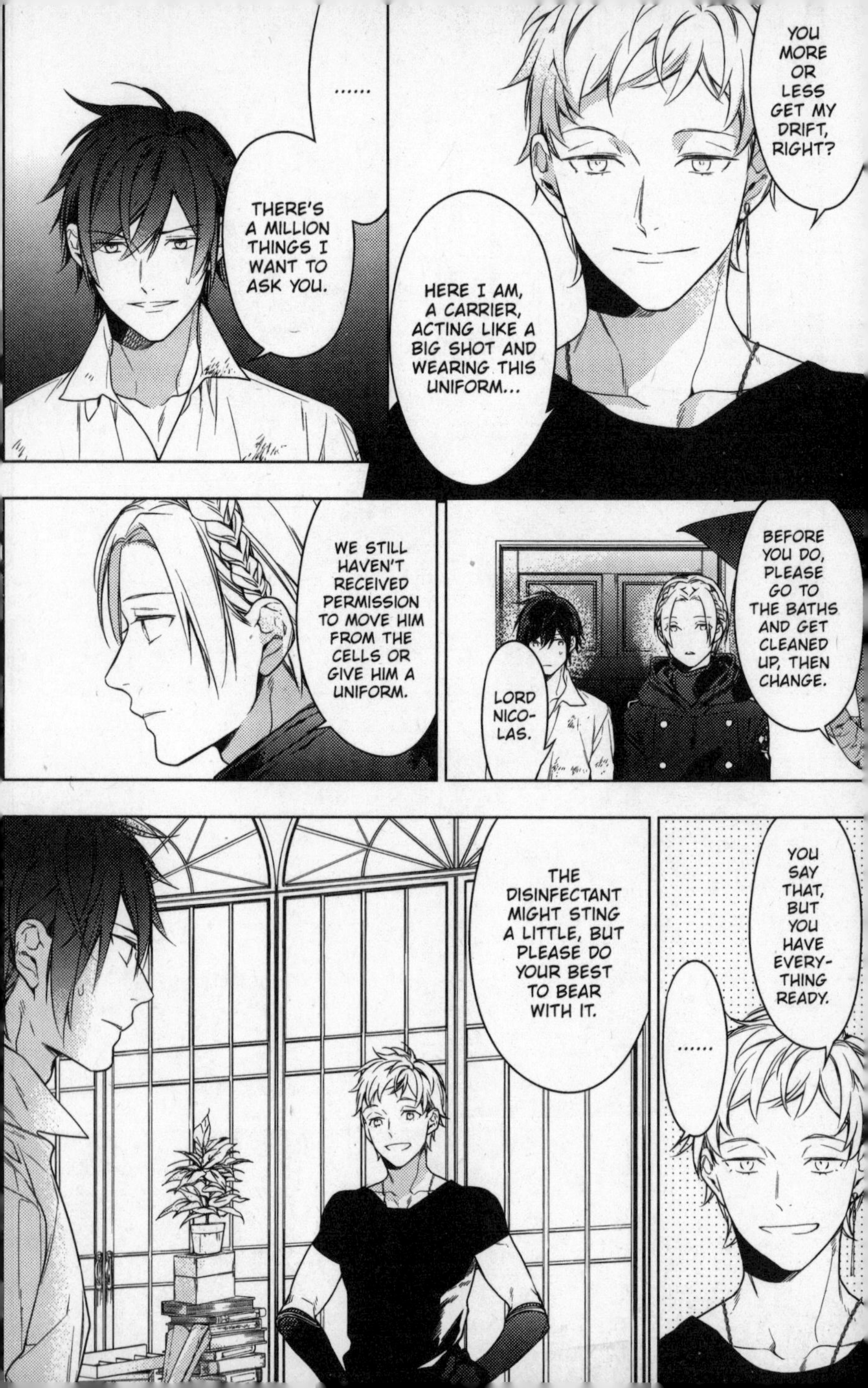
YOU MORE OR LESS GET MY DRIFT, RIGHT?
HERE I AM, A CARRIER, ACTING LIKE A BIG SHOT AND WEARING THIS UNIFORM...
......
THERE'S A MILLION THINGS I WANT TO ASK YOU.
BEFORE YOU DO, PLEASE GO TO THE BATHS AND GET CLEANED UP, THEN CHANGE.
LORD NICO-LAS.
WE STILL HAVEN'T RECEIVED PERMISSION TO MOVE HIM FROM THE CELLS OR GIVE HIM A UNIFORM.
YOU SAY THAT, BUT YOU HAVE EVERY-THING READY.
......
THE DISINFECTANT MIGHT STING A LITTLE, BUT PLEASE DO YOUR BEST TO BEAR WITH IT.

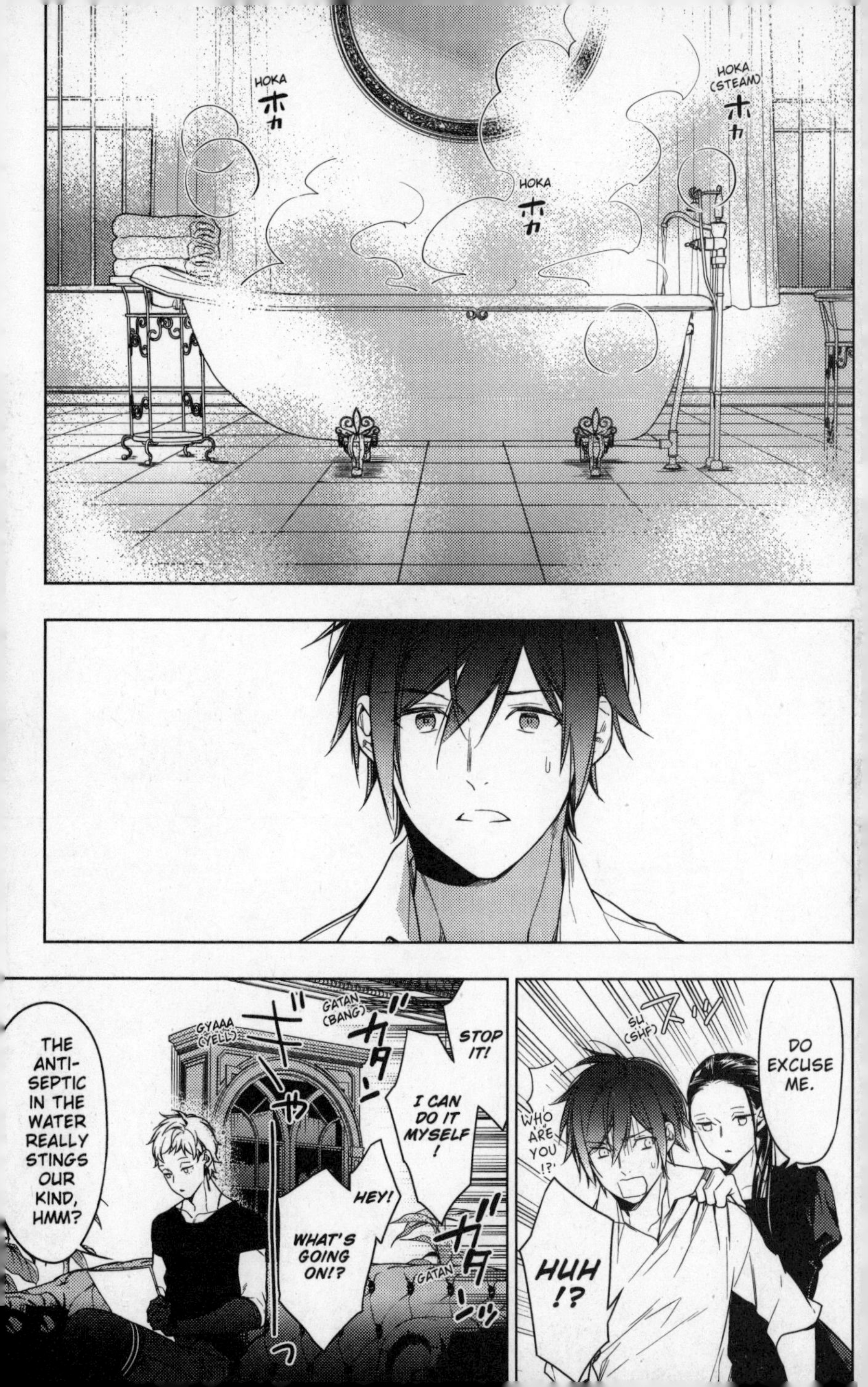
HOKA (STEAM)
ホカ
HOKA
ホカ
HOKA
ホカ
SU (SHF)
スッ
DO EXCUSE ME.
WHO ARE YOU !?
HUH !?
STOP IT!
GATAN (BANG)
ガタン
I CAN DO IT MYSELF !
GYAAA (YELL)
ギャーッ
HEY!
WHAT'S GOING ON!?
GATAN
ガタンッ
THE ANTI-SEPTIC IN THE WATER REALLY STINGS OUR KIND, HMM?

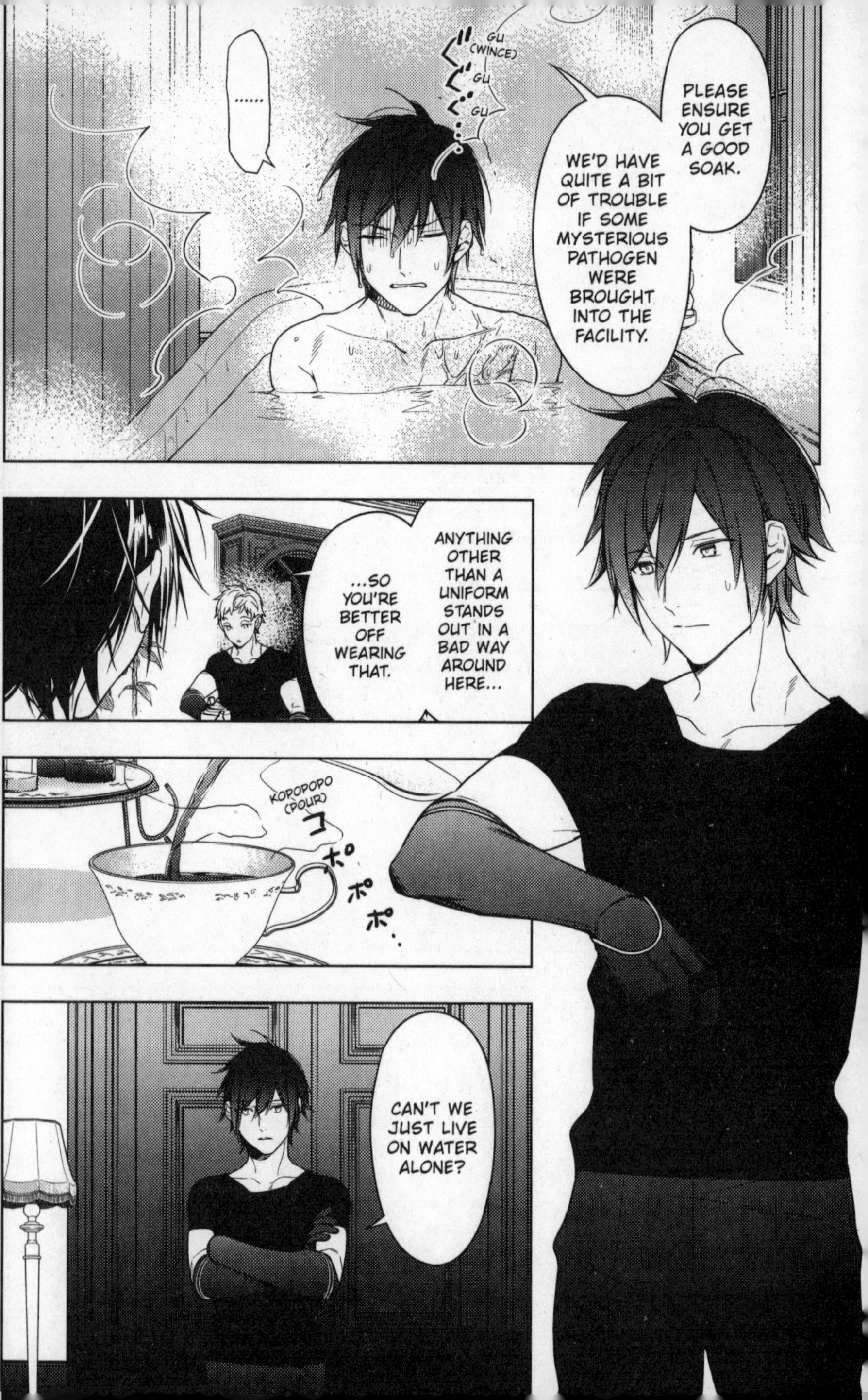
PLEASE ENSURE YOU GET A GOOD SOAK.
WE'D HAVE QUITE A BIT OF TROUBLE IF SOME MYSTERIOUS PATHOGEN WERE BROUGHT INTO THE FACILITY.
GU (WINCE) GU GU
......
ANYTHING OTHER THAN A UNIFORM STANDS OUT IN A BAD WAY AROUND HERE...
...SO YOU'RE BETTER OFF WEARING THAT.
KOPOPOPO (POUR)
CAN'T WE JUST LIVE ON WATER ALONE?

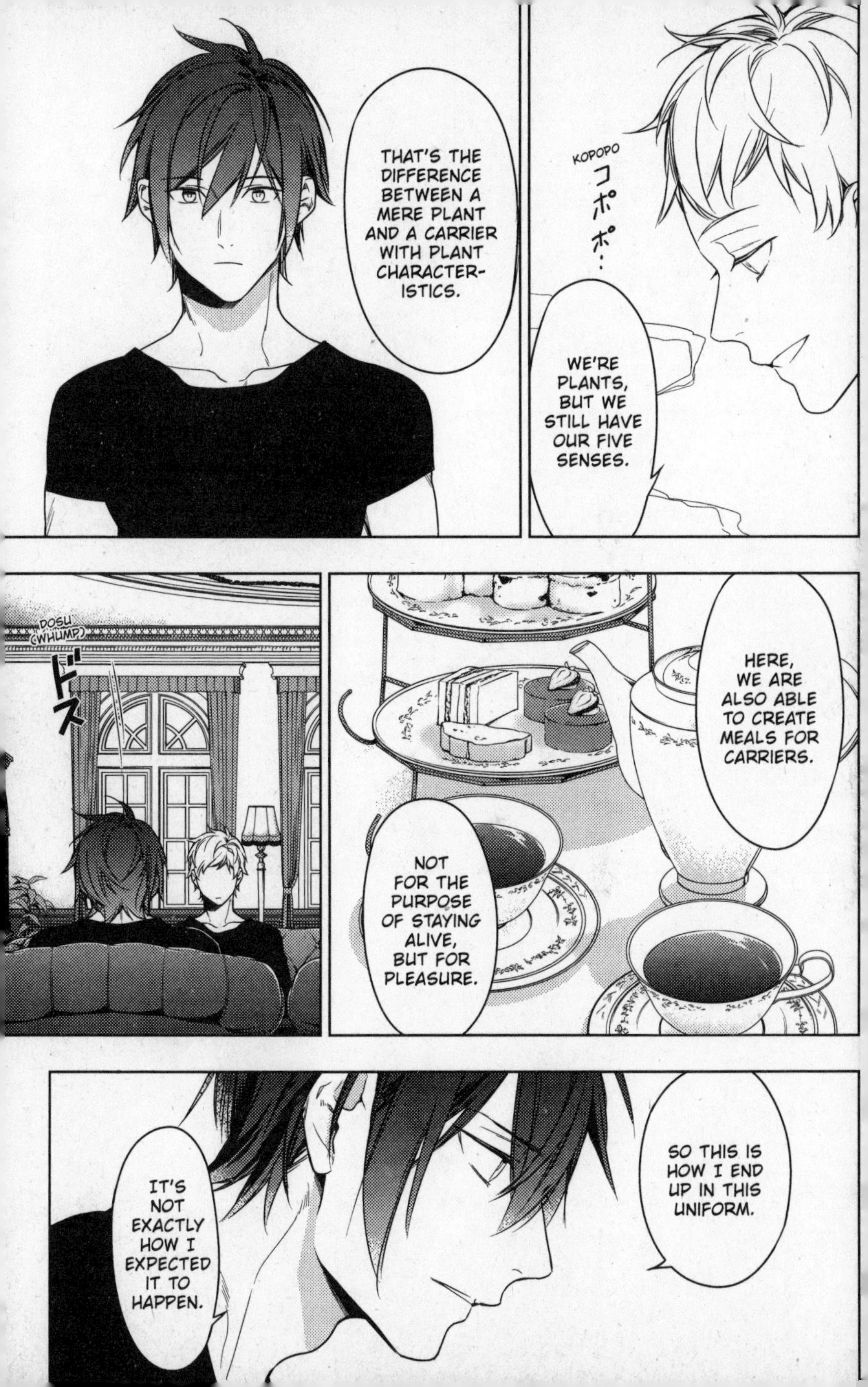
KOPOPO
コポポ…
WE'RE PLANTS, BUT WE STILL HAVE OUR FIVE SENSES.
THAT'S THE DIFFERENCE BETWEEN A MERE PLANT AND A CARRIER WITH PLANT CHARACTER-ISTICS.
HERE, WE ARE ALSO ABLE TO CREATE MEALS FOR CARRIERS.
NOT FOR THE PURPOSE OF STAYING ALIVE, BUT FOR PLEASURE.
DOSU (WHUMP)
ドス
SO THIS IS HOW I END UP IN THIS UNIFORM.
IT'S NOT EXACTLY HOW I EXPECTED IT TO HAPPEN.

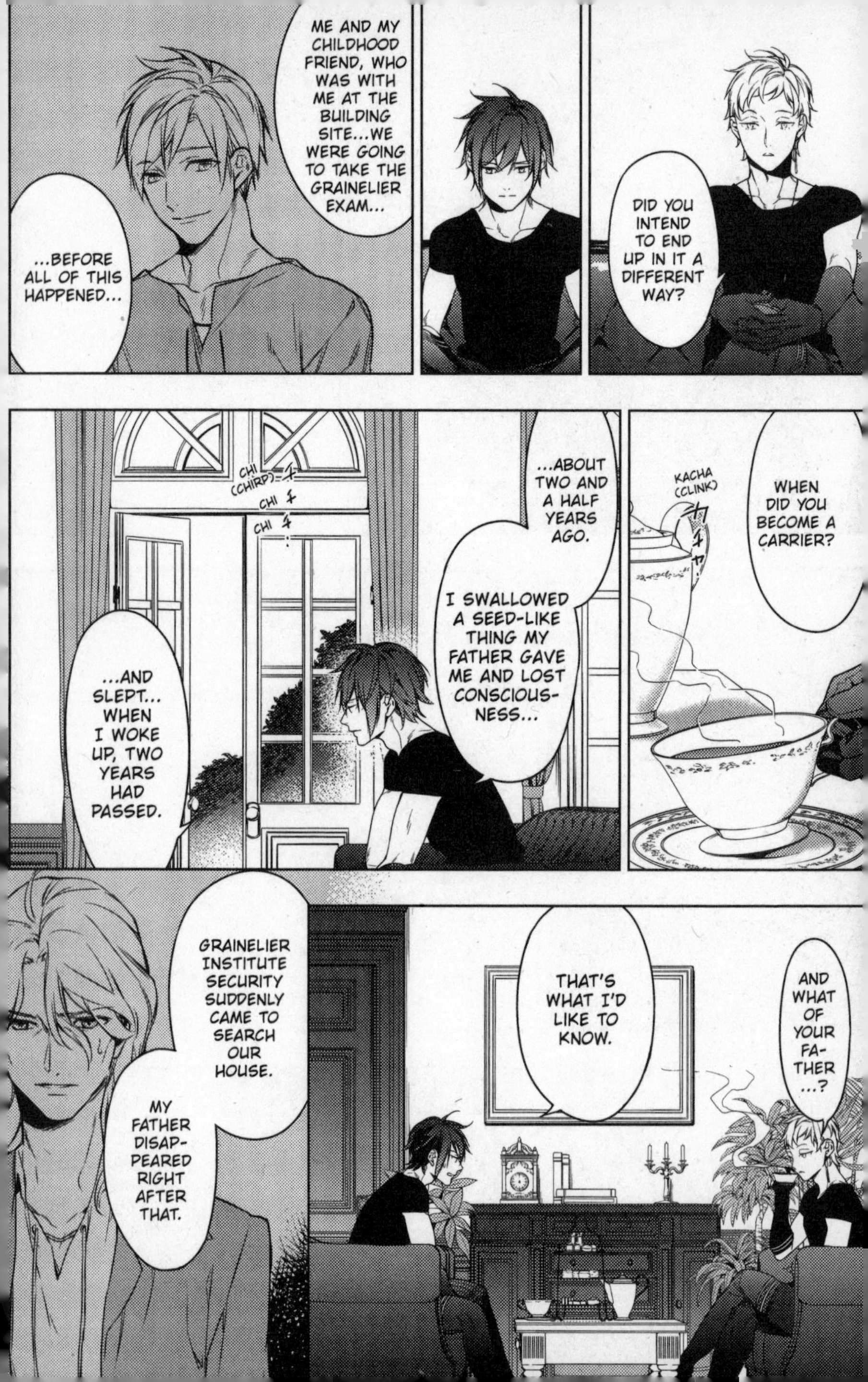
DID YOU INTEND TO END UP IN IT A DIFFERENT WAY?
ME AND MY CHILDHOOD FRIEND, WHO WAS WITH ME AT THE BUILDING SITE...WE WERE GOING TO TAKE THE GRAINELIER EXAM...
...BEFORE ALL OF THIS HAPPENED...
WHEN DID YOU BECOME A CARRIER?
KACHA (CLINK)
...ABOUT TWO AND A HALF YEARS AGO.
I SWALLOWED A SEED-LIKE THING MY FATHER GAVE ME AND LOST CONSCIOUS-NESS...
CHI (CHIRP) CHI CHI
...AND SLEPT... WHEN I WOKE UP, TWO YEARS HAD PASSED.
AND WHAT OF YOUR FA-THER...?
THAT'S WHAT I'D LIKE TO KNOW.
GRAINELIER INSTITUTE SECURITY SUDDENLY CAME TO SEARCH OUR HOUSE.
MY FATHER DISAP-PEARED RIGHT AFTER THAT.

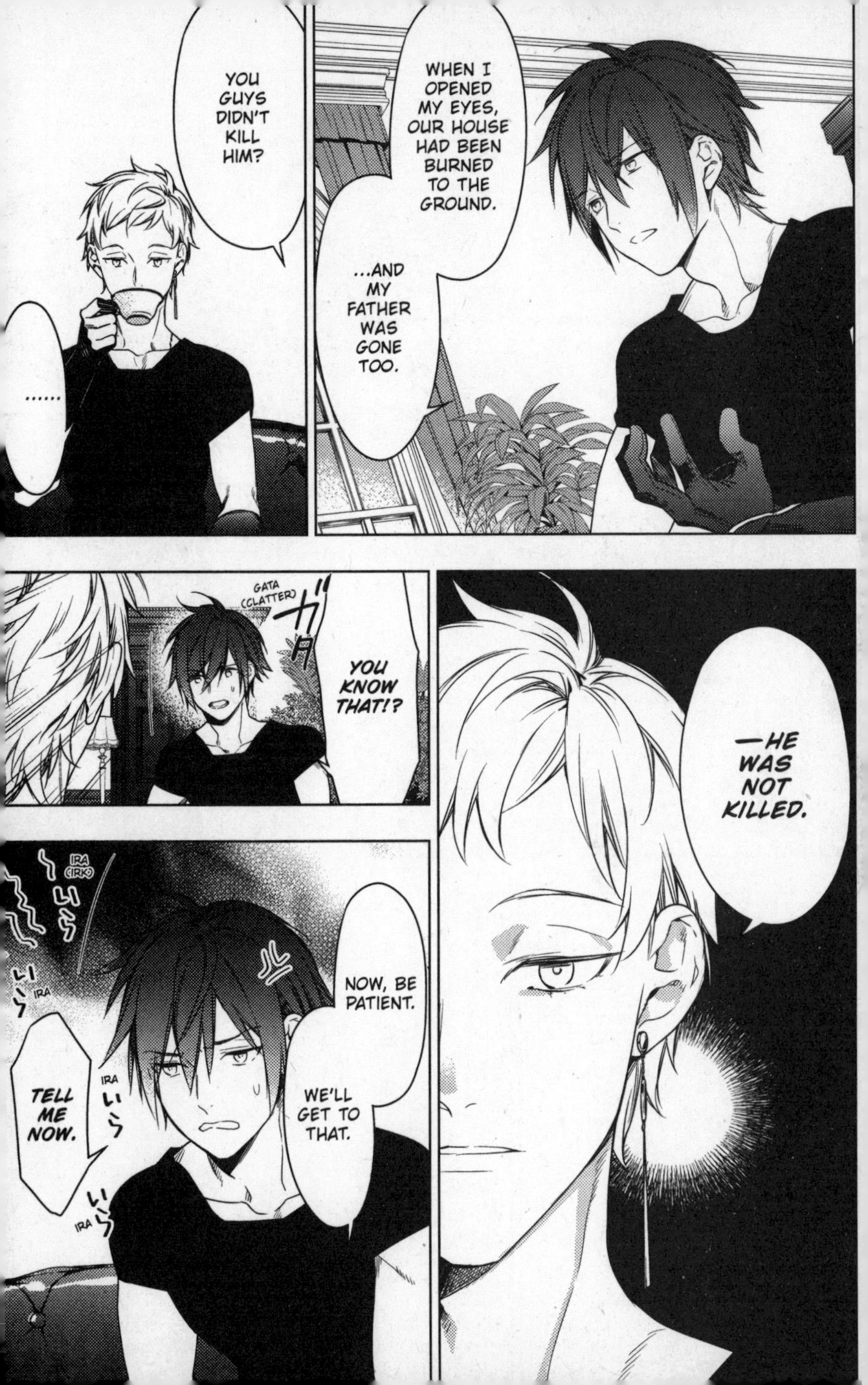
WHEN I OPENED MY EYES, OUR HOUSE HAD BEEN BURNED TO THE GROUND.
...AND MY FATHER WAS GONE TOO.
YOU GUYS DIDN'T KILL HIM?
......
—HE WAS NOT KILLED.
GATA (CLATTER)
ガタ
YOU KNOW THAT!?
NOW, BE PATIENT.
WE'LL GET TO THAT.
IRA (IRK)
いら
IRA
いら
IRA
いら
TELL ME NOW.
IRA
いら

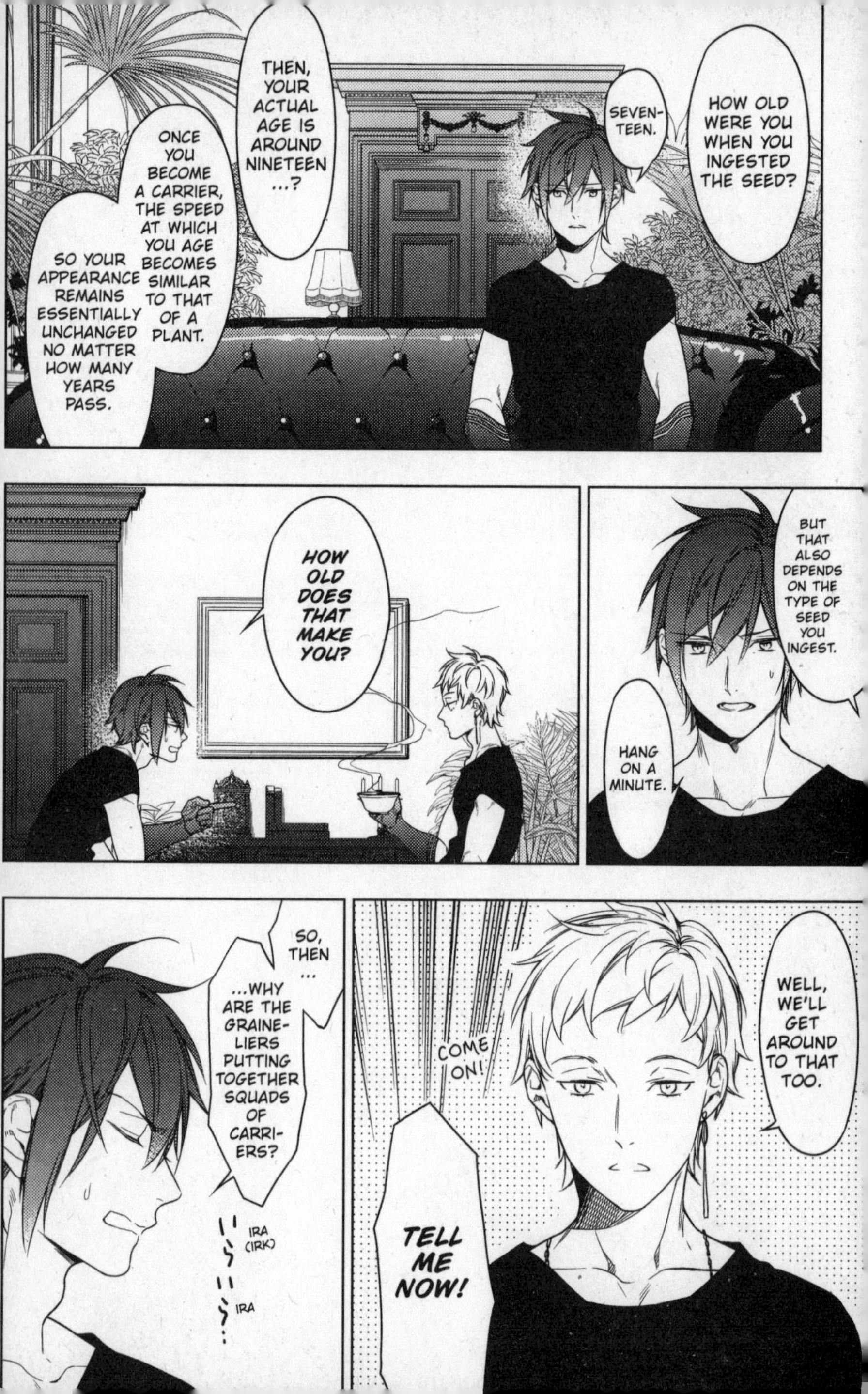
HOW OLD WERE YOU WHEN YOU INGESTED THE SEED?
SEVEN-TEEN.
THEN, YOUR ACTUAL AGE IS AROUND NINETEEN ...?
ONCE YOU BECOME A CARRIER, THE SPEED AT WHICH YOU AGE BECOMES SIMILAR TO THAT OF A PLANT.
SO YOUR APPEARANCE REMAINS ESSENTIALLY UNCHANGED NO MATTER HOW MANY YEARS PASS.
BUT THAT ALSO DEPENDS ON THE TYPE OF SEED YOU INGEST.
HANG ON A MINUTE.
HOW OLD DOES THAT MAKE YOU?
WELL, WE'LL GET AROUND TO THAT TOO.
COME ON!
TELL ME NOW!
SO, THEN ...
...WHY ARE THE GRAINE-LIERS PUTTING TOGETHER SQUADS OF CARRI-ERS?
いらいら
IRA (IRK)
IRA

Episode 24

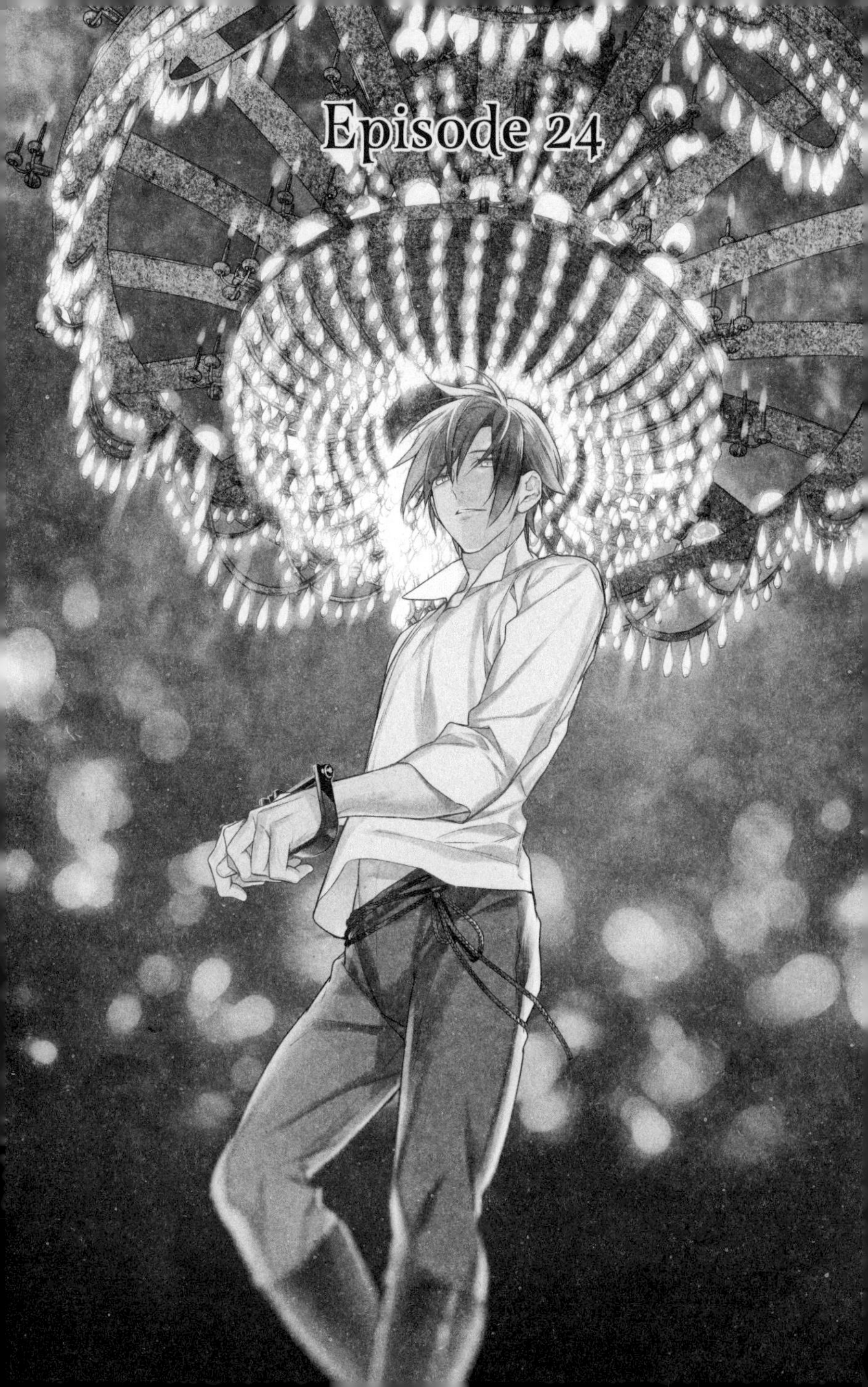

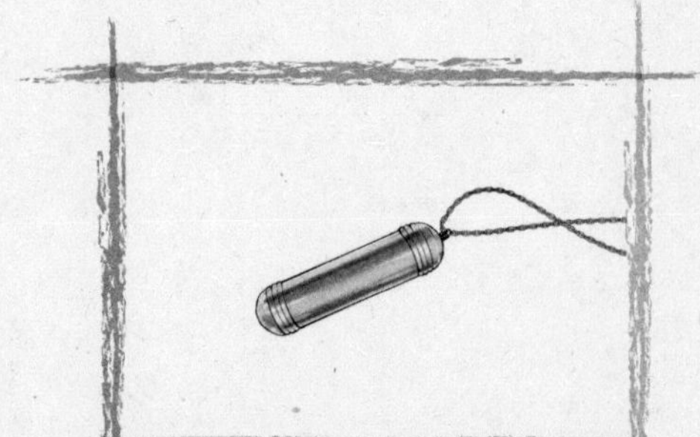

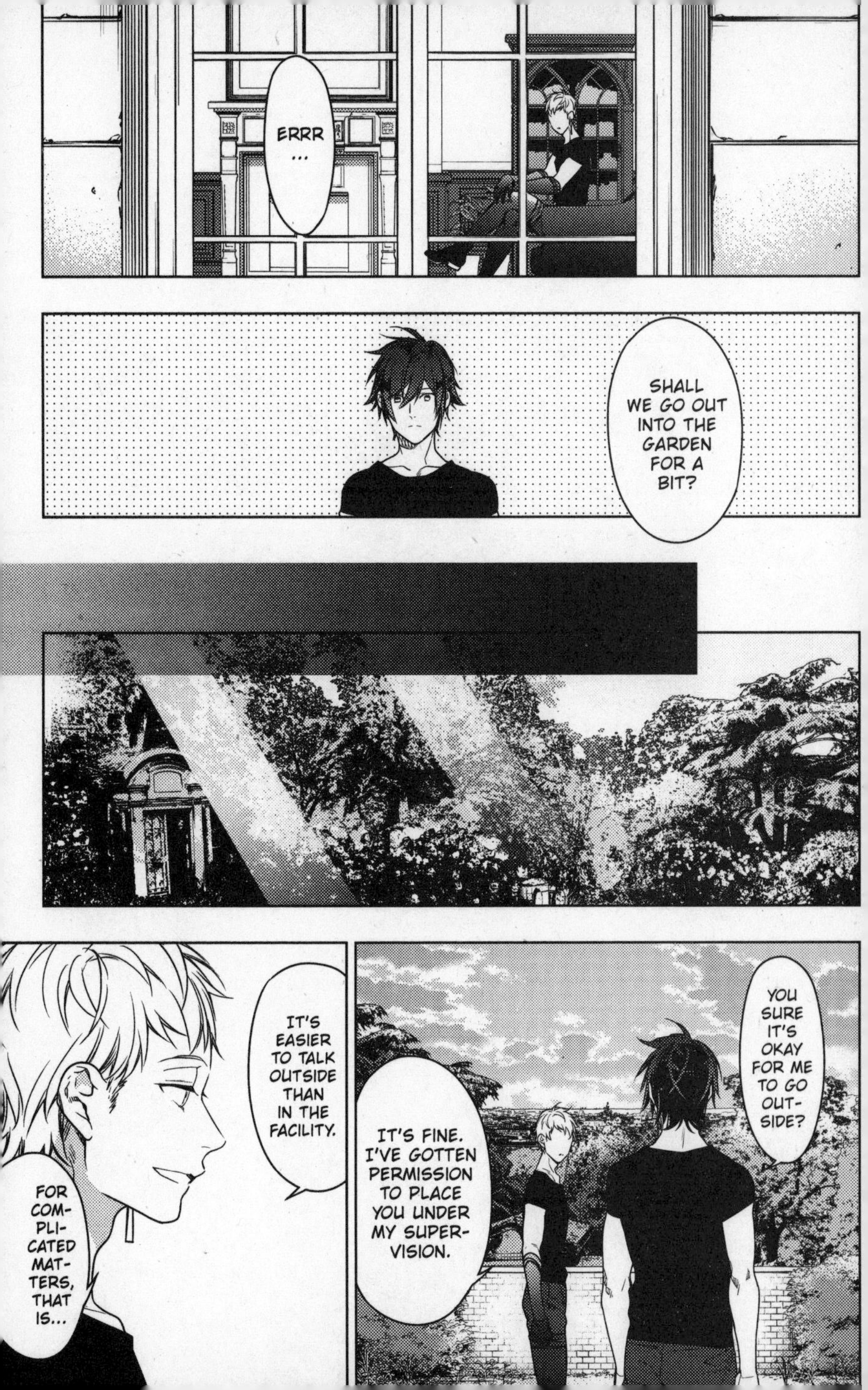
ERRR ...
SHALL WE GO OUT INTO THE GARDEN FOR A BIT?
YOU SURE IT'S OKAY FOR ME TO GO OUTSIDE?
IT'S FINE. I'VE GOTTEN PERMISSION TO PLACE YOU UNDER MY SUPERVISION.
IT'S EASIER TO TALK OUTSIDE THAN IN THE FACILITY.
FOR COMPLICATED MATTERS, THAT IS...

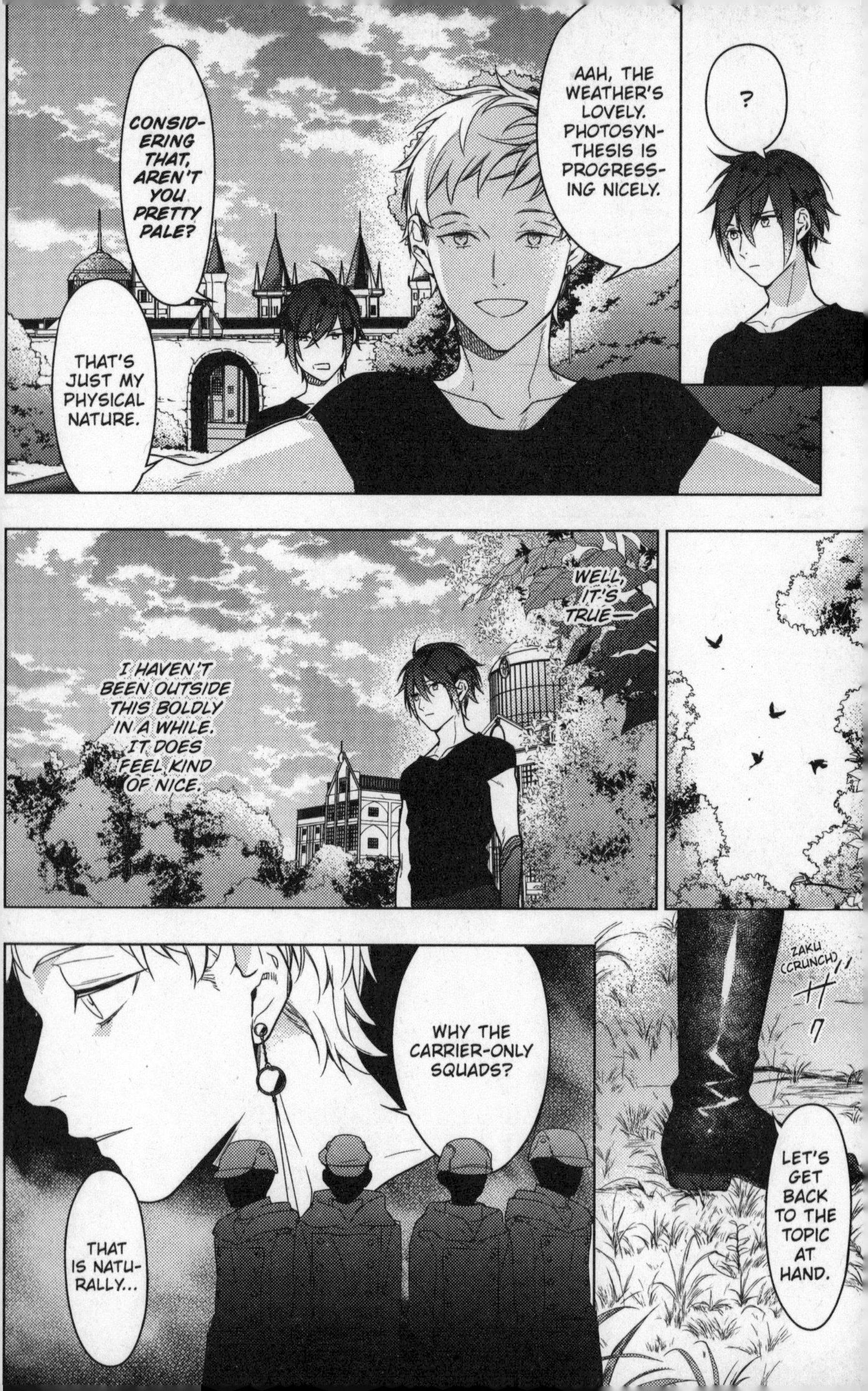
?
AAH, THE WEATHER'S LOVELY. PHOTOSYNTHESIS IS PROGRESSING NICELY.
CONSIDERING THAT, AREN'T YOU PRETTY PALE?
THAT'S JUST MY PHYSICAL NATURE.
WELL, IT'S TRUE—
I HAVEN'T BEEN OUTSIDE THIS BOLDLY IN A WHILE. IT DOES FEEL KIND OF NICE.
ZAKU (CRUNCH)
LET'S GET BACK TO THE TOPIC AT HAND.
WHY THE CARRIER-ONLY SQUADS?
THAT IS NATURALLY...

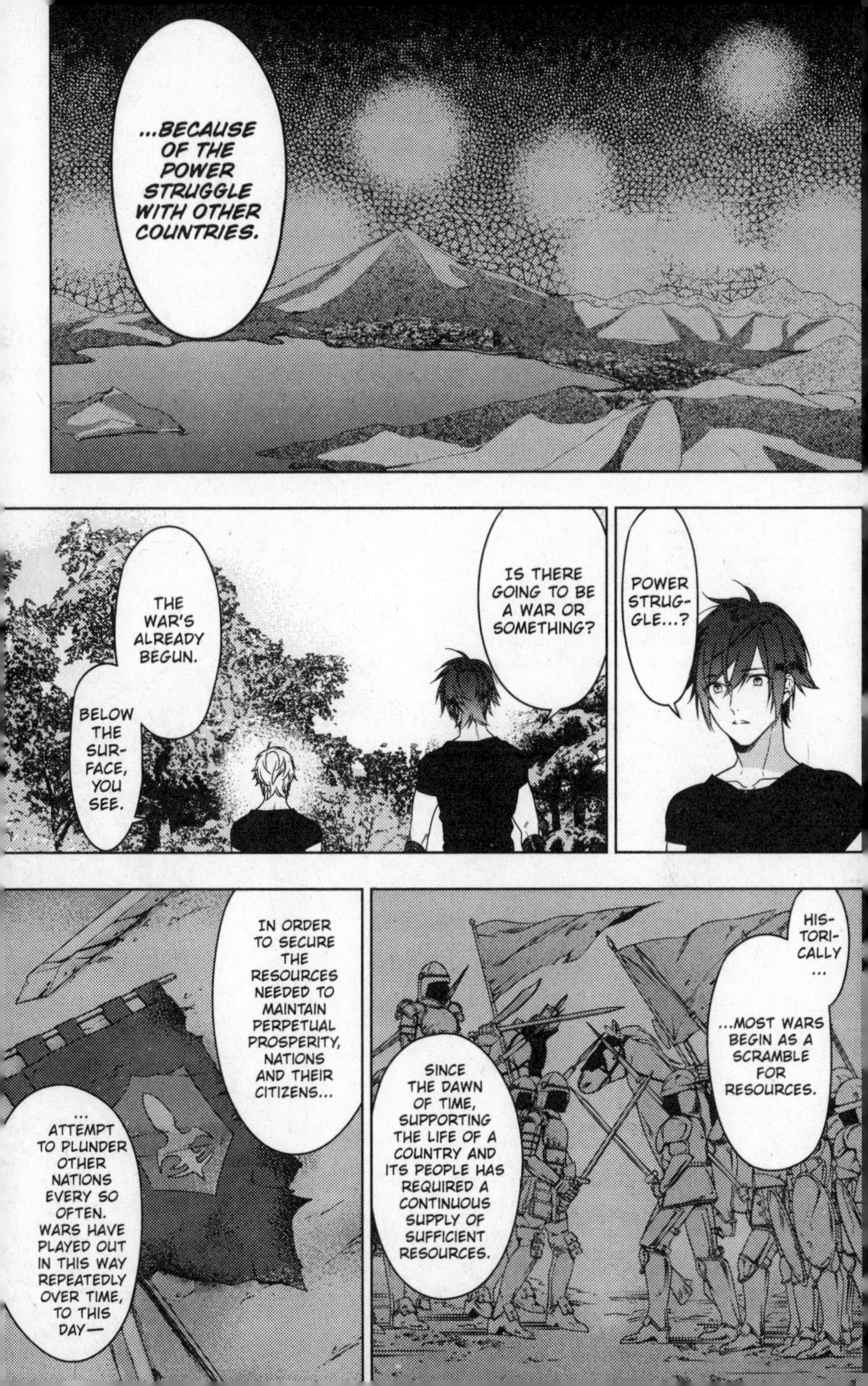
...BECAUSE OF THE POWER STRUGGLE WITH OTHER COUNTRIES.
POWER STRUG-GLE...?
IS THERE GOING TO BE A WAR OR SOMETHING?
THE WAR'S ALREADY BEGUN.
BELOW THE SUR-FACE, YOU SEE.
HIS-TORI-CALLY...
...MOST WARS BEGIN AS A SCRAMBLE FOR RESOURCES.
SINCE THE DAWN OF TIME, SUPPORTING THE LIFE OF A COUNTRY AND ITS PEOPLE HAS REQUIRED A CONTINUOUS SUPPLY OF SUFFICIENT RESOURCES.
IN ORDER TO SECURE THE RESOURCES NEEDED TO MAINTAIN PERPETUAL PROSPERITY, NATIONS AND THEIR CITIZENS...
...ATTEMPT TO PLUNDER OTHER NATIONS EVERY SO OFTEN. WARS HAVE PLAYED OUT IN THIS WAY REPEATEDLY OVER TIME, TO THIS DAY—

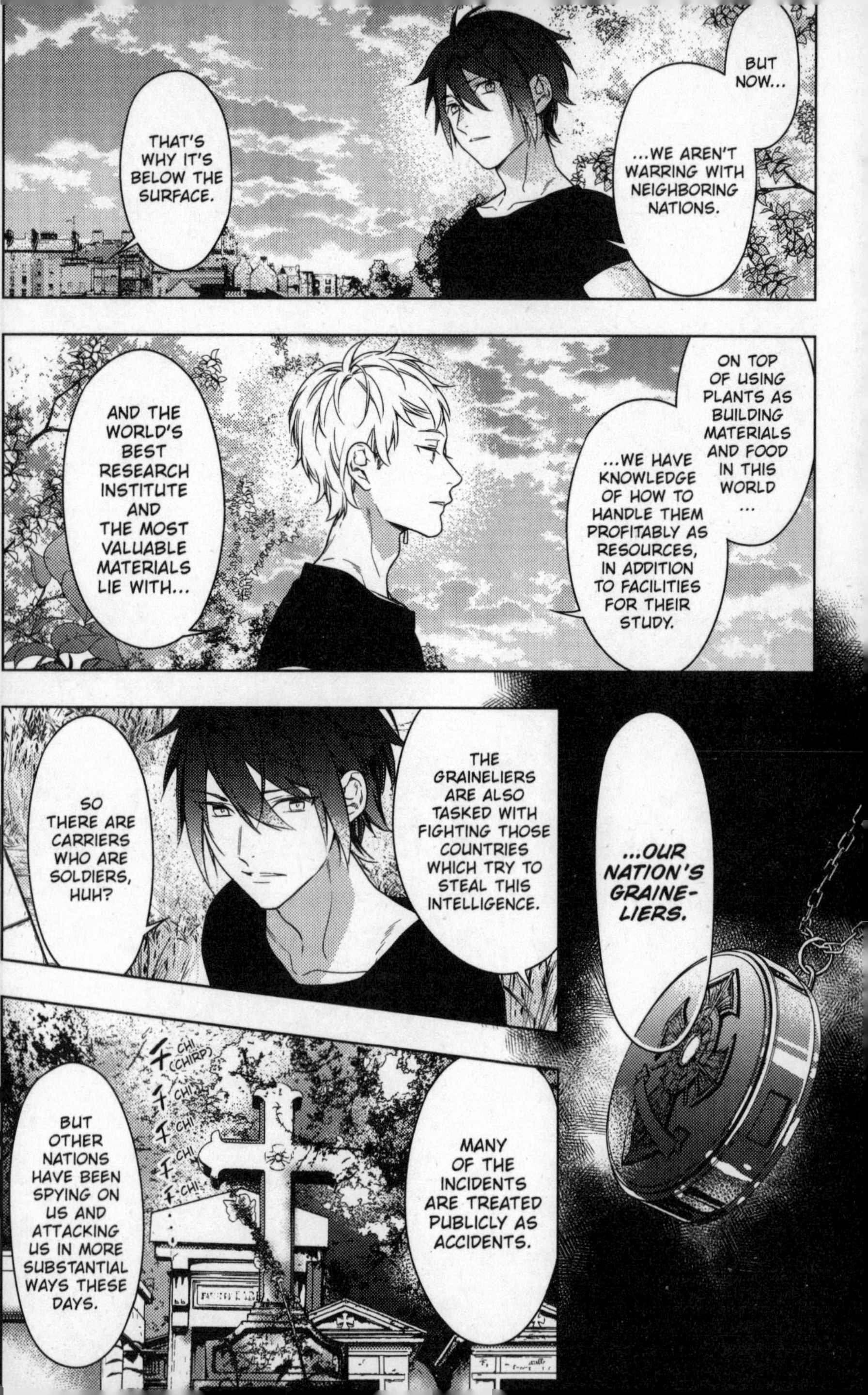
BUT NOW...
...WE AREN'T WARRING WITH NEIGHBORING NATIONS.
THAT'S WHY IT'S BELOW THE SURFACE.
ON TOP OF USING PLANTS AS BUILDING MATERIALS AND FOOD IN THIS WORLD...
...WE HAVE KNOWLEDGE OF HOW TO HANDLE THEM PROFITABLY AS RESOURCES, IN ADDITION TO FACILITIES FOR THEIR STUDY.
AND THE WORLD'S BEST RESEARCH INSTITUTE AND THE MOST VALUABLE MATERIALS LIE WITH...
...OUR NATION'S GRAINE-LIERS.
THE GRAINELIERS ARE ALSO TASKED WITH FIGHTING THOSE COUNTRIES WHICH TRY TO STEAL THIS INTELLIGENCE.
SO THERE ARE CARRIERS WHO ARE SOLDIERS, HUH?
チ CHI (CHIRP)
チ CHI
チ CHI
チ CHI
チ CHI
MANY OF THE INCIDENTS ARE TREATED PUBLICLY AS ACCIDENTS.
BUT OTHER NATIONS HAVE BEEN SPYING ON US AND ATTACKING US IN MORE SUBSTANTIAL WAYS THESE DAYS.

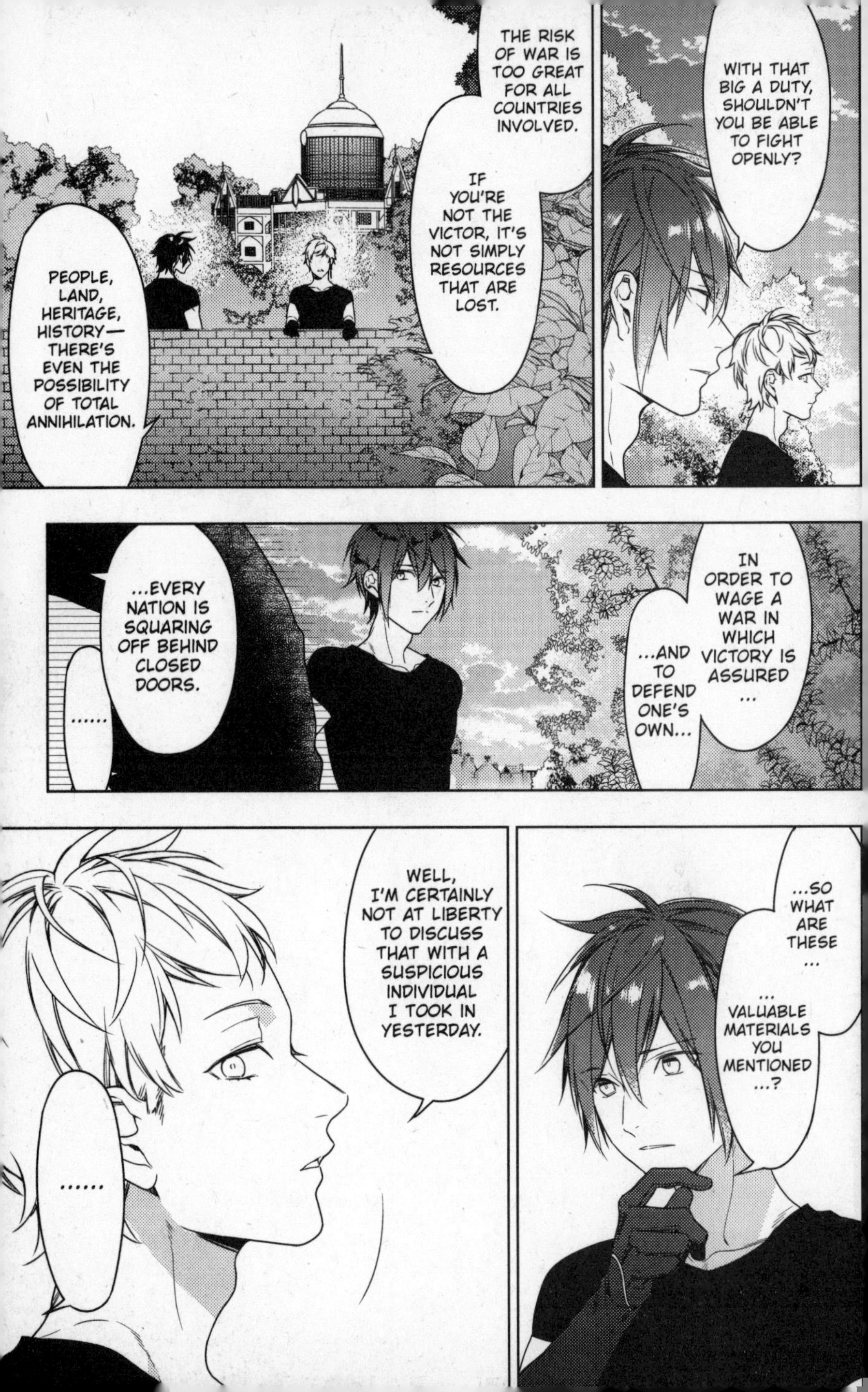
WITH THAT BIG A DUTY, SHOULDN'T YOU BE ABLE TO FIGHT OPENLY?
THE RISK OF WAR IS TOO GREAT FOR ALL COUNTRIES INVOLVED.
IF YOU'RE NOT THE VICTOR, IT'S NOT SIMPLY RESOURCES THAT ARE LOST.
PEOPLE, LAND, HERITAGE, HISTORY—THERE'S EVEN THE POSSIBILITY OF TOTAL ANNIHILATION.
IN ORDER TO WAGE A WAR IN WHICH VICTORY IS ASSURED...
...AND TO DEFEND ONE'S OWN...
...EVERY NATION IS SQUARING OFF BEHIND CLOSED DOORS.
......
...SO WHAT ARE THESE... ...VALUABLE MATERIALS YOU MENTIONED...?
WELL, I'M CERTAINLY NOT AT LIBERTY TO DISCUSS THAT WITH A SUSPICIOUS INDIVIDUAL I TOOK IN YESTERDAY.
......

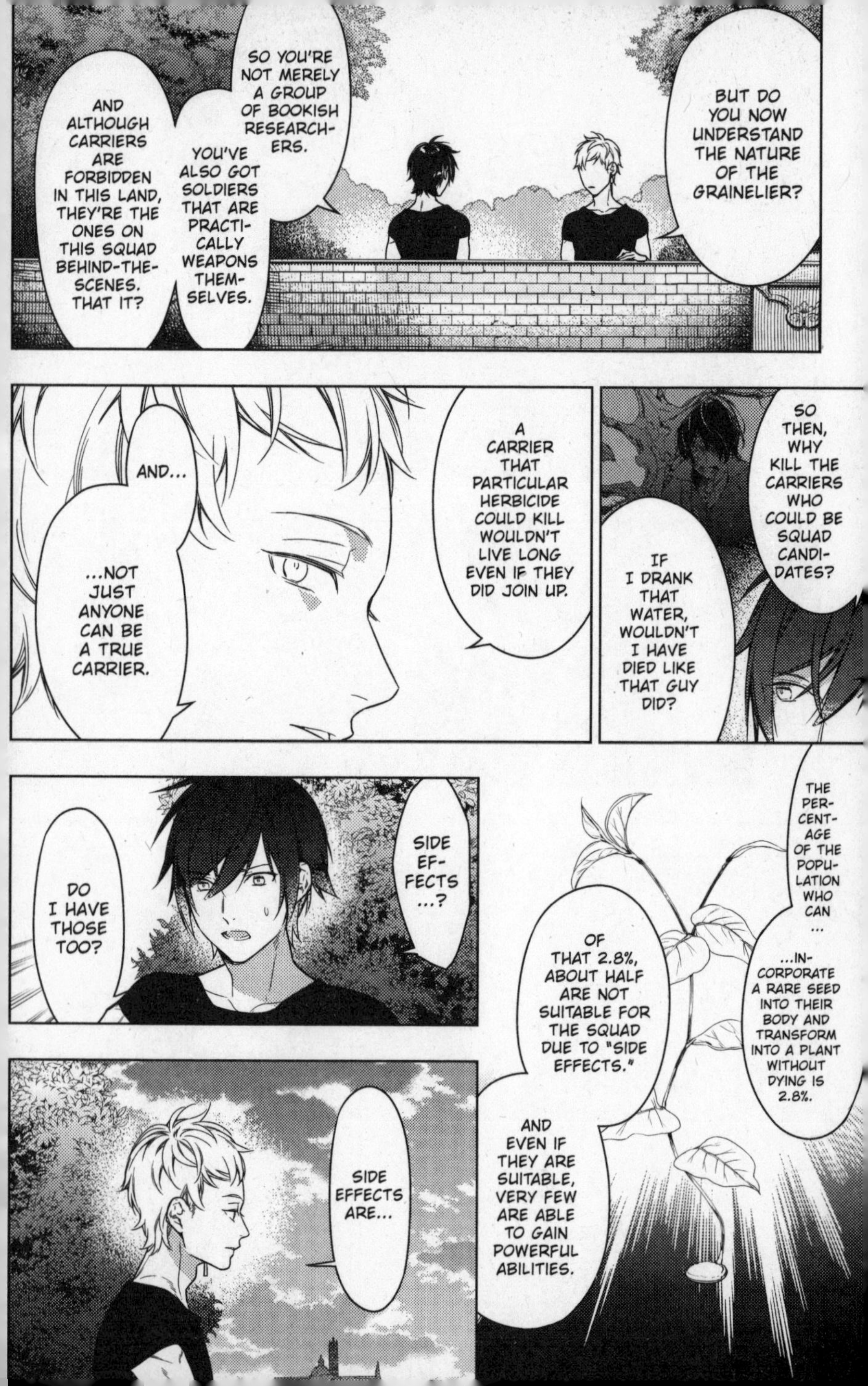
BUT DO YOU NOW UNDERSTAND THE NATURE OF THE GRAINELIER?
SO YOU'RE NOT MERELY A GROUP OF BOOKISH RESEARCHERS.
YOU'VE ALSO GOT SOLDIERS THAT ARE PRACTICALLY WEAPONS THEMSELVES.
AND ALTHOUGH CARRIERS ARE FORBIDDEN IN THIS LAND, THEY'RE THE ONES ON THIS SQUAD BEHIND-THE-SCENES. THAT IT?
SO THEN, WHY KILL THE CARRIERS WHO COULD BE SQUAD CANDIDATES?
IF I DRANK THAT WATER, WOULDN'T I HAVE DIED LIKE THAT GUY DID?
A CARRIER THAT PARTICULAR HERBICIDE COULD KILL WOULDN'T LIVE LONG EVEN IF THEY DID JOIN UP.
AND...
...NOT JUST ANYONE CAN BE A TRUE CARRIER.
THE PERCENTAGE OF THE POPULATION WHO CAN...
...INCORPORATE A RARE SEED INTO THEIR BODY AND TRANSFORM INTO A PLANT WITHOUT DYING IS 2.8%.
OF THAT 2.8%, ABOUT HALF ARE NOT SUITABLE FOR THE SQUAD DUE TO "SIDE EFFECTS."
AND EVEN IF THEY ARE SUITABLE, VERY FEW ARE ABLE TO GAIN POWERFUL ABILITIES.
SIDE EFFECTS...?
DO I HAVE THOSE TOO?
SIDE EFFECTS ARE...

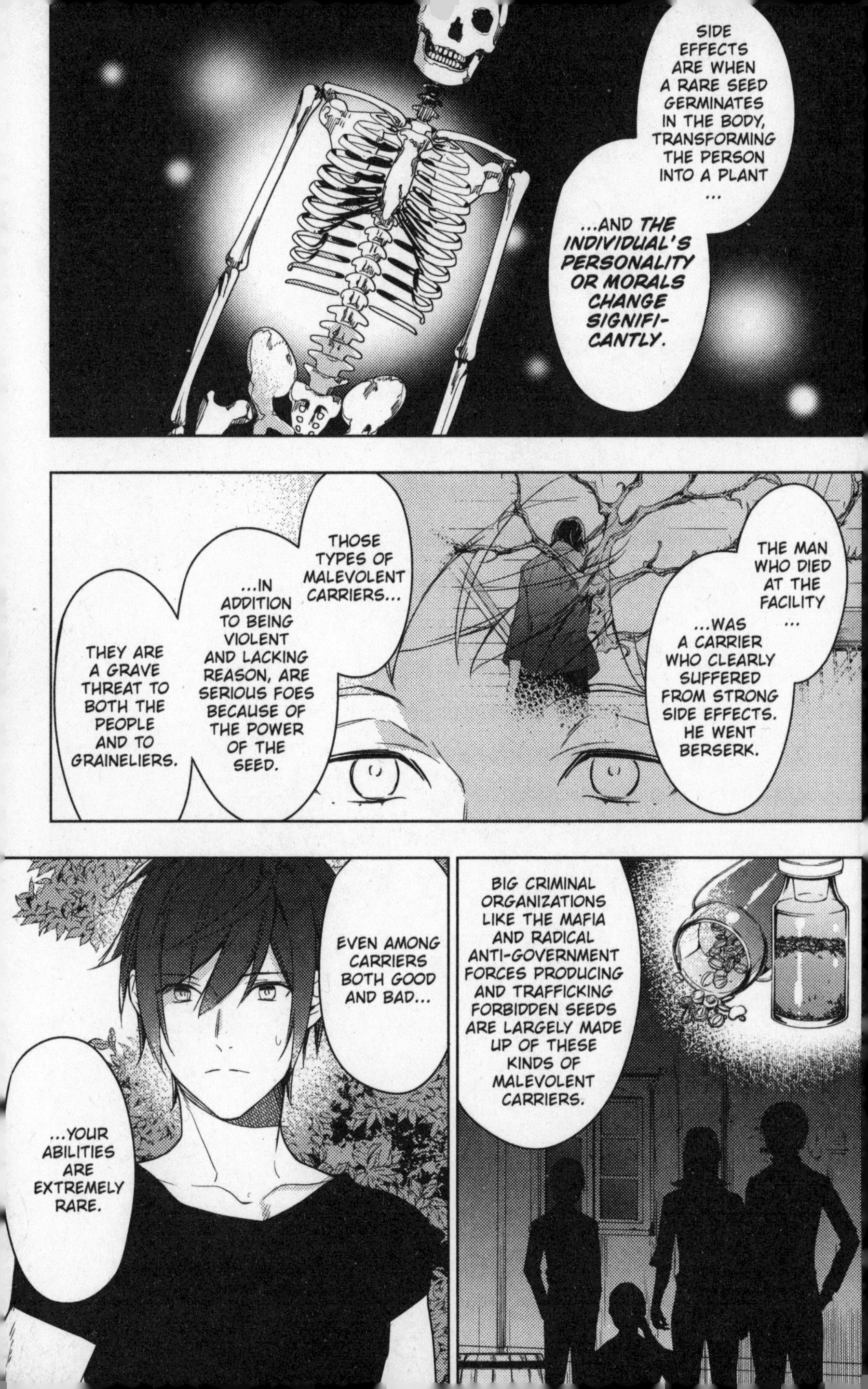
SIDE EFFECTS ARE WHEN A RARE SEED GERMINATES IN THE BODY, TRANSFORMING THE PERSON INTO A PLANT ...
...AND *THE INDIVIDUAL'S PERSONALITY OR MORALS CHANGE SIGNIFICANTLY.*
THE MAN WHO DIED AT THE FACILITY ...
...WAS A CARRIER WHO CLEARLY SUFFERED FROM STRONG SIDE EFFECTS. HE WENT BERSERK.
THOSE TYPES OF MALEVOLENT CARRIERS...
...IN ADDITION TO BEING VIOLENT AND LACKING REASON, ARE SERIOUS FOES BECAUSE OF THE POWER OF THE SEED.
THEY ARE A GRAVE THREAT TO BOTH THE PEOPLE AND TO GRAINELIERS.
BIG CRIMINAL ORGANIZATIONS LIKE THE MAFIA AND RADICAL ANTI-GOVERNMENT FORCES PRODUCING AND TRAFFICKING FORBIDDEN SEEDS ARE LARGELY MADE UP OF THESE KINDS OF MALEVOLENT CARRIERS.
EVEN AMONG CARRIERS BOTH GOOD AND BAD...
...YOUR ABILITIES ARE EXTREMELY RARE.

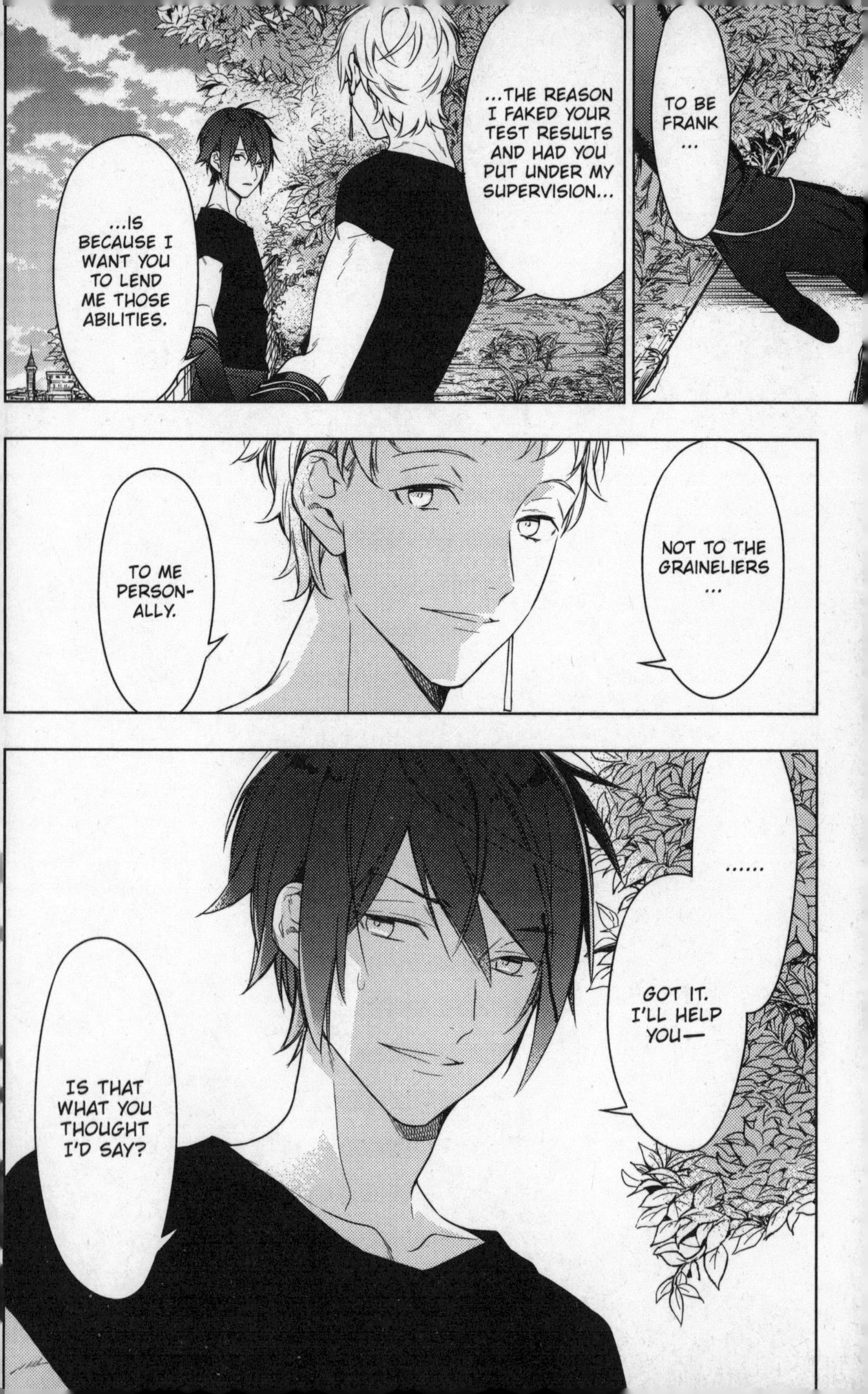
TO BE FRANK...
...THE REASON I FAKED YOUR TEST RESULTS AND HAD YOU PUT UNDER MY SUPERVISION...
...IS BECAUSE I WANT YOU TO LEND ME THOSE ABILITIES.
NOT TO THE GRAINELIERS...
TO ME PERSON-ALLY.
......
GOT IT. I'LL HELP YOU—
IS THAT WHAT YOU THOUGHT I'D SAY?

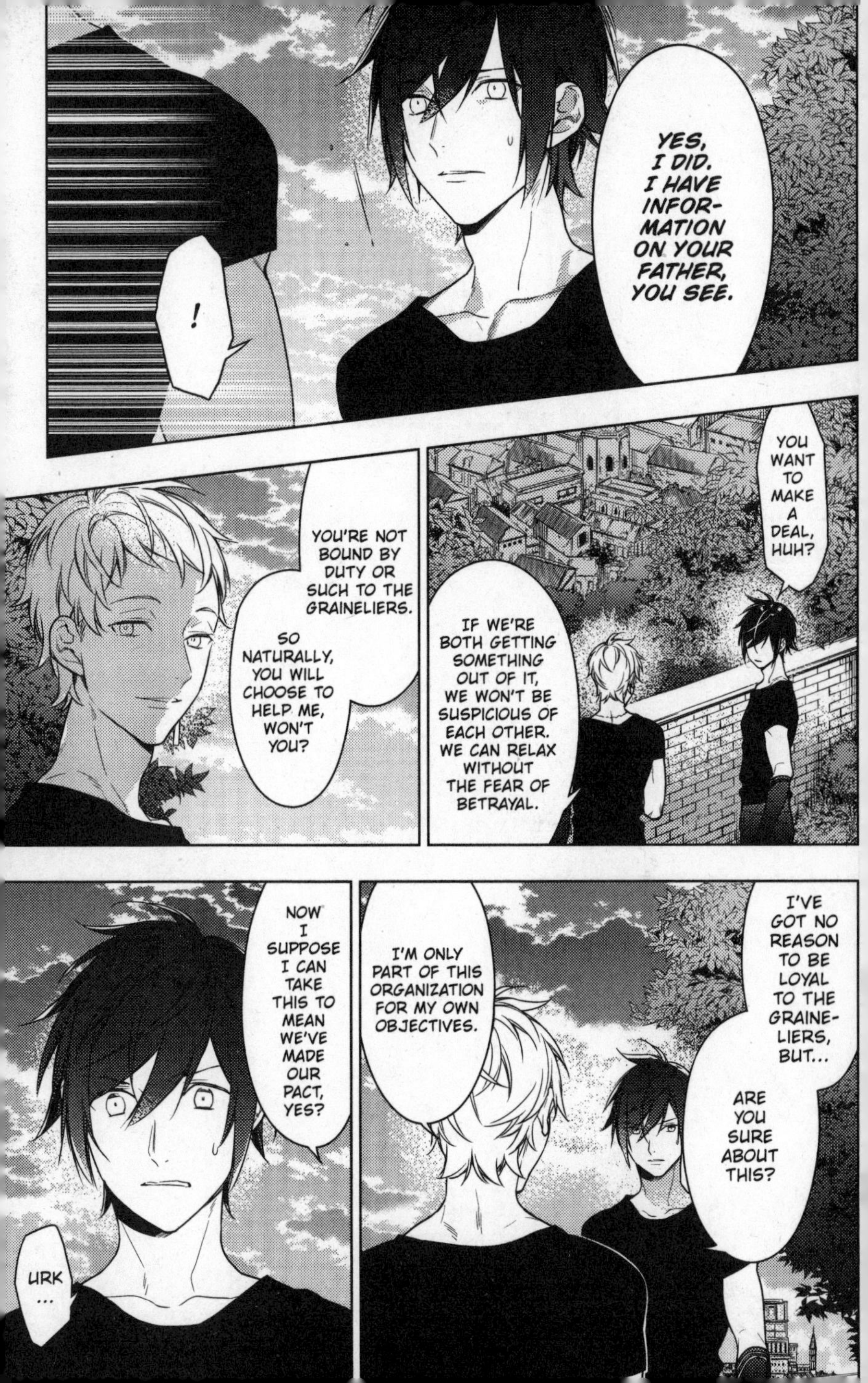

YES, I DID. I HAVE INFORMATION ON YOUR FATHER, YOU SEE.
!
YOU WANT TO MAKE A DEAL, HUH?
IF WE'RE BOTH GETTING SOMETHING OUT OF IT, WE WON'T BE SUSPICIOUS OF EACH OTHER. WE CAN RELAX WITHOUT THE FEAR OF BETRAYAL.
YOU'RE NOT BOUND BY DUTY OR SUCH TO THE GRAINELIERS.
SO NATURALLY, YOU WILL CHOOSE TO HELP ME, WON'T YOU?
I'VE GOT NO REASON TO BE LOYAL TO THE GRAINELIERS, BUT...
ARE YOU SURE ABOUT THIS?
I'M ONLY PART OF THIS ORGANIZATION FOR MY OWN OBJECTIVES.
NOW I SUPPOSE I CAN TAKE THIS TO MEAN WE'VE MADE OUR PACT, YES?
URK...

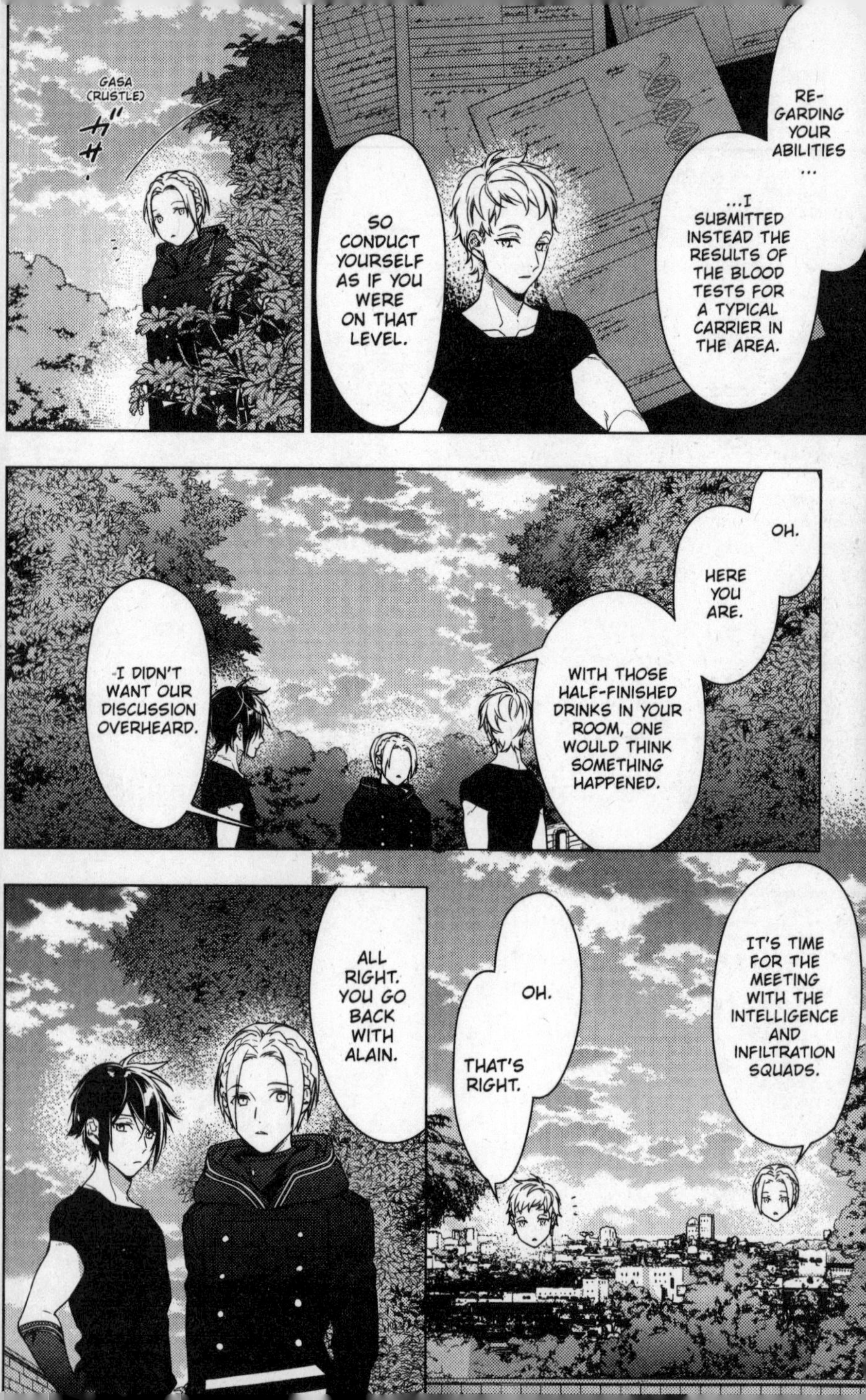
REGARDING YOUR ABILITIES...
...I SUBMITTED INSTEAD THE RESULTS OF THE BLOOD TESTS FOR A TYPICAL CARRIER IN THE AREA.
SO CONDUCT YOURSELF AS IF YOU WERE ON THAT LEVEL.
GASA (RUSTLE)
OH.
HERE YOU ARE.
WITH THOSE HALF-FINISHED DRINKS IN YOUR ROOM, ONE WOULD THINK SOMETHING HAPPENED.
-I DIDN'T WANT OUR DISCUSSION OVERHEARD.
IT'S TIME FOR THE MEETING WITH THE INTELLIGENCE AND INFILTRATION SQUADS.
OH.
THAT'S RIGHT.
ALL RIGHT. YOU GO BACK WITH ALAIN.

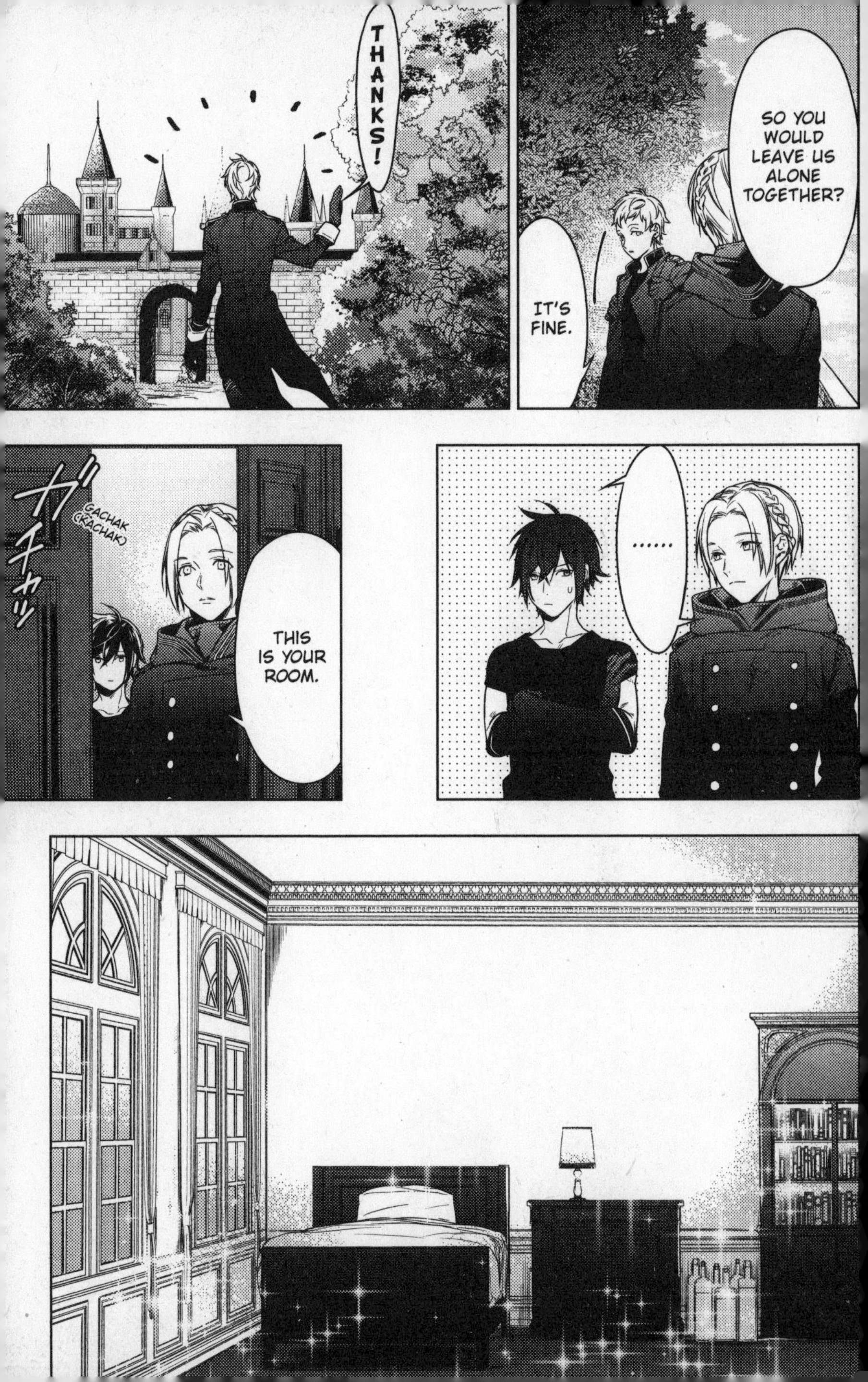
SO YOU WOULD LEAVE US ALONE TOGETHER?
IT'S FINE.
THANKS!
......
ガチャッ
GACHAK (KACHAK)
THIS IS YOUR ROOM.

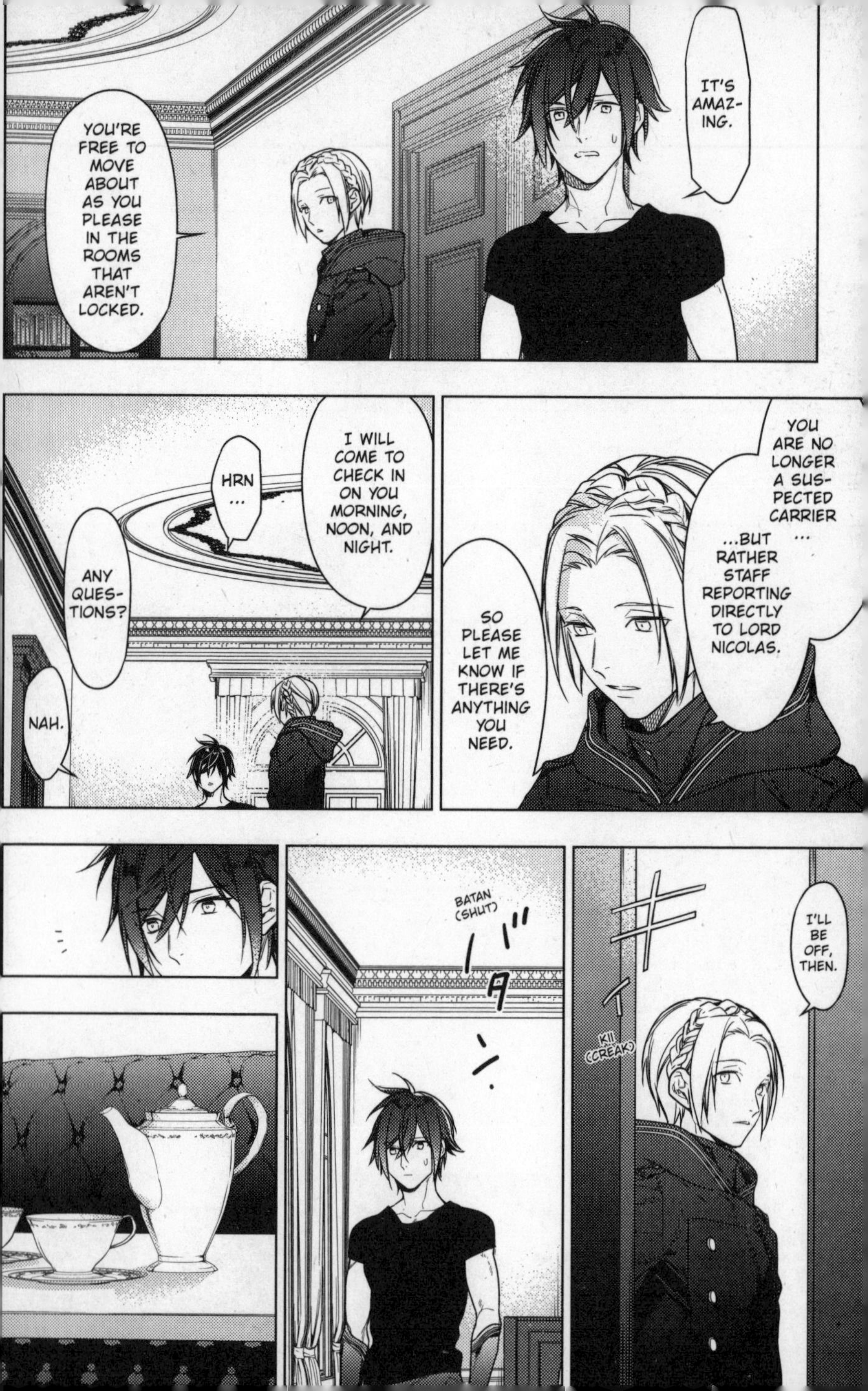
IT'S AMAZ-ING.
YOU'RE FREE TO MOVE ABOUT AS YOU PLEASE IN THE ROOMS THAT AREN'T LOCKED.
YOU ARE NO LONGER A SUS-PECTED CARRIER...
...BUT RATHER STAFF REPORTING DIRECTLY TO LORD NICOLAS.
SO PLEASE LET ME KNOW IF THERE'S ANYTHING YOU NEED.
I WILL COME TO CHECK IN ON YOU MORNING, NOON, AND NIGHT.
HRN...
ANY QUES-TIONS?
NAH.
I'LL BE OFF, THEN.
KII (CREAK)
BATAN (SHUT)

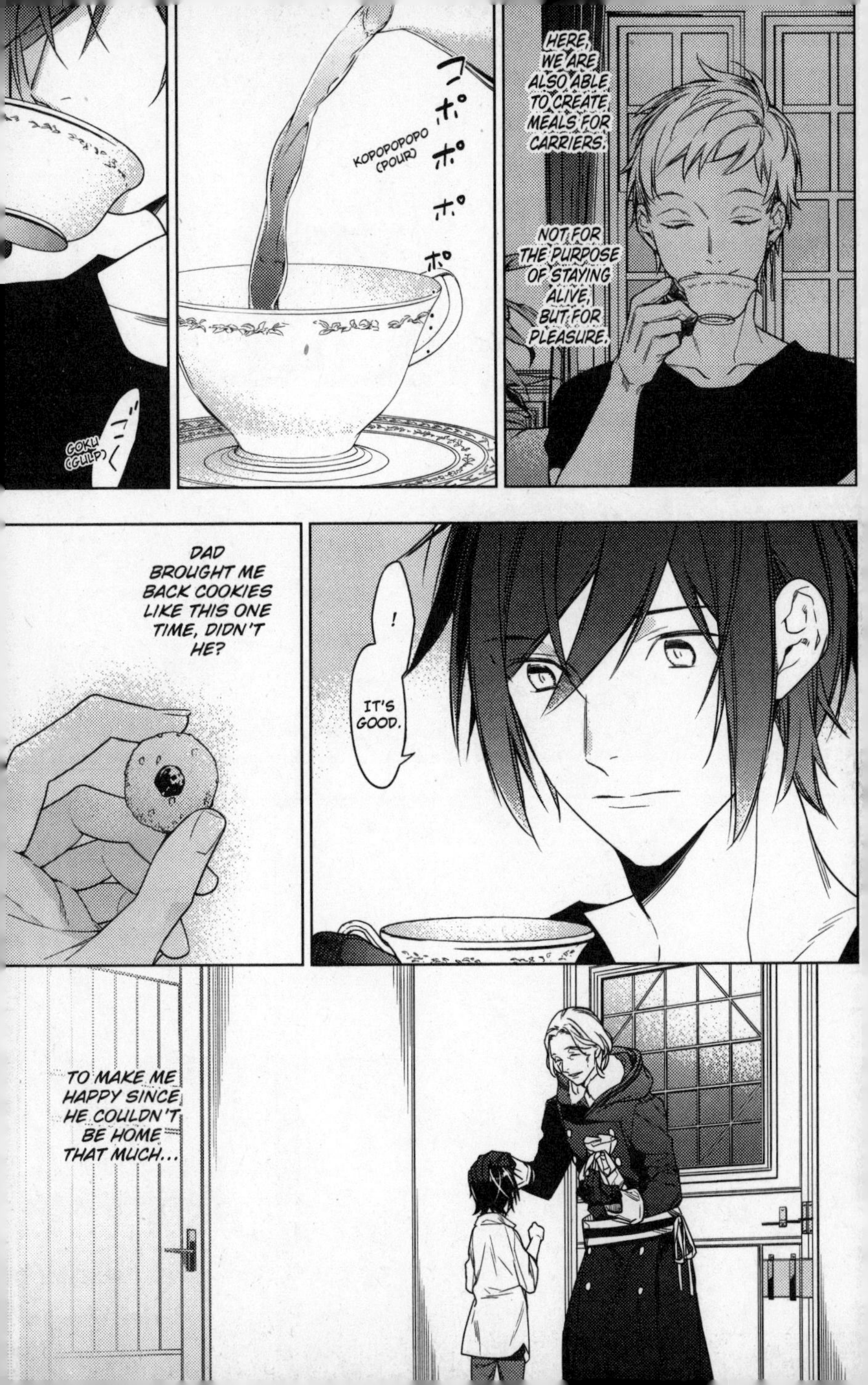
HERE, WE ARE ALSO ABLE TO CREATE MEALS FOR CARRIERS.
NOT FOR THE PURPOSE OF STAYING ALIVE, BUT FOR PLEASURE.
コポポポポ
KOPOPOPOPO (POUR)
ゴく
GOKU (GULP)
!
IT'S GOOD.
DAD BROUGHT ME BACK COOKIES LIKE THIS ONE TIME, DIDN'T HE?
TO MAKE ME HAPPY SINCE HE COULDN'T BE HOME THAT MUCH...

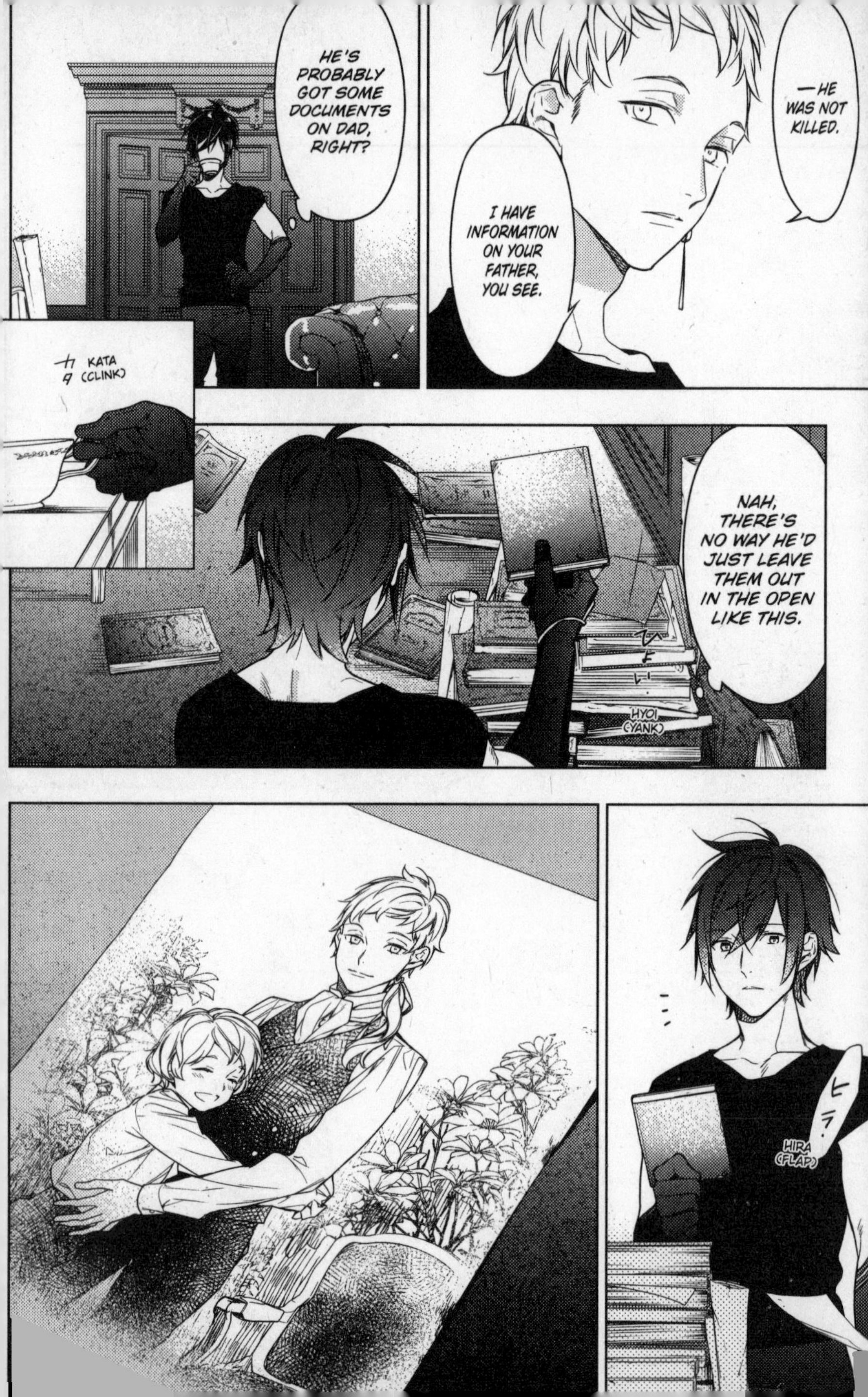
—HE WAS NOT KILLED.
I HAVE INFORMATION ON YOUR FATHER, YOU SEE.
HE'S PROBABLY GOT SOME DOCUMENTS ON DAD, RIGHT?
NAH, THERE'S NO WAY HE'D JUST LEAVE THEM OUT IN THE OPEN LIKE THIS.
ひょい
HYOI (YANK)
カタ KATA (CLINK)
...
ヒラ
HIRA (FLAP)

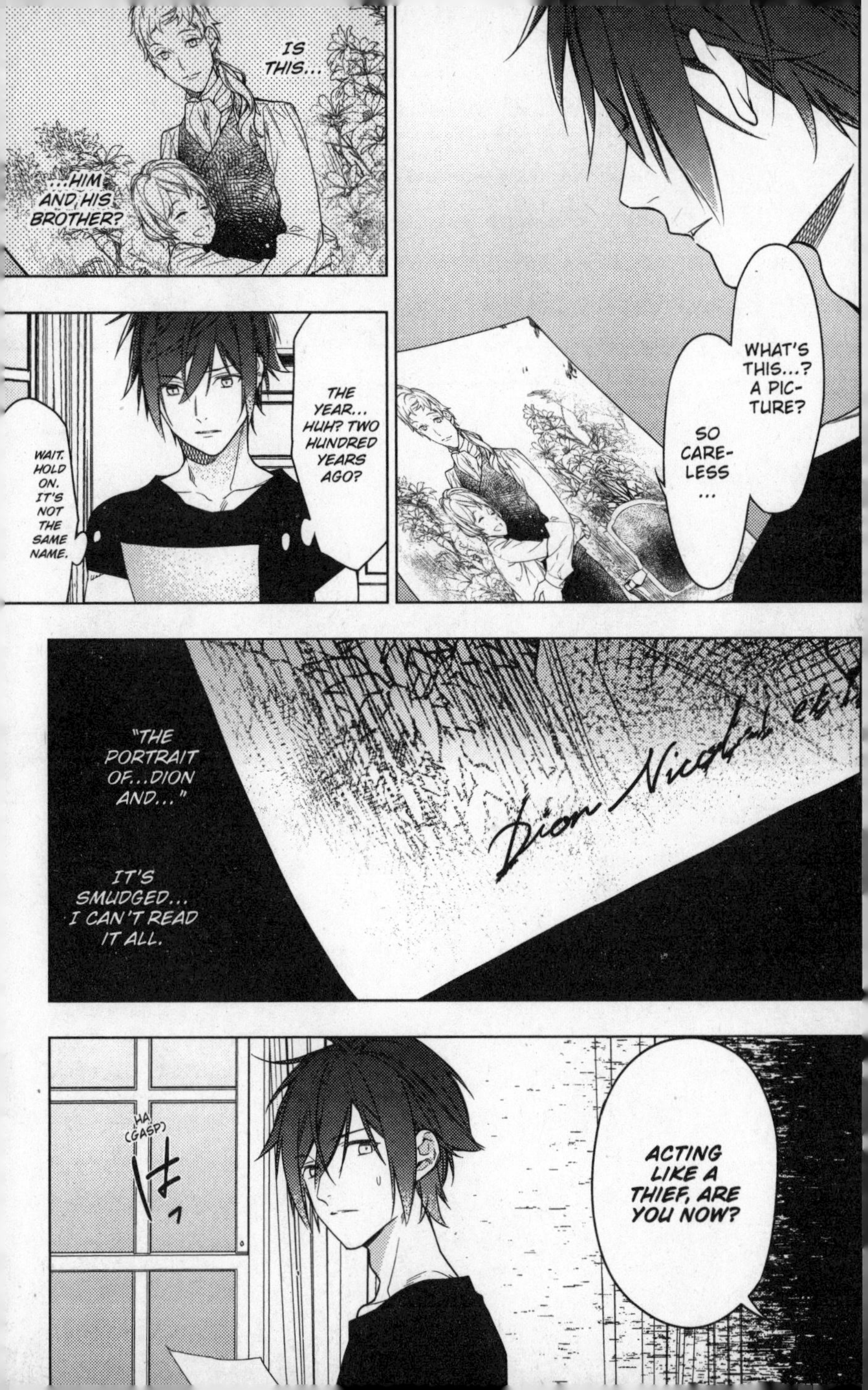
WHAT'S THIS...? A PIC-TURE?
SO CARE-LESS...
IS THIS...
...HIM AND HIS BROTHER?
THE YEAR... HUH? TWO HUNDRED YEARS AGO?
WAIT. HOLD ON. IT'S NOT THE SAME NAME.
Dion
"THE PORTRAIT OF...DION AND..."
IT'S SMUDGED... I CAN'T READ IT ALL.
ACTING LIKE A THIEF, ARE YOU NOW?
HA (GASP)
はっ

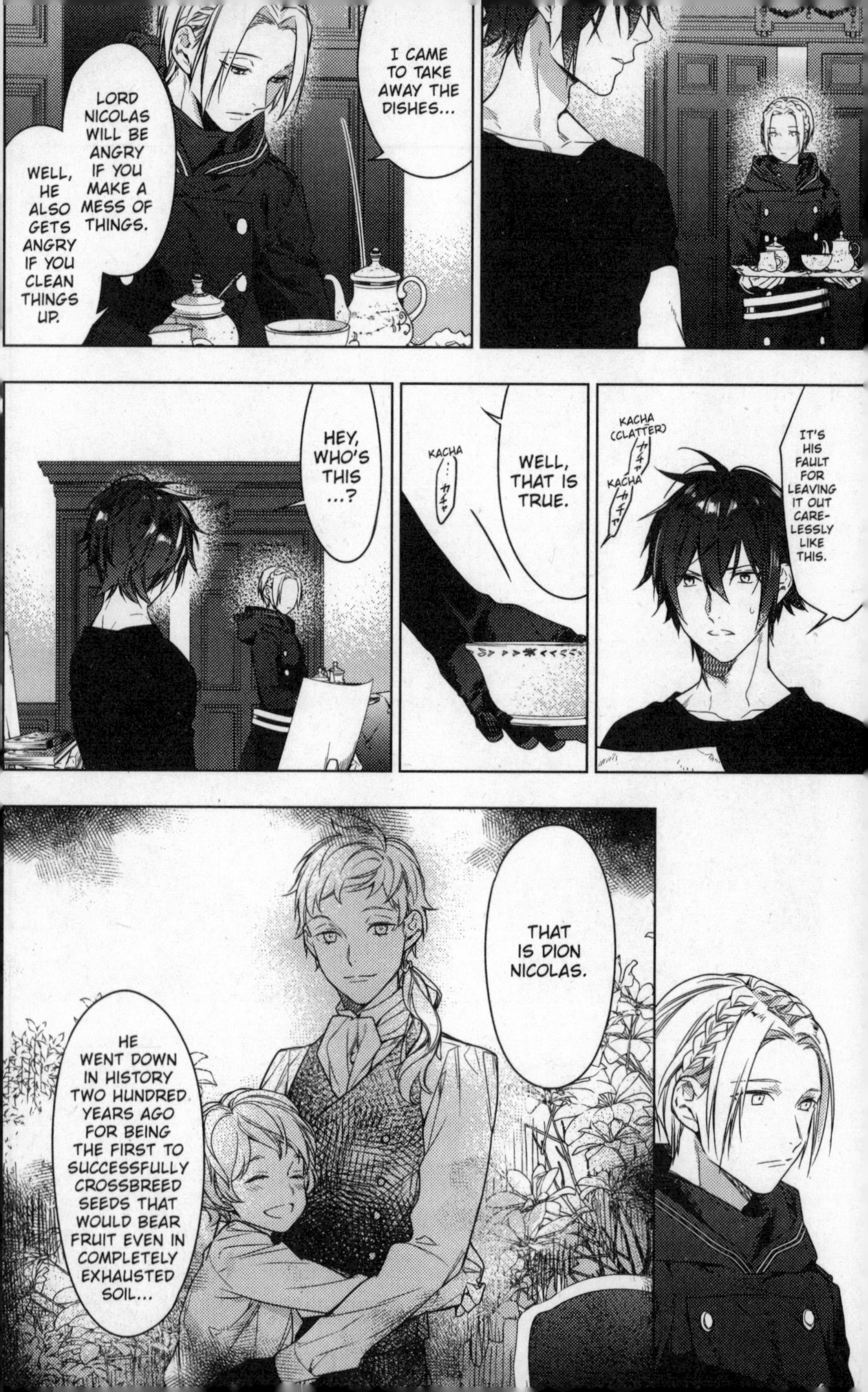
I CAME TO TAKE AWAY THE DISHES...
LORD NICOLAS WILL BE ANGRY IF YOU MAKE A MESS OF THINGS.
WELL, HE ALSO GETS ANGRY IF YOU CLEAN THINGS UP.
KACHA (CLATTER)
KACHA
IT'S HIS FAULT FOR LEAVING IT OUT CARELESSLY LIKE THIS.
KACHA
WELL, THAT IS TRUE.
HEY, WHO'S THIS ...?
THAT IS DION NICOLAS.
HE WENT DOWN IN HISTORY TWO HUNDRED YEARS AGO FOR BEING THE FIRST TO SUCCESSFULLY CROSSBREED SEEDS THAT WOULD BEAR FRUIT EVEN IN COMPLETELY EXHAUSTED SOIL...

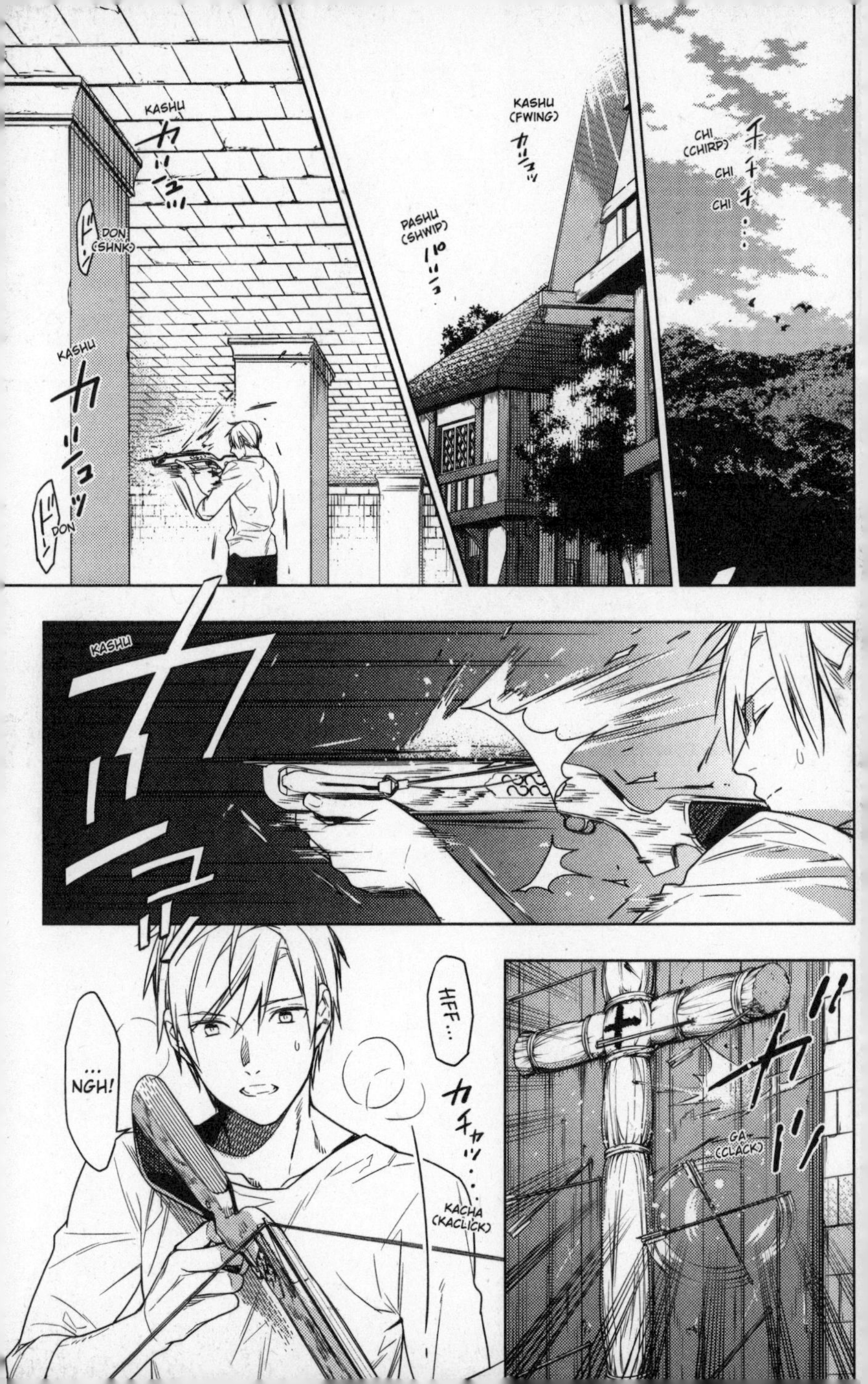
CHI (CHIRP)
CHI
CHI
KASHU (FWING)
PASHU (SHWIP)
KASHU
DON (SHNK)
KASHU
DON
KASHU
GA (CLACK)
HFF...
...NGH!
KACHA (KACLICK)

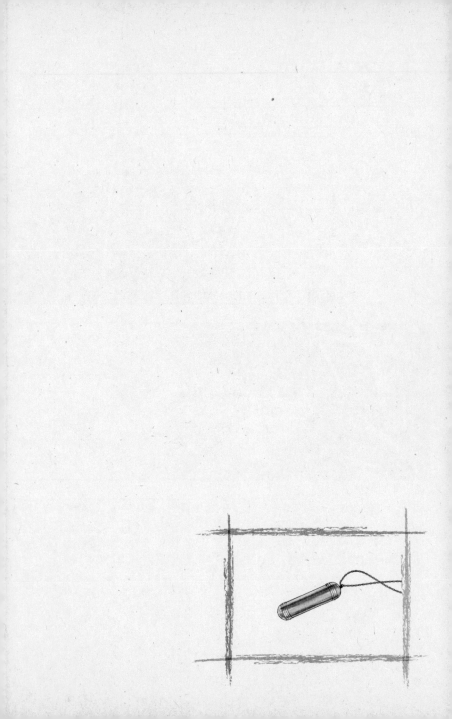

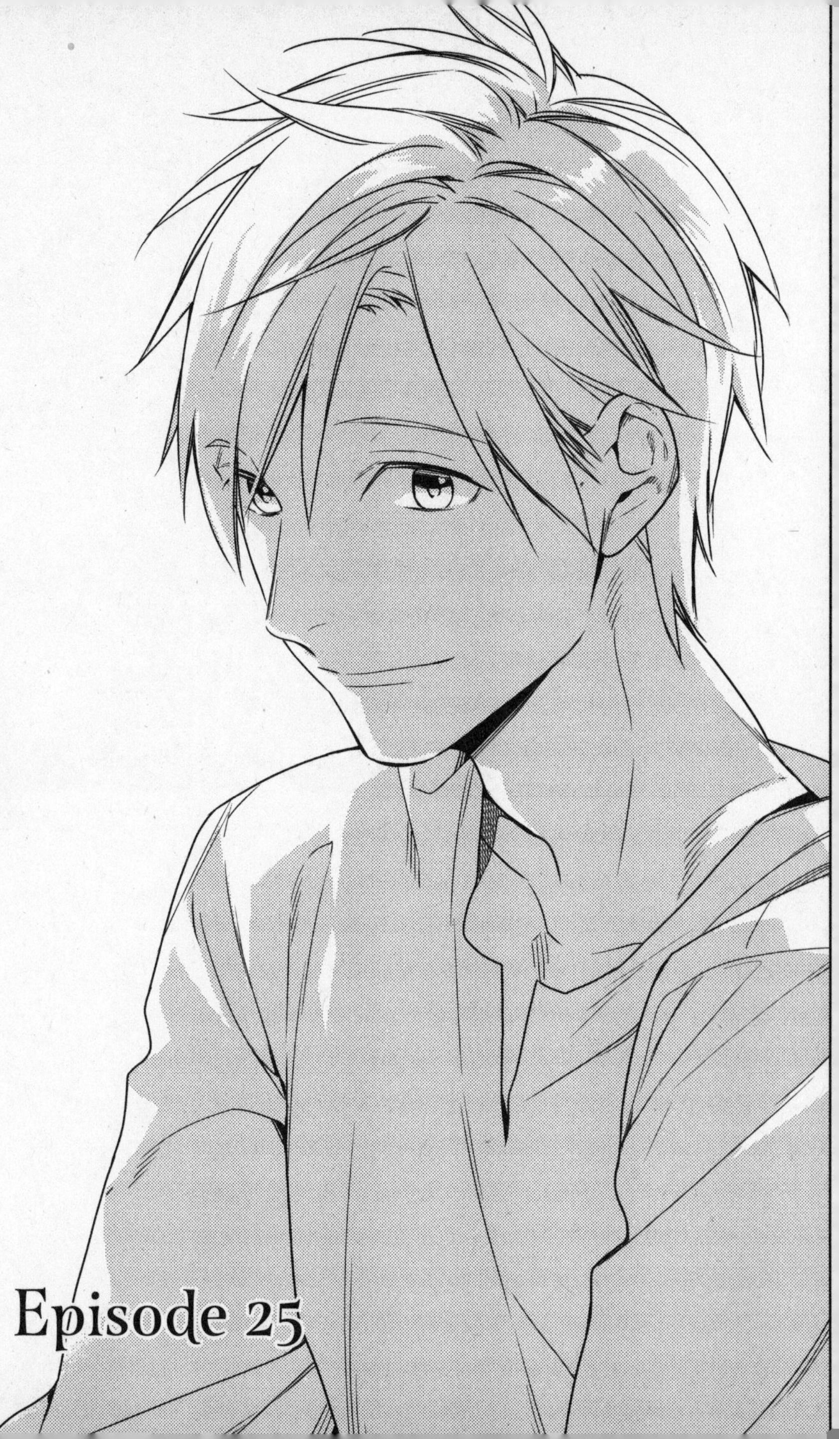

Episode 25

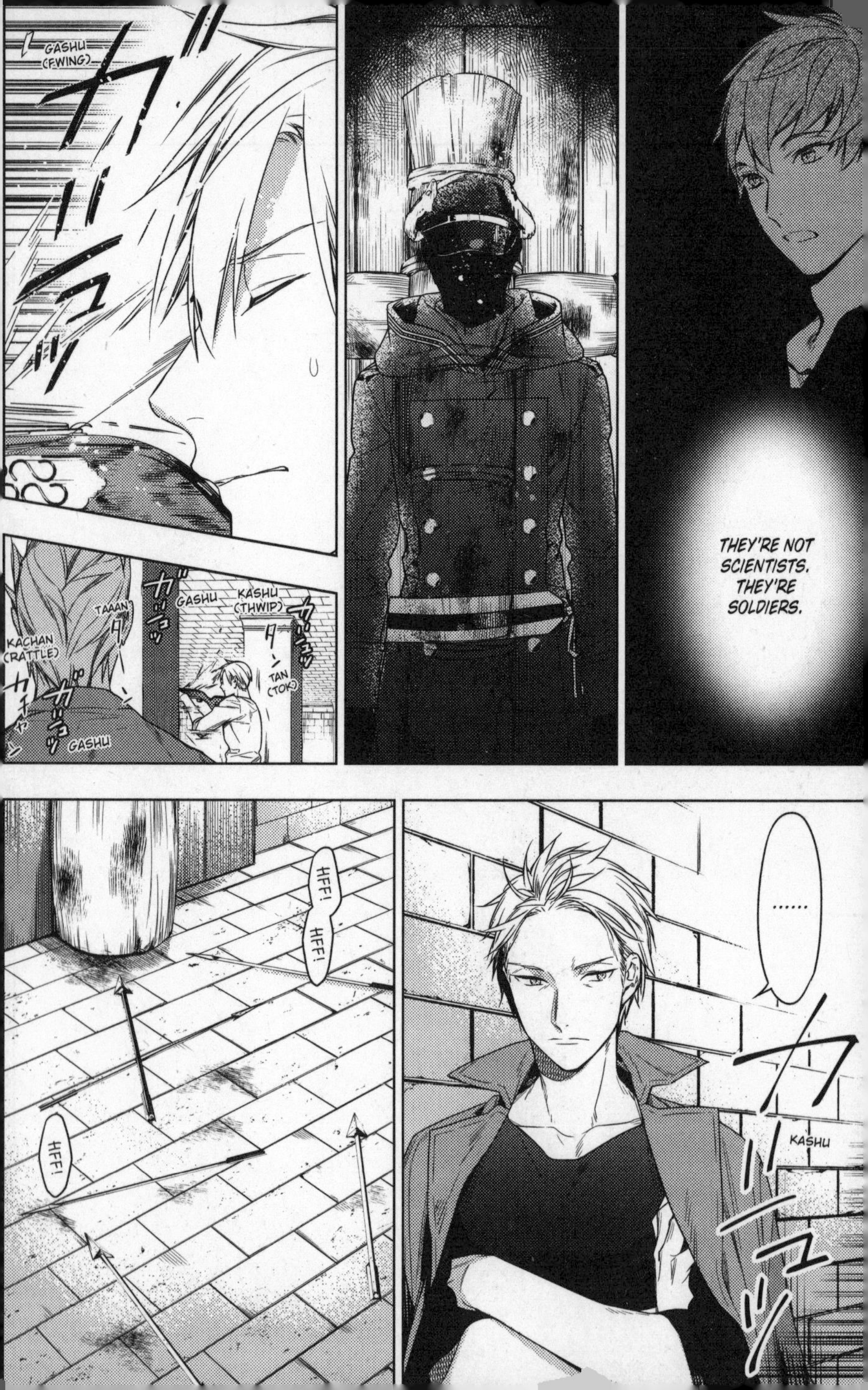
THEY'RE NOT SCIENTISTS. THEY'RE SOLDIERS.
GASHU (FWING)
KASHU (THWIP)
TAN (TOK)
GASHU
TAAAN
KACHAN (RATTLE)
GASHU
......
KASHU
HFF! HFF!
HFF!

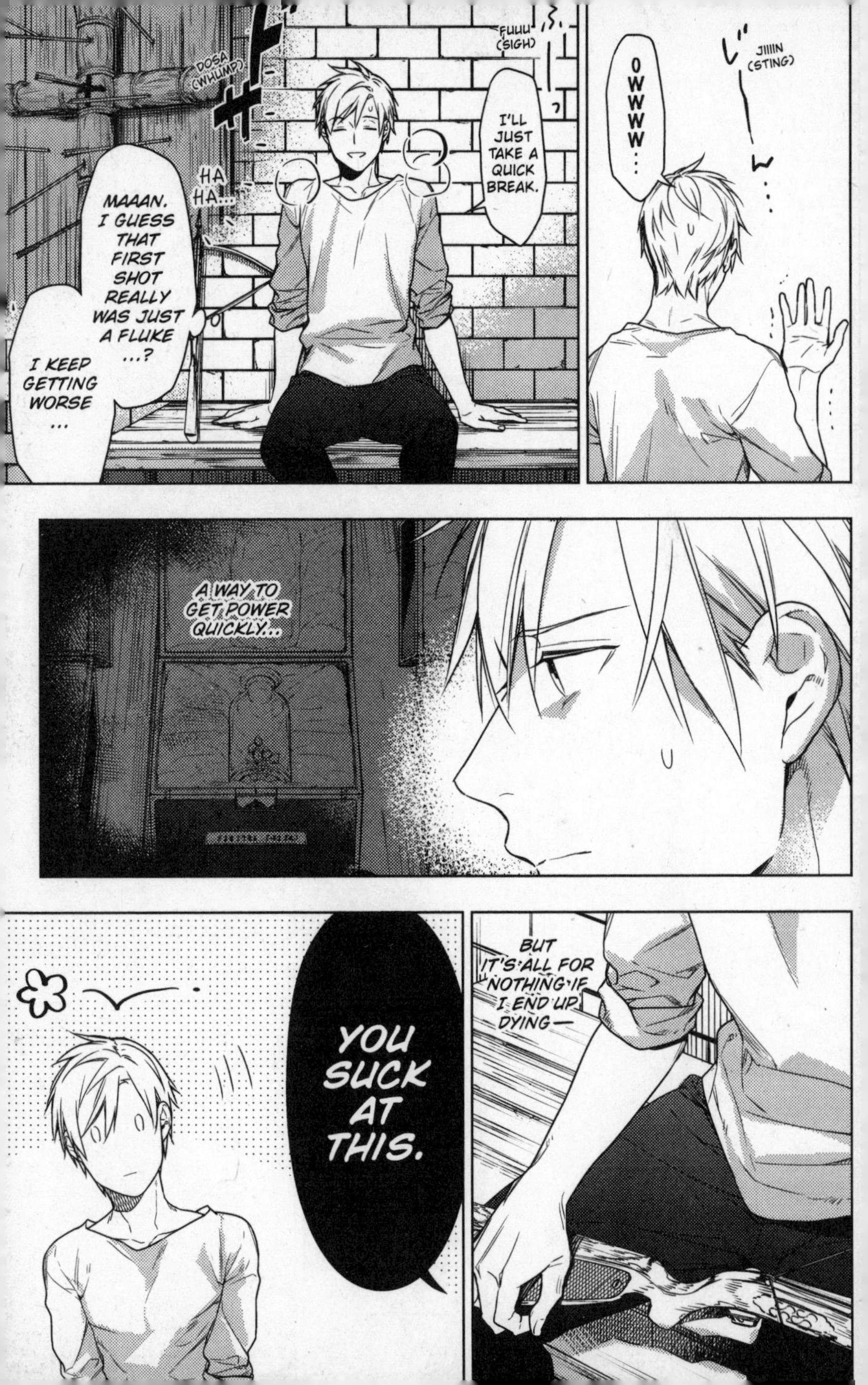
JIIIN (STING)
OWWWW...
FUUU (SIGH)
I'LL JUST TAKE A QUICK BREAK.
DOSA (WHUMP)
HA HA...
MAAAN. I GUESS THAT FIRST SHOT REALLY WAS JUST A FLUKE...?
I KEEP GETTING WORSE...
A WAY TO GET POWER QUICKLY...
BUT IT'S ALL FOR NOTHING IF I END UP DYING—
YOU SUCK AT THIS.

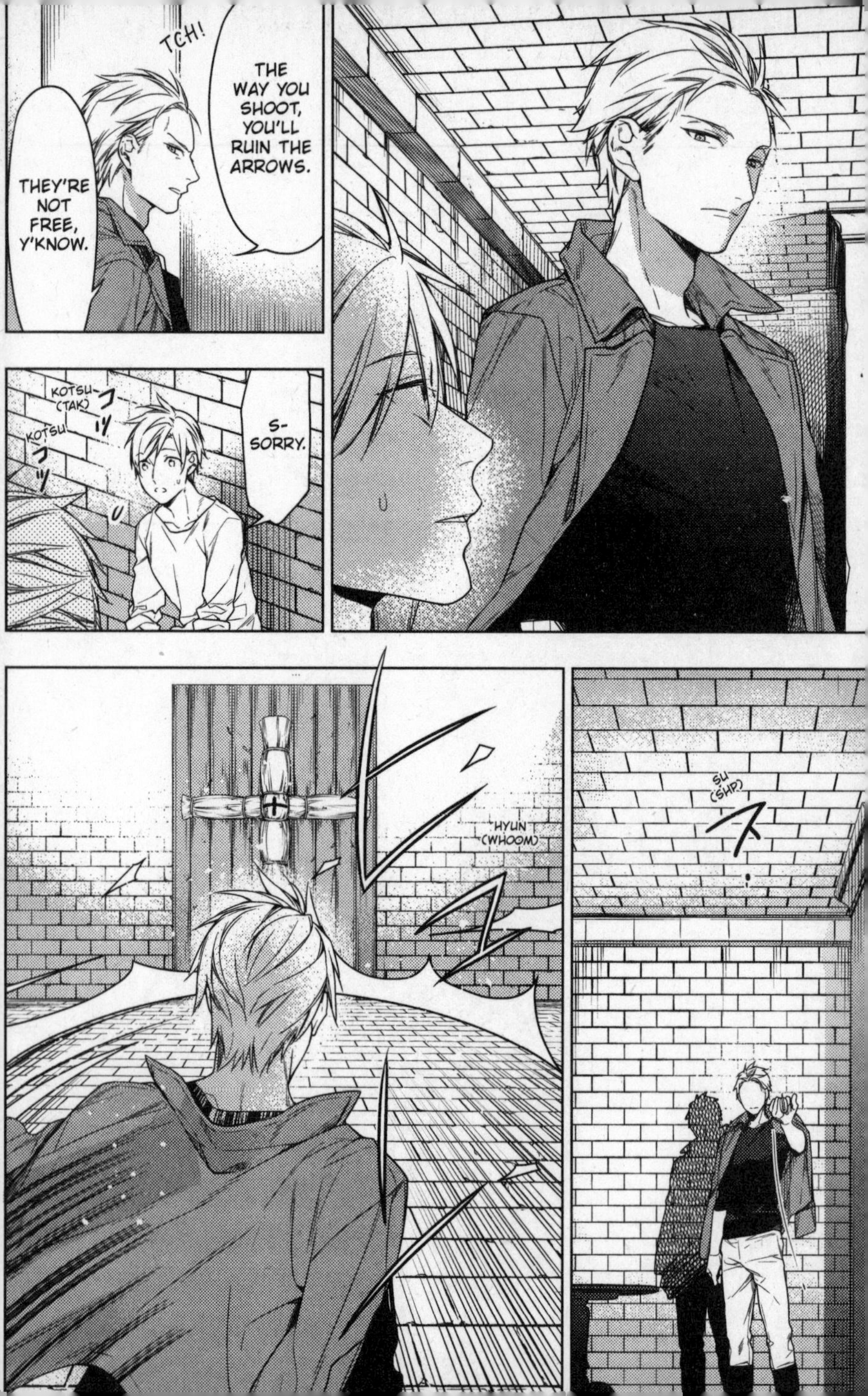
TCH!
THE WAY YOU SHOOT, YOU'LL RUIN THE ARROWS.
THEY'RE NOT FREE, Y'KNOW.
S-SORRY.
KOTSU (TAK)
KOTSU
SU (SHP)
HYUN (WHOOM)

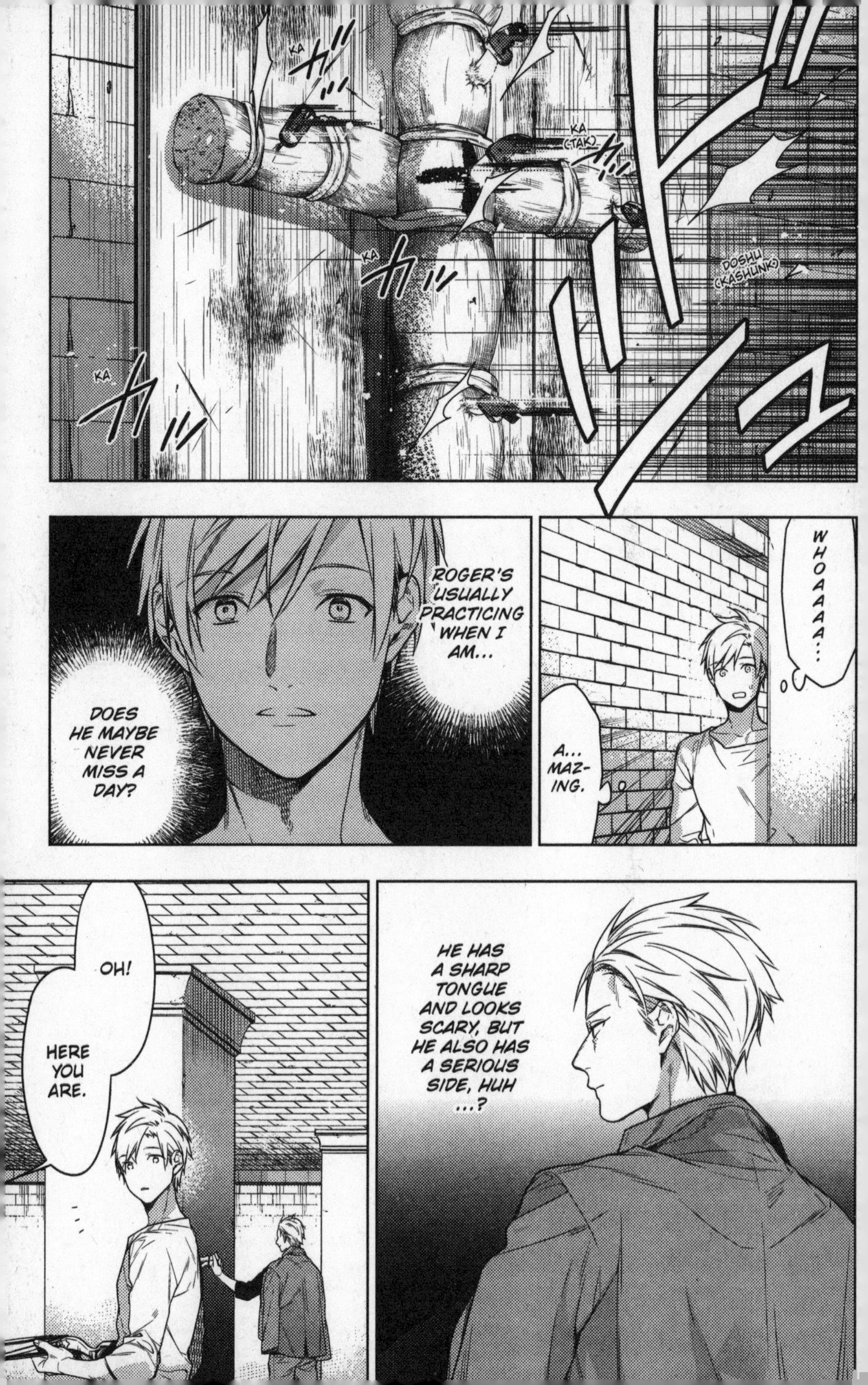
KA
KA (TAK)
KA
KA
DOSHU (KASHUNK)
WHOAAAAA...
A... MAZ-ING.
ROGER'S USUALLY PRACTICING WHEN I AM...
DOES HE MAYBE NEVER MISS A DAY?
HE HAS A SHARP TONGUE AND LOOKS SCARY, BUT HE ALSO HAS A SERIOUS SIDE, HUH ...?
OH!
HERE YOU ARE.
...

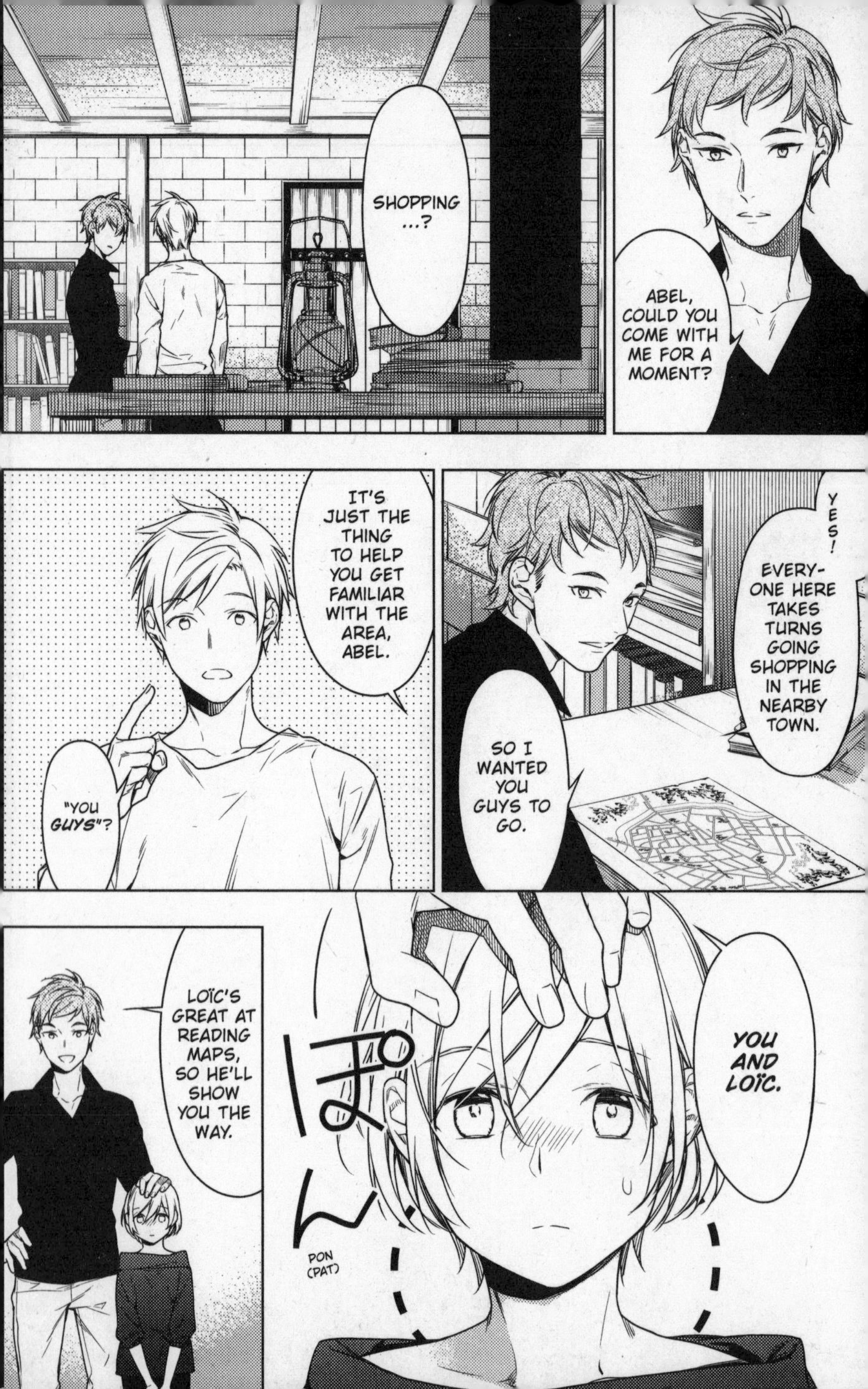
ABEL, COULD YOU COME WITH ME FOR A MOMENT?
SHOPPING ...?
YES!
EVERYONE HERE TAKES TURNS GOING SHOPPING IN THE NEARBY TOWN.
SO I WANTED YOU GUYS TO GO.
IT'S JUST THE THING TO HELP YOU GET FAMILIAR WITH THE AREA, ABEL.
"YOU *GUYS*"?
YOU AND LOÏC.
ぽん
PON (PAT)
...
LOÏC'S GREAT AT READING MAPS, SO HE'LL SHOW YOU THE WAY.

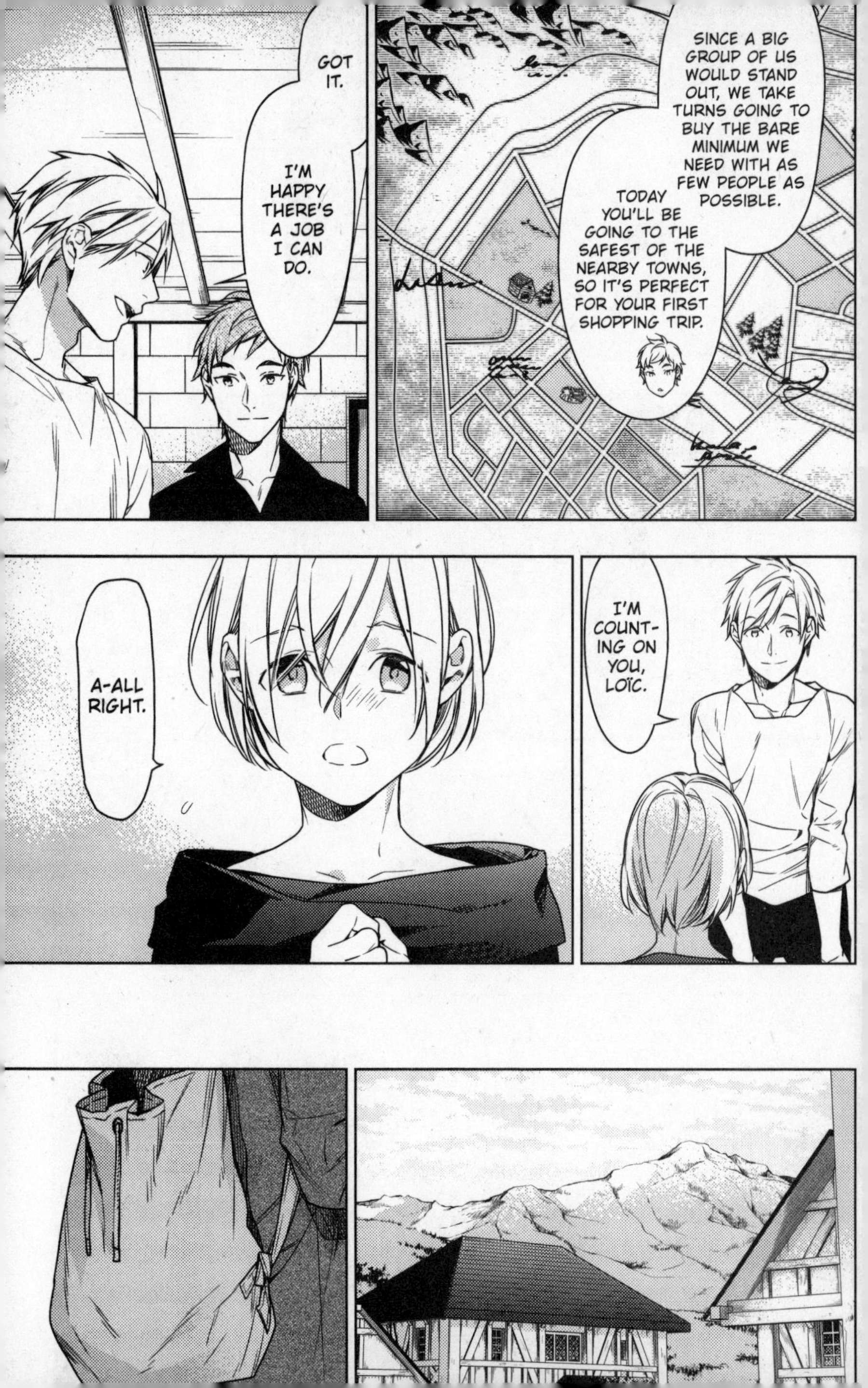
SINCE A BIG GROUP OF US WOULD STAND OUT, WE TAKE TURNS GOING TO BUY THE BARE MINIMUM WE NEED WITH AS FEW PEOPLE AS POSSIBLE.
TODAY YOU'LL BE GOING TO THE SAFEST OF THE NEARBY TOWNS, SO IT'S PERFECT FOR YOUR FIRST SHOPPING TRIP.
GOT IT.
I'M HAPPY THERE'S A JOB I CAN DO.
I'M COUNTING ON YOU, LOÏC.
A-ALL RIGHT.

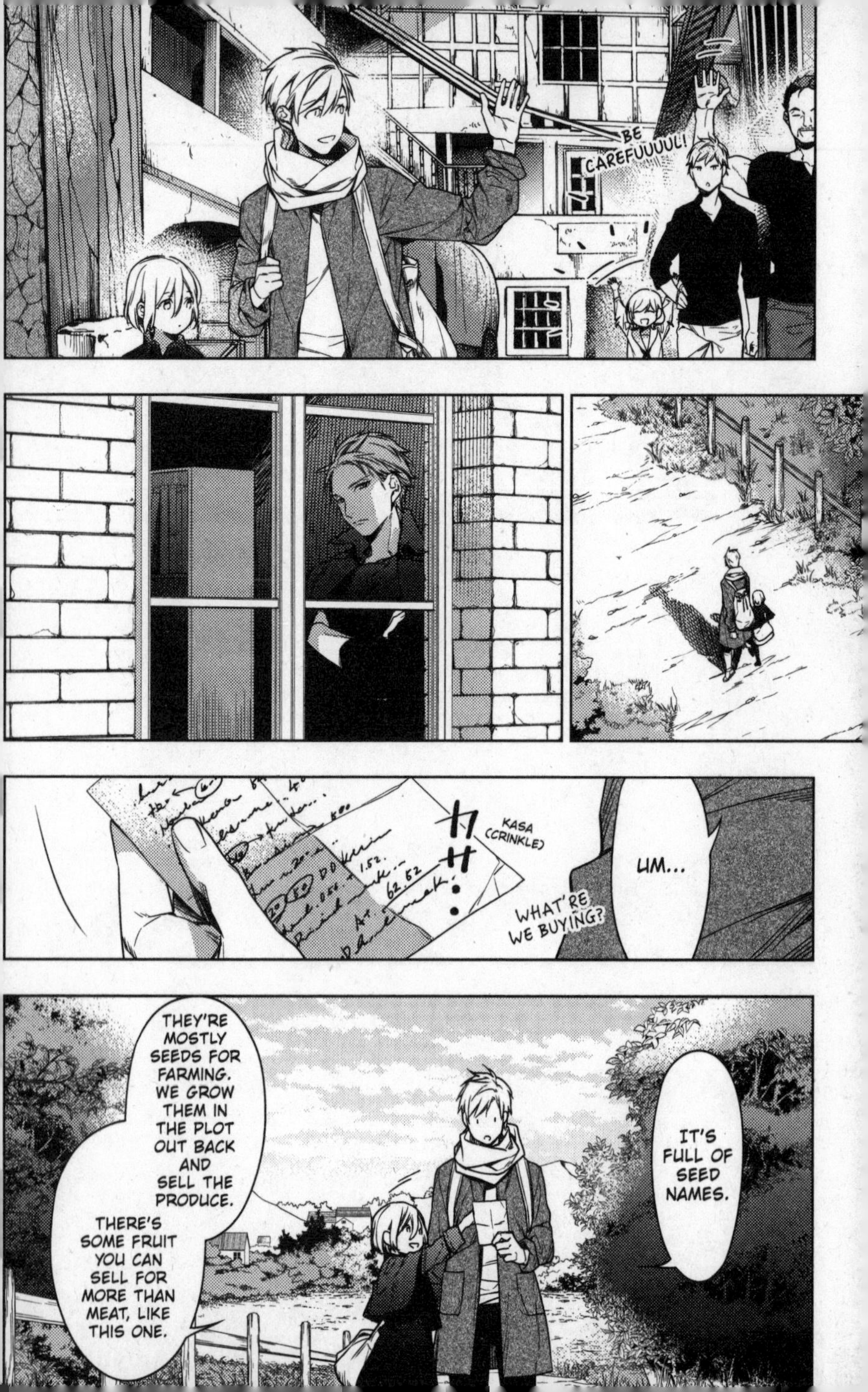
BE CAREFUUUUL!
UM...
WHAT'RE WE BUYING?
KASA (CRINKLE)
IT'S FULL OF SEED NAMES.
THEY'RE MOSTLY SEEDS FOR FARMING. WE GROW THEM IN THE PLOT OUT BACK AND SELL THE PRODUCE.
THERE'S SOME FRUIT YOU CAN SELL FOR MORE THAN MEAT, LIKE THIS ONE.

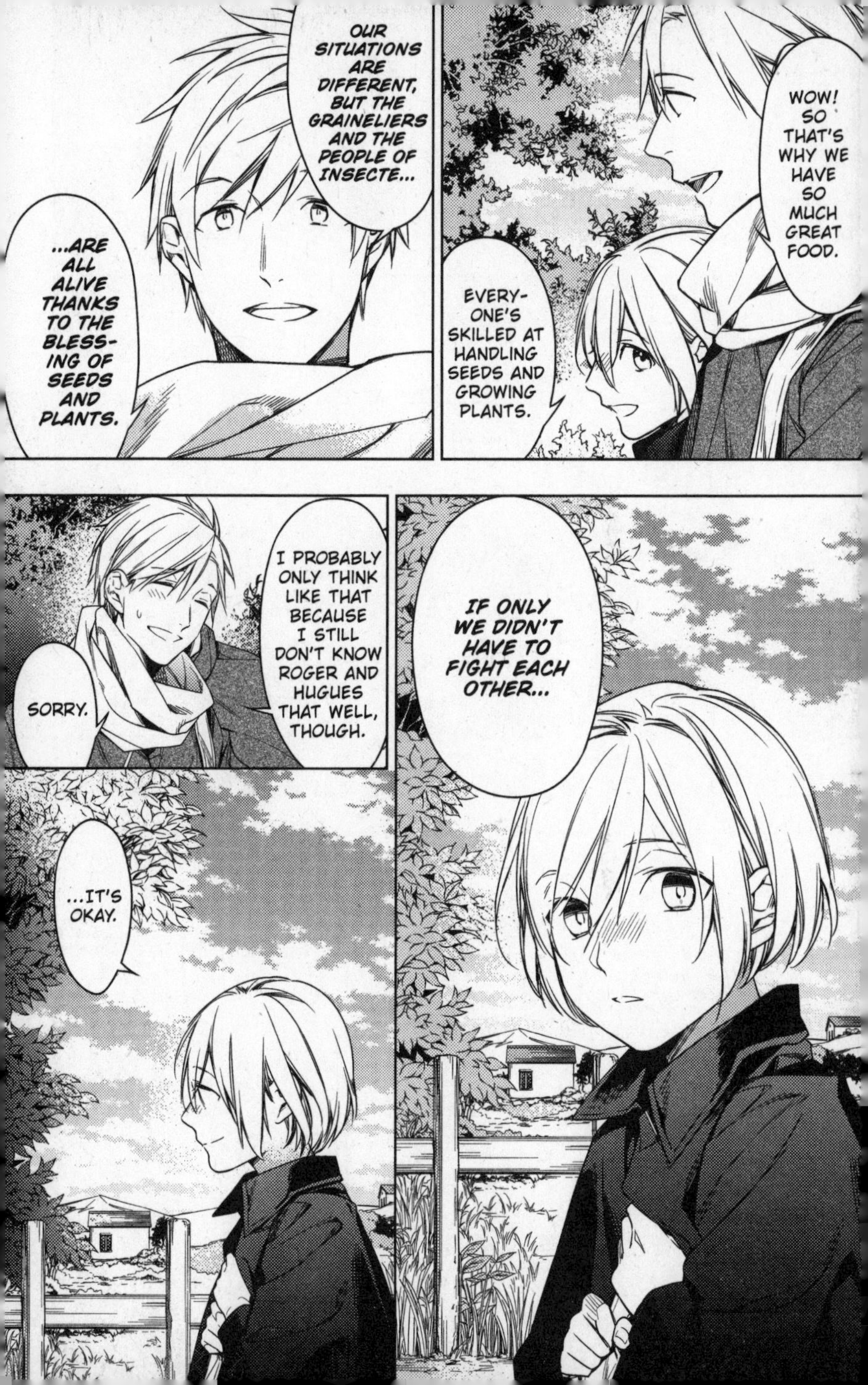
WOW! SO THAT'S WHY WE HAVE SO MUCH GREAT FOOD.
EVERY-ONE'S SKILLED AT HANDLING SEEDS AND GROWING PLANTS.
OUR SITUATIONS ARE DIFFERENT, BUT THE GRAINELIERS AND THE PEOPLE OF INSECTE...
...ARE ALL ALIVE THANKS TO THE BLESS-ING OF SEEDS AND PLANTS.
IF ONLY WE DIDN'T HAVE TO FIGHT EACH OTHER...
I PROBABLY ONLY THINK LIKE THAT BECAUSE I STILL DON'T KNOW ROGER AND HUGUES THAT WELL, THOUGH.
SORRY.
...IT'S OKAY.

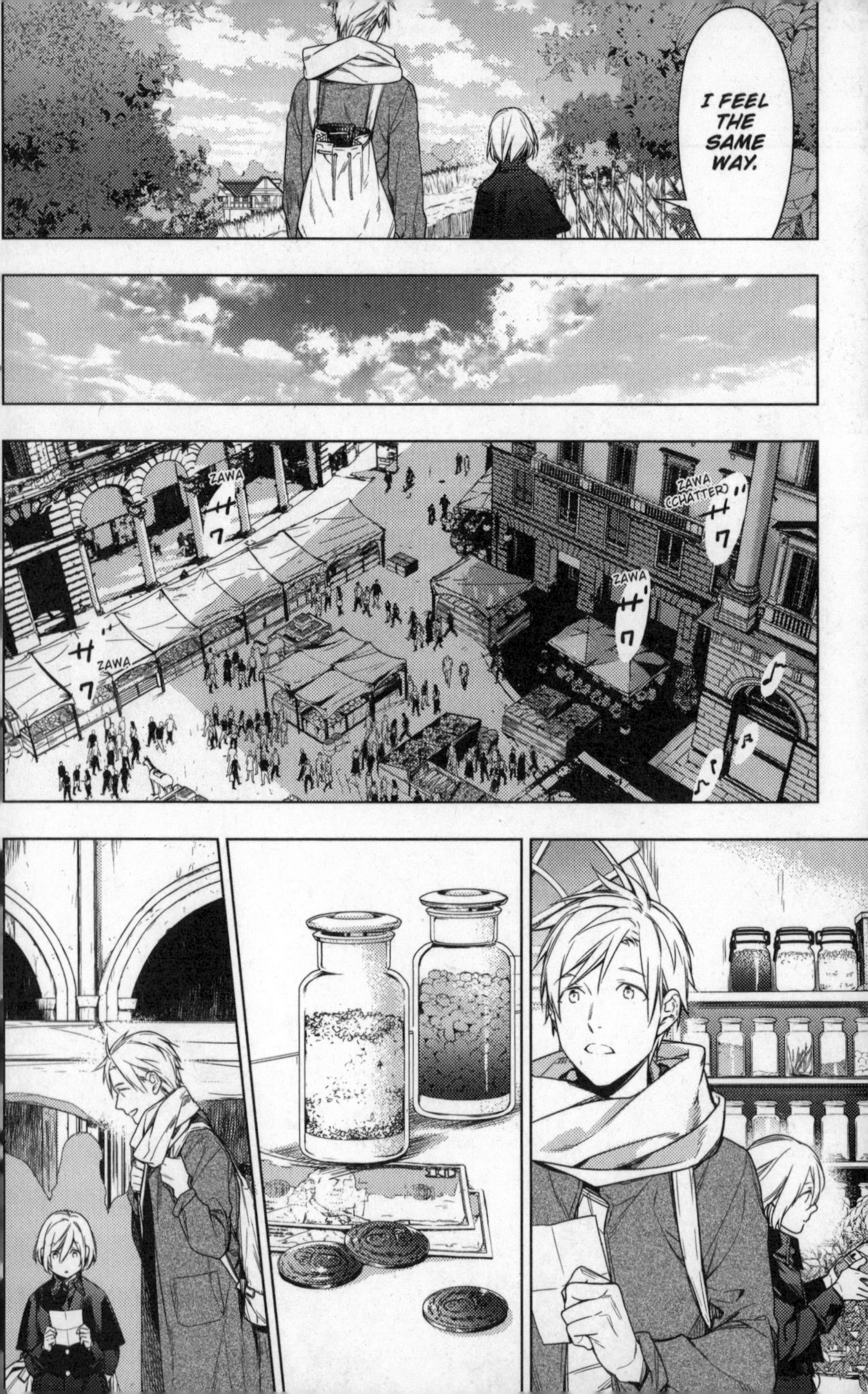
I FEEL THE SAME WAY.
ZAWA (CHATTER)
ZAWA
ZAWA
ZAWA

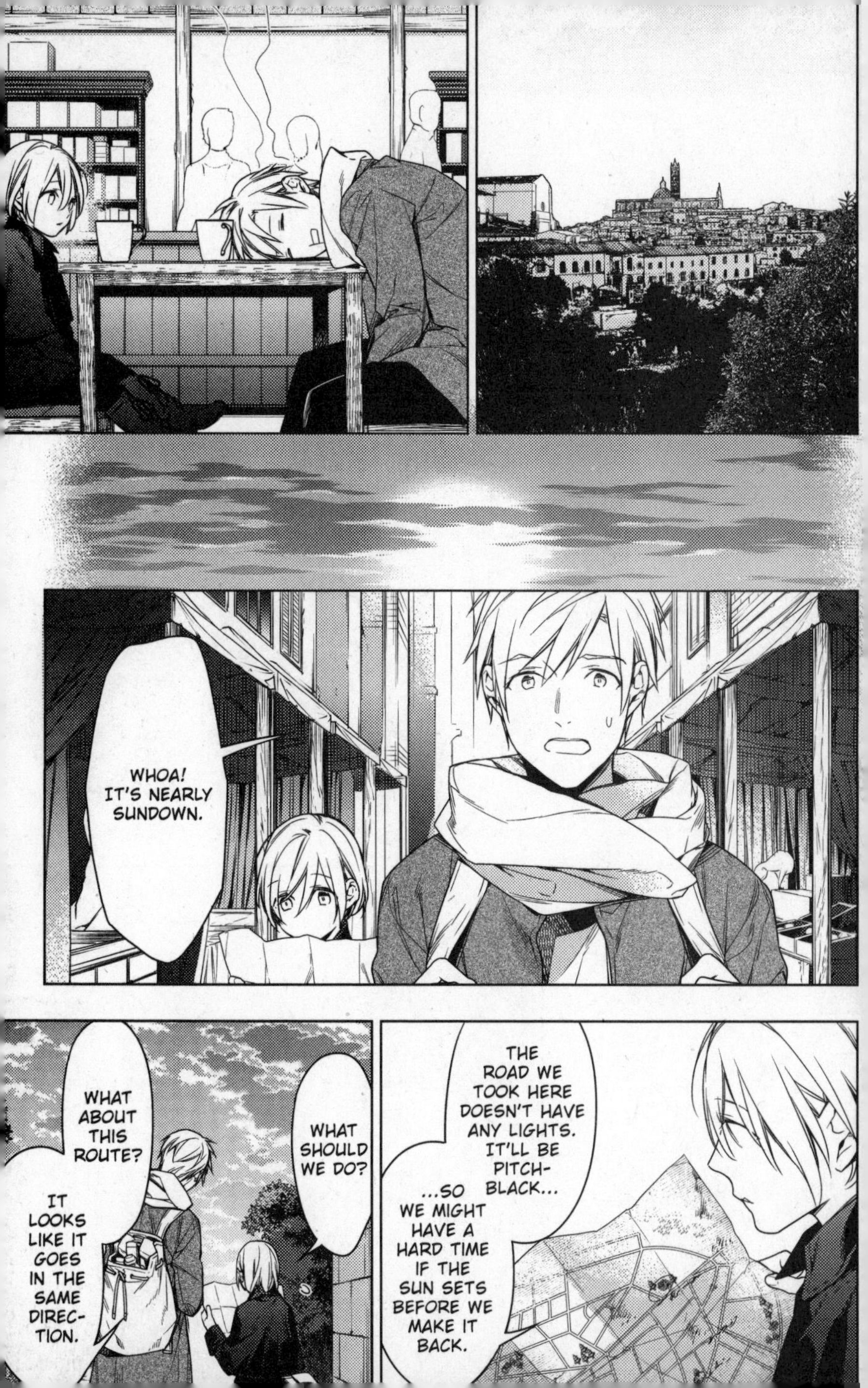
WHOA! IT'S NEARLY SUNDOWN.
THE ROAD WE TOOK HERE DOESN'T HAVE ANY LIGHTS. IT'LL BE PITCH-BLACK...
...SO WE MIGHT HAVE A HARD TIME IF THE SUN SETS BEFORE WE MAKE IT BACK.
WHAT SHOULD WE DO?
WHAT ABOUT THIS ROUTE?
IT LOOKS LIKE IT GOES IN THE SAME DIRECTION.

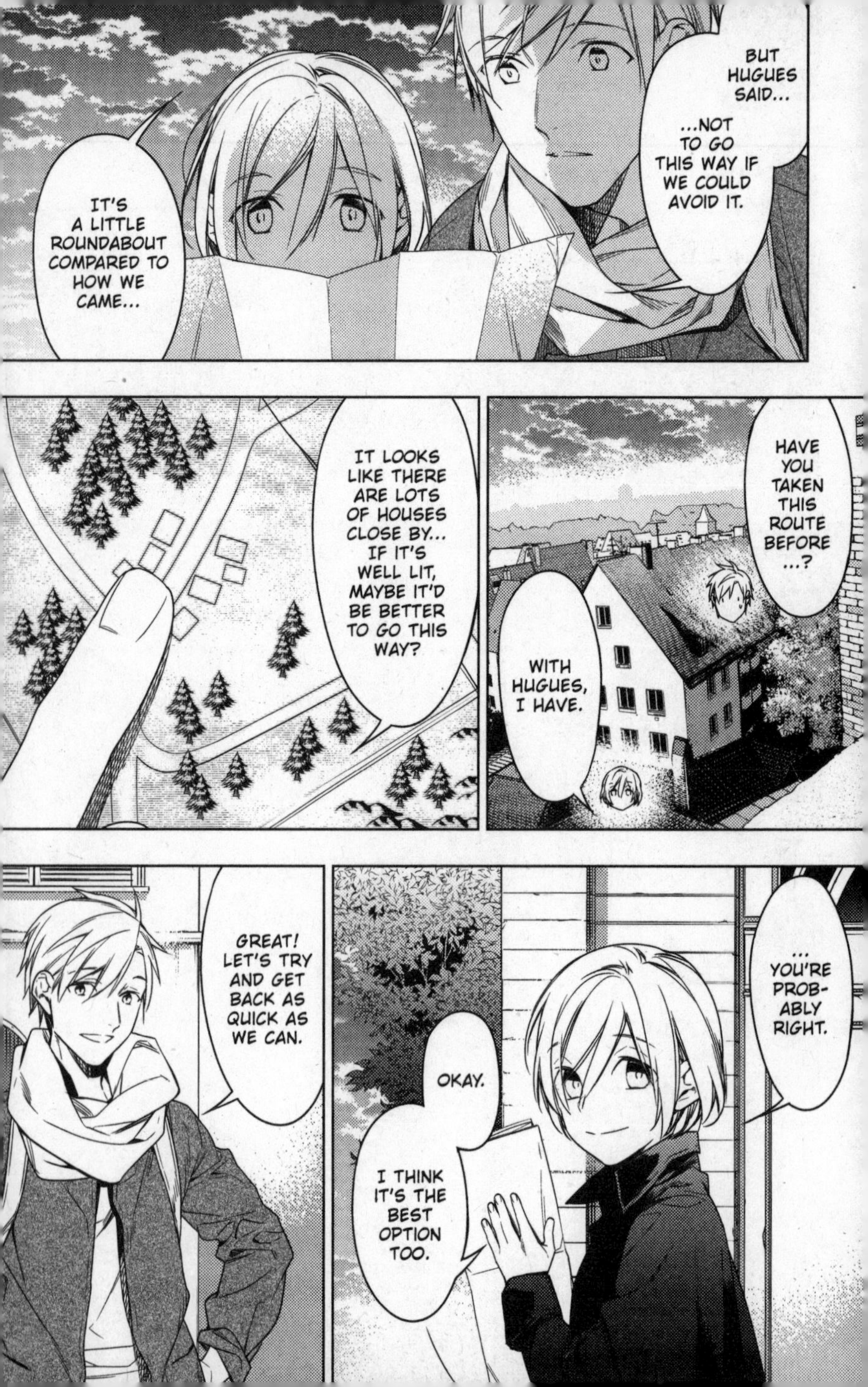
BUT HUGUES SAID...
...NOT TO GO THIS WAY IF WE COULD AVOID IT.
IT'S A LITTLE ROUNDABOUT COMPARED TO HOW WE CAME...
HAVE YOU TAKEN THIS ROUTE BEFORE ...?
WITH HUGUES, I HAVE.
IT LOOKS LIKE THERE ARE LOTS OF HOUSES CLOSE BY... IF IT'S WELL LIT, MAYBE IT'D BE BETTER TO GO THIS WAY?
... YOU'RE PROB-ABLY RIGHT.
OKAY.
I THINK IT'S THE BEST OPTION TOO.
GREAT! LET'S TRY AND GET BACK AS QUICK AS WE CAN.

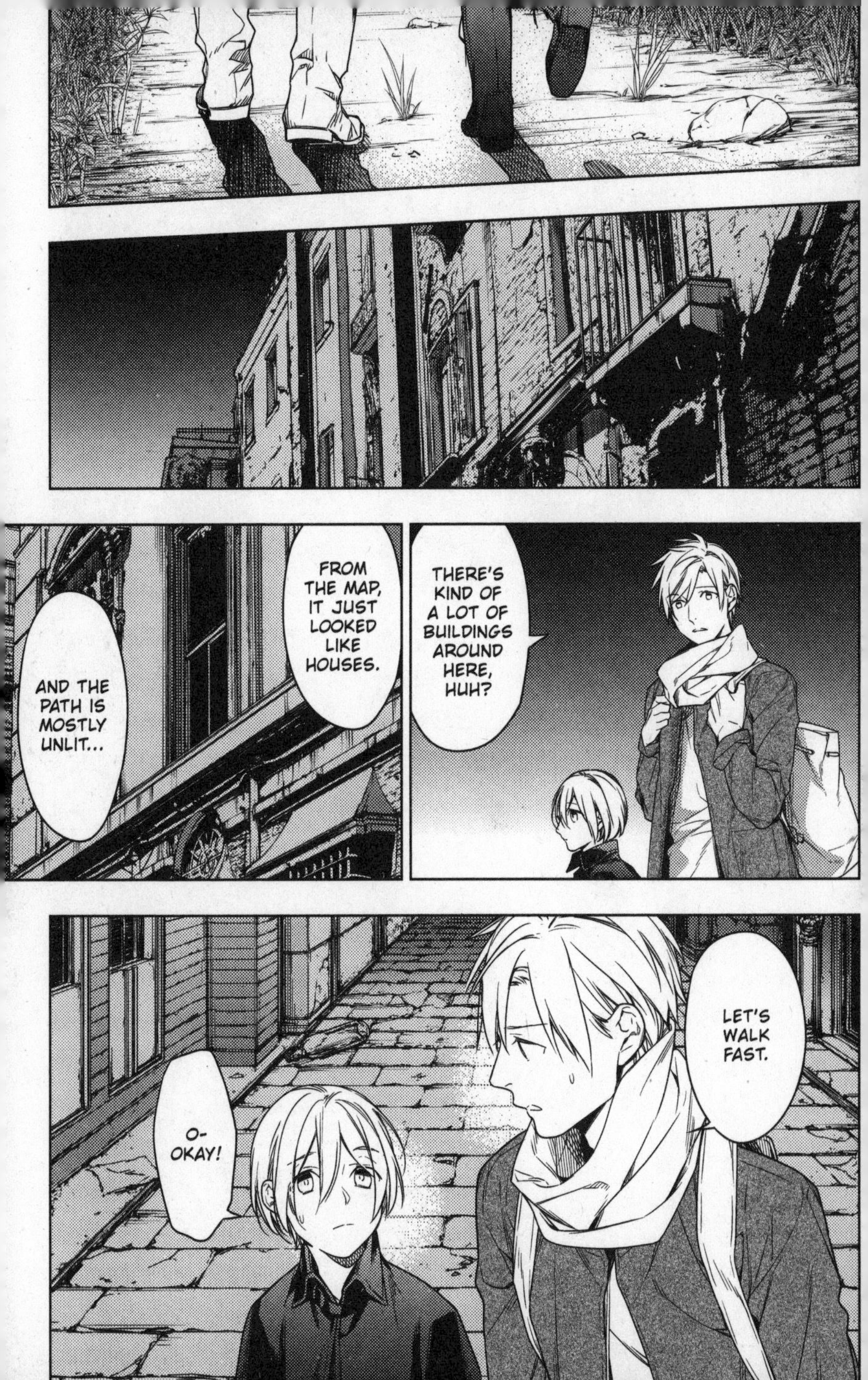
THERE'S KIND OF A LOT OF BUILDINGS AROUND HERE, HUH?
FROM THE MAP, IT JUST LOOKED LIKE HOUSES.
AND THE PATH IS MOSTLY UNLIT...
LET'S WALK FAST.
O-OKAY!

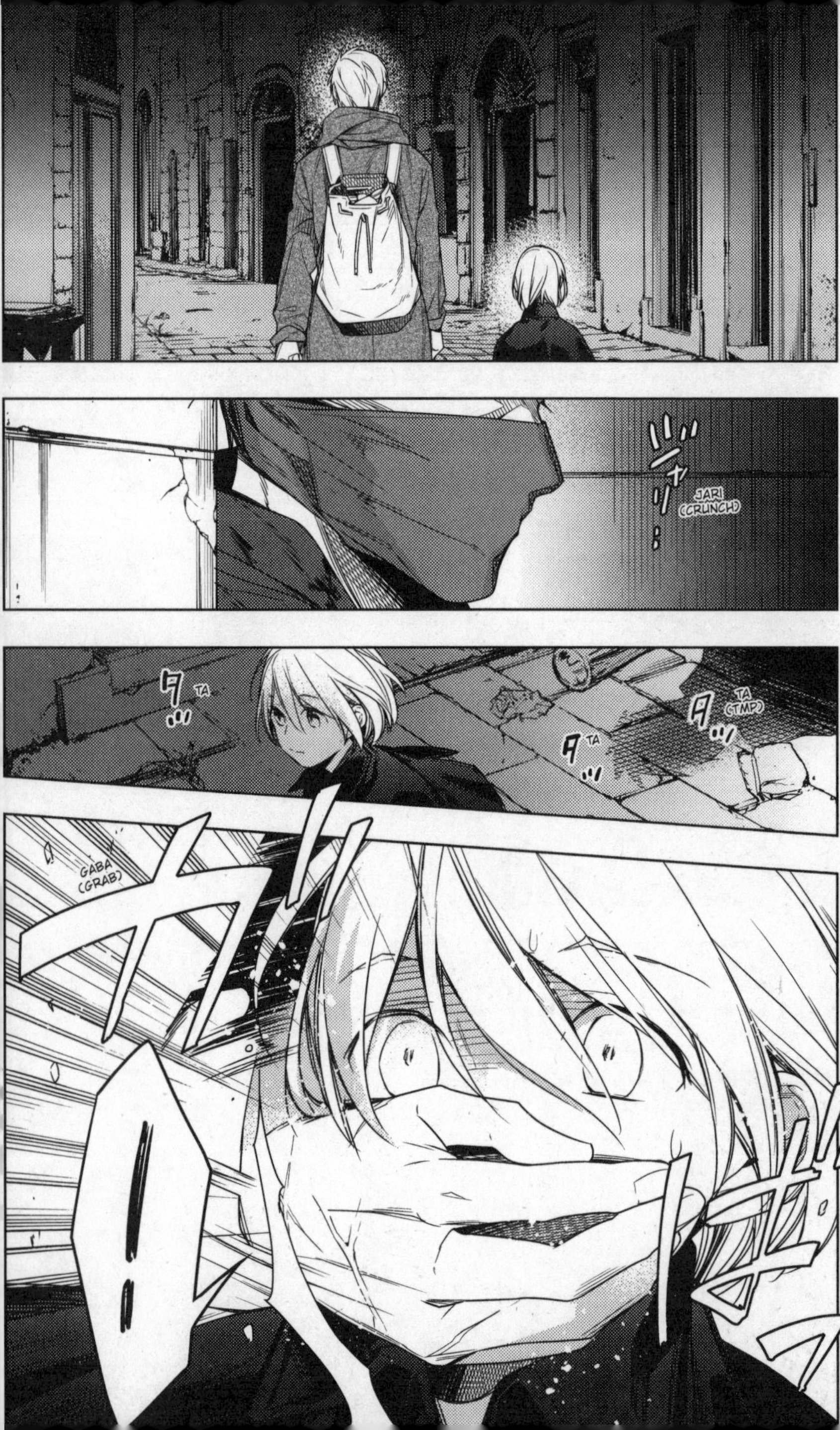
JARI (CRUNCH)
TA (TMP)
TA
TA
GABA (GRAB)

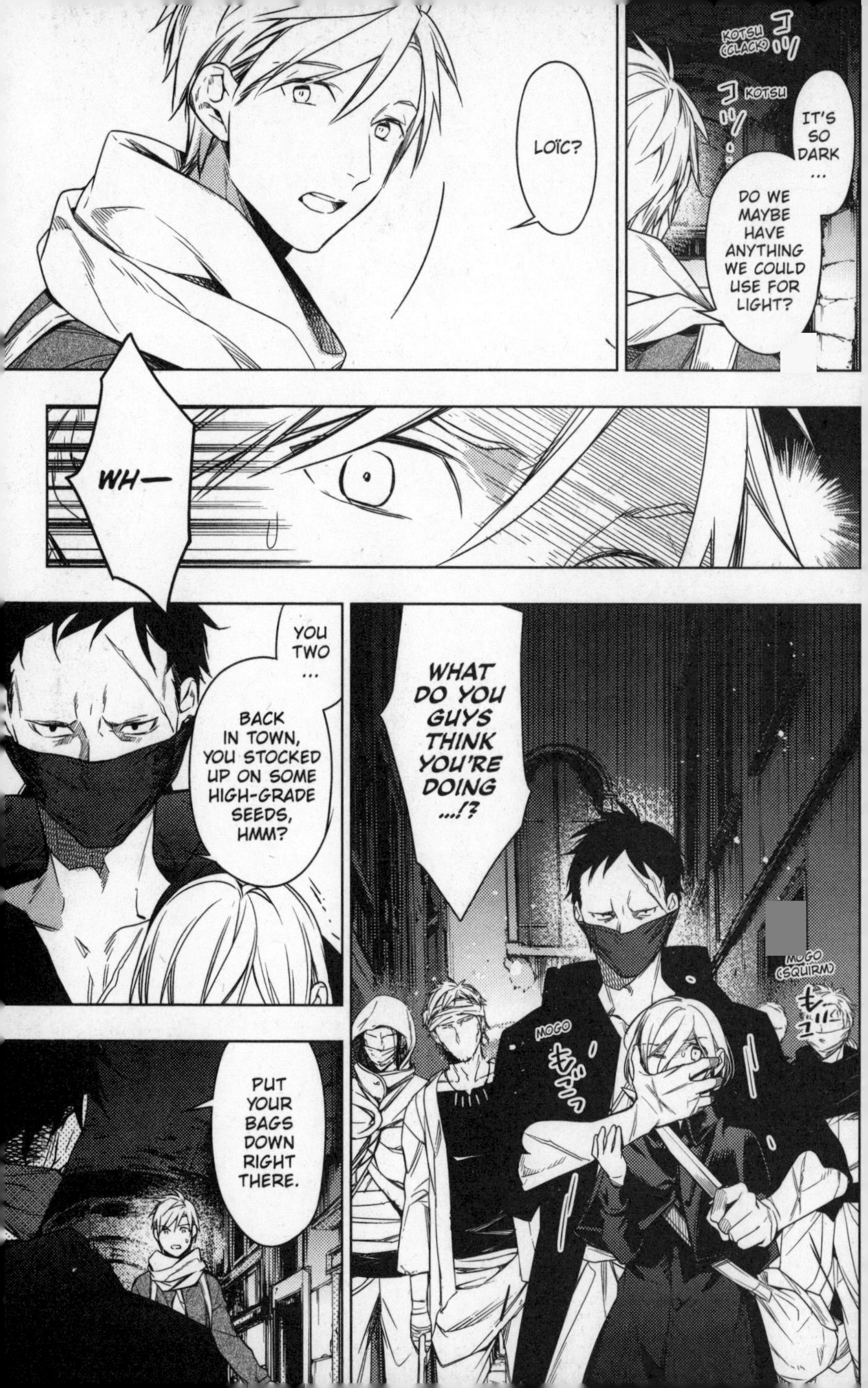
KOTSU (CLACK)
KOTSU
IT'S SO DARK...
DO WE MAYBE HAVE ANYTHING WE COULD USE FOR LIGHT?
LOÏC?
WH—
WHAT DO YOU GUYS THINK YOU'RE DOING...!?
MOGO (SQUIRM)
MOGO
YOU TWO...
BACK IN TOWN, YOU STOCKED UP ON SOME HIGH-GRADE SEEDS, HMM?
PUT YOUR BAGS DOWN RIGHT THERE.

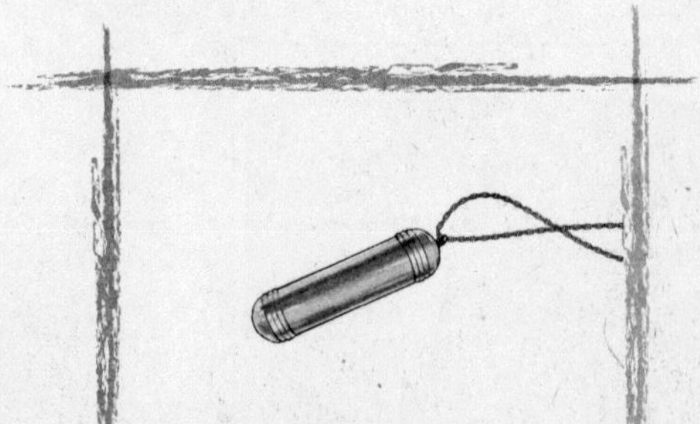

Episode 26

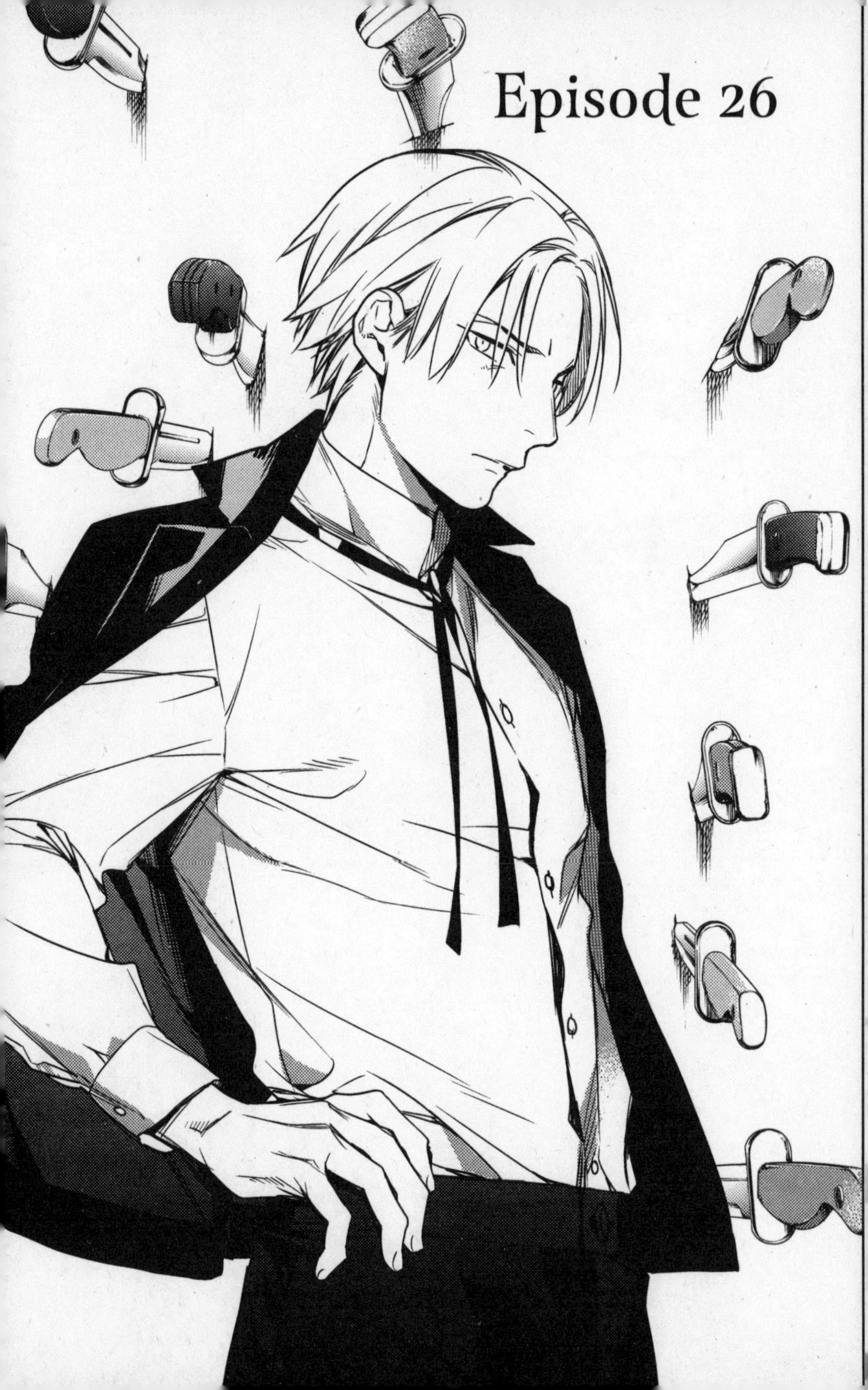

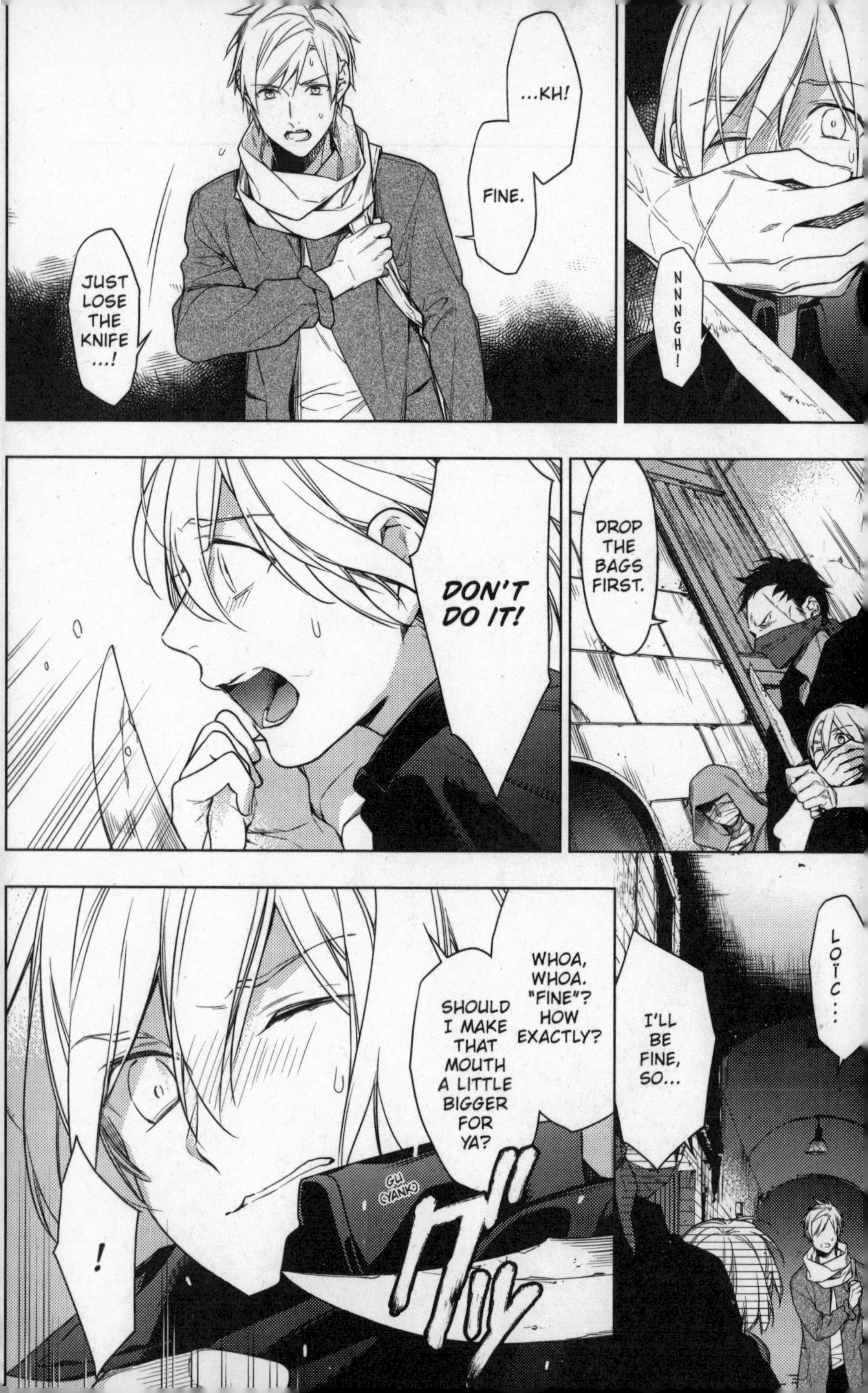
NNNGH!
...KH!
FINE.
JUST LOSE THE KNIFE ...!
DROP THE BAGS FIRST.
DON'T DO IT!
LOÏC...
I'LL BE FINE, SO...
WHOA, WHOA. "FINE"? HOW EXACTLY?
SHOULD I MAKE THAT MOUTH A LITTLE BIGGER FOR YA?
GU (YANK)
!

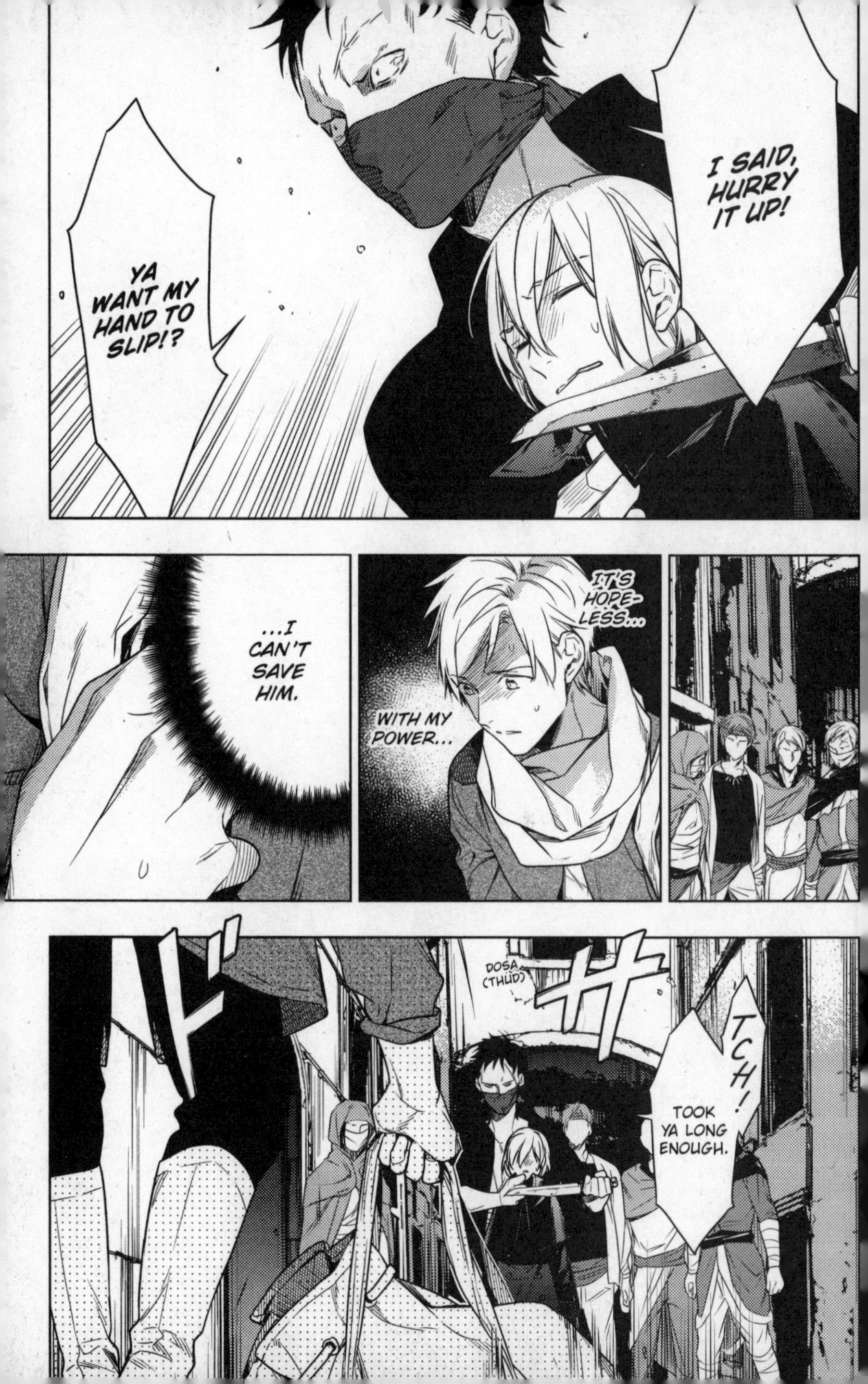
I SAID, HURRY IT UP!
YA WANT MY HAND TO SLIP!?
IT'S HOPE-LESS...
WITH MY POWER...
...I CAN'T SAVE HIM.
TCH!
TOOK YA LONG ENOUGH.
DOSA (THUD)

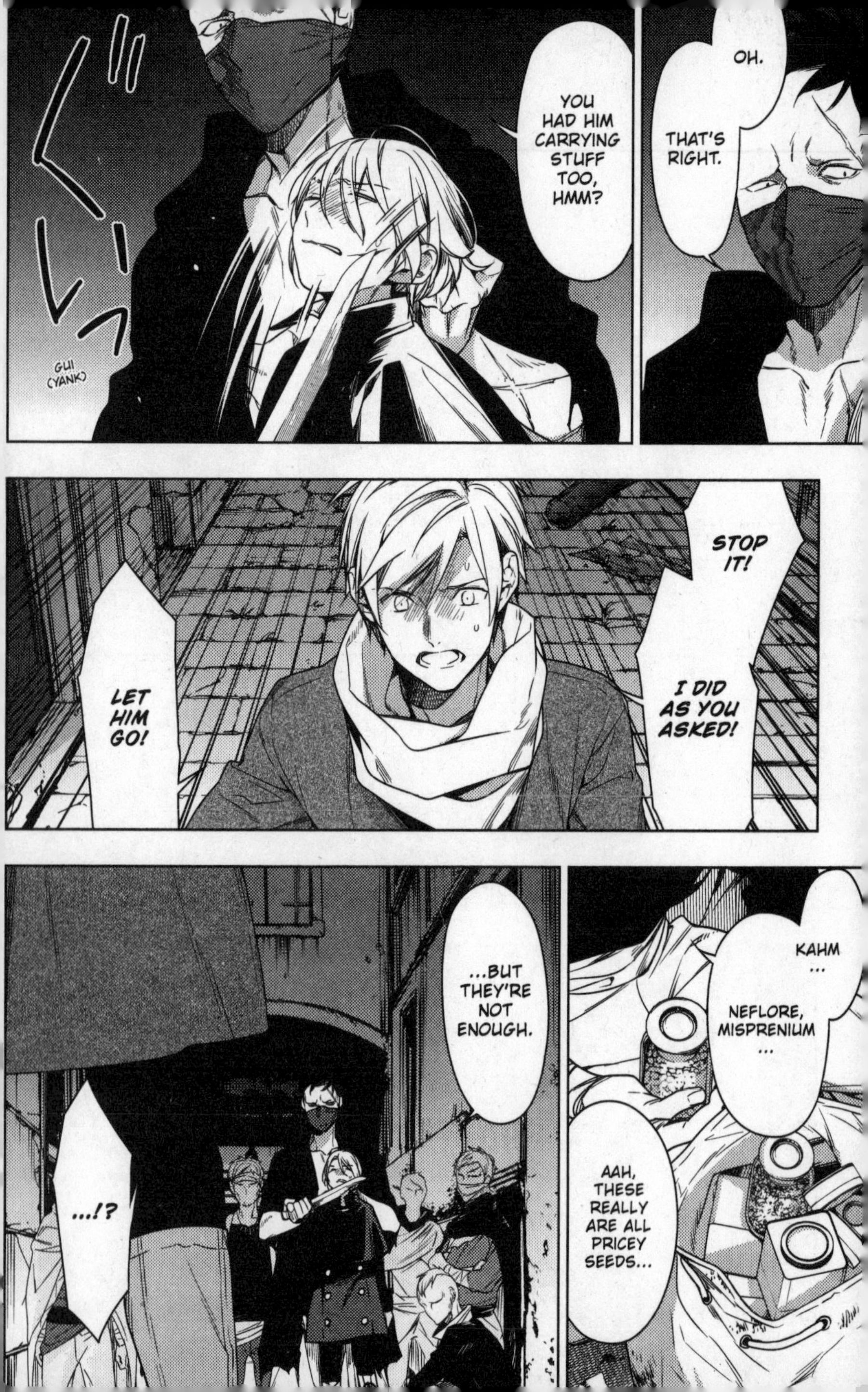
OH.
THAT'S RIGHT.
YOU HAD HIM CARRYING STUFF TOO, HMM?
GUI (YANK)
STOP IT!
I DID AS YOU ASKED!
LET HIM GO!
KAHM...
NEFLORE, MISPRENIUM...
AAH, THESE REALLY ARE ALL PRICEY SEEDS...
...BUT THEY'RE NOT ENOUGH.
...!?

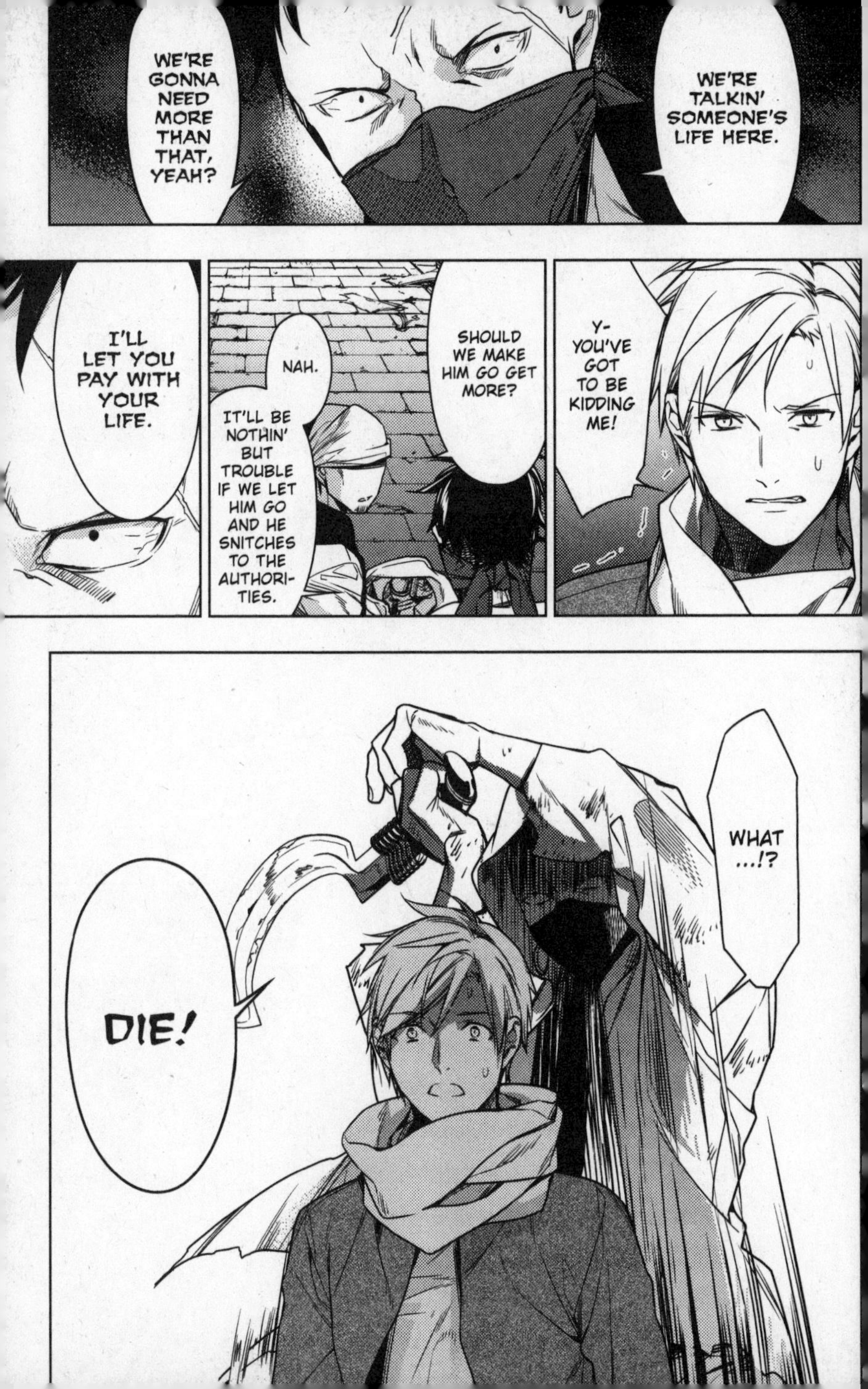
WE'RE TALKIN' SOMEONE'S LIFE HERE.
WE'RE GONNA NEED MORE THAN THAT, YEAH?
Y-YOU'VE GOT TO BE KIDDING ME!
SHOULD WE MAKE HIM GO GET MORE?
NAH.
IT'LL BE NOTHIN' BUT TROUBLE IF WE LET HIM GO AND HE SNITCHES TO THE AUTHORITIES.
I'LL LET YOU PAY WITH YOUR LIFE.
WHAT ...!?
DIE!

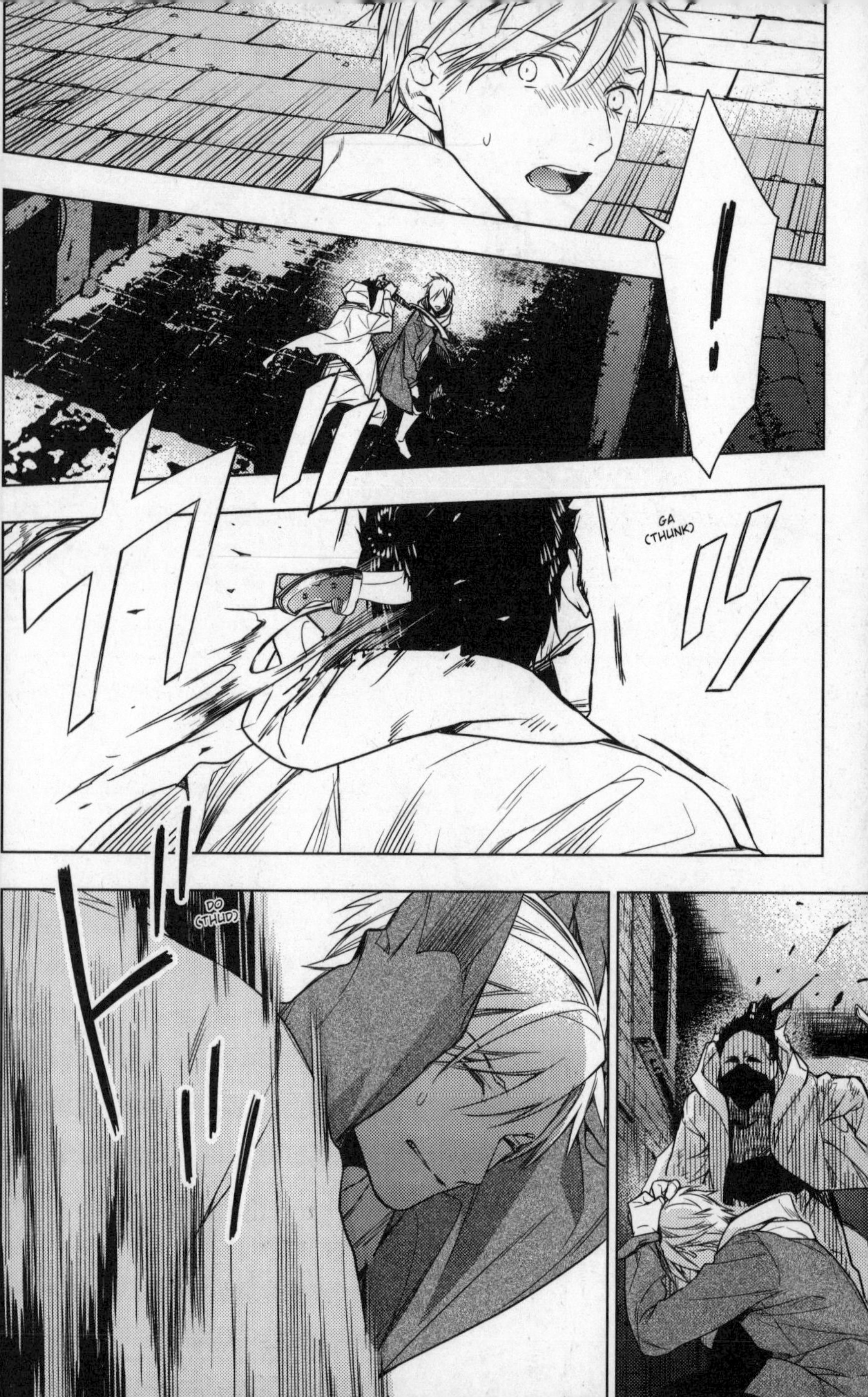
!!
GA
(THUNK)
DO
(THUD)

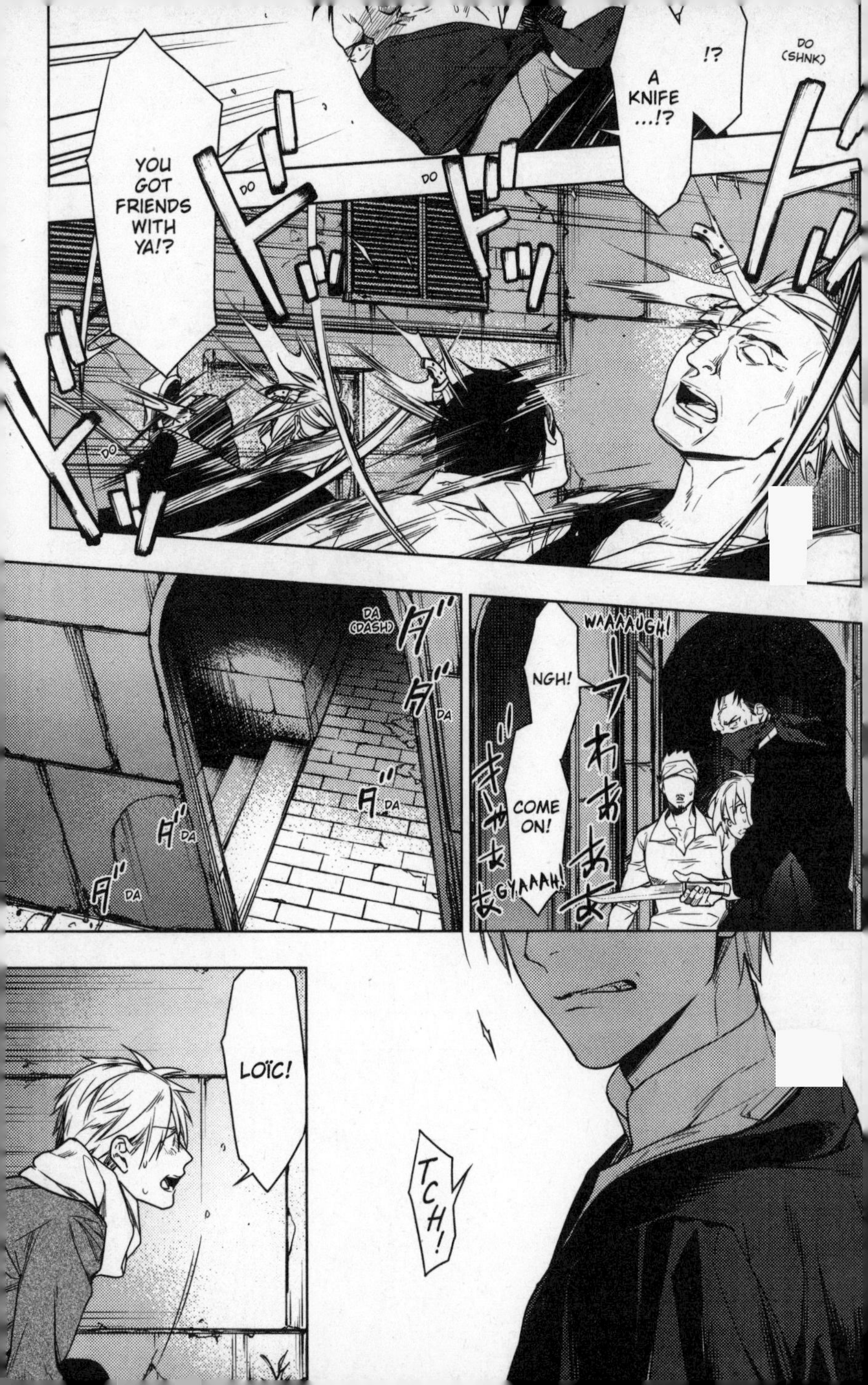
DO (SHNK)
!?
A KNIFE ...!?
DO
DO
YOU GOT FRIENDS WITH YA!?
DO
WAAAAUGH!
NGH!
COME ON!
GYAAAH!
DA (DASH)
DA
DA
DA
DA
TCH!
LOÏC!

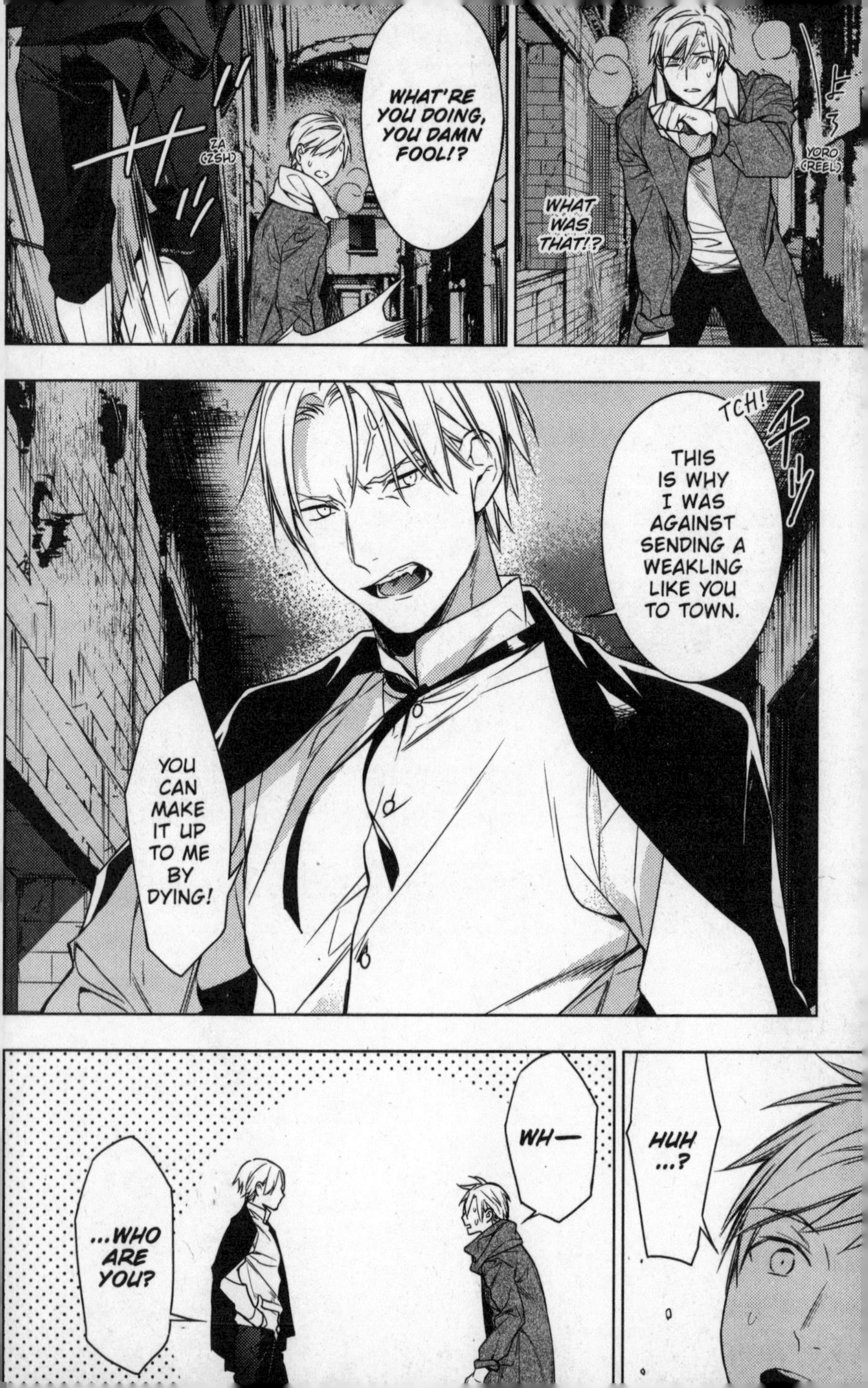
YORO (REEL)
WHAT WAS THAT!?
WHAT'RE YOU DOING, YOU DAMN FOOL!?
ZA (ZSH)
TCH!
THIS IS WHY I WAS AGAINST SENDING A WEAKLING LIKE YOU TO TOWN.
YOU CAN MAKE IT UP TO ME BY DYING!
HUH ...?
WH—
...WHO ARE YOU?

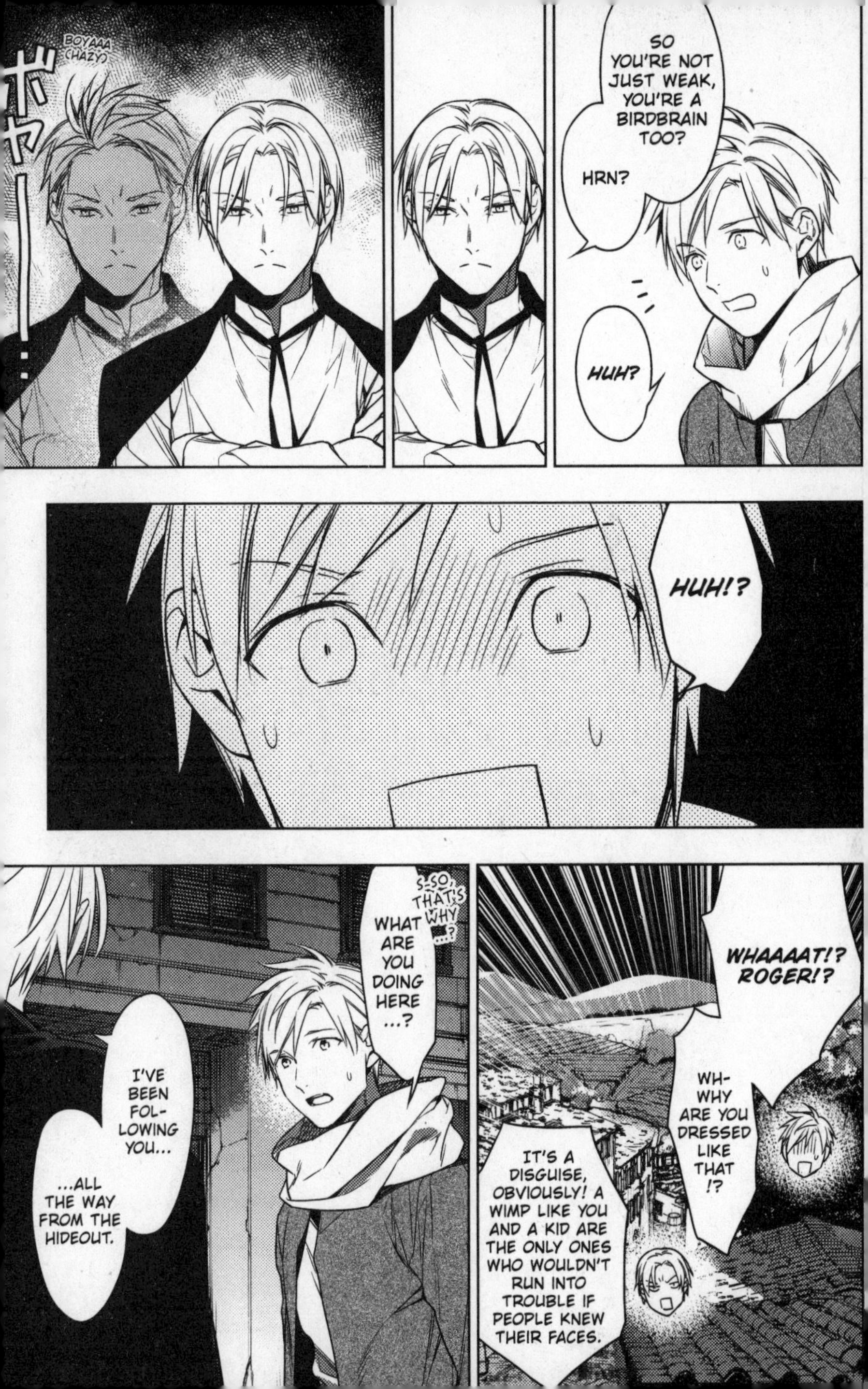
SO YOU'RE NOT JUST WEAK, YOU'RE A BIRDBRAIN TOO?
HRN?
HUH?
BOYAAA (HAZY)
ボヤー…
HUH!?
WHAAAAT!? ROGER!?
WH-WHY ARE YOU DRESSED LIKE THAT!?
IT'S A DISGUISE, OBVIOUSLY! A WIMP LIKE YOU AND A KID ARE THE ONLY ONES WHO WOULDN'T RUN INTO TROUBLE IF PEOPLE KNEW THEIR FACES.
S-SO, THAT'S WHY...?
WHAT ARE YOU DOING HERE...?
I'VE BEEN FOL-LOWING YOU...
...ALL THE WAY FROM THE HIDEOUT.

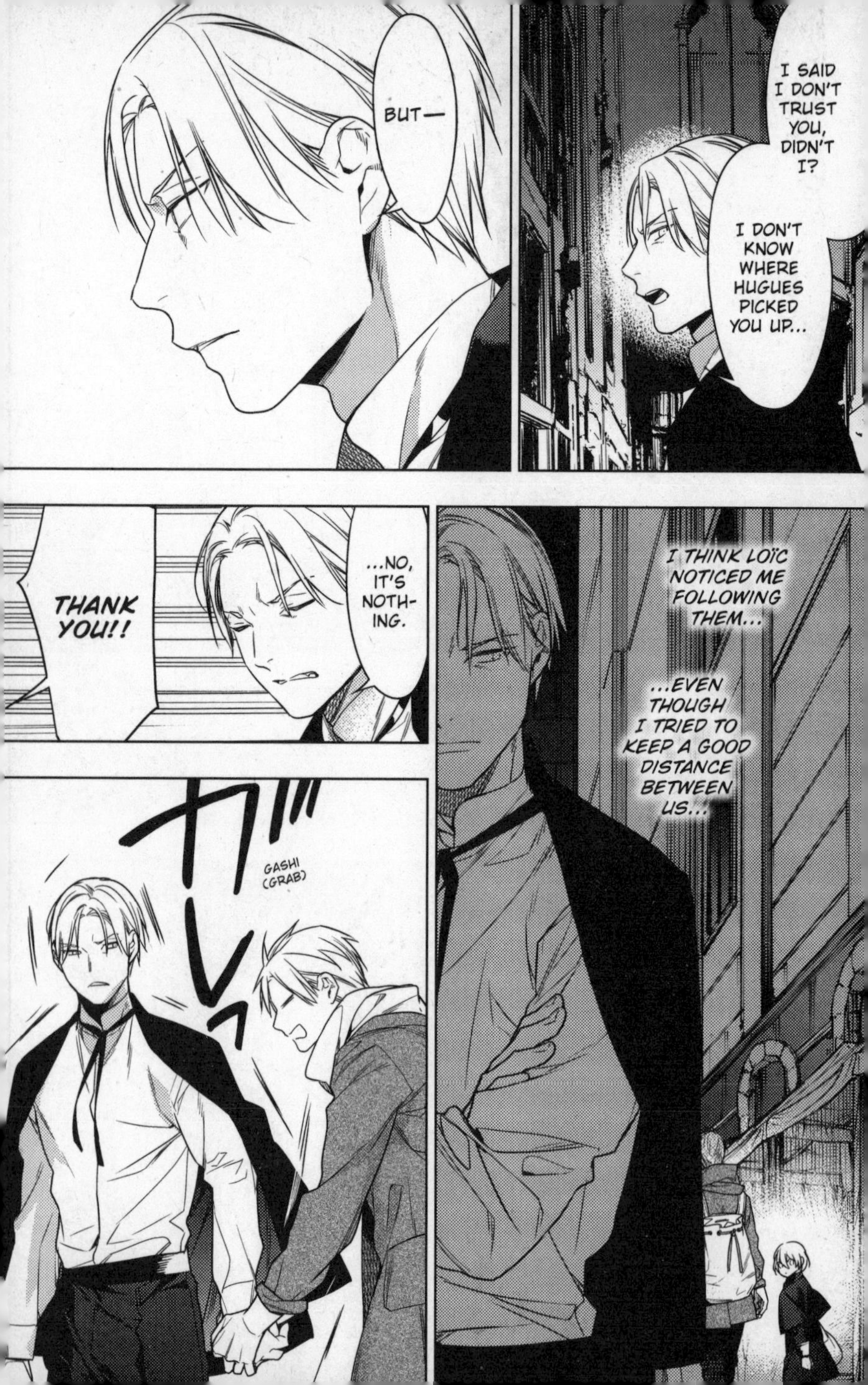
I SAID I DON'T TRUST YOU, DIDN'T I?
I DON'T KNOW WHERE HUGUES PICKED YOU UP...
BUT—
I THINK LOÏC NOTICED ME FOLLOWING THEM...
...EVEN THOUGH I TRIED TO KEEP A GOOD DISTANCE BETWEEN US...
...NO, IT'S NOTH-ING.
THANK YOU!!
GASHI (GRAB)

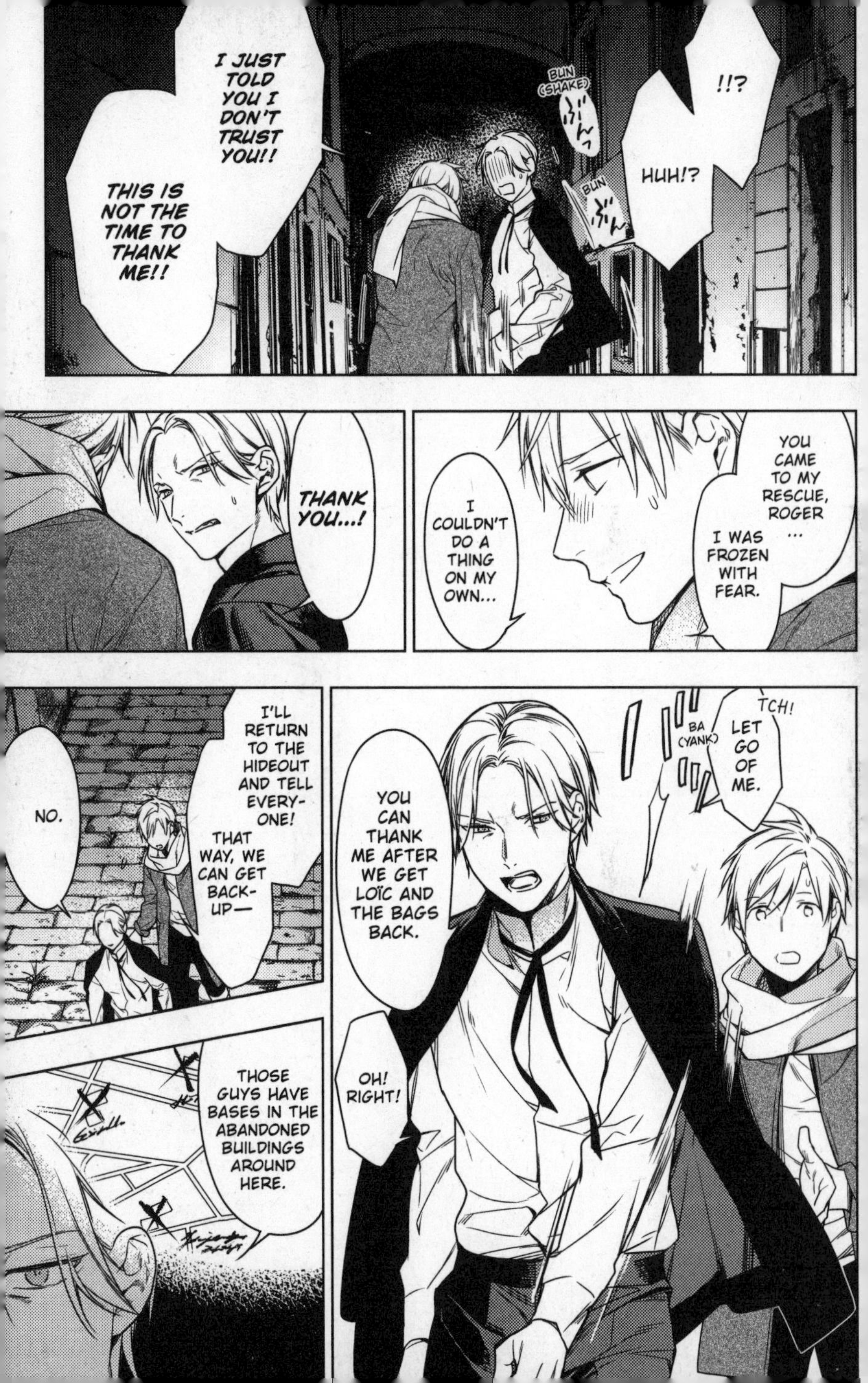
!!?
BUN (SHAKE)
BUN
HUH!?
I JUST TOLD YOU I DON'T TRUST YOU!!
THIS IS NOT THE TIME TO THANK ME!!
YOU CAME TO MY RESCUE, ROGER...
I WAS FROZEN WITH FEAR.
I COULDN'T DO A THING ON MY OWN...
THANK YOU...!
TCH!
LET GO OF ME.
BA (YANK)
YOU CAN THANK ME AFTER WE GET LOÏC AND THE BAGS BACK.
OH! RIGHT!
I'LL RETURN TO THE HIDEOUT AND TELL EVERY-ONE!
THAT WAY, WE CAN GET BACK-UP—
NO.
THOSE GUYS HAVE BASES IN THE ABANDONED BUILDINGS AROUND HERE.

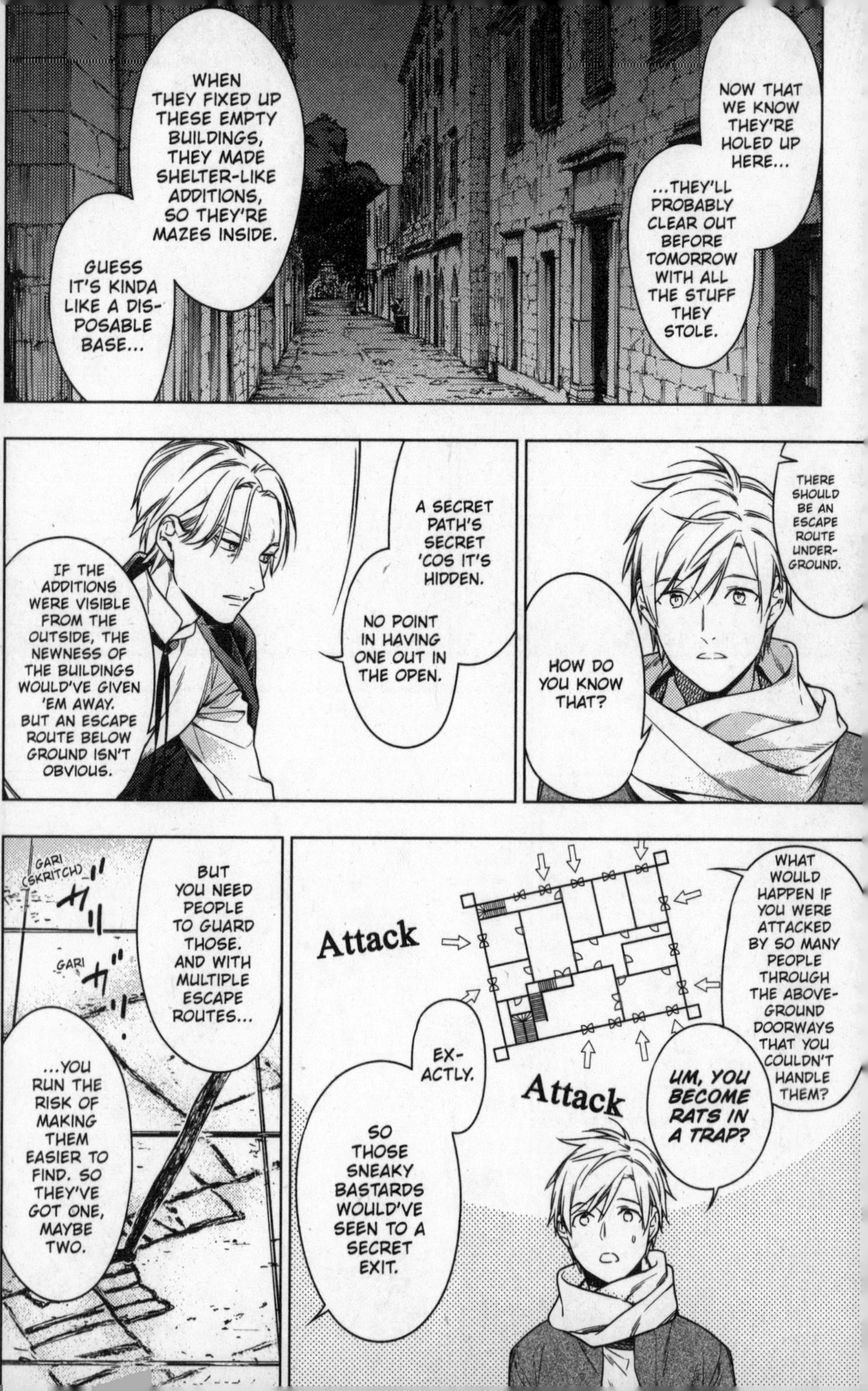
NOW THAT WE KNOW THEY'RE HOLED UP HERE...
...THEY'LL PROBABLY CLEAR OUT BEFORE TOMORROW WITH ALL THE STUFF THEY STOLE.
WHEN THEY FIXED UP THESE EMPTY BUILDINGS, THEY MADE SHELTER-LIKE ADDITIONS, SO THEY'RE MAZES INSIDE.
GUESS IT'S KINDA LIKE A DIS-POSABLE BASE...
THERE SHOULD BE AN ESCAPE ROUTE UNDER-GROUND.
HOW DO YOU KNOW THAT?
A SECRET PATH'S SECRET 'COS IT'S HIDDEN.
NO POINT IN HAVING ONE OUT IN THE OPEN.
IF THE ADDITIONS WERE VISIBLE FROM THE OUTSIDE, THE NEWNESS OF THE BUILDINGS WOULD'VE GIVEN 'EM AWAY. BUT AN ESCAPE ROUTE BELOW GROUND ISN'T OBVIOUS.
Attack
Attack
WHAT WOULD HAPPEN IF YOU WERE ATTACKED BY SO MANY PEOPLE THROUGH THE ABOVE-GROUND DOORWAYS THAT YOU COULDN'T HANDLE THEM?
UM, YOU BECOME RATS IN A TRAP?
EX-ACTLY.
SO THOSE SNEAKY BASTARDS WOULD'VE SEEN TO A SECRET EXIT.
BUT YOU NEED PEOPLE TO GUARD THOSE. AND WITH MULTIPLE ESCAPE ROUTES...
GARI (SKRITCH)
GARI
...YOU RUN THE RISK OF MAKING THEM EASIER TO FIND. SO THEY'VE GOT ONE, MAYBE TWO.

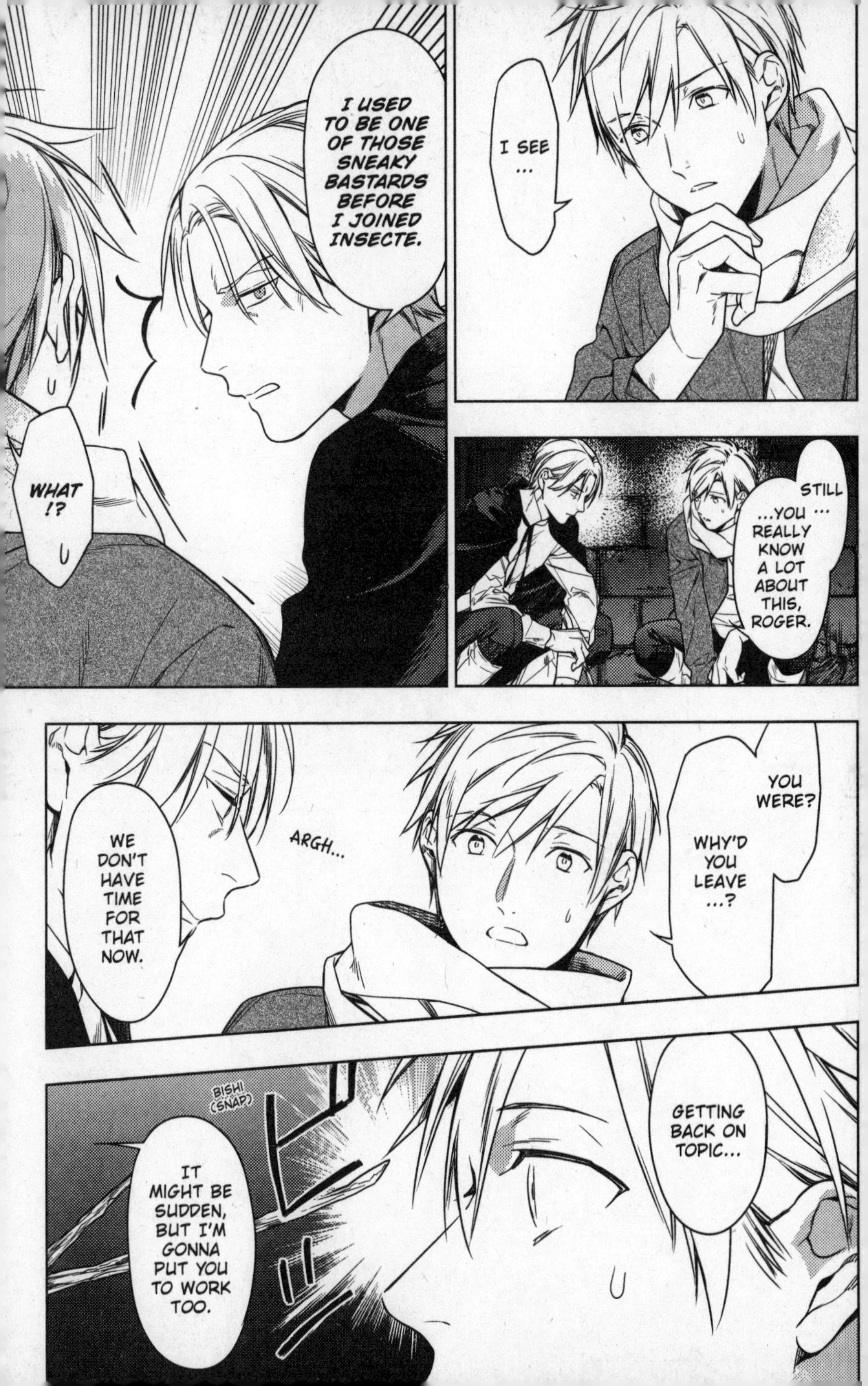
I SEE ...
STILL ... ...YOU REALLY KNOW A LOT ABOUT THIS, ROGER.
I USED TO BE ONE OF THOSE SNEAKY BASTARDS BEFORE I JOINED INSECTE.
WHAT !?
YOU WERE?
WHY'D YOU LEAVE ...?
ARGH...
WE DON'T HAVE TIME FOR THAT NOW.
GETTING BACK ON TOPIC...
BISHI (SNAP)
IT MIGHT BE SUDDEN, BUT I'M GONNA PUT YOU TO WORK TOO.

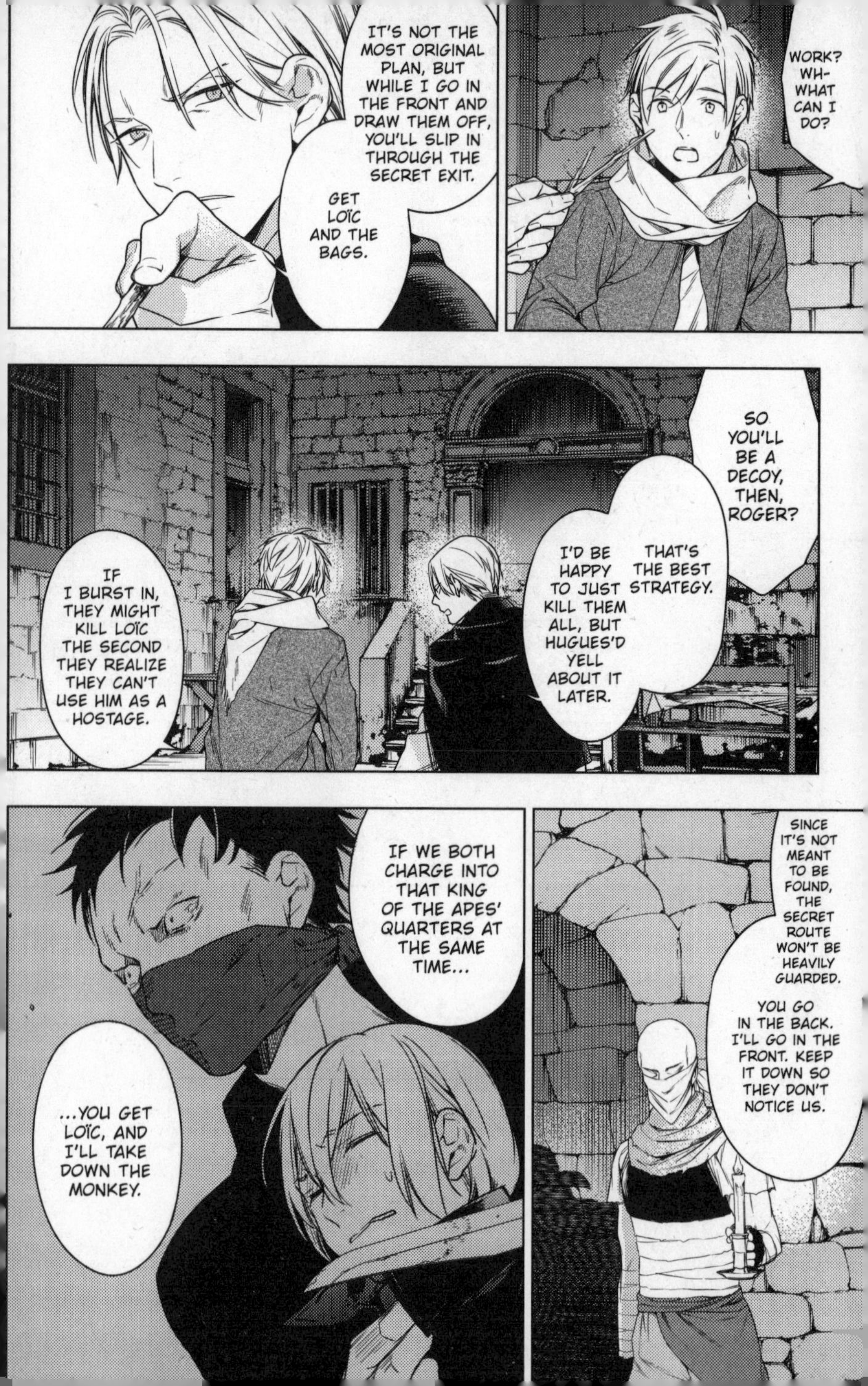
WORK? WH-WHAT CAN I DO?
IT'S NOT THE MOST ORIGINAL PLAN, BUT WHILE I GO IN THE FRONT AND DRAW THEM OFF, YOU'LL SLIP IN THROUGH THE SECRET EXIT.
GET LOÏC AND THE BAGS.
SO YOU'LL BE A DECOY, THEN, ROGER?
THAT'S THE BEST STRATEGY.
I'D BE HAPPY TO JUST KILL THEM ALL, BUT HUGUES'D YELL ABOUT IT LATER.
IF I BURST IN, THEY MIGHT KILL LOÏC THE SECOND THEY REALIZE THEY CAN'T USE HIM AS A HOSTAGE.
SINCE IT'S NOT MEANT TO BE FOUND, THE SECRET ROUTE WON'T BE HEAVILY GUARDED.
YOU GO IN THE BACK. I'LL GO IN THE FRONT. KEEP IT DOWN SO THEY DON'T NOTICE US.
IF WE BOTH CHARGE INTO THAT KING OF THE APES' QUARTERS AT THE SAME TIME...
...YOU GET LOÏC, AND I'LL TAKE DOWN THE MONKEY.

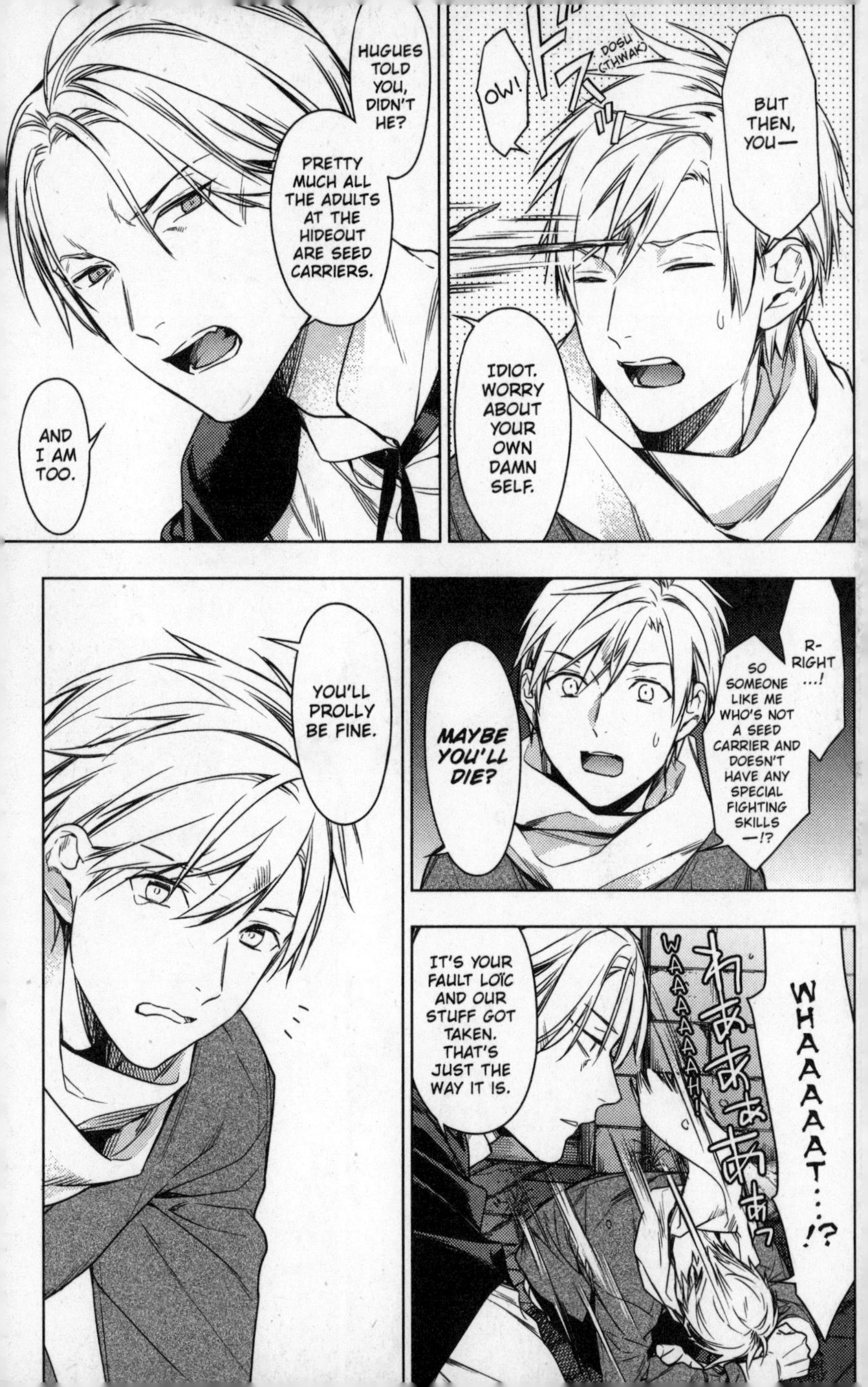
BUT THEN, YOU—
OW!
ドス
DOSU (THWAK)
IDIOT. WORRY ABOUT YOUR OWN DAMN SELF.
HUGUES TOLD YOU, DIDN'T HE?
PRETTY MUCH ALL THE ADULTS AT THE HIDEOUT ARE SEED CARRIERS.
AND I AM TOO.
R-RIGHT...!
SO SOMEONE LIKE ME WHO'S NOT A SEED CARRIER AND DOESN'T HAVE ANY SPECIAL FIGHTING SKILLS—!?
MAYBE YOU'LL DIE?
WHAAAAAT...!?
わあああぁっ
WAAAAAAAH!
IT'S YOUR FAULT LOÏC AND OUR STUFF GOT TAKEN. THAT'S JUST THE WAY IT IS.
YOU'LL PROLLY BE FINE.

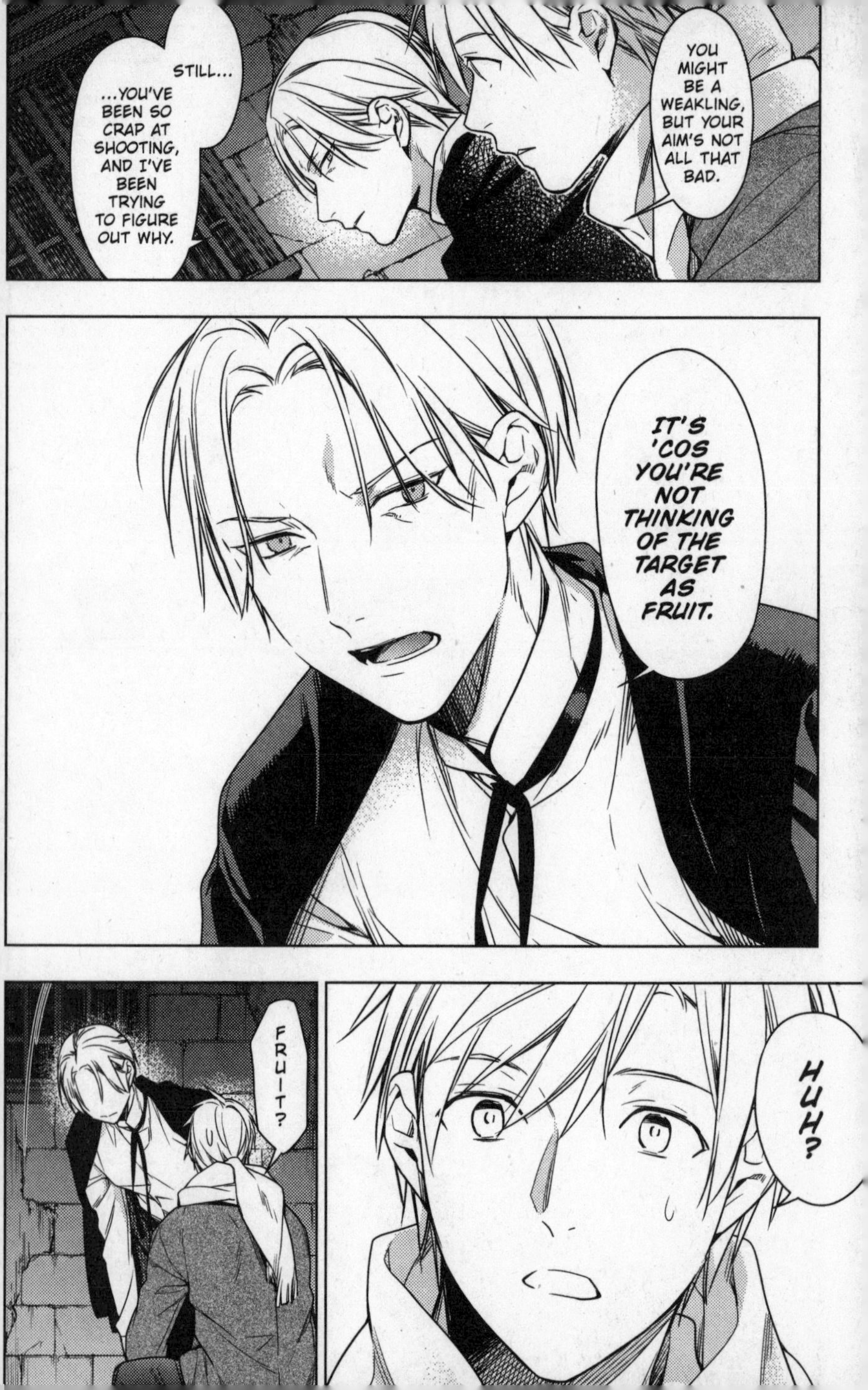
YOU MIGHT BE A WEAKLING, BUT YOUR AIM'S NOT ALL THAT BAD.
STILL...
...YOU'VE BEEN SO CRAP AT SHOOTING, AND I'VE BEEN TRYING TO FIGURE OUT WHY.
IT'S 'COS YOU'RE NOT THINKING OF THE TARGET AS FRUIT.
HUH?
FRUIT?

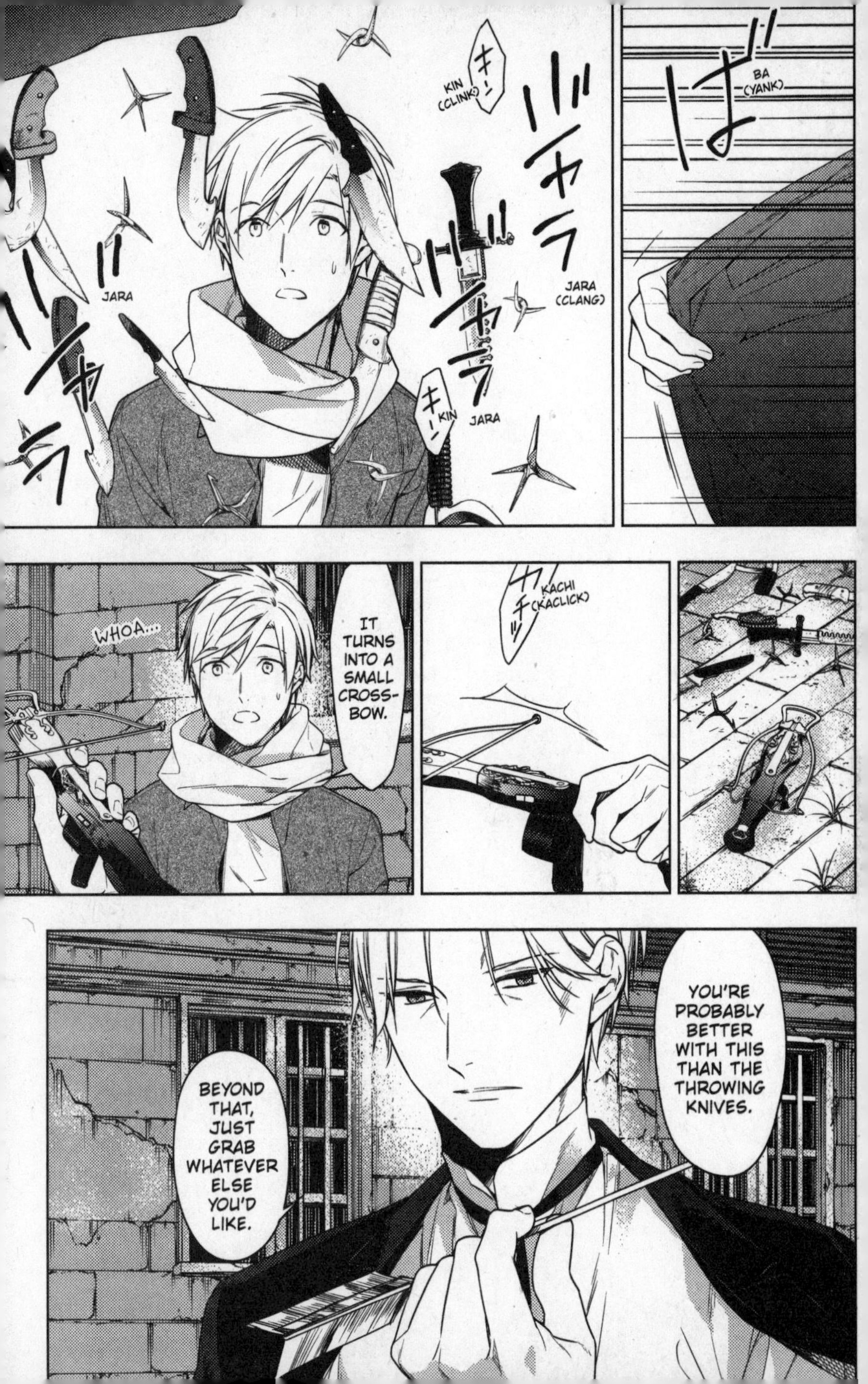
ば
BA (YANK)
ジャラ
JARA (CLANG)
キン
KIN (CLINK)
ジャラ
JARA
キン
KIN
ジャラ
JARA
カチッ
KACHI (KACLICK)
IT TURNS INTO A SMALL CROSS-BOW.
WHOA...
YOU'RE PROBABLY BETTER WITH THIS THAN THE THROWING KNIVES.
BEYOND THAT, JUST GRAB WHATEVER ELSE YOU'D LIKE.

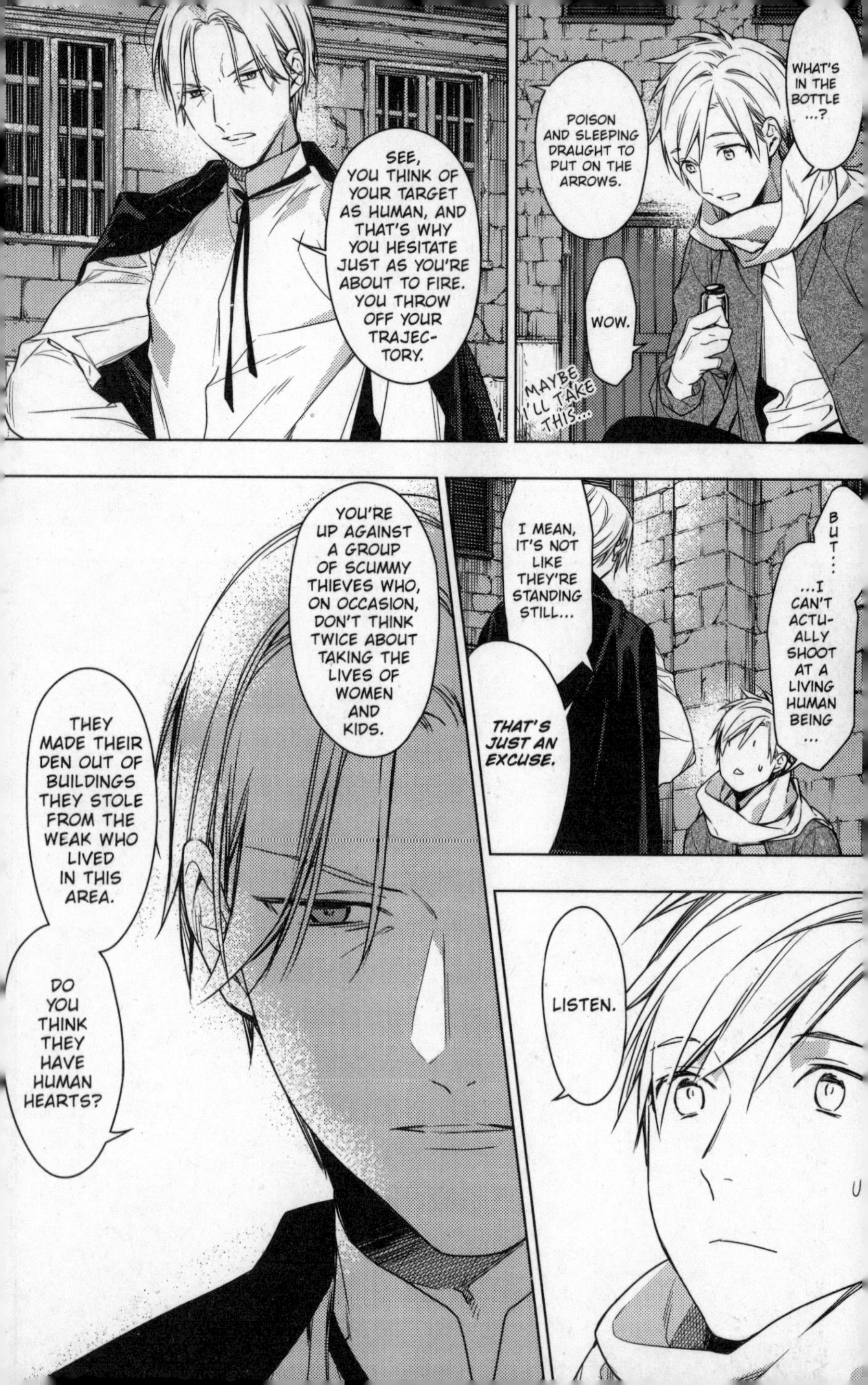
WHAT'S IN THE BOTTLE ...?
POISON AND SLEEPING DRAUGHT TO PUT ON THE ARROWS.
WOW.
MAYBE I'LL TAKE THIS...
SEE, YOU THINK OF YOUR TARGET AS HUMAN, AND THAT'S WHY YOU HESITATE JUST AS YOU'RE ABOUT TO FIRE. YOU THROW OFF YOUR TRAJEC-TORY.
BUT... ...I CAN'T ACTU-ALLY SHOOT AT A LIVING HUMAN BEING...
I MEAN, IT'S NOT LIKE THEY'RE STANDING STILL...
THAT'S JUST AN EXCUSE.
LISTEN.
YOU'RE UP AGAINST A GROUP OF SCUMMY THIEVES WHO, ON OCCASION, DON'T THINK TWICE ABOUT TAKING THE LIVES OF WOMEN AND KIDS.
THEY MADE THEIR DEN OUT OF BUILDINGS THEY STOLE FROM THE WEAK WHO LIVED IN THIS AREA.
DO YOU THINK THEY HAVE HUMAN HEARTS?

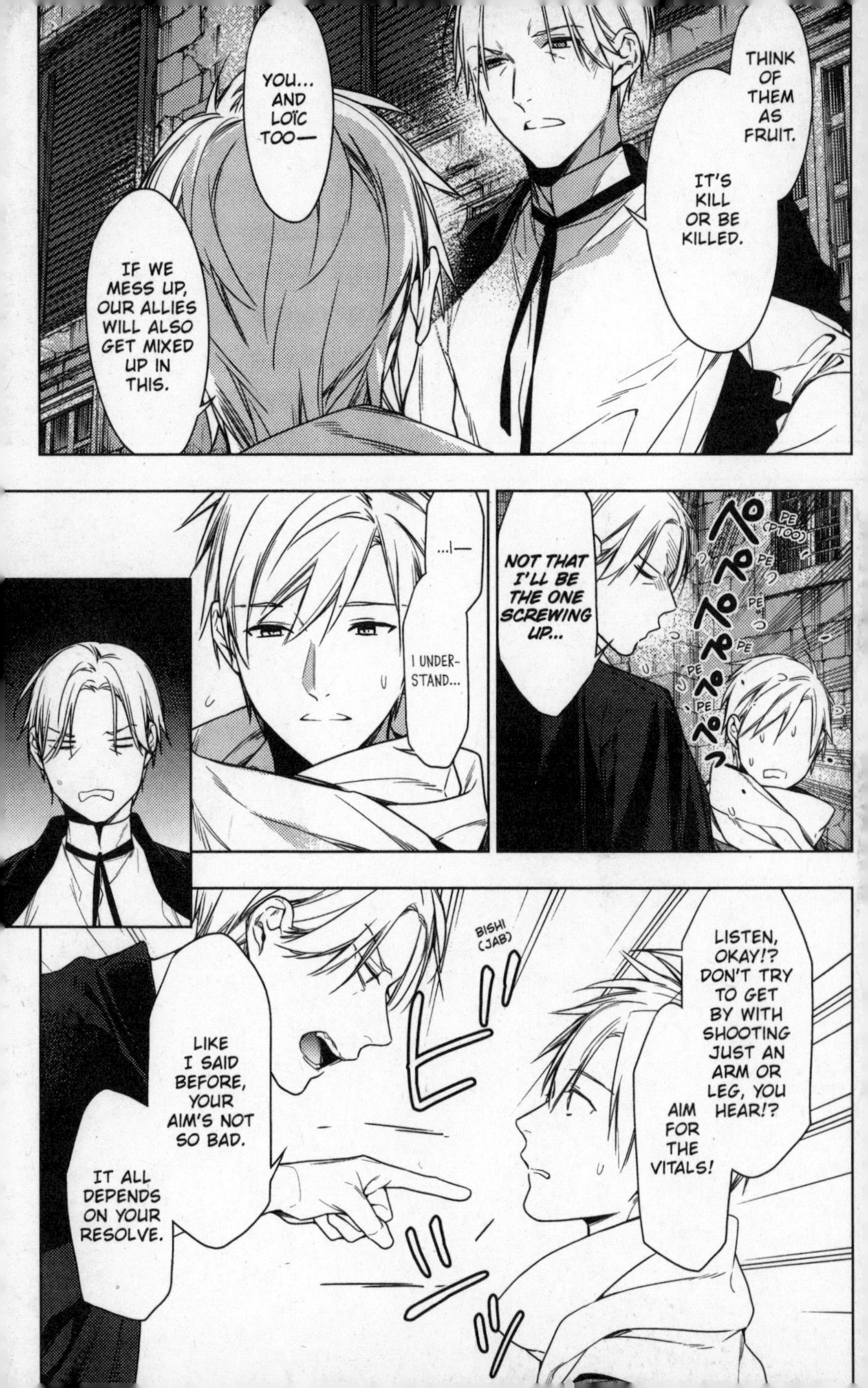
THINK OF THEM AS FRUIT.
IT'S KILL OR BE KILLED.
YOU... AND LOÏC TOO—
IF WE MESS UP, OUR ALLIES WILL ALSO GET MIXED UP IN THIS.
NOT THAT I'LL BE THE ONE SCREWING UP...
PE (PTOO)
PE
PE
PE
PE
PE
...I—
I UNDERSTAND...
LISTEN, OKAY!? DON'T TRY TO GET BY WITH SHOOTING JUST AN ARM OR LEG, YOU HEAR!?
AIM FOR THE VITALS!
BISHI (JAB)
LIKE I SAID BEFORE, YOUR AIM'S NOT SO BAD.
IT ALL DEPENDS ON YOUR RESOLVE.

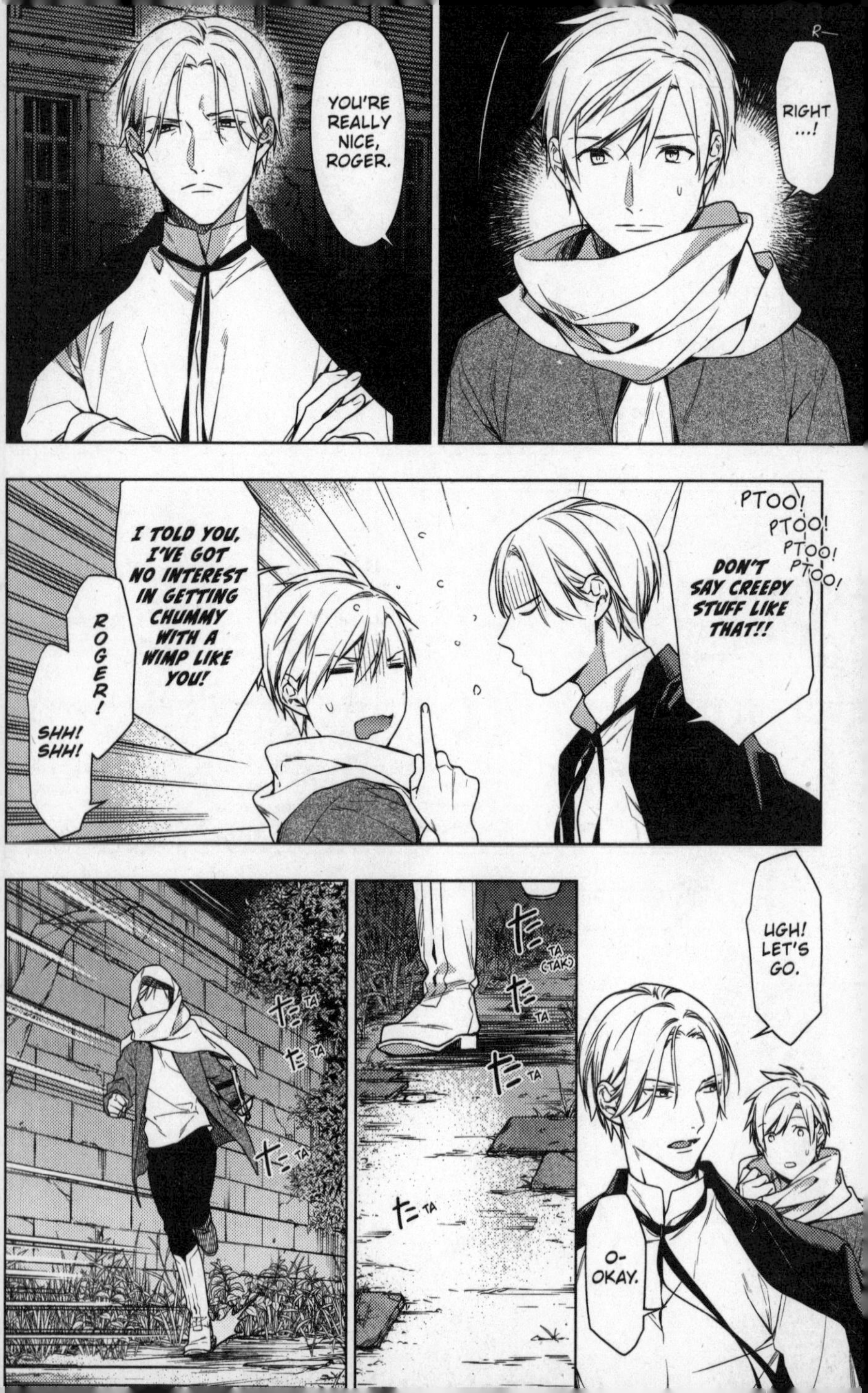

R—
RIGHT ...!
YOU'RE REALLY NICE, ROGER.
PTOO! PTOO! PTOO! PTOO!
DON'T SAY CREEPY STUFF LIKE THAT!!
I TOLD YOU, I'VE GOT NO INTEREST IN GETTING CHUMMY WITH A WIMP LIKE YOU!
ROGER!
SHH! SHH!
UGH! LET'S GO.
O-OKAY.
TA (TAK)
TA
TA
TA
TA
TA
TA

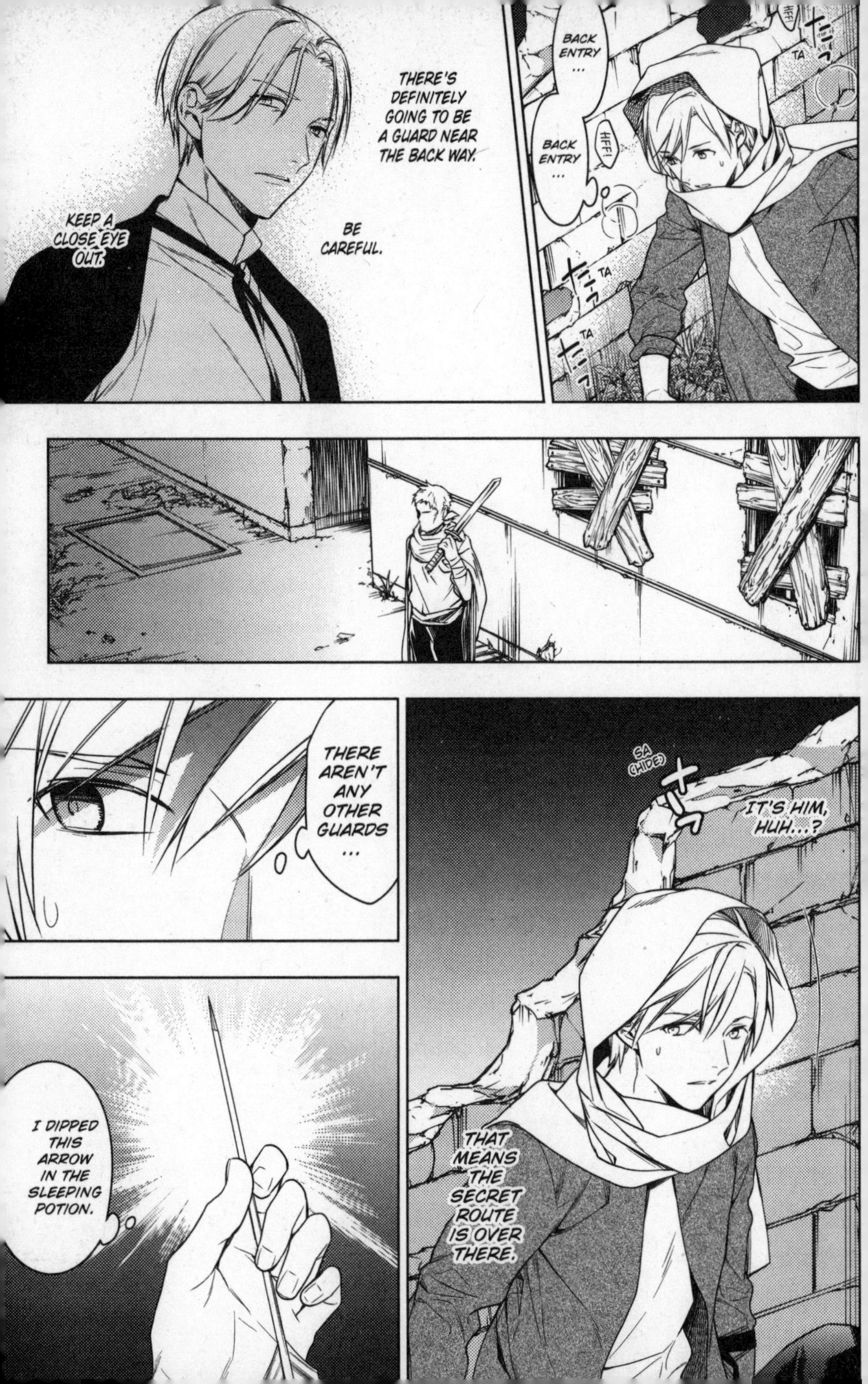
HFF!
BACK ENTRY ...
TA
BACK ENTRY ...
HFF!
TA
TA
THERE'S DEFINITELY GOING TO BE A GUARD NEAR THE BACK WAY.
BE CAREFUL.
KEEP A CLOSE EYE OUT.
SA (HIDE)
IT'S HIM, HUH...?
THAT MEANS THE SECRET ROUTE IS OVER THERE.
THERE AREN'T ANY OTHER GUARDS ...
I DIPPED THIS ARROW IN THE SLEEPING POTION.

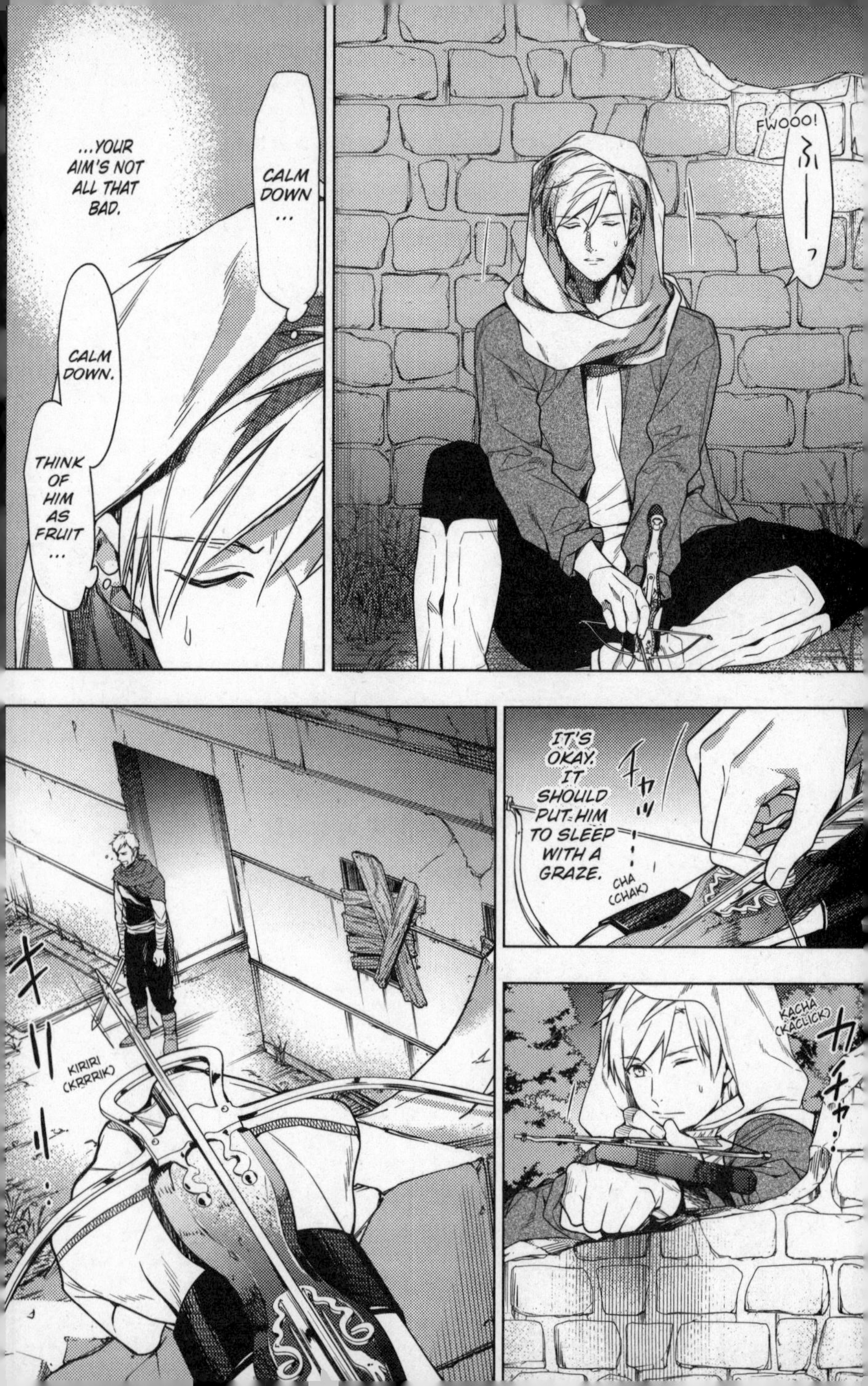
ふーーっ
FWOOO!
CALM DOWN...
...YOUR AIM'S NOT ALL THAT BAD.
CALM DOWN.
THINK OF HIM AS FRUIT...
チャッ
CHA (CHAK)
IT'S OKAY. IT SHOULD PUT HIM TO SLEEP WITH A GRAZE.
カチャ...
KACHA (KACLICK)
キリリ
KIRIRI (KRRRIK)

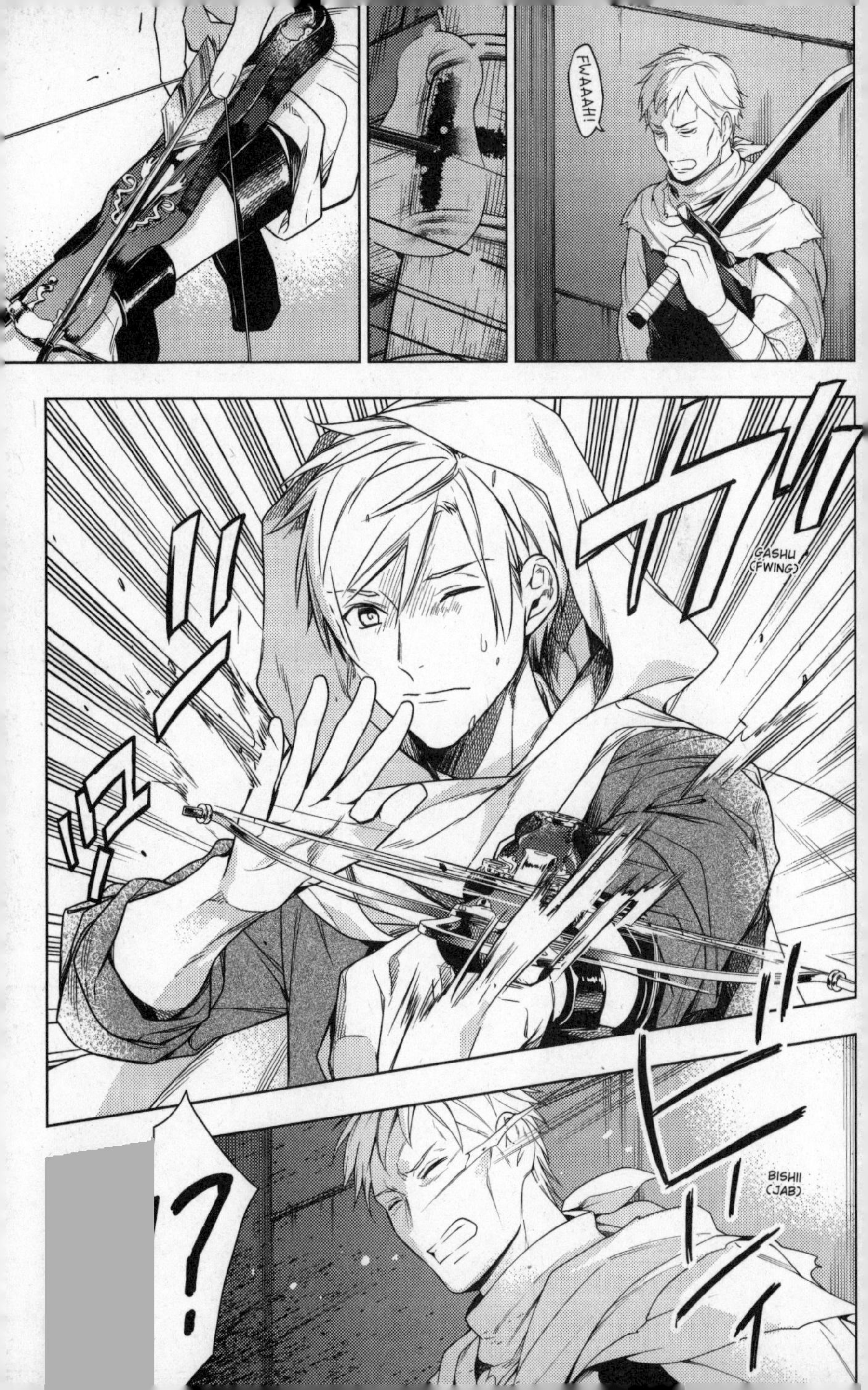
FWAAAH!
GASHU (FWING)
BISHII (JAB)
?

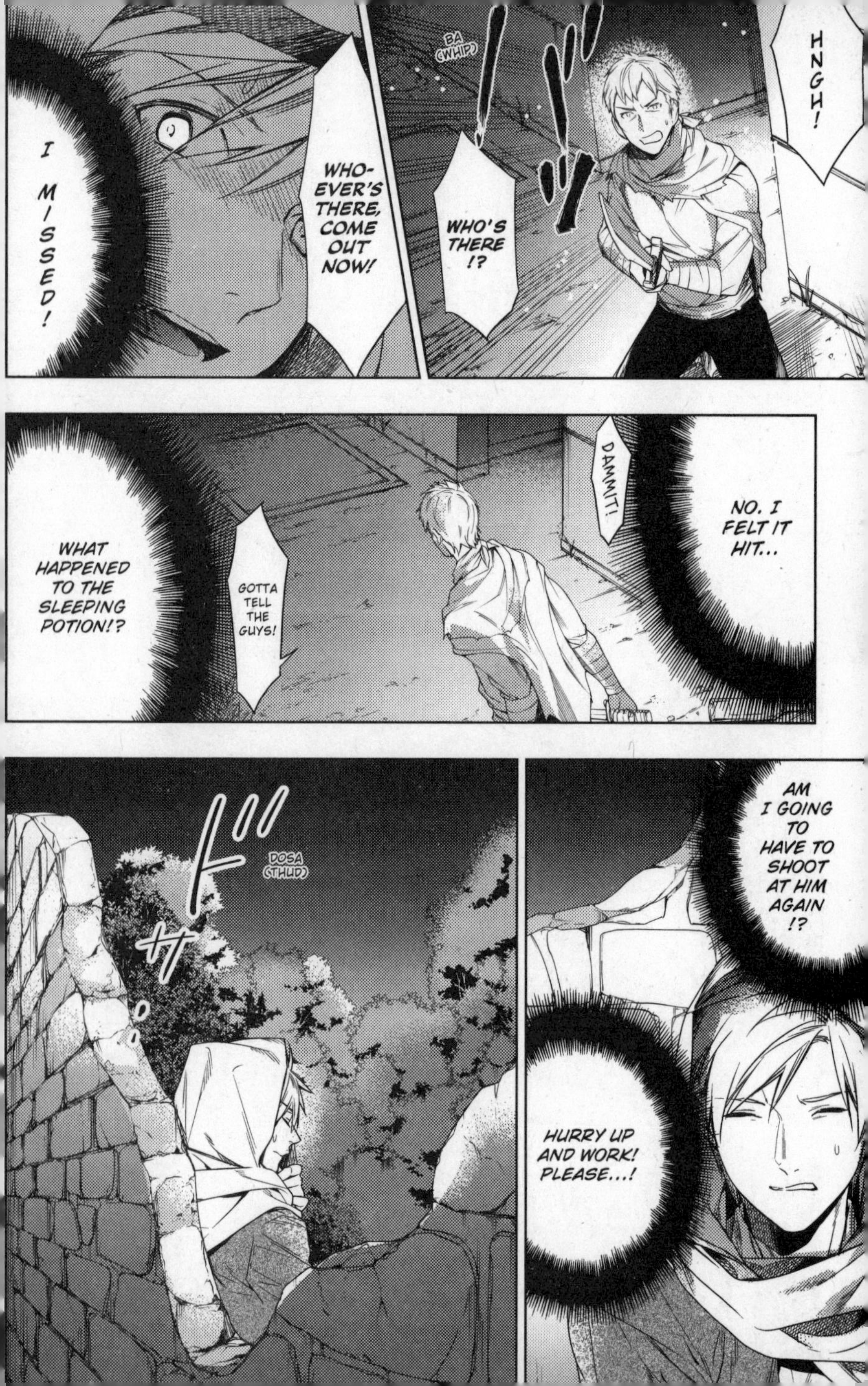
HNGH!
BA (WHIP)
WHO'S THERE !?
WHO-EVER'S THERE, COME OUT NOW!
I MISSED!
NO. I FELT IT HIT...
DAMMIT!
GOTTA TELL THE GUYS!
WHAT HAPPENED TO THE SLEEPING POTION!?
AM I GOING TO HAVE TO SHOOT AT HIM AGAIN !?
HURRY UP AND WORK! PLEASE...!
DOSA (THUD)

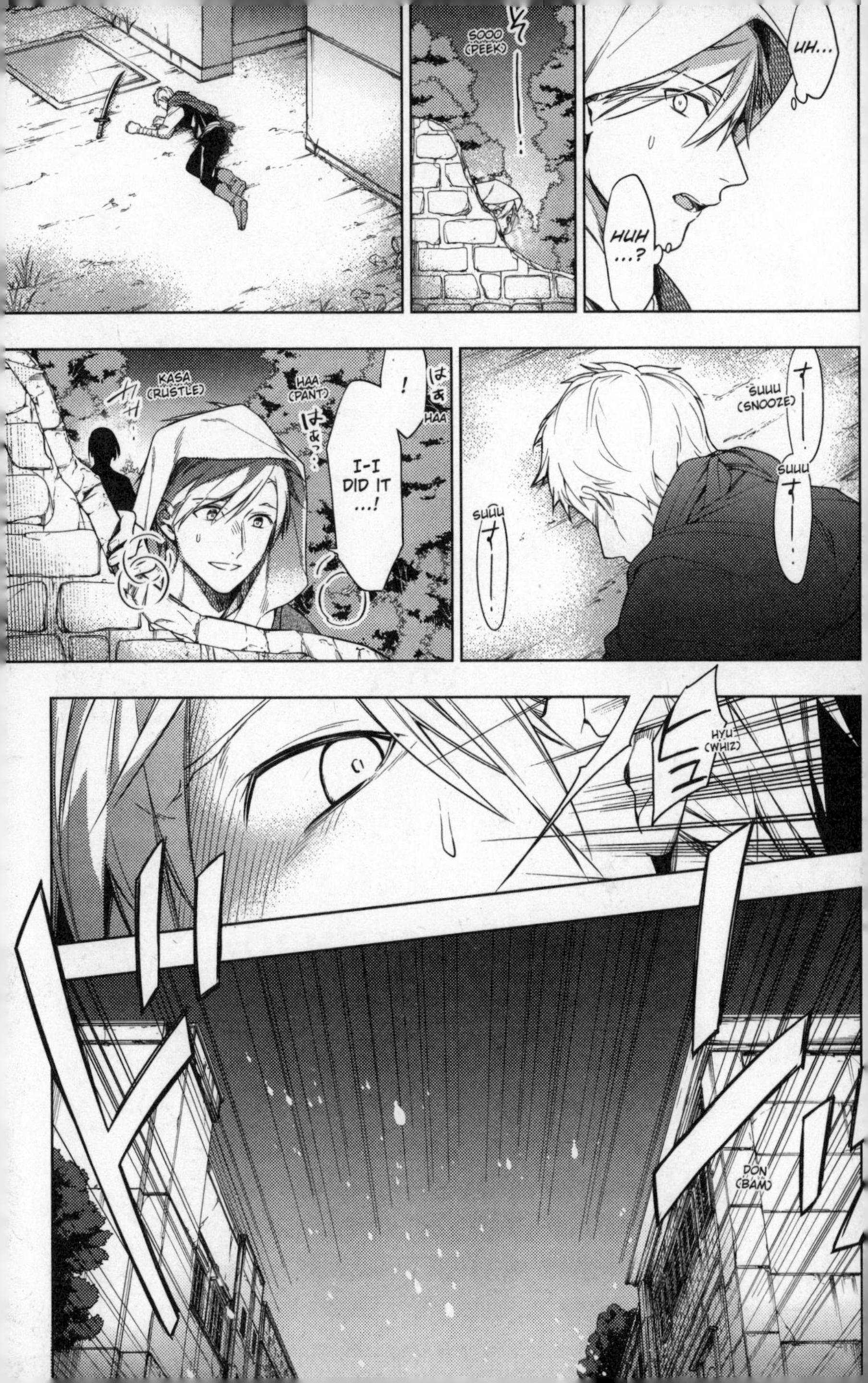
UH...
HUH ...?
SOOO (PEEK)
そーー…
I-I DID IT ...!
!
HAA (PANT)
はぁ HAA はぁっ…
KASA (RUSTLE)
カサ…
SUUU (SNOOZE)
すー…
SUUU すー…
SUUU すー…
HYU (WHIZ)
ヒュ
DON (BAM)
ドン

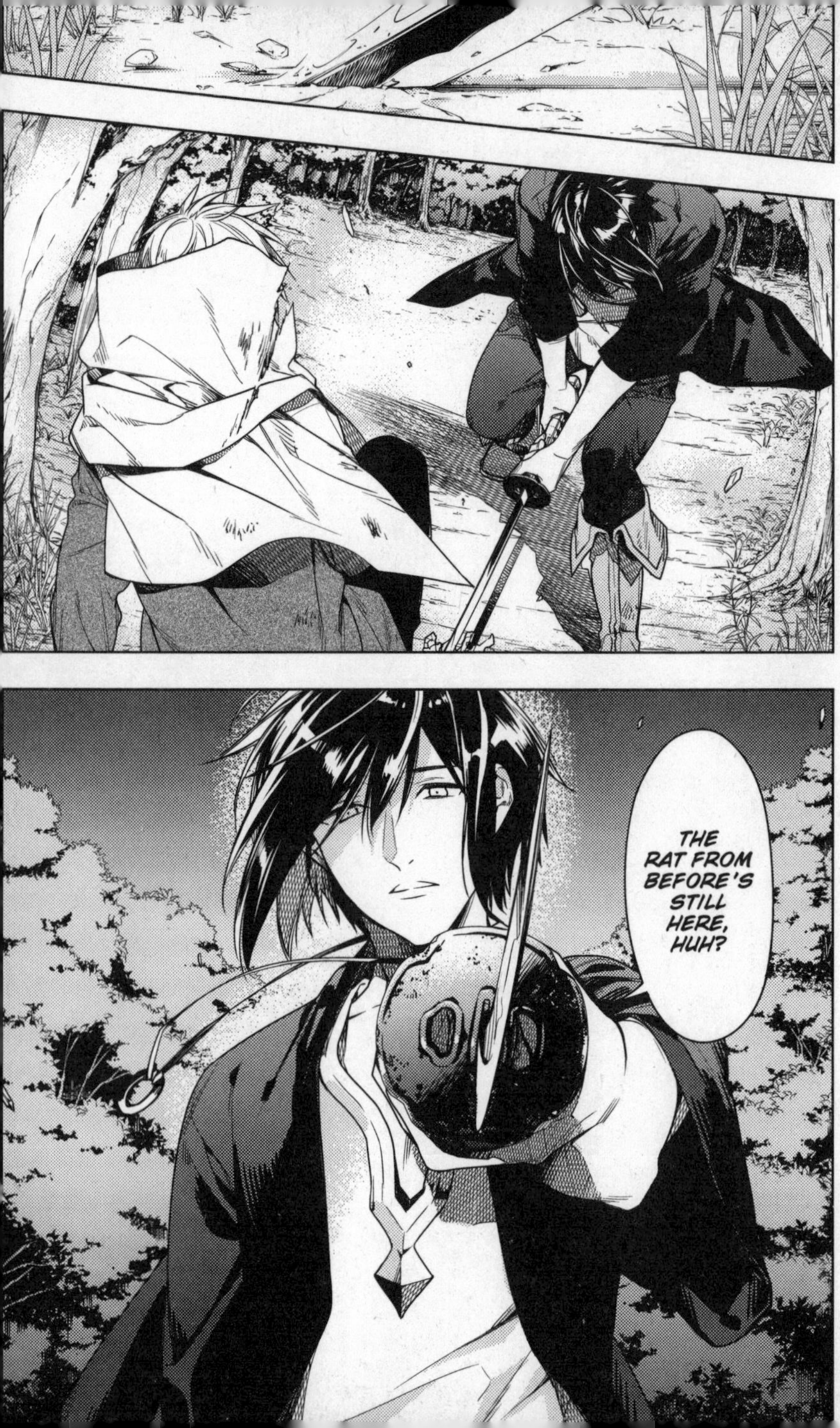
THE RAT FROM BEFORE'S STILL HERE, HUH?

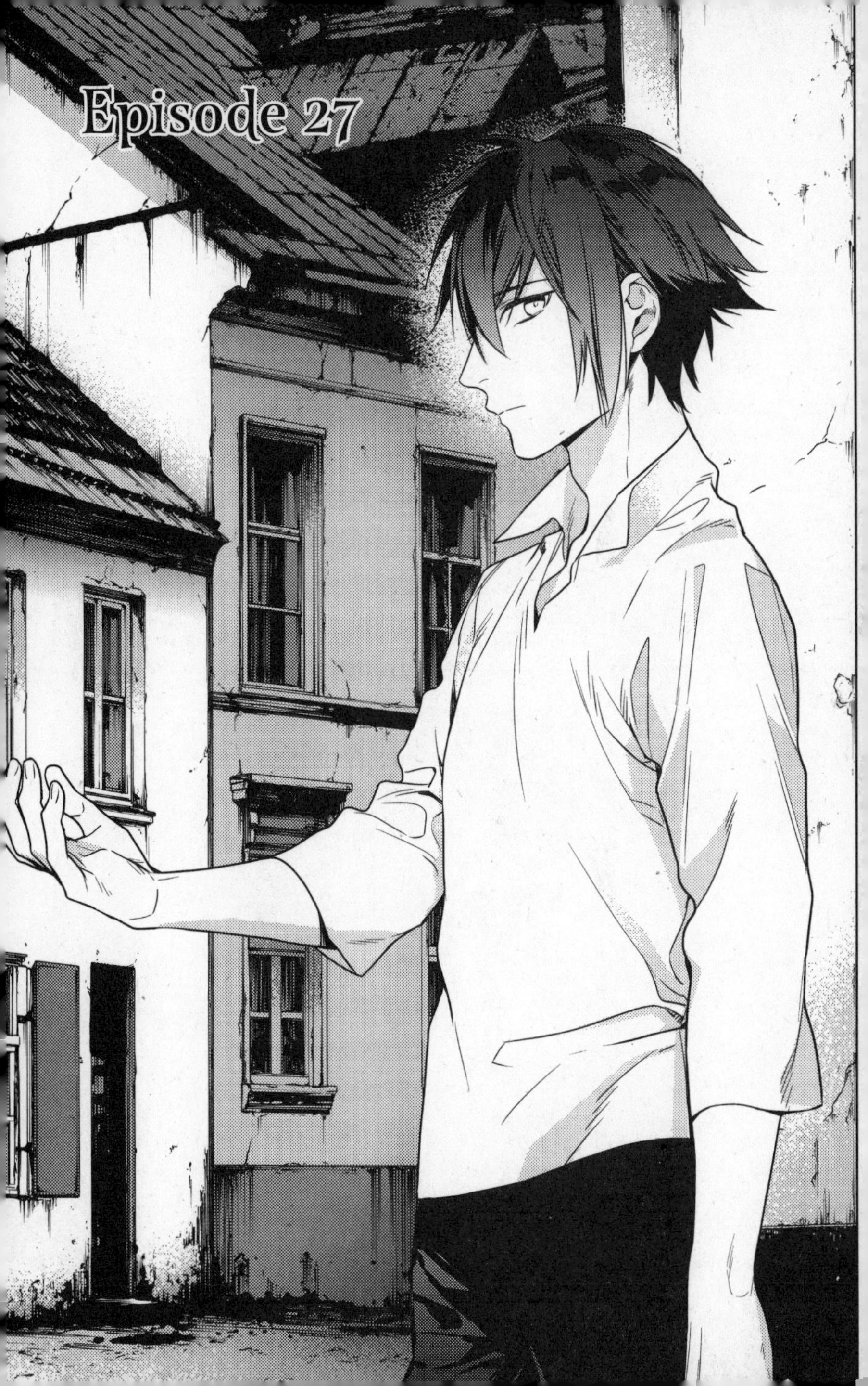
Episode 27

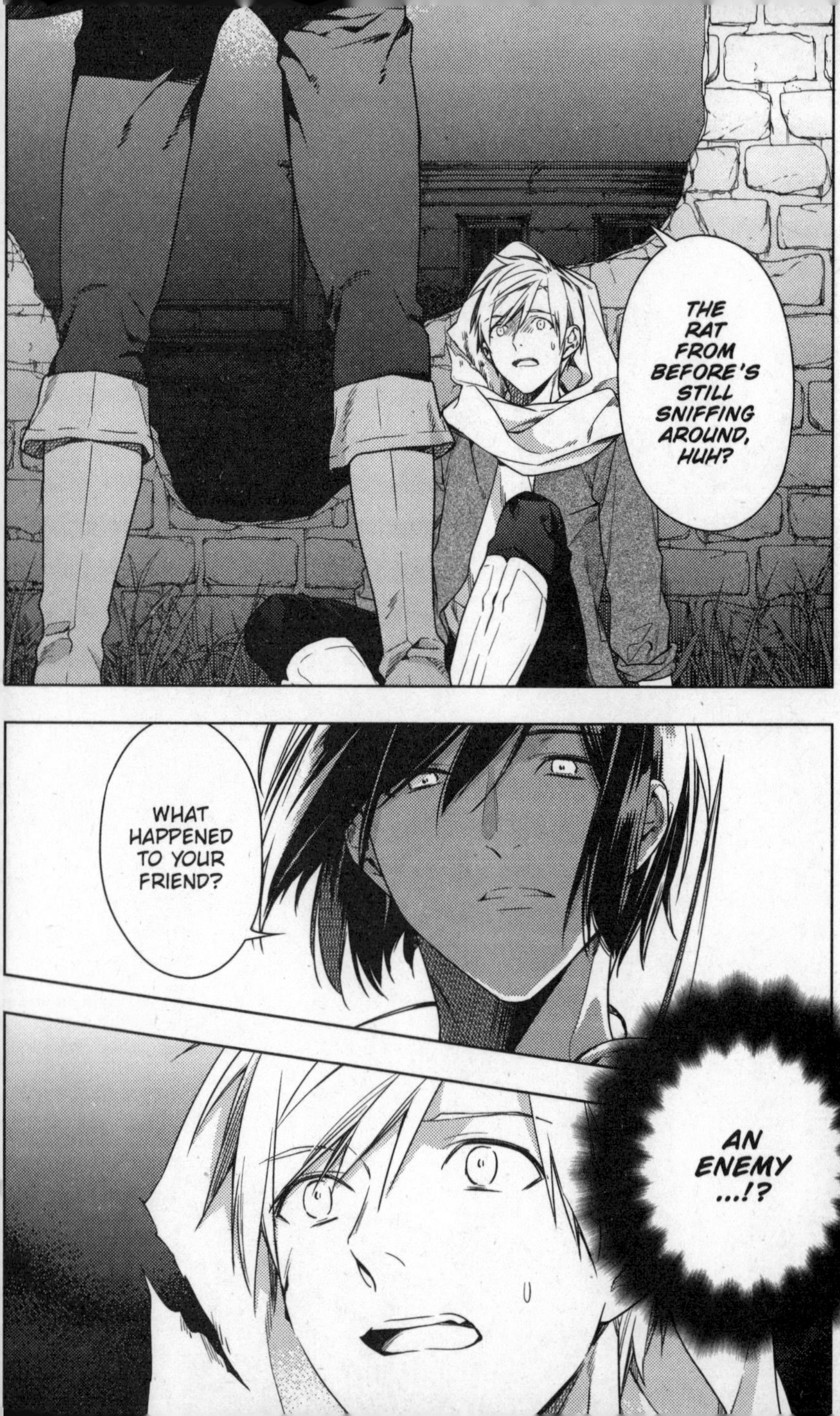
THE RAT FROM BEFORE'S STILL SNIFFING AROUND, HUH?
WHAT HAPPENED TO YOUR FRIEND?
AN ENEMY ...!?

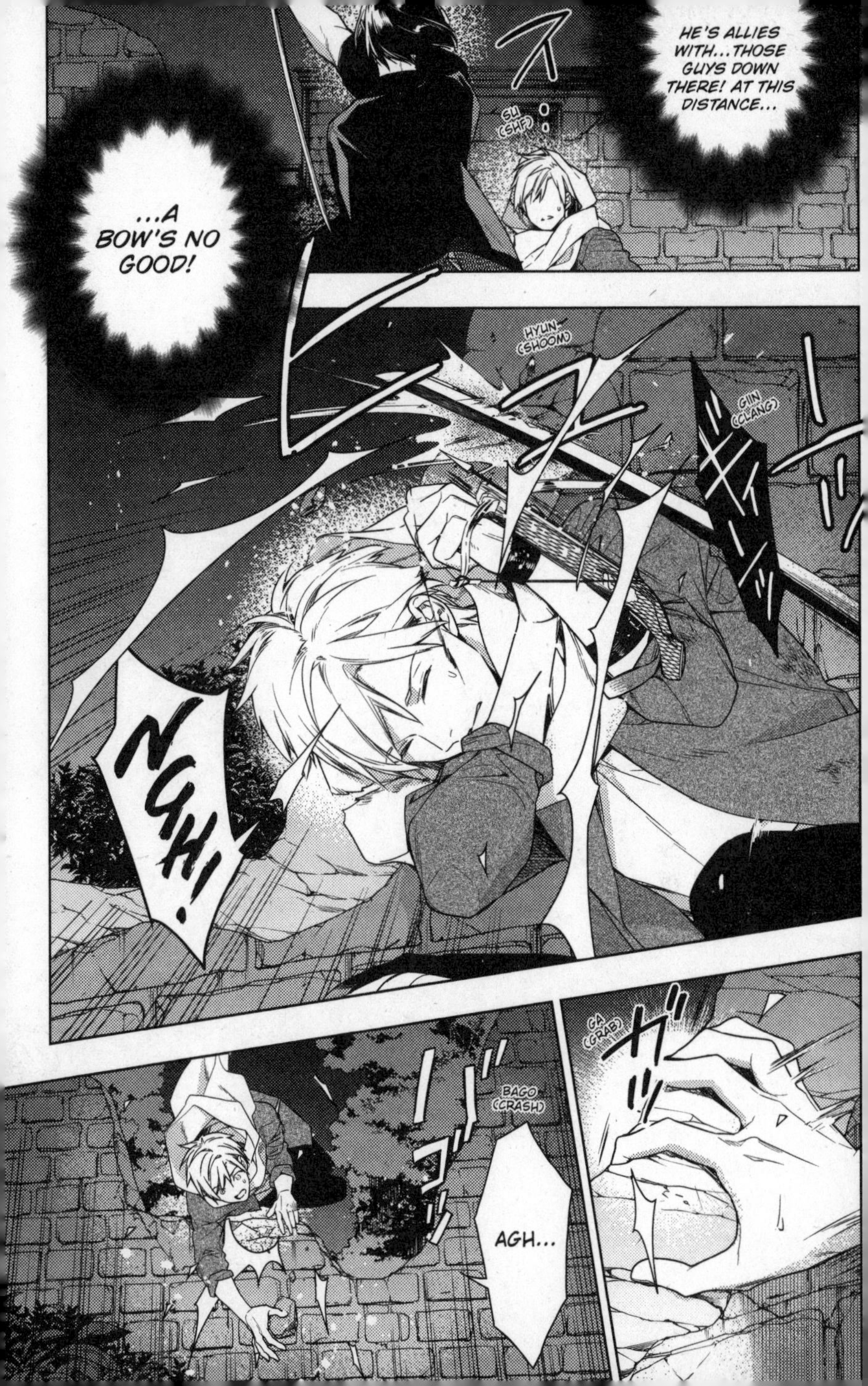
HE'S ALLIES WITH...THOSE GUYS DOWN THERE! AT THIS DISTANCE...
SU (SHF)
...A BOW'S NO GOOD!
HYLUN (SHOOM)
GIIN (CLANG)
NGH!
GA (GRAB)
BAGO (CRASH)
AGH...

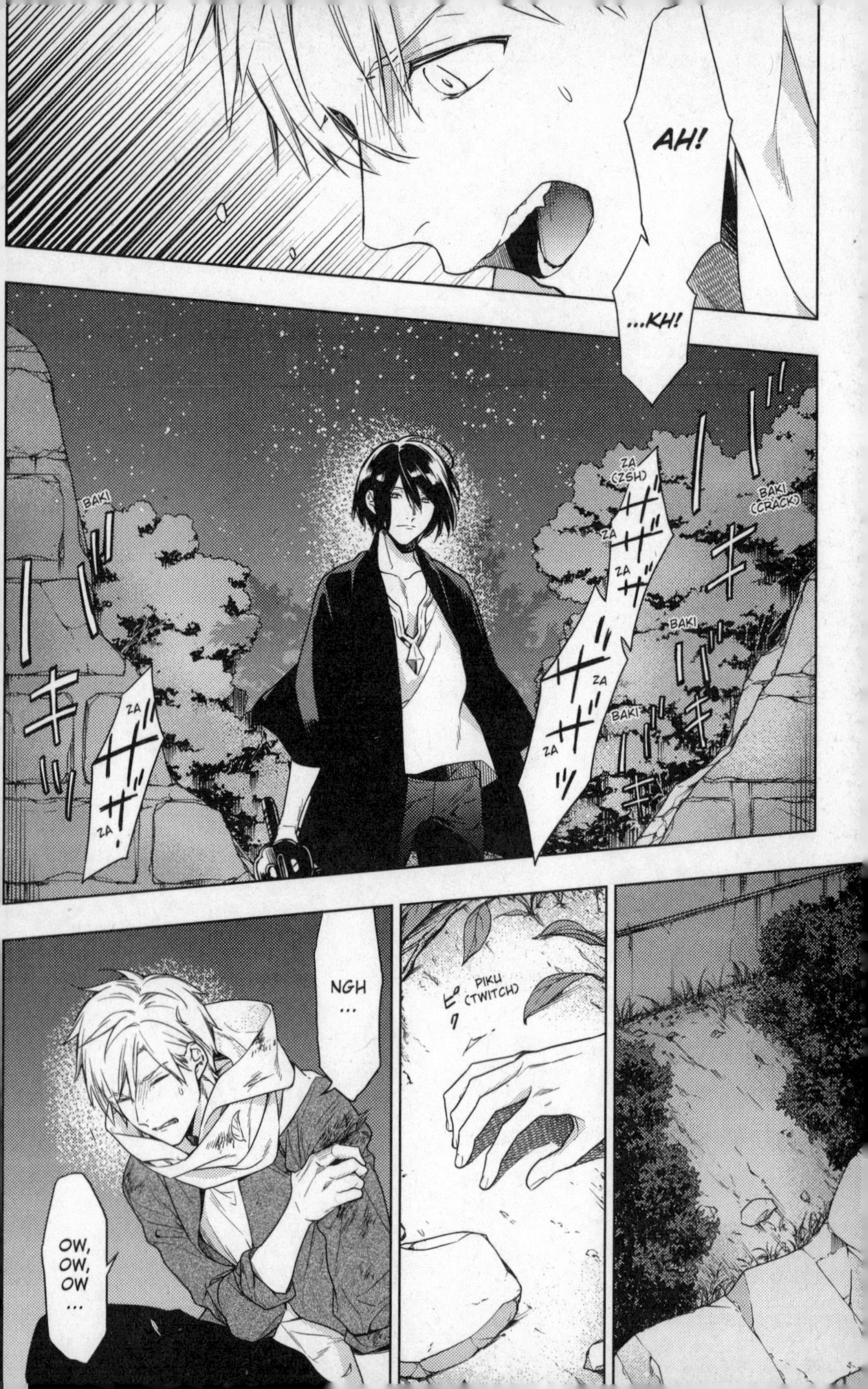

AH!
...KH!
ZA (ZSH)
BAKI (CRACK)
ZA
ZA
BAKI
ZA
BAKI
ZA
BAKI
ZA
ZA
PIKU (TWITCH)
NGH ...
OW, OW, OW ...

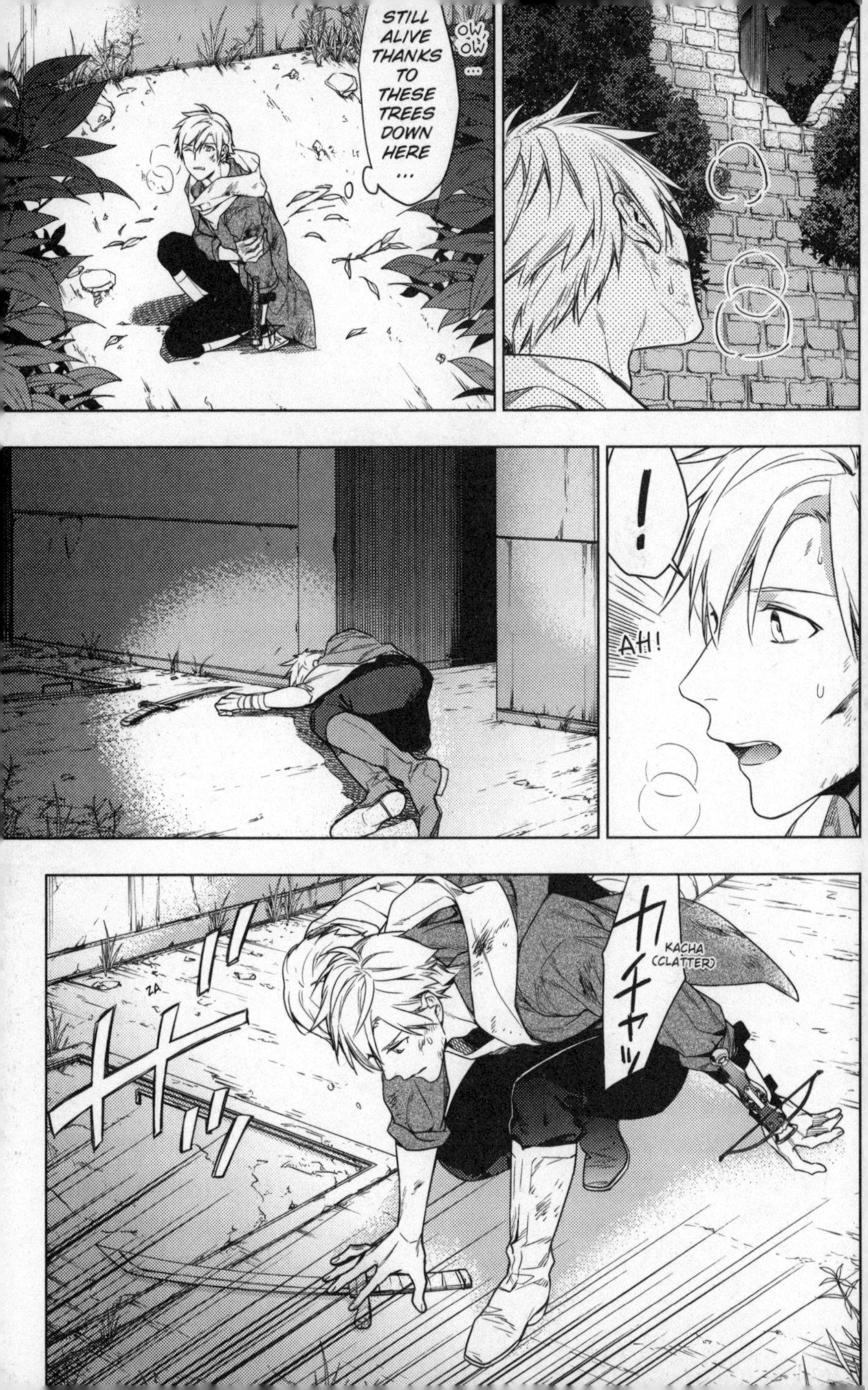
OW, OW ...
STILL ALIVE THANKS TO THESE TREES DOWN HERE ...
!
AH!
KACHA (CLATTER)
ZA

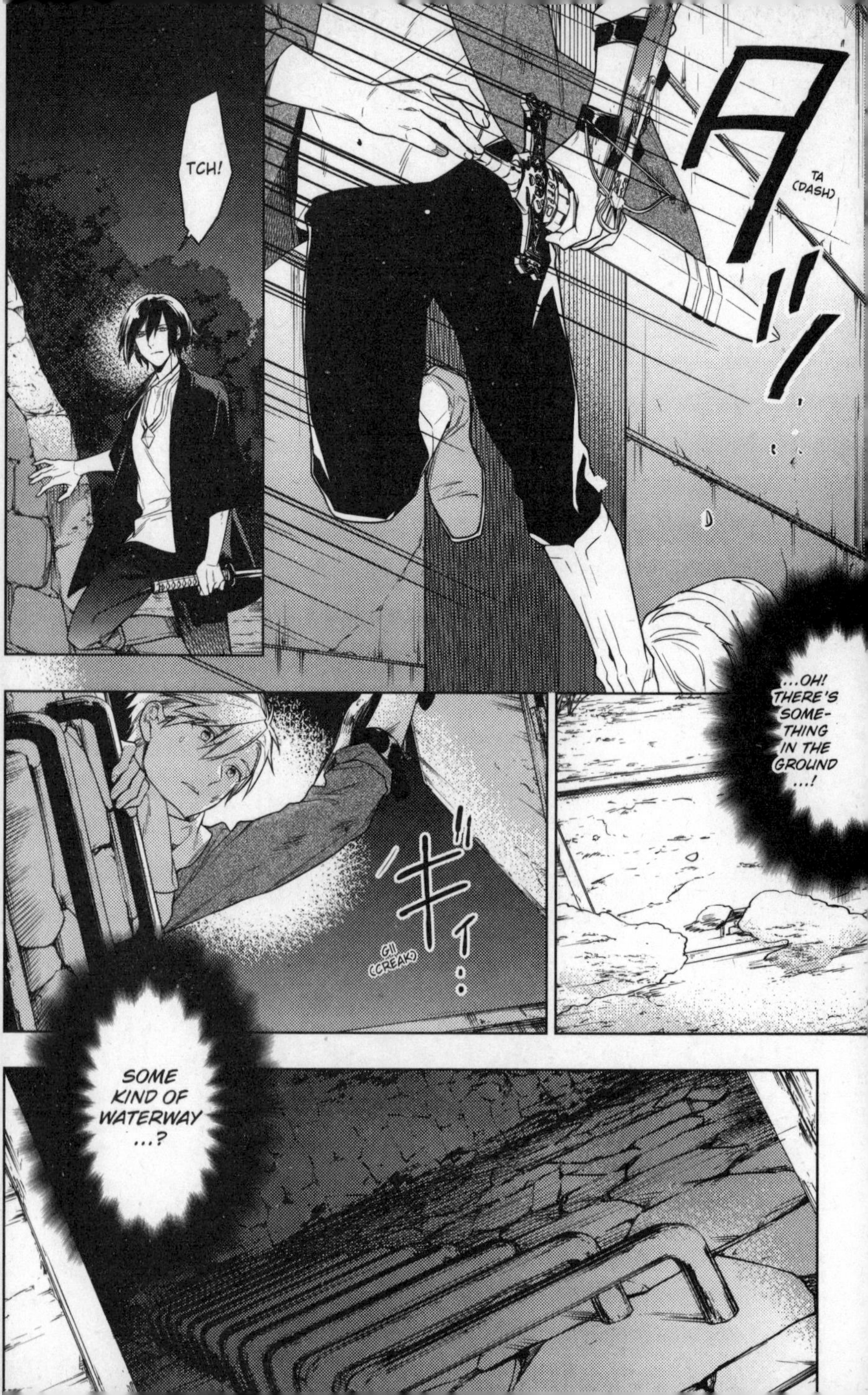
TA (DASH)
TCH!
...OH! THERE'S SOME-THING IN THE GROUND ...!
GII (CREAK)
SOME KIND OF WATERWAY ...?

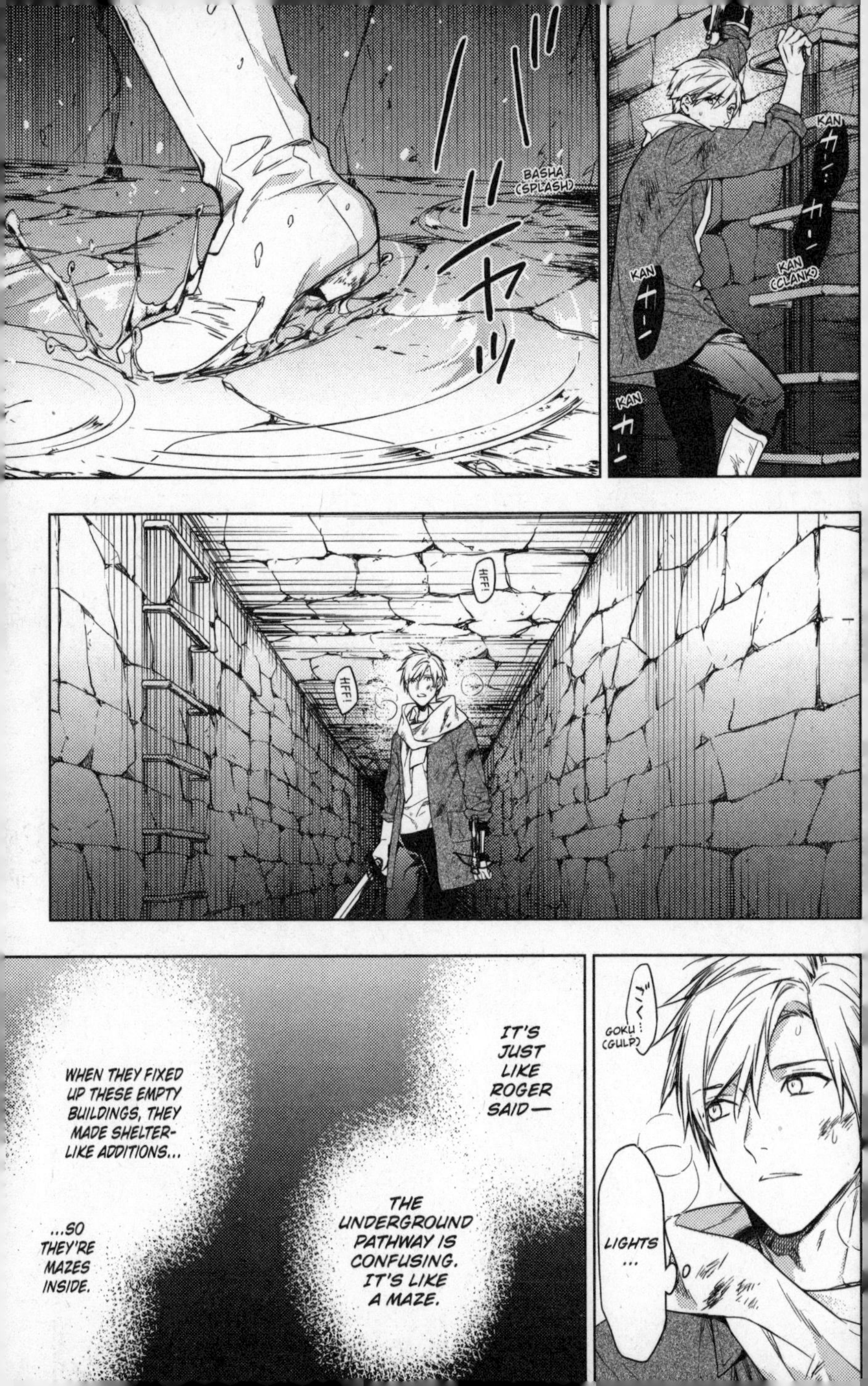
KAN
KAN (CLANK)
KAN
KAN
BASHA (SPLASH)
HFF!
HFF!
GOKU (GULP)
LIGHTS...
IT'S JUST LIKE ROGER SAID—
THE UNDERGROUND PATHWAY IS CONFUSING. IT'S LIKE A MAZE.
WHEN THEY FIXED UP THESE EMPTY BUILDINGS, THEY MADE SHELTER-LIKE ADDITIONS...
...SO THEY'RE MAZES INSIDE.

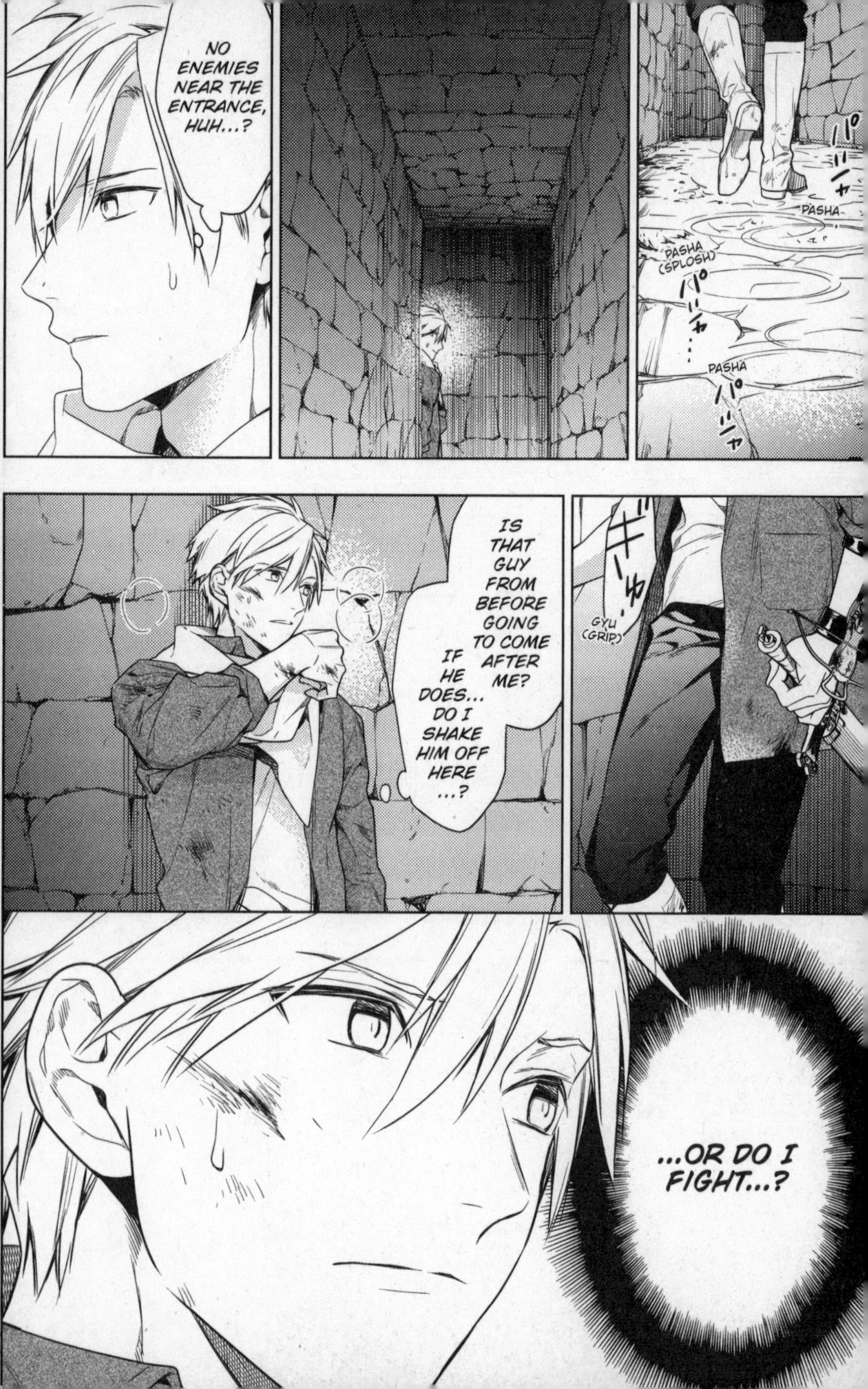
PASHA
PASHA (SPLOSH)
PASHA
NO ENEMIES NEAR THE ENTRANCE, HUH...?
GYU (GRIP)
IS THAT GUY FROM BEFORE GOING TO COME AFTER ME?
IF HE DOES... DO I SHAKE HIM OFF HERE ...?
...OR DO I FIGHT...?

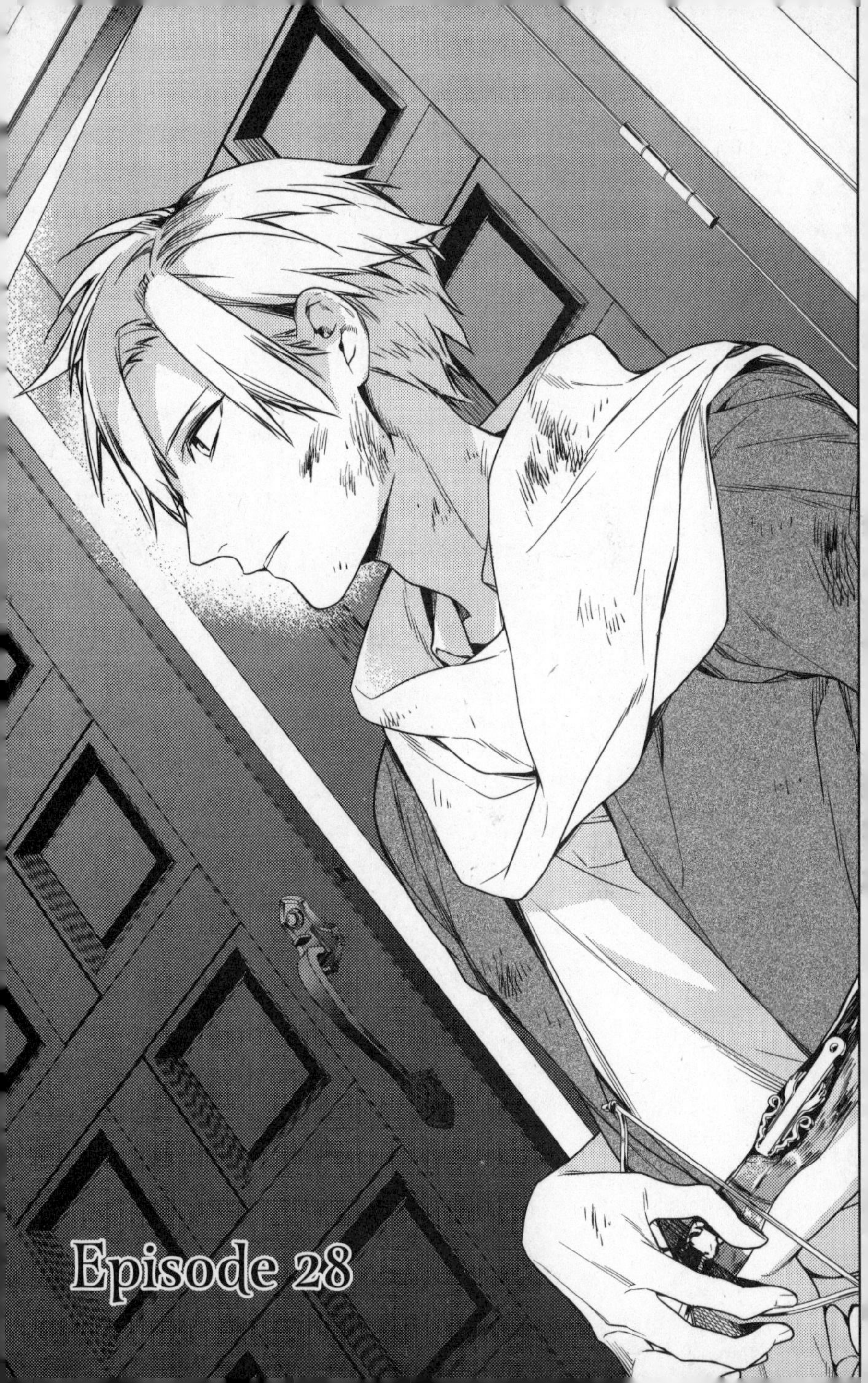
Episode 28

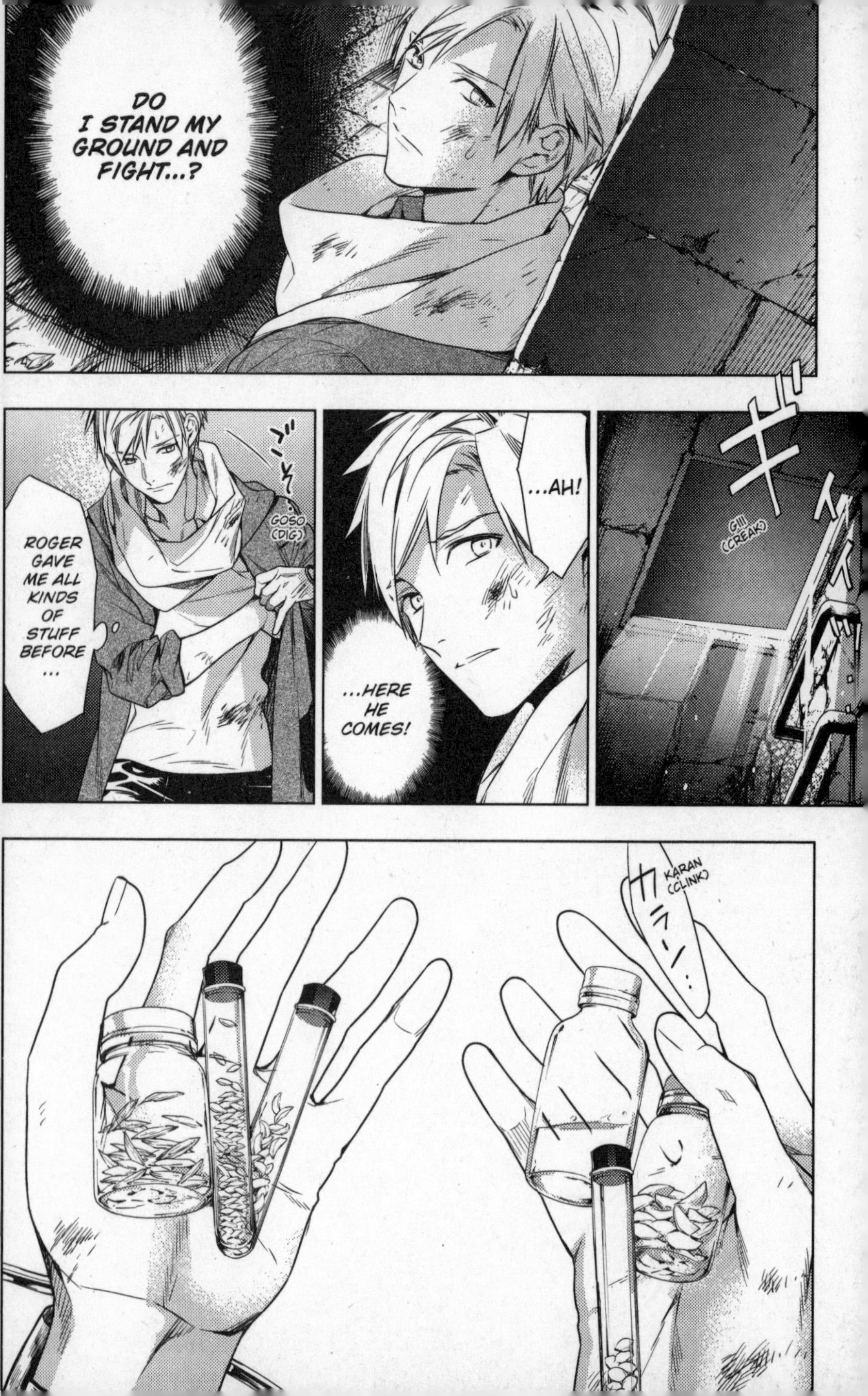
DO I STAND MY GROUND AND FIGHT...?
GII (CREAK)
...AH!
...HERE HE COMES!
GOSO (DIG)
ROGER GAVE ME ALL KINDS OF STUFF BEFORE ...
KARAN (CLINK)

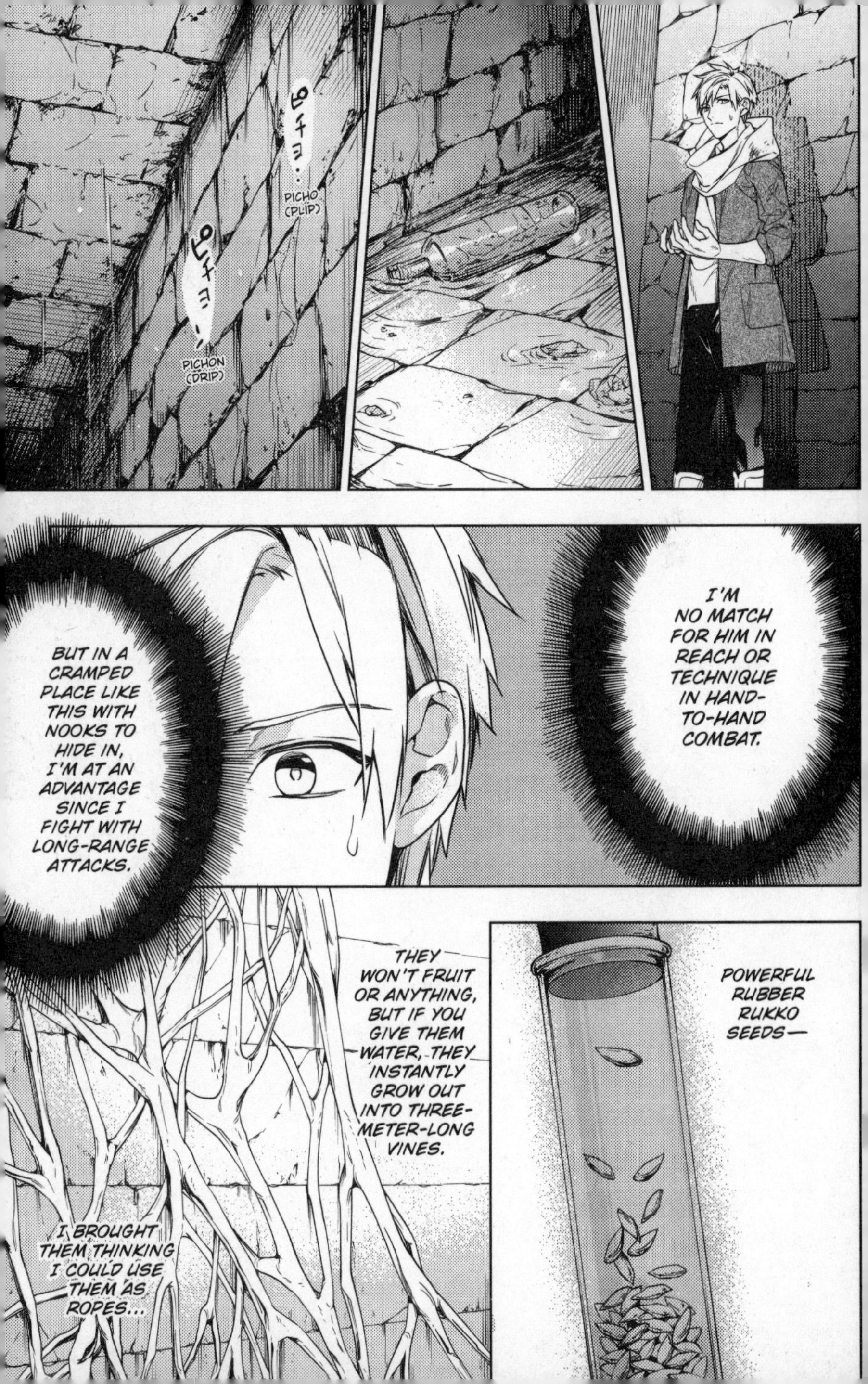
PICHO (PLIP)
PICHON (DRIP)
I'M NO MATCH FOR HIM IN REACH OR TECHNIQUE IN HAND-TO-HAND COMBAT.
BUT IN A CRAMPED PLACE LIKE THIS WITH NOOKS TO HIDE IN, I'M AT AN ADVANTAGE SINCE I FIGHT WITH LONG-RANGE ATTACKS.
POWERFUL RUBBER RUKKO SEEDS—
THEY WON'T FRUIT OR ANYTHING, BUT IF YOU GIVE THEM WATER, THEY INSTANTLY GROW OUT INTO THREE-METER-LONG VINES.
I BROUGHT THEM THINKING I COULD USE THEM AS ROPES...

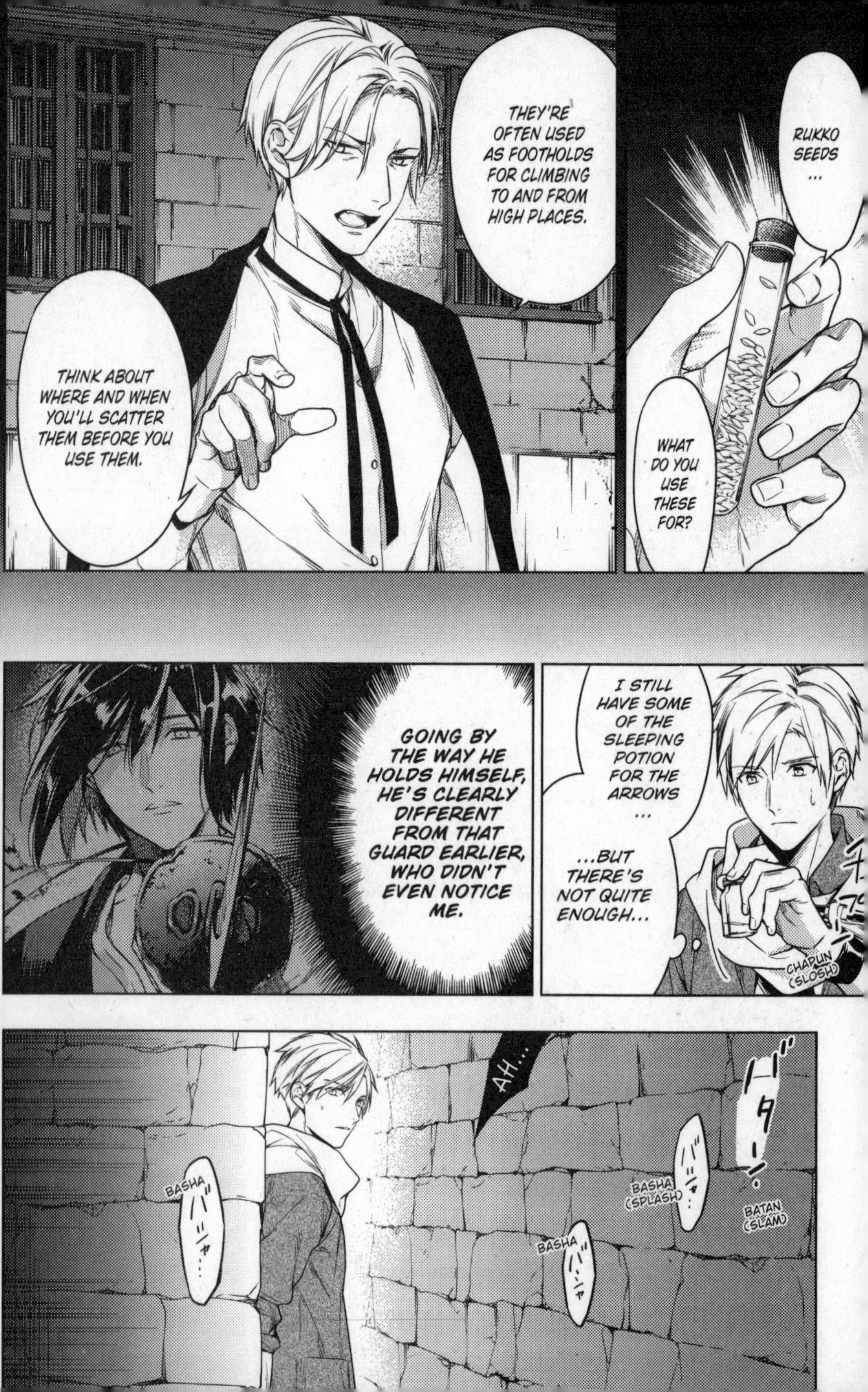
RUKKO SEEDS ...
WHAT DO YOU USE THESE FOR?
THEY'RE OFTEN USED AS FOOTHOLDS FOR CLIMBING TO AND FROM HIGH PLACES.
THINK ABOUT WHERE AND WHEN YOU'LL SCATTER THEM BEFORE YOU USE THEM.
I STILL HAVE SOME OF THE SLEEPING POTION FOR THE ARROWS ...
...BUT THERE'S NOT QUITE ENOUGH...
CHAPUN (SLOSH)
GOING BY THE WAY HE HOLDS HIMSELF, HE'S CLEARLY DIFFERENT FROM THAT GUARD EARLIER, WHO DIDN'T EVEN NOTICE ME.
BATAN (SLAM)
BASHA (SPLASH)
AH...
BASHA
BASHA

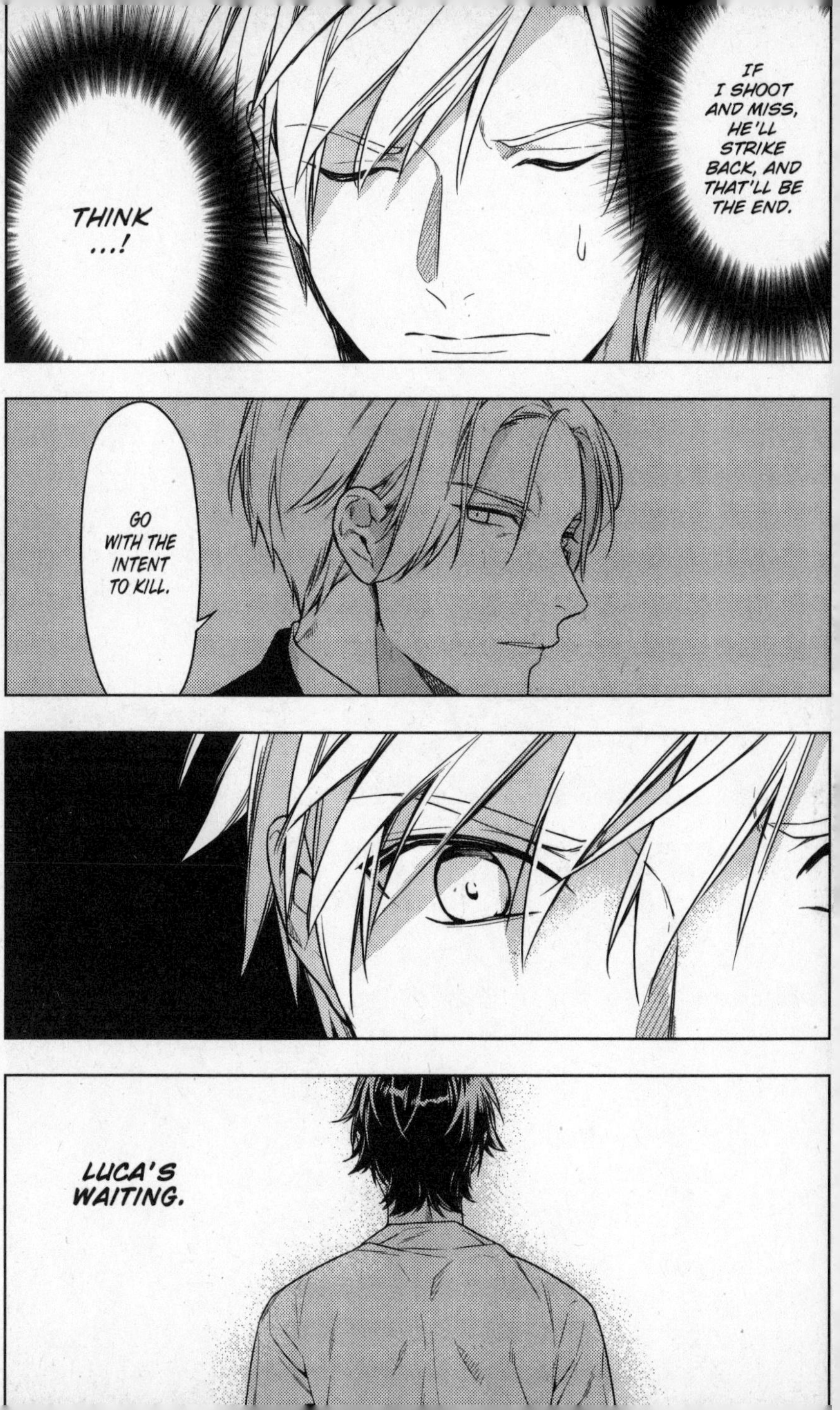
IF I SHOOT AND MISS, HE'LL STRIKE BACK, AND THAT'LL BE THE END.
THINK ...!
GO WITH THE INTENT TO KILL.
LUCA'S WAITING.

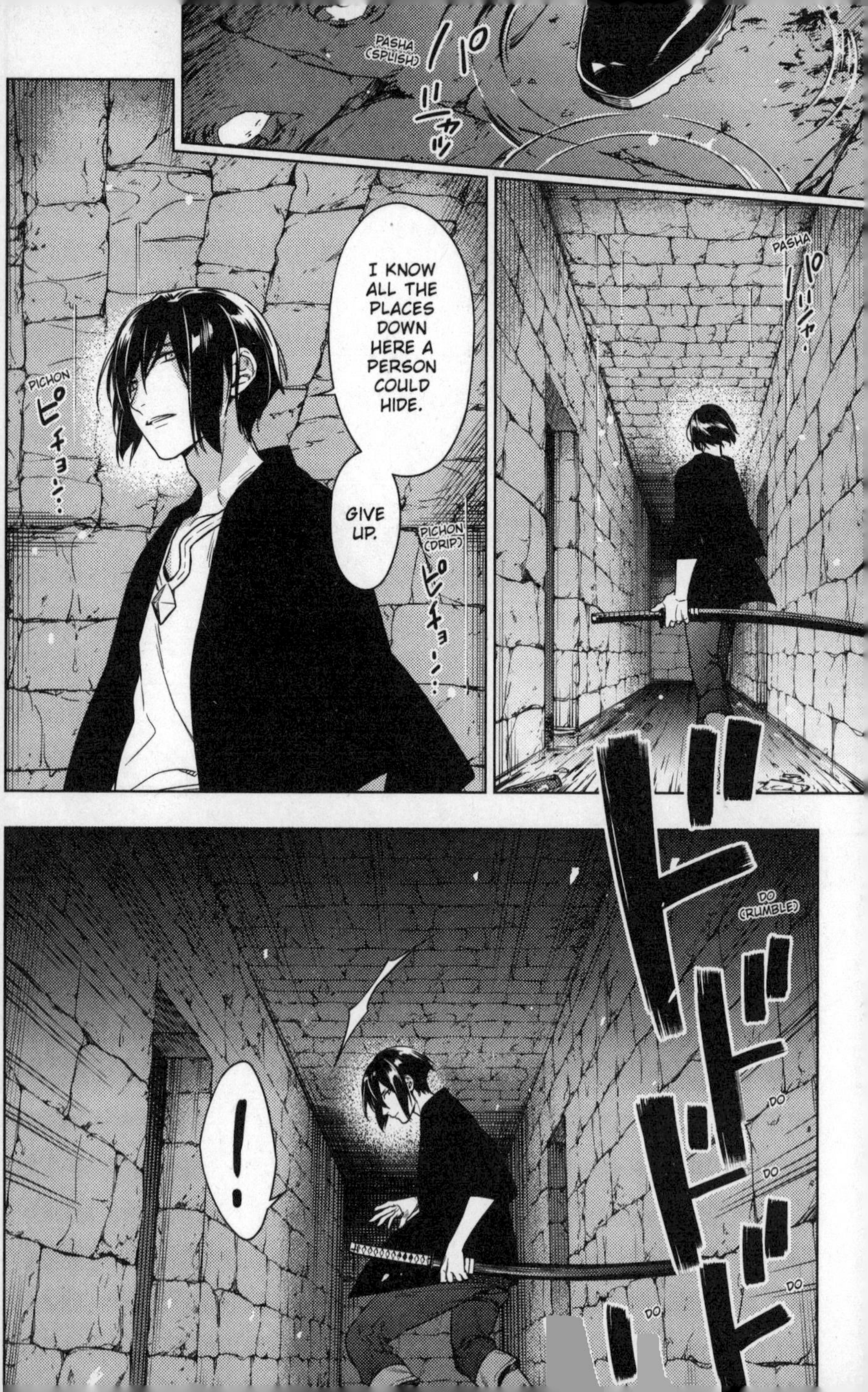
PASHA (SPLISH)
PASHA
I KNOW ALL THE PLACES DOWN HERE A PERSON COULD HIDE.
GIVE UP.
PICHON (DRIP)
PICHON
DO (RUMBLE)
DO
DO
DO
DO
!

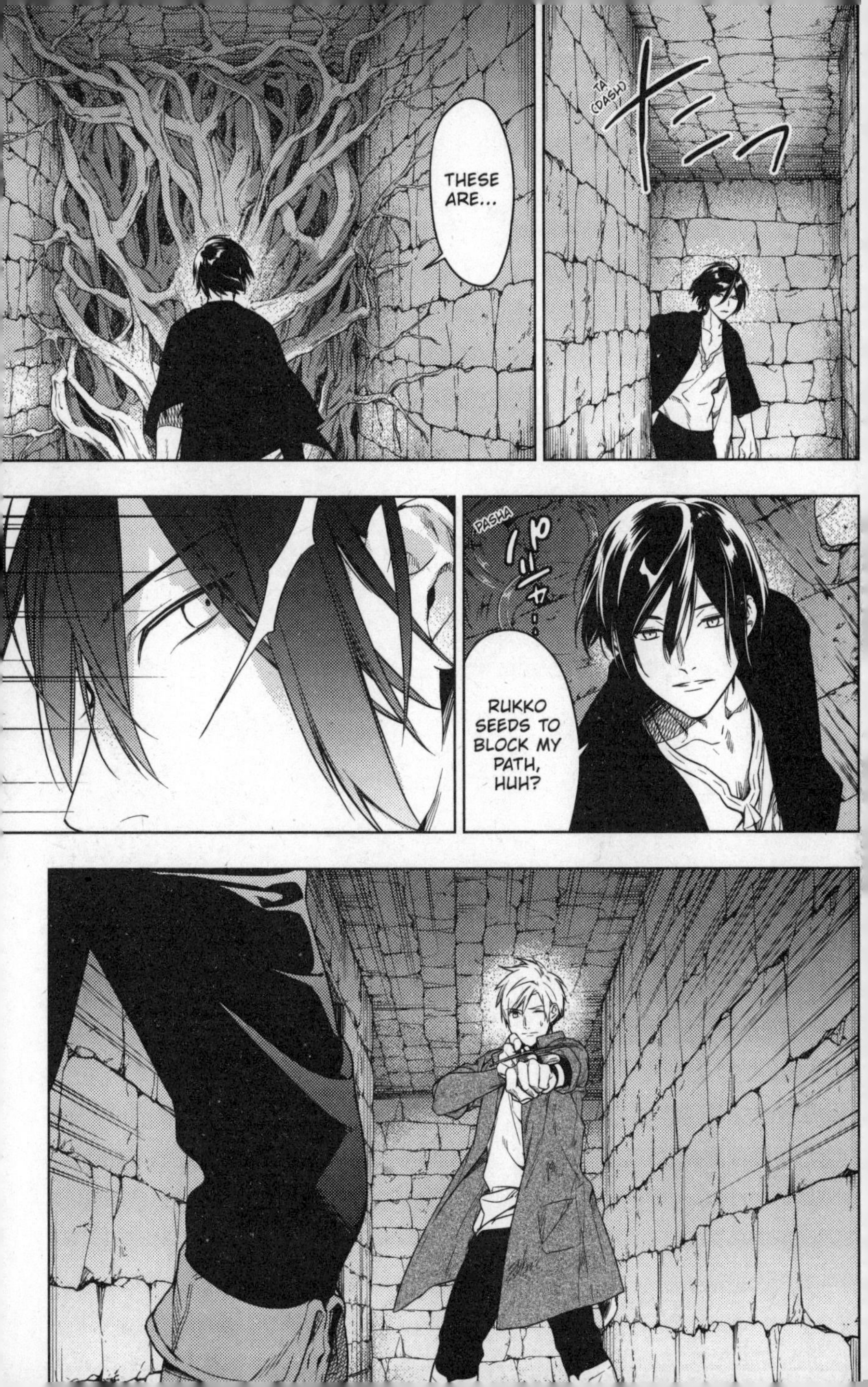
TA (DASH)
THESE ARE...
PASHA
RUKKO SEEDS TO BLOCK MY PATH, HUH?

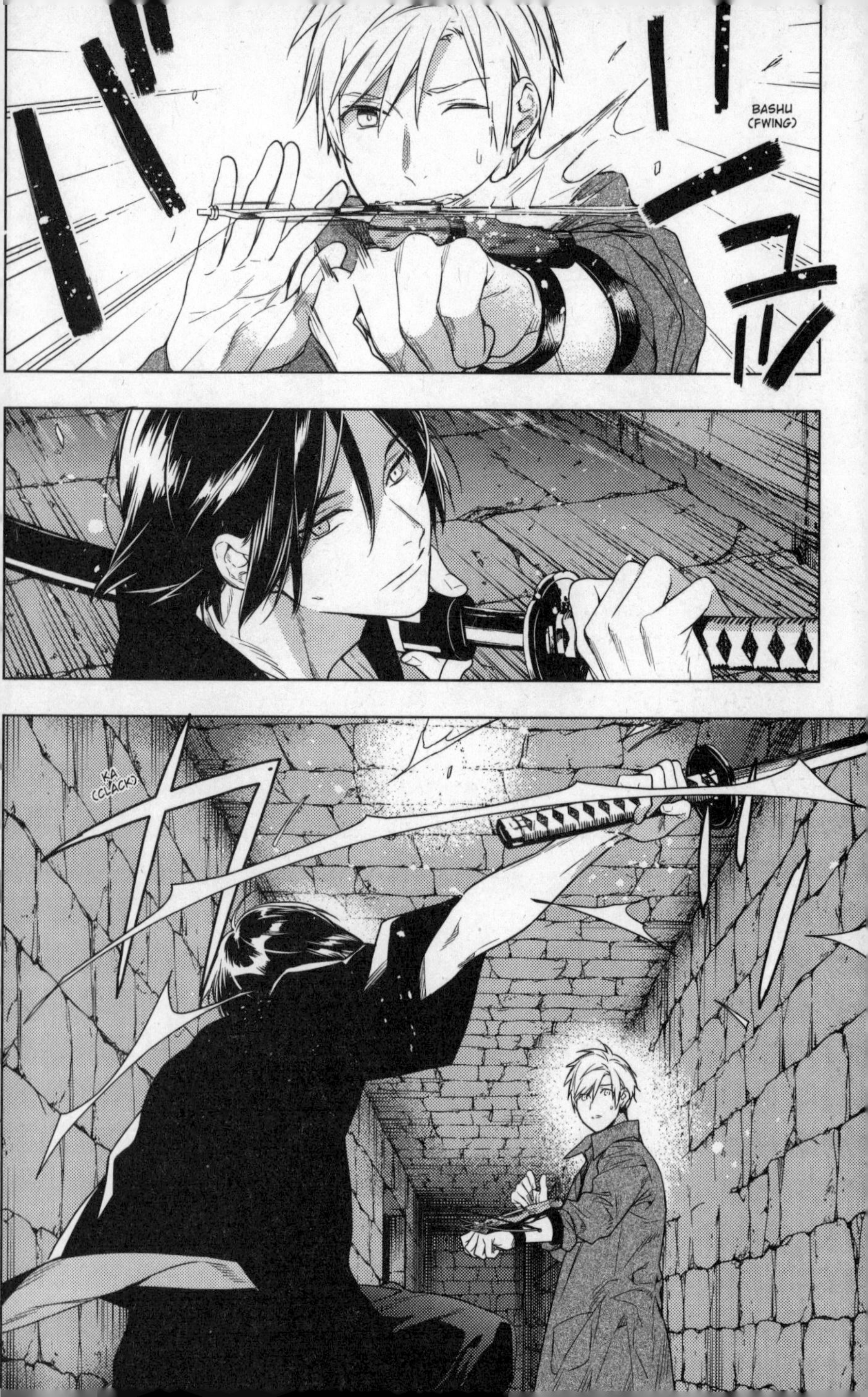
BASHU
(FWING)
KA
(CLACK)

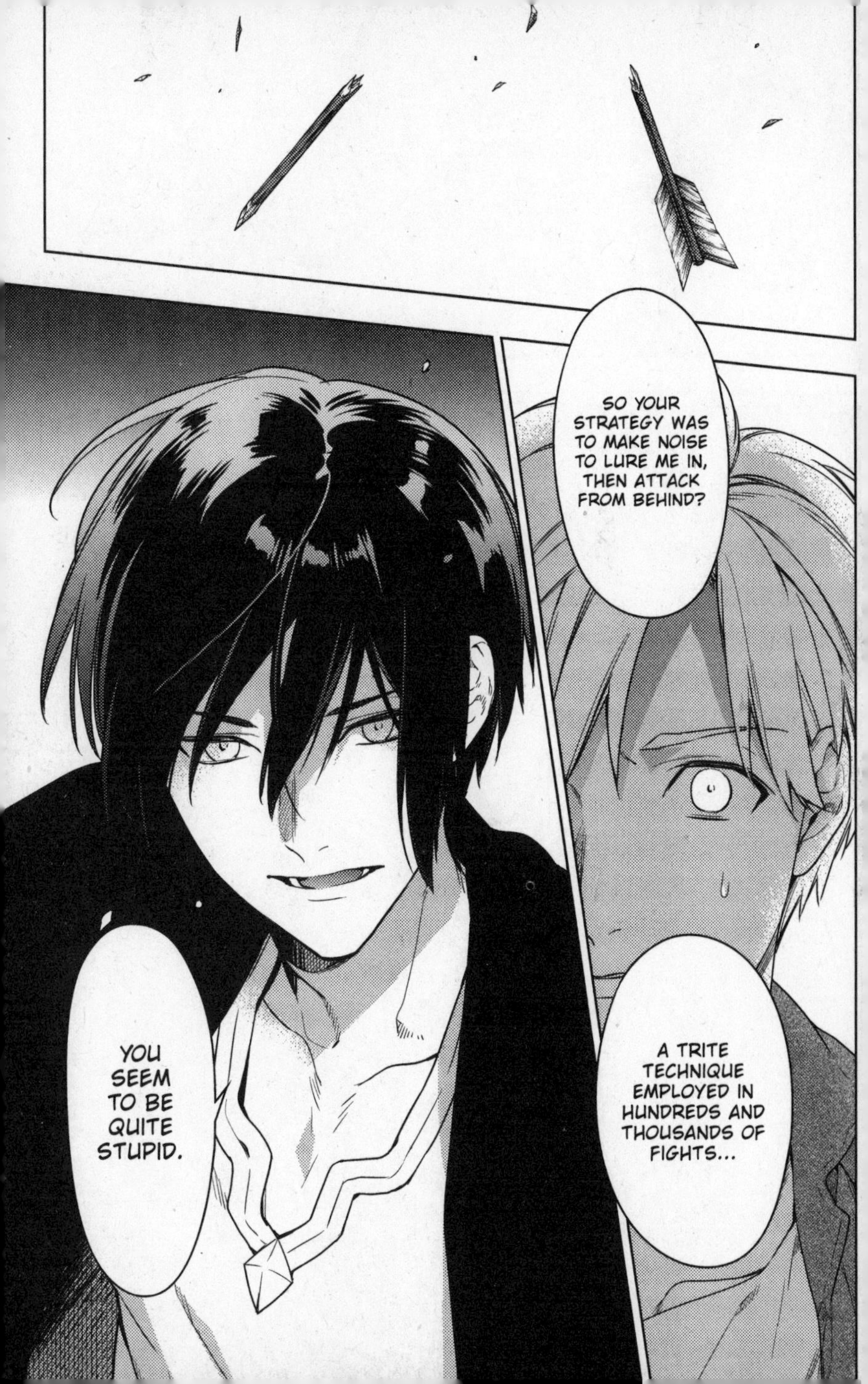
SO YOUR STRATEGY WAS TO MAKE NOISE TO LURE ME IN, THEN ATTACK FROM BEHIND?
A TRITE TECHNIQUE EMPLOYED IN HUNDREDS AND THOUSANDS OF FIGHTS...
YOU SEEM TO BE QUITE STUPID.

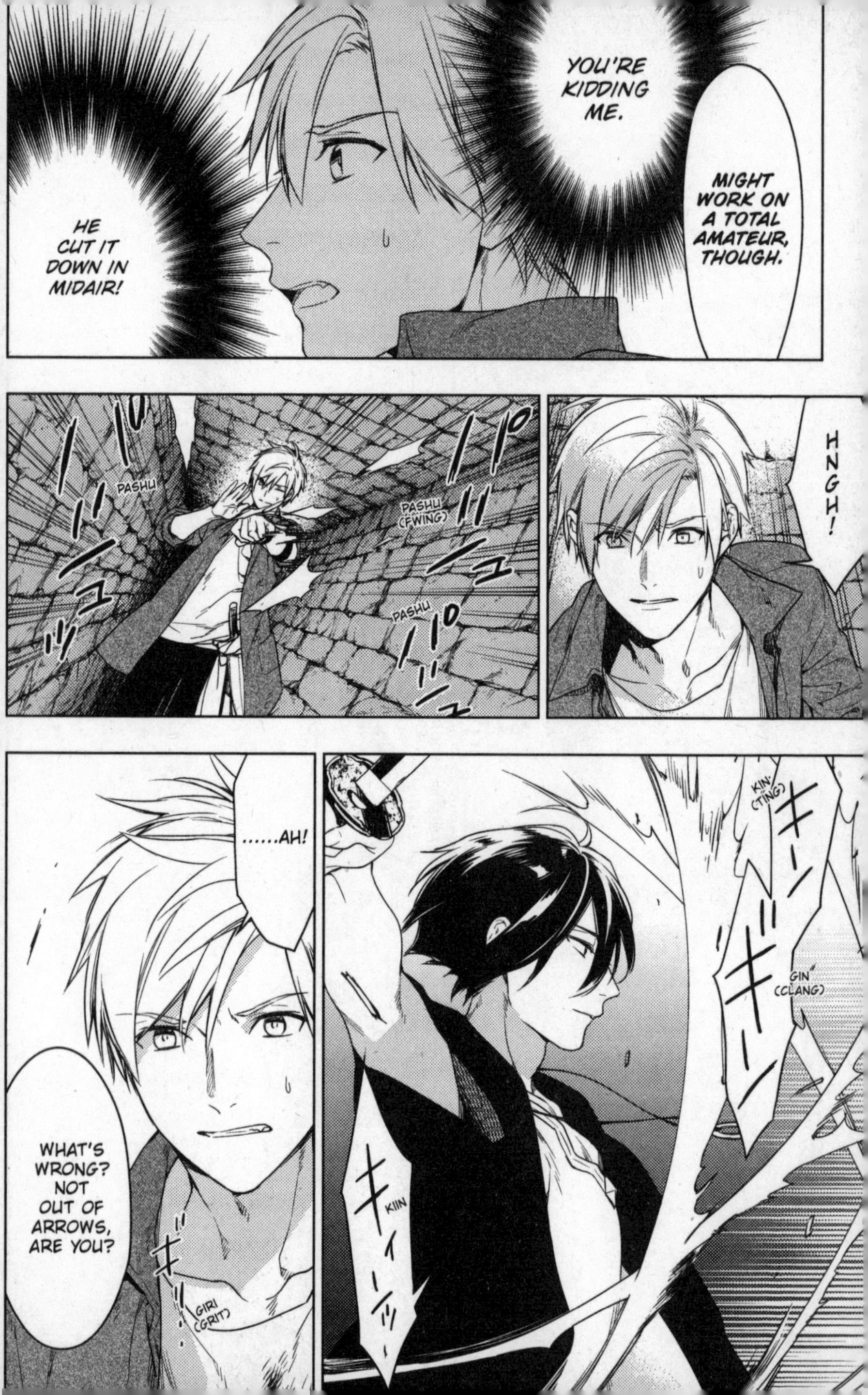
YOU'RE KIDDING ME.
MIGHT WORK ON A TOTAL AMATEUR, THOUGH.
HE CUT IT DOWN IN MIDAIR!
HNGH!
PASHU (FWING)
PASHU
PASHU
KIN (TING)
GIN (CLANG)
KIIN
......AH!
WHAT'S WRONG? NOT OUT OF ARROWS, ARE YOU?
GIRI (GRIT)

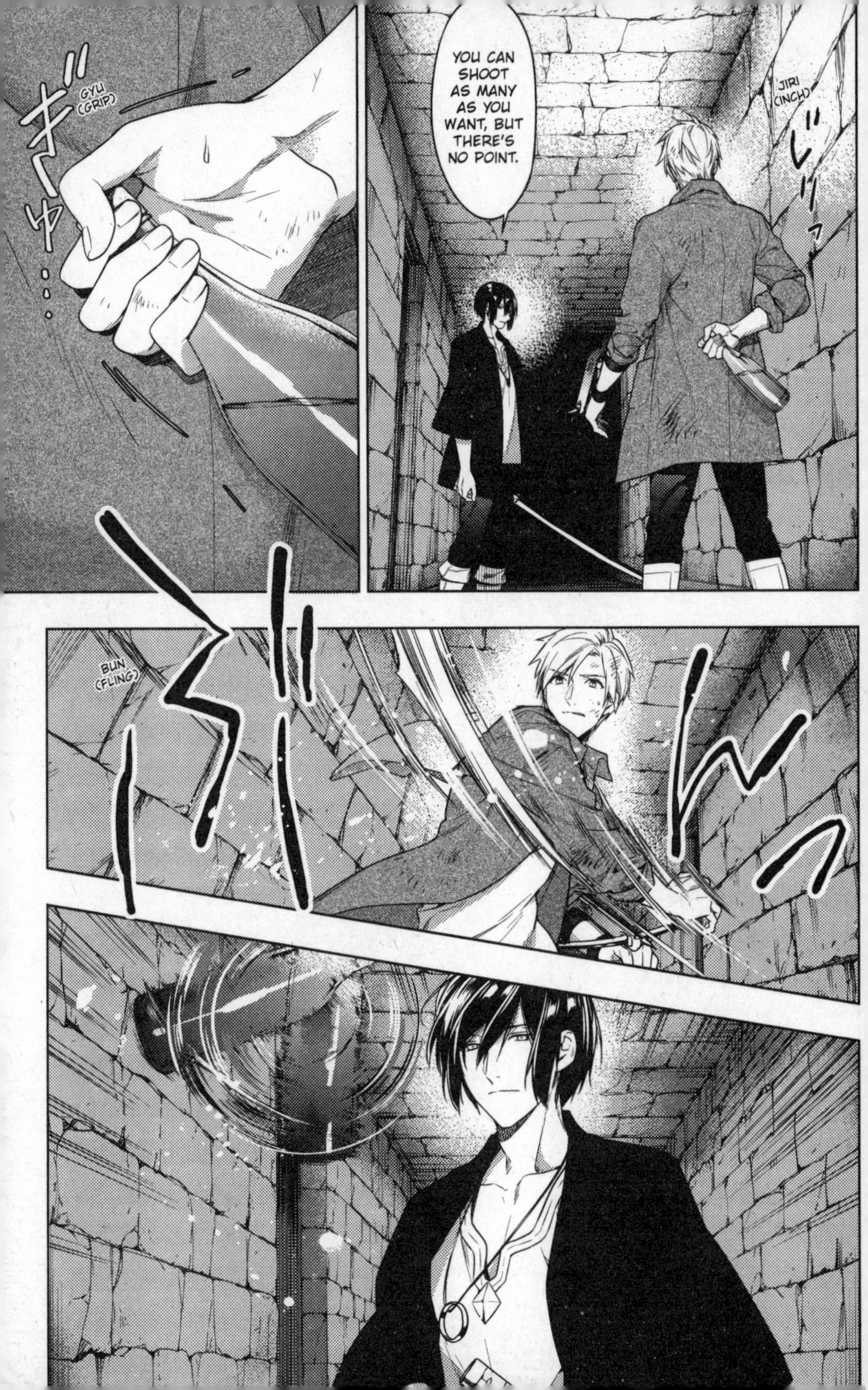
YOU CAN SHOOT AS MANY AS YOU WANT, BUT THERE'S NO POINT.
JIRI (INCH)
GYU (GRIP)
BUN (FLING)

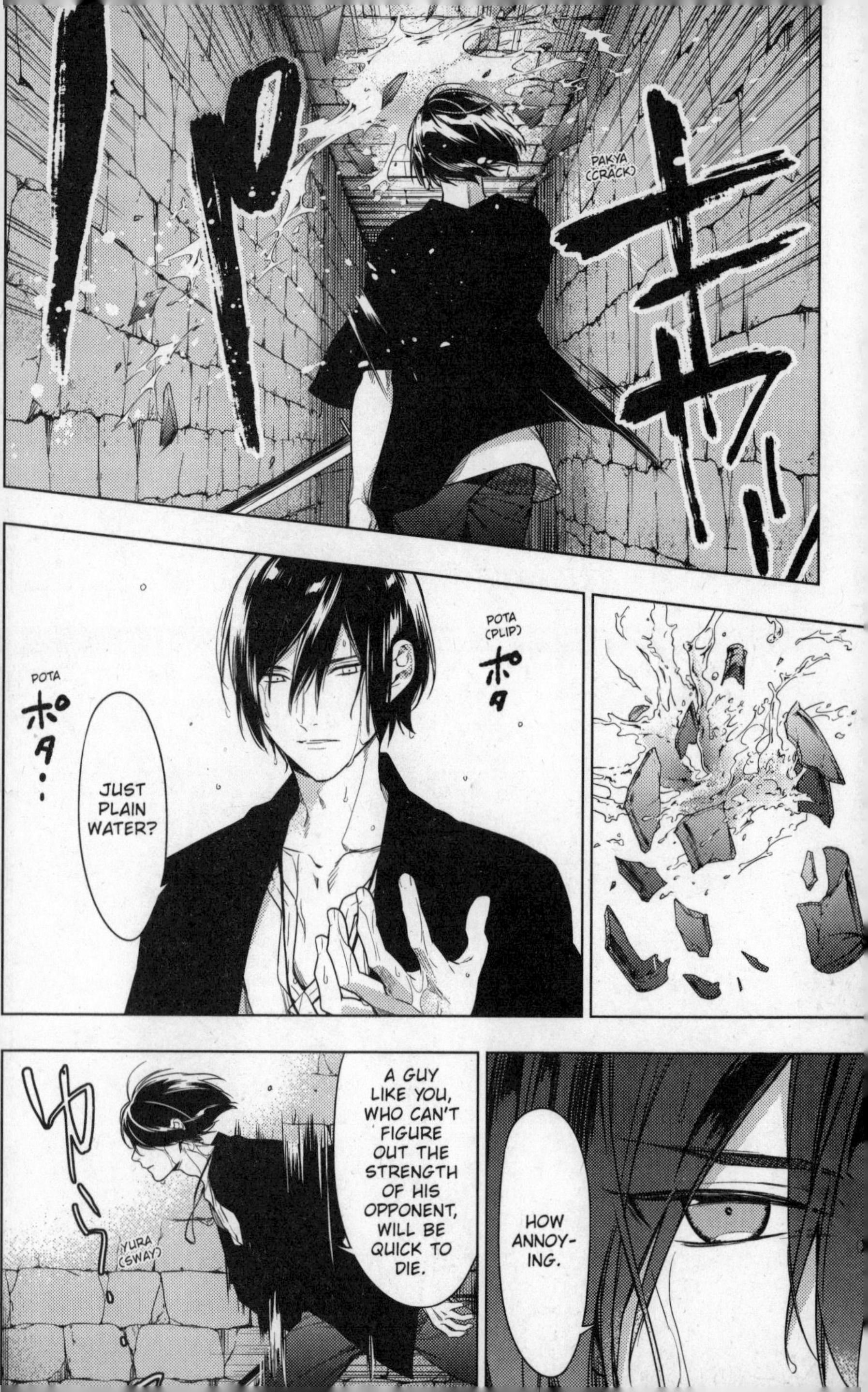
PAKYA (CRACK)
POTA (PLIP)
ポタ
POTA
ポタ・・
JUST PLAIN WATER?
HOW ANNOY-ING.
A GUY LIKE YOU, WHO CAN'T FIGURE OUT THE STRENGTH OF HIS OPPONENT, WILL BE QUICK TO DIE.
YURA (SWAY)

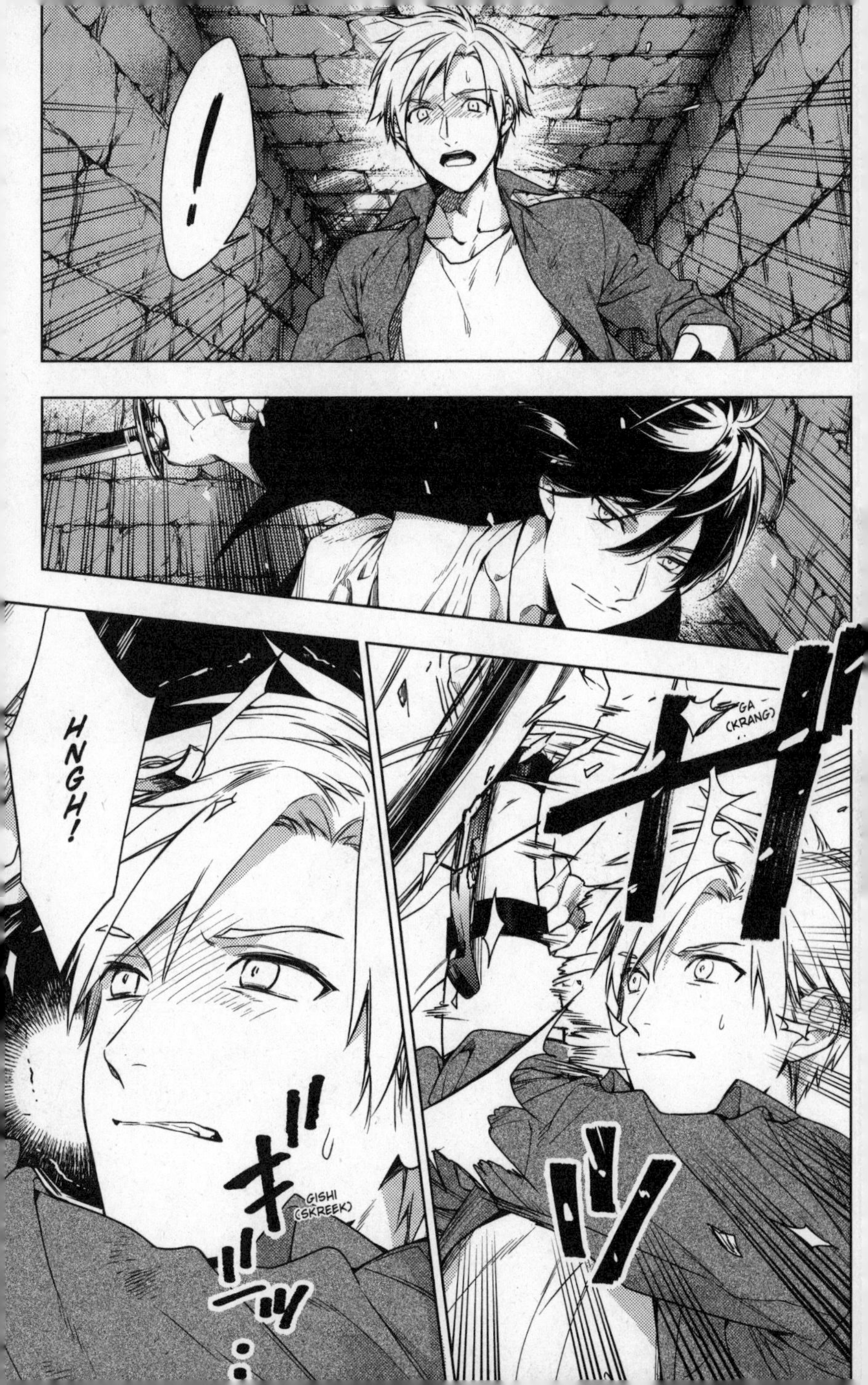
!
GA
(KRANG)
HNGH!
GISHI
(SKREEK)

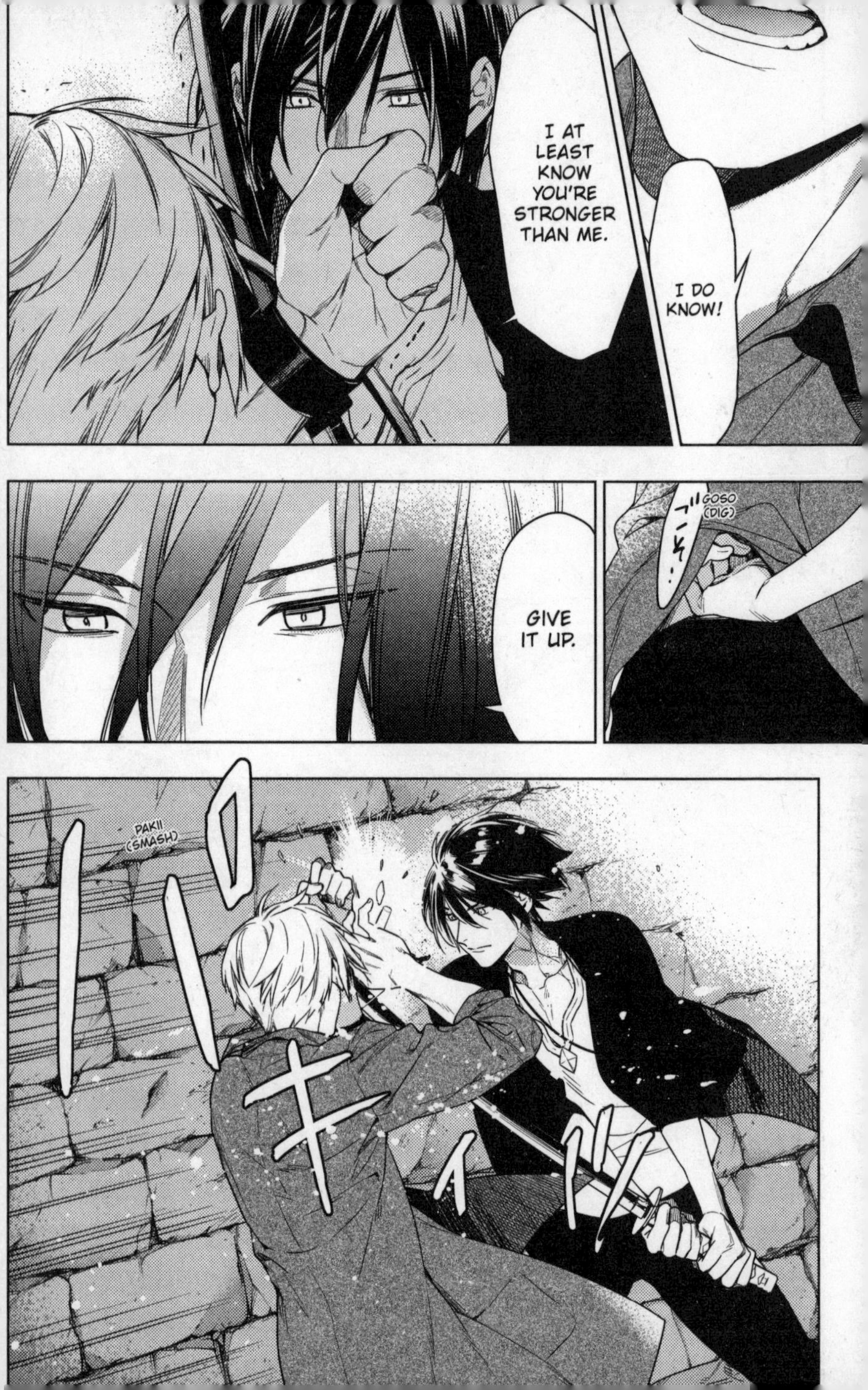
I AT LEAST KNOW YOU'RE STRONGER THAN ME.
I DO KNOW!
GOSO (DIG)
GIVE IT UP.
PAKII (SMASH)

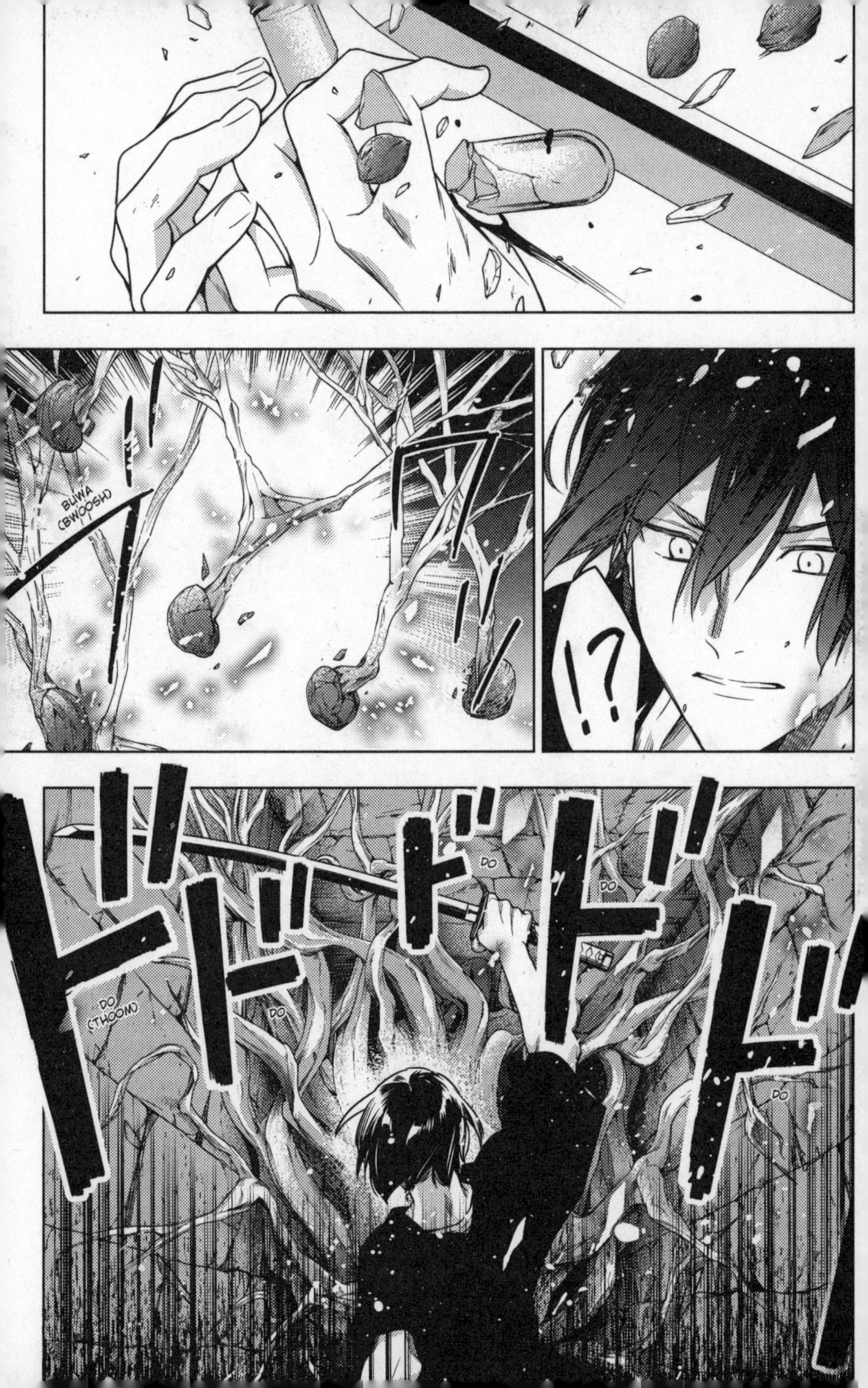
!?
BUWA
(BWOOSH)
DO
DO
DO
DO
DO
(THOOM)

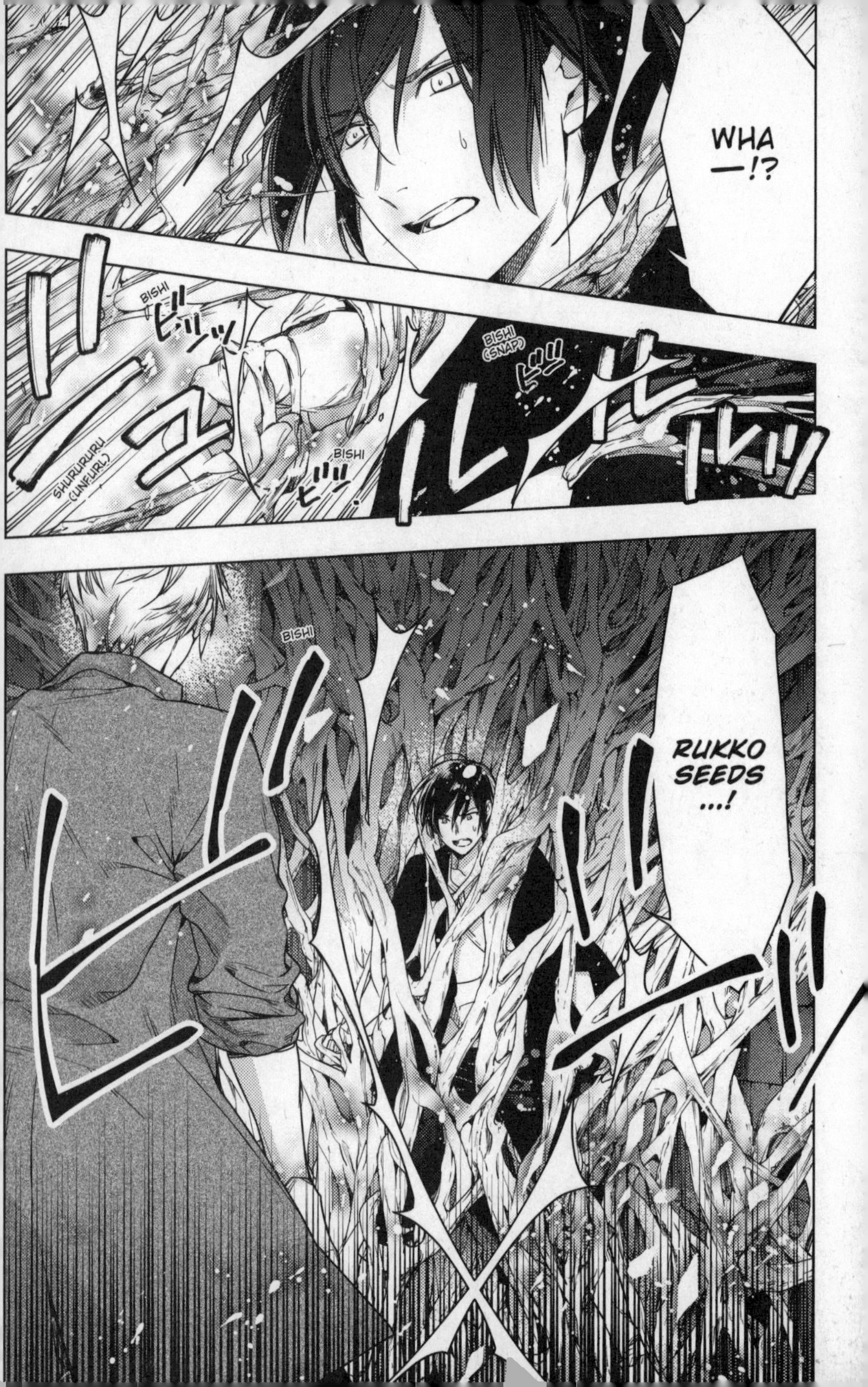
WHA—!?
BISHI (SNAP)
BISHI
BISHI
SHURURURU (UNFURL)
RUKKO SEEDS ...!
BISHI

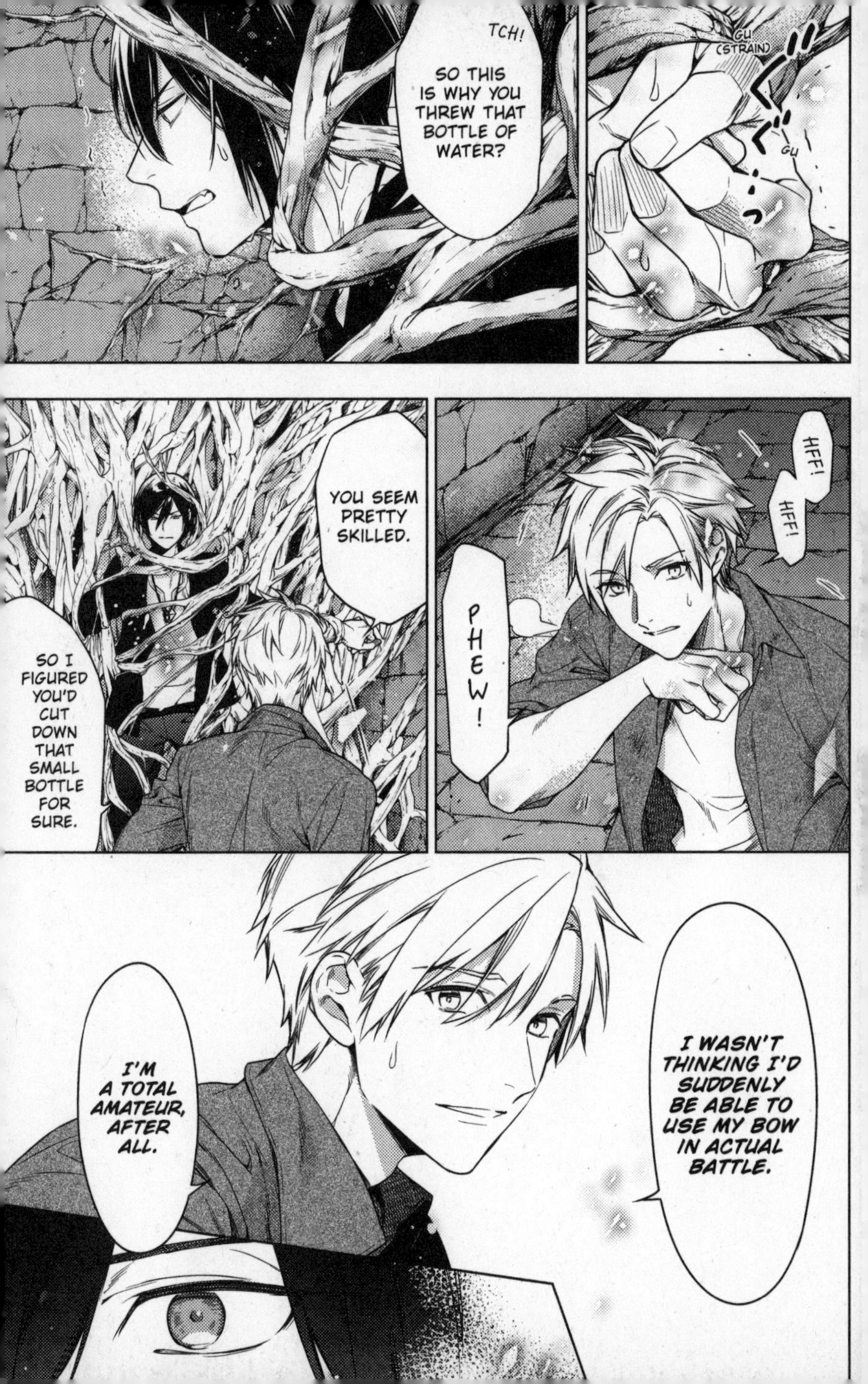
GU (STRAIN)
GU
TCH!
SO THIS IS WHY YOU THREW THAT BOTTLE OF WATER?
HFF!
HFF!
PHEW!
YOU SEEM PRETTY SKILLED.
SO I FIGURED YOU'D CUT DOWN THAT SMALL BOTTLE FOR SURE.
I WASN'T THINKING I'D SUDDENLY BE ABLE TO USE MY BOW IN ACTUAL BATTLE.
I'M A TOTAL AMATEUR, AFTER ALL.

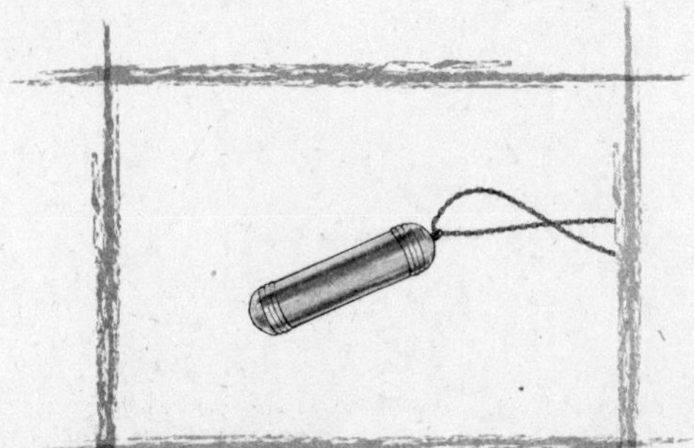

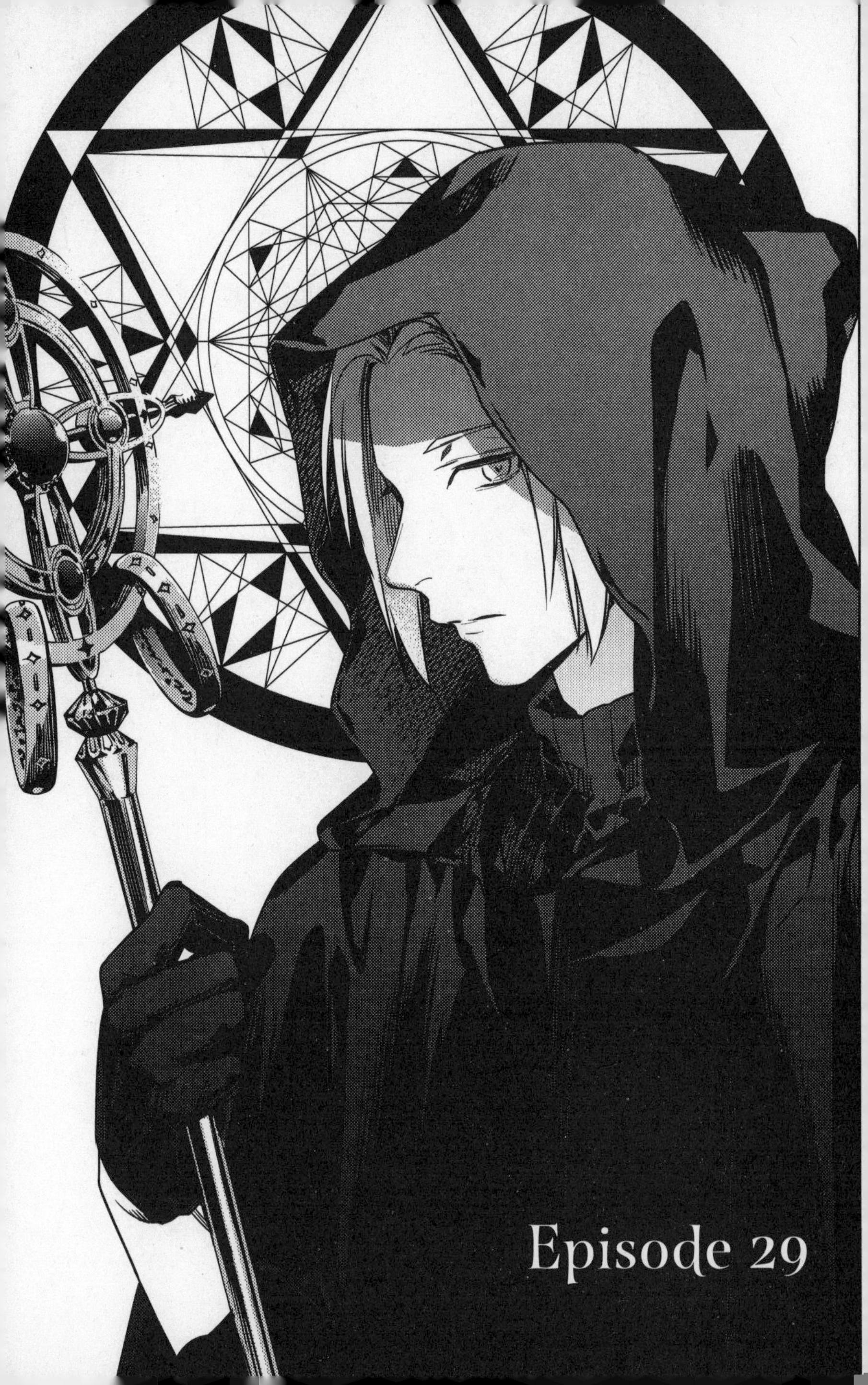
Episode 29

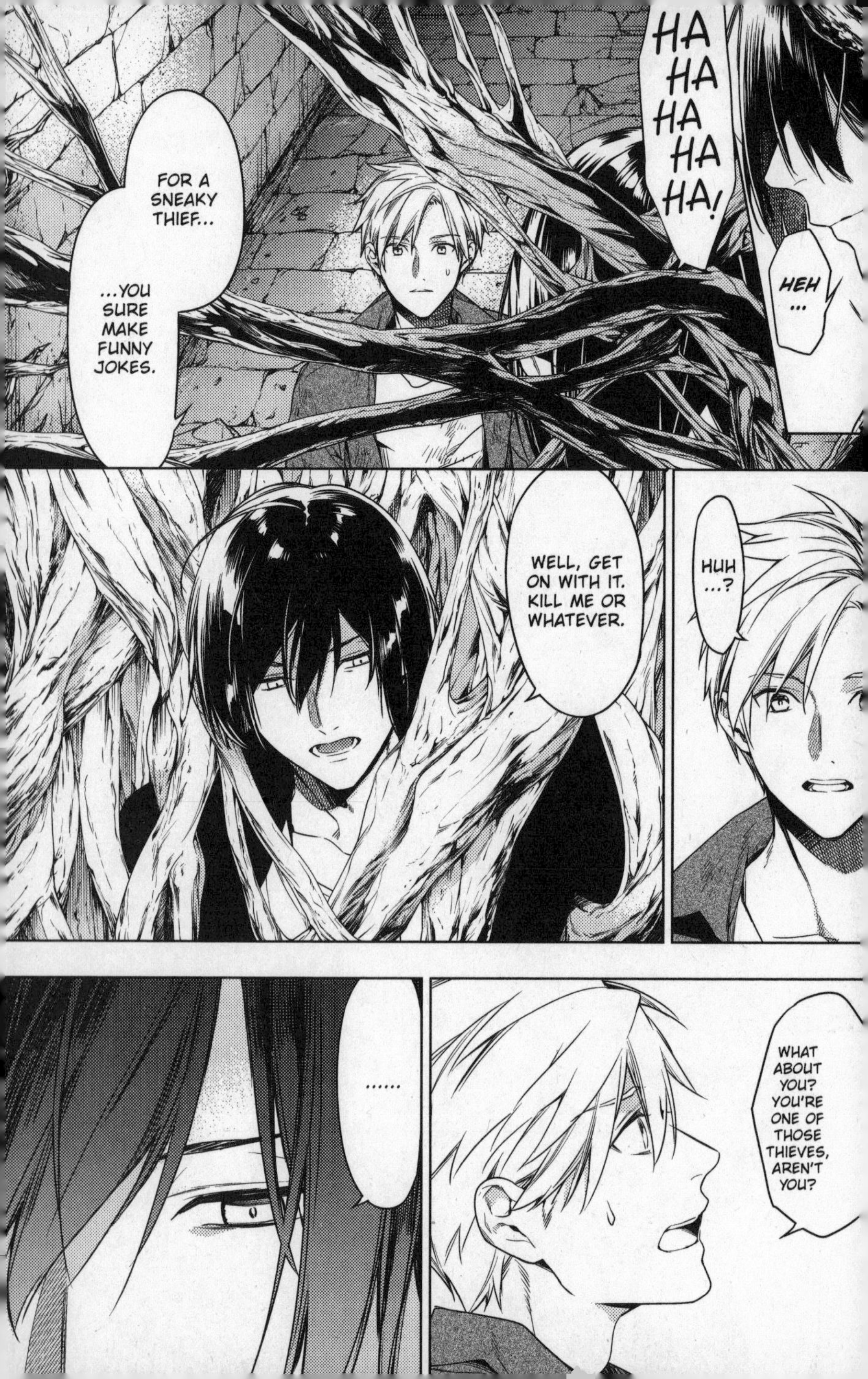
HA HA HA HA HA!
HEH...
FOR A SNEAKY THIEF...
...YOU SURE MAKE FUNNY JOKES.
HUH...?
WELL, GET ON WITH IT. KILL ME OR WHATEVER.
WHAT ABOUT YOU? YOU'RE ONE OF THOSE THIEVES, AREN'T YOU?
......

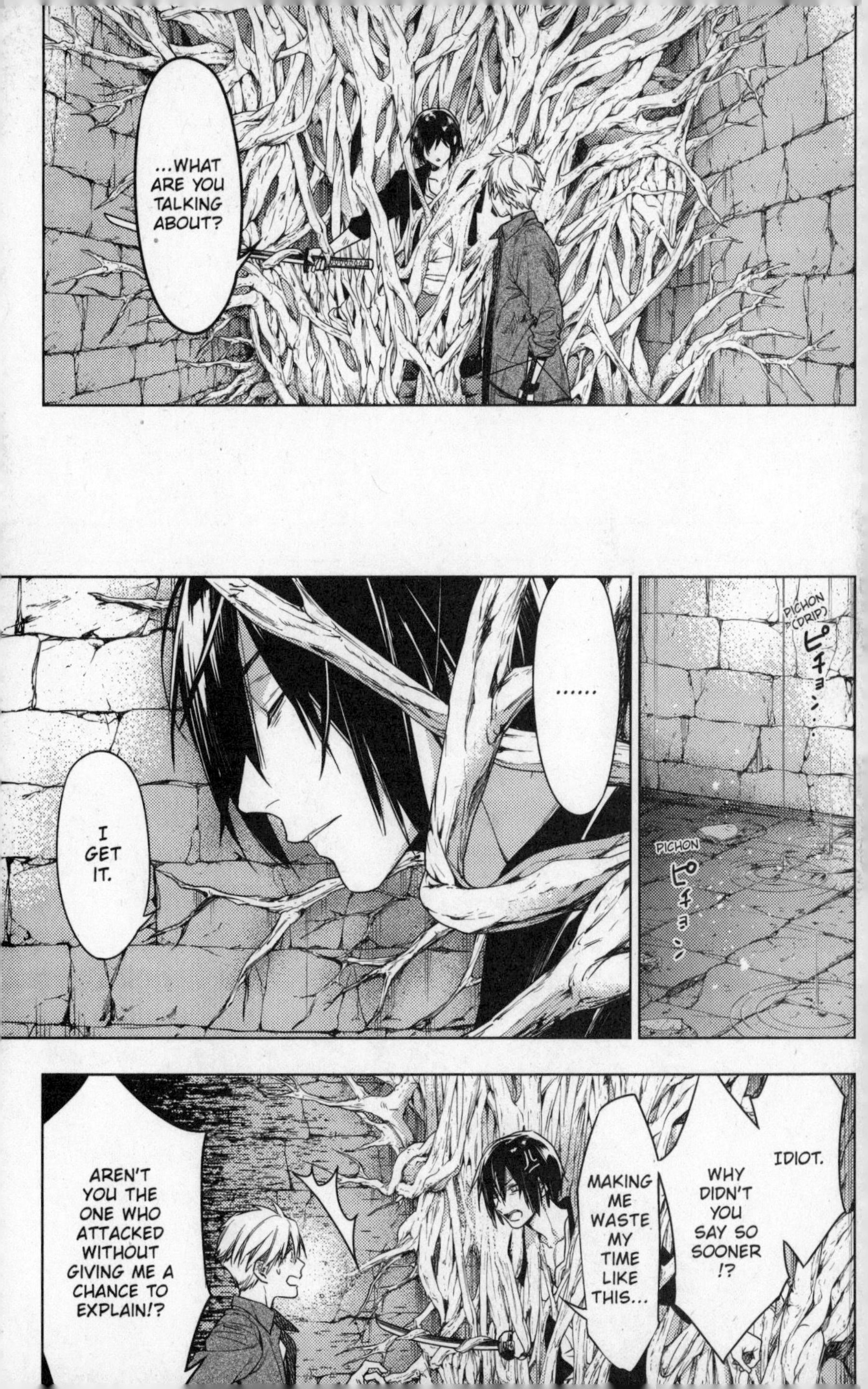
...WHAT ARE YOU TALKING ABOUT?
PICHON (DRIP)
ピチョン
PICHON
ピチョン
......
I GET IT.
IDIOT.
WHY DIDN'T YOU SAY SO SOONER!?
MAKING ME WASTE MY TIME LIKE THIS...
AREN'T YOU THE ONE WHO ATTACKED WITHOUT GIVING ME A CHANCE TO EXPLAIN!?

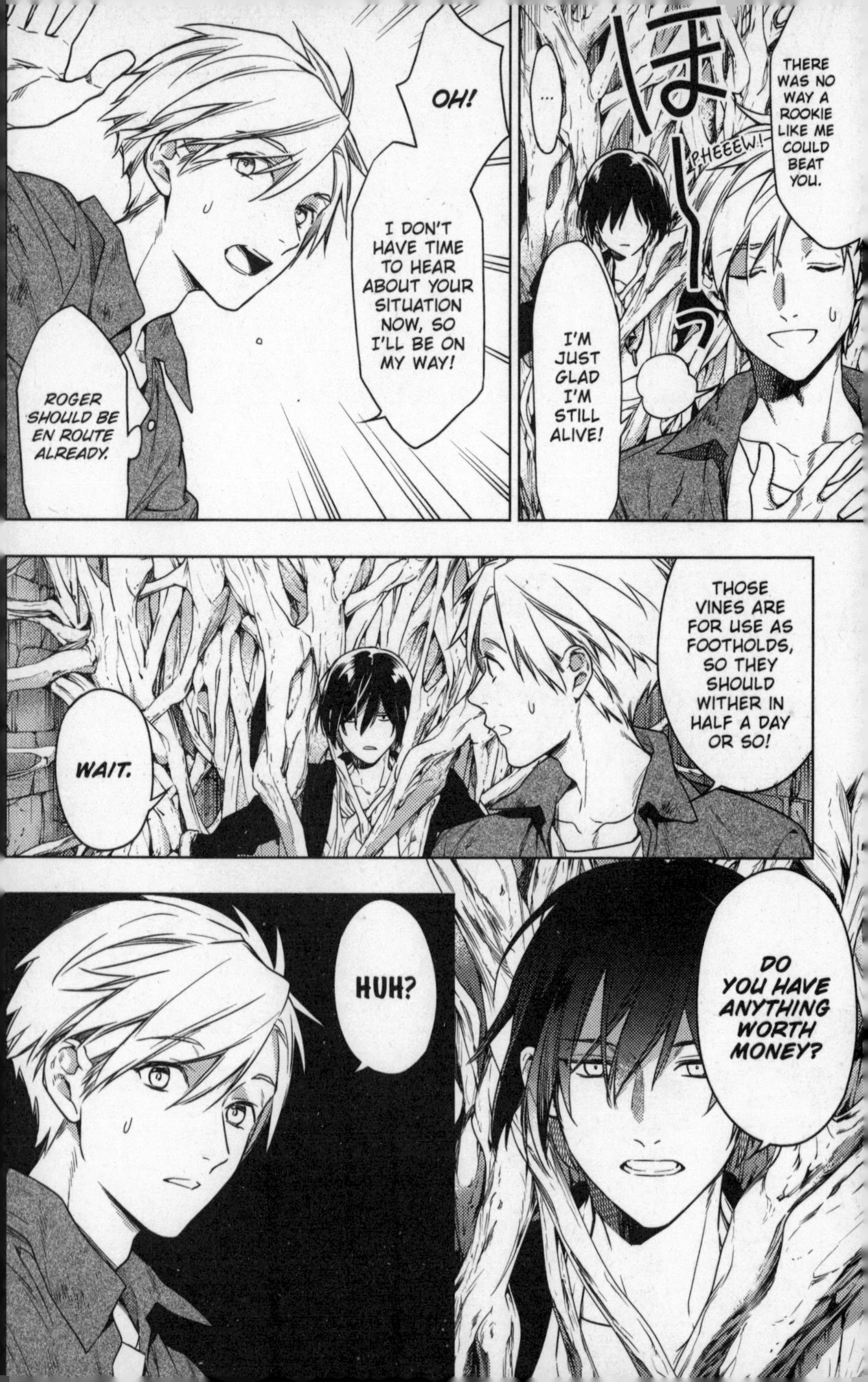
THERE WAS NO WAY A ROOKIE LIKE ME COULD BEAT YOU.
...
ほ〜っ
PHEEEW!
I'M JUST GLAD I'M STILL ALIVE!
OH!
I DON'T HAVE TIME TO HEAR ABOUT YOUR SITUATION NOW, SO I'LL BE ON MY WAY!
ROGER SHOULD BE EN ROUTE ALREADY.
THOSE VINES ARE FOR USE AS FOOTHOLDS, SO THEY SHOULD WITHER IN HALF A DAY OR SO!
WAIT.
DO YOU HAVE ANYTHING WORTH MONEY?
HUH?

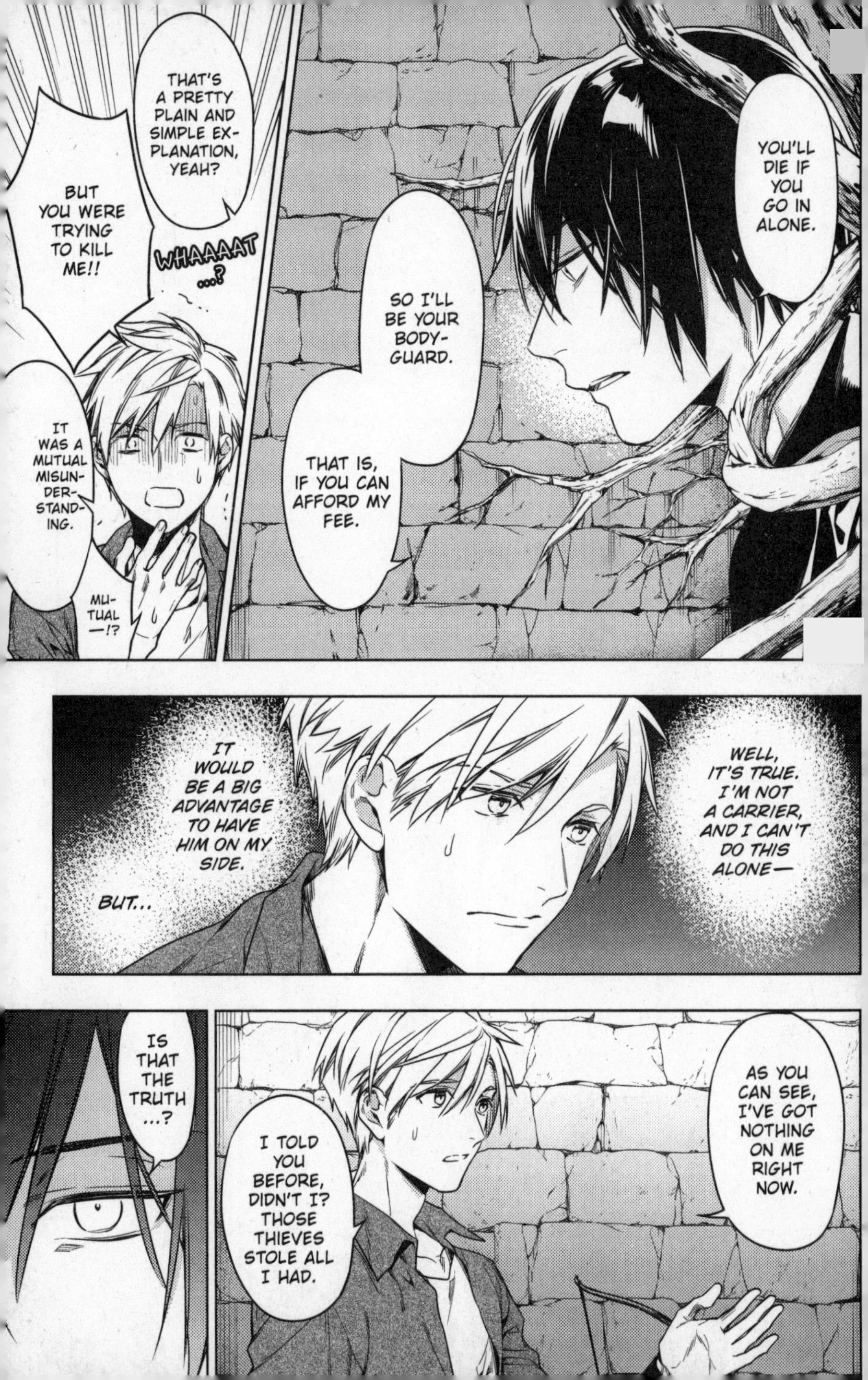
YOU'LL DIE IF YOU GO IN ALONE.
SO I'LL BE YOUR BODYGUARD.
THAT IS, IF YOU CAN AFFORD MY FEE.
THAT'S A PRETTY PLAIN AND SIMPLE EXPLANATION, YEAH?
BUT YOU WERE TRYING TO KILL ME!!
WHAAAAT...?
IT WAS A MUTUAL MISUNDERSTANDING.
MUTUAL—!?
WELL, IT'S TRUE. I'M NOT A CARRIER, AND I CAN'T DO THIS ALONE—
IT WOULD BE A BIG ADVANTAGE TO HAVE HIM ON MY SIDE.
BUT...
AS YOU CAN SEE, I'VE GOT NOTHING ON ME RIGHT NOW.
I TOLD YOU BEFORE, DIDN'T I? THOSE THIEVES STOLE ALL I HAD.
IS THAT THE TRUTH...?

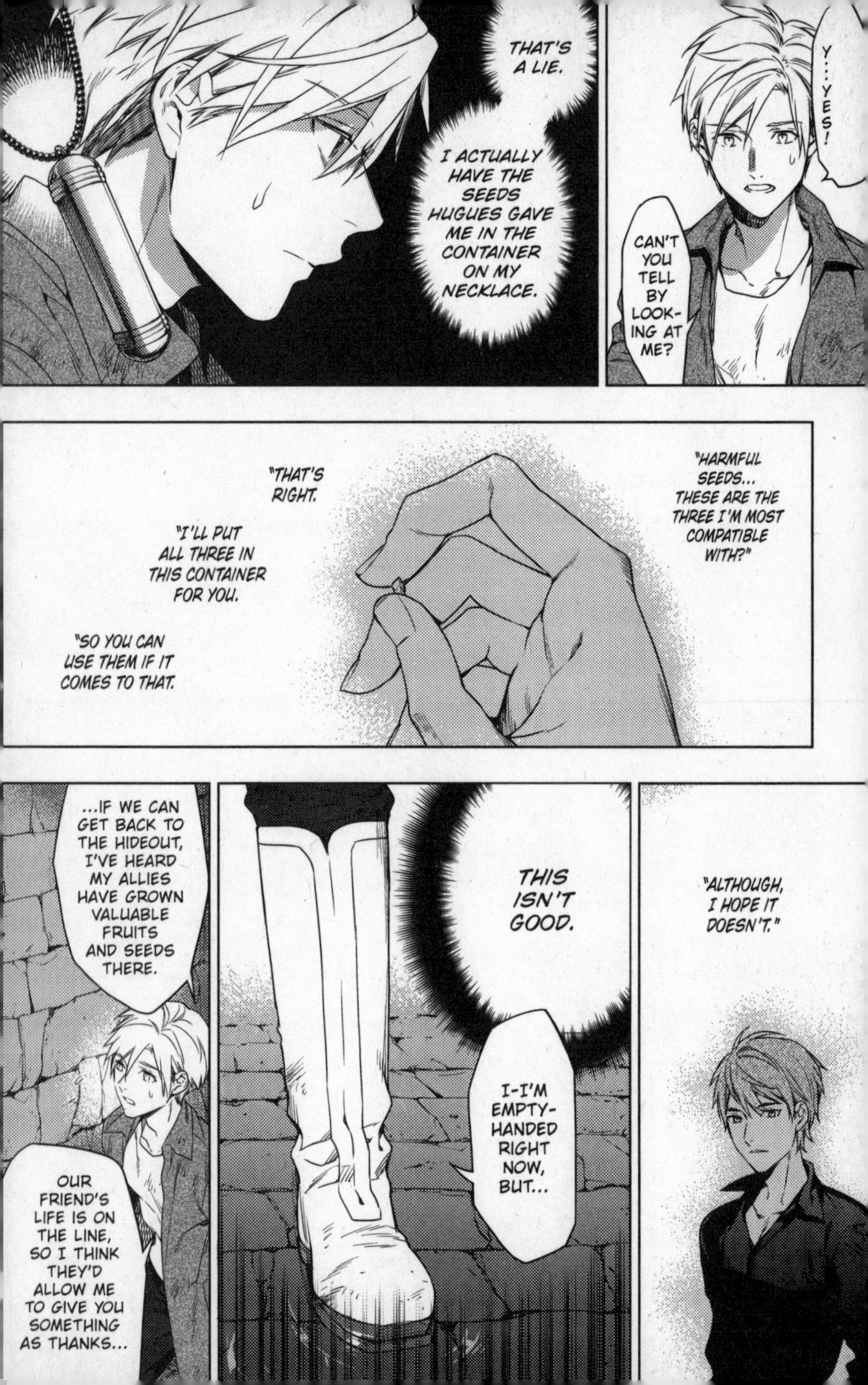
Y...YES!
CAN'T YOU TELL BY LOOKING AT ME?
THAT'S A LIE.
I ACTUALLY HAVE THE SEEDS HUGUES GAVE ME IN THE CONTAINER ON MY NECKLACE.
"HARMFUL SEEDS... THESE ARE THE THREE I'M MOST COMPATIBLE WITH?"
"THAT'S RIGHT.
"I'LL PUT ALL THREE IN THIS CONTAINER FOR YOU.
"SO YOU CAN USE THEM IF IT COMES TO THAT.
"ALTHOUGH, I HOPE IT DOESN'T."
THIS ISN'T GOOD.
I-I'M EMPTY-HANDED RIGHT NOW, BUT...
...IF WE CAN GET BACK TO THE HIDEOUT, I'VE HEARD MY ALLIES HAVE GROWN VALUABLE FRUITS AND SEEDS THERE.
OUR FRIEND'S LIFE IS ON THE LINE, SO I THINK THEY'D ALLOW ME TO GIVE YOU SOMETHING AS THANKS...

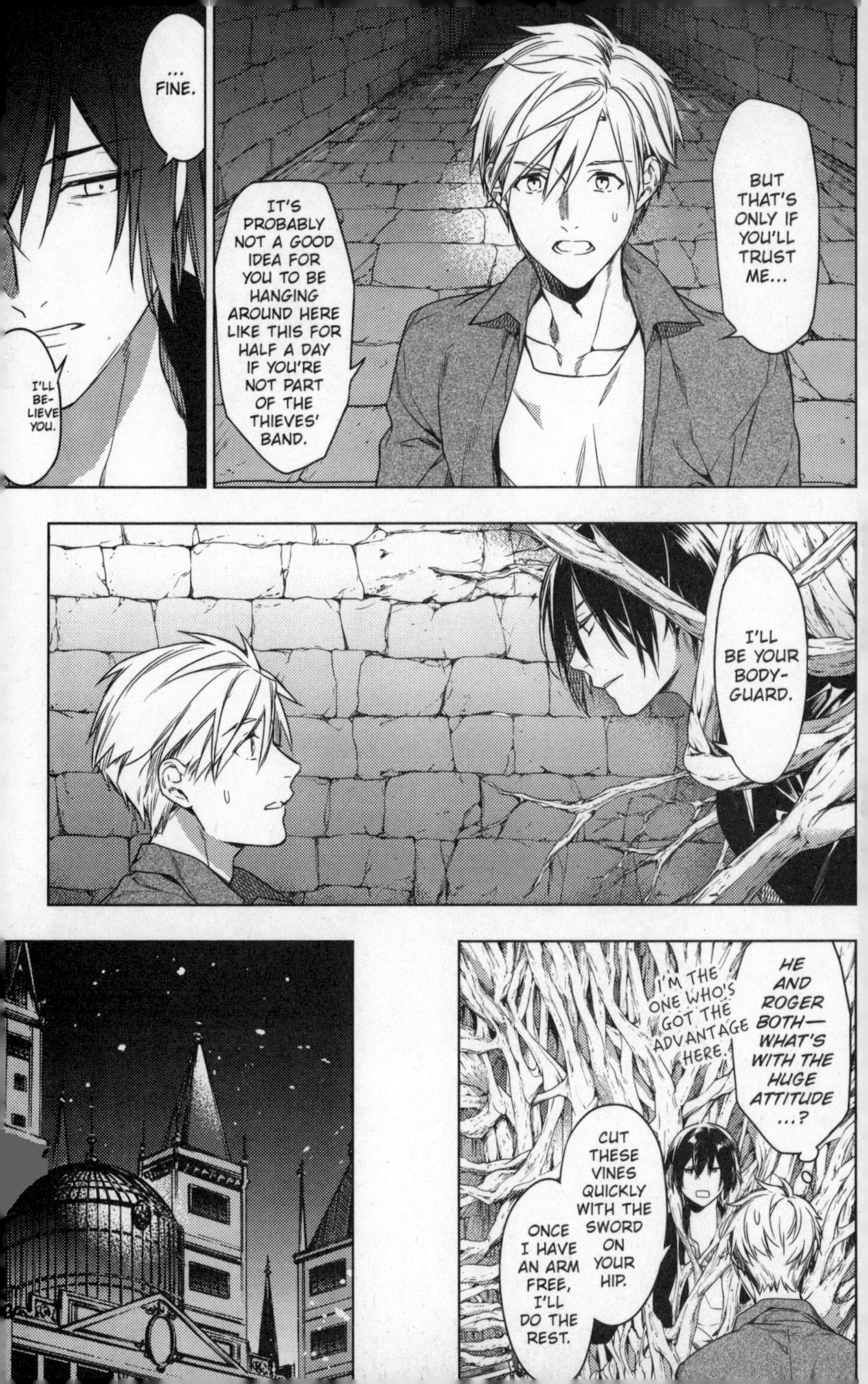
BUT THAT'S ONLY IF YOU'LL TRUST ME...
IT'S PROBABLY NOT A GOOD IDEA FOR YOU TO BE HANGING AROUND HERE LIKE THIS FOR HALF A DAY IF YOU'RE NOT PART OF THE THIEVES' BAND.
... FINE.
I'LL BE-LIEVE YOU.
I'LL BE YOUR BODY-GUARD.
HE AND ROGER BOTH—WHAT'S WITH THE HUGE ATTITUDE ...?
I'M THE ONE WHO'S GOT THE ADVANTAGE HERE.
CUT THESE VINES QUICKLY WITH THE SWORD ON YOUR HIP.
ONCE I HAVE AN ARM FREE, I'LL DO THE REST.

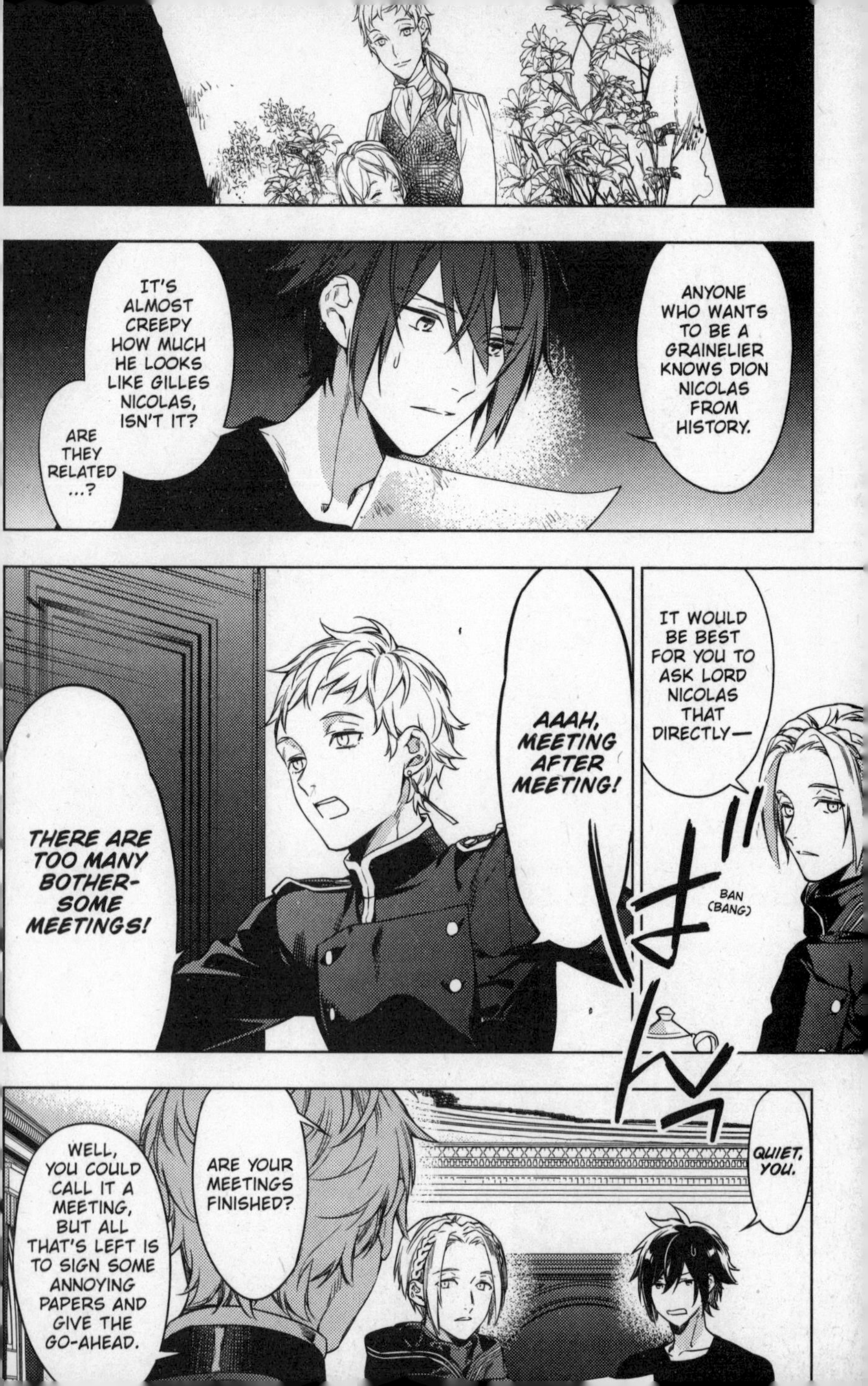
ANYONE WHO WANTS TO BE A GRAINELIER KNOWS DION NICOLAS FROM HISTORY.
IT'S ALMOST CREEPY HOW MUCH HE LOOKS LIKE GILLES NICOLAS, ISN'T IT?
ARE THEY RELATED ...?
IT WOULD BE BEST FOR YOU TO ASK LORD NICOLAS THAT DIRECTLY—
BAN (BANG)
AAAH, MEETING AFTER MEETING!
THERE ARE TOO MANY BOTHER-SOME MEETINGS!
QUIET, YOU.
ARE YOUR MEETINGS FINISHED?
WELL, YOU COULD CALL IT A MEETING, BUT ALL THAT'S LEFT IS TO SIGN SOME ANNOYING PAPERS AND GIVE THE GO-AHEAD.

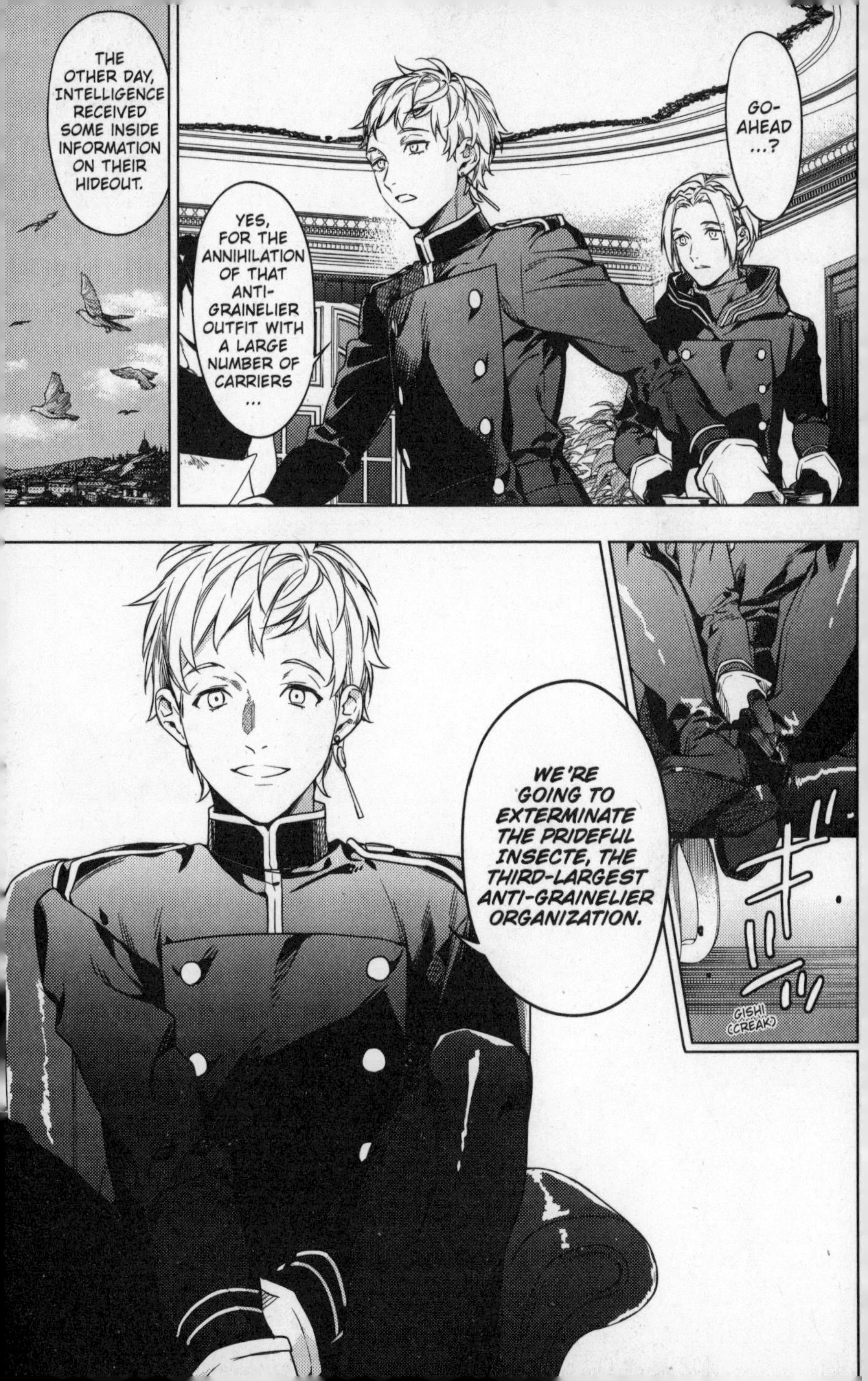
GO-AHEAD ...?
YES, FOR THE ANNIHILATION OF THAT ANTI-GRAINELIER OUTFIT WITH A LARGE NUMBER OF CARRIERS ...
THE OTHER DAY, INTELLIGENCE RECEIVED SOME INSIDE INFORMATION ON THEIR HIDEOUT.
GISHI (CREAK)
WE'RE GOING TO EXTERMINATE THE PRIDEFUL INSECTE, THE THIRD-LARGEST ANTI-GRAINELIER ORGANIZATION.

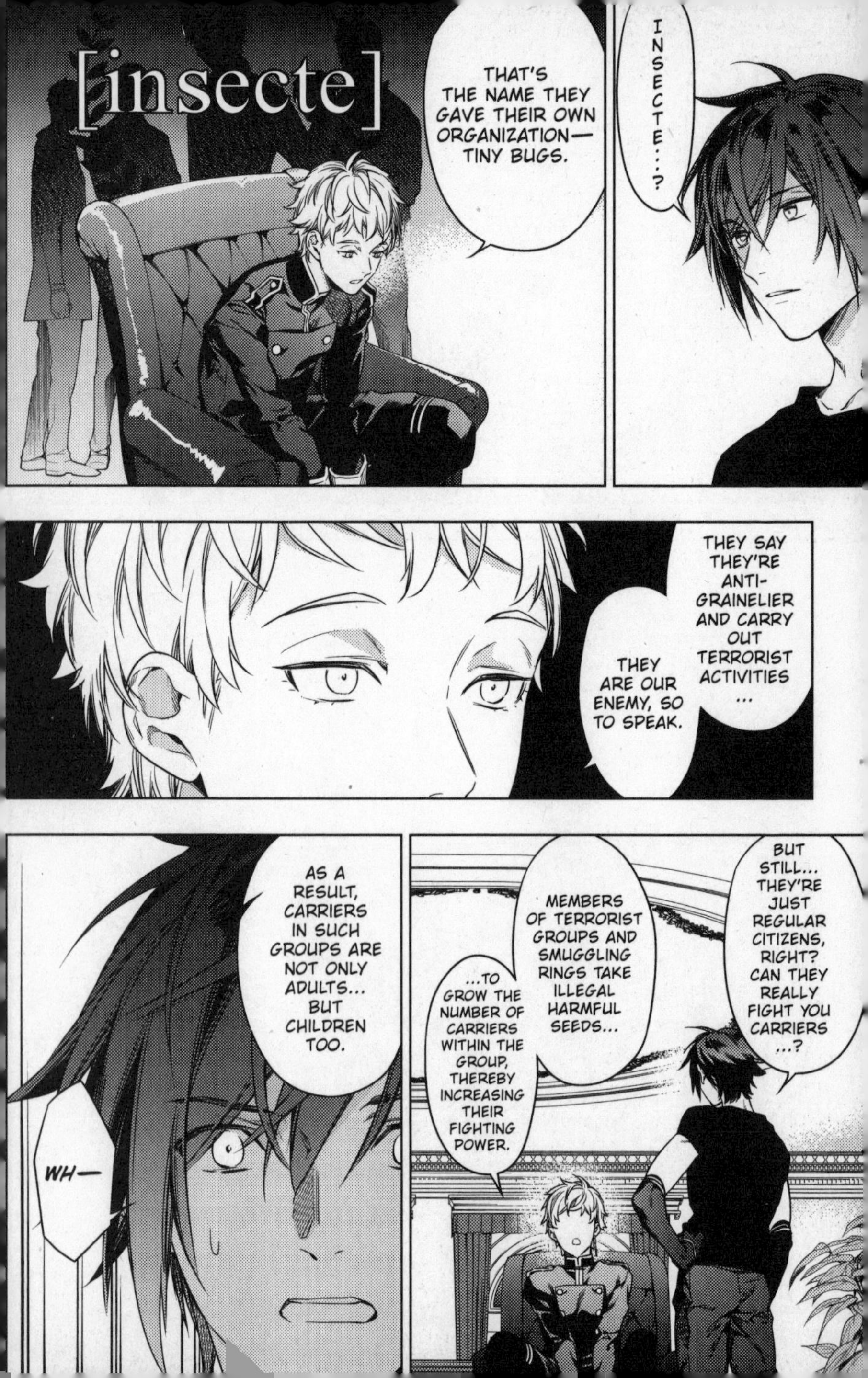
INSECTE...?
THAT'S THE NAME THEY GAVE THEIR OWN ORGANIZATION—TINY BUGS.
[insecte]
THEY SAY THEY'RE ANTI-GRAINELIER AND CARRY OUT TERRORIST ACTIVITIES ...
THEY ARE OUR ENEMY, SO TO SPEAK.
BUT STILL... THEY'RE JUST REGULAR CITIZENS, RIGHT? CAN THEY REALLY FIGHT YOU CARRIERS ...?
MEMBERS OF TERRORIST GROUPS AND SMUGGLING RINGS TAKE ILLEGAL HARMFUL SEEDS...
...TO GROW THE NUMBER OF CARRIERS WITHIN THE GROUP, THEREBY INCREASING THEIR FIGHTING POWER.
AS A RESULT, CARRIERS IN SUCH GROUPS ARE NOT ONLY ADULTS... BUT CHILDREN TOO.
WH—

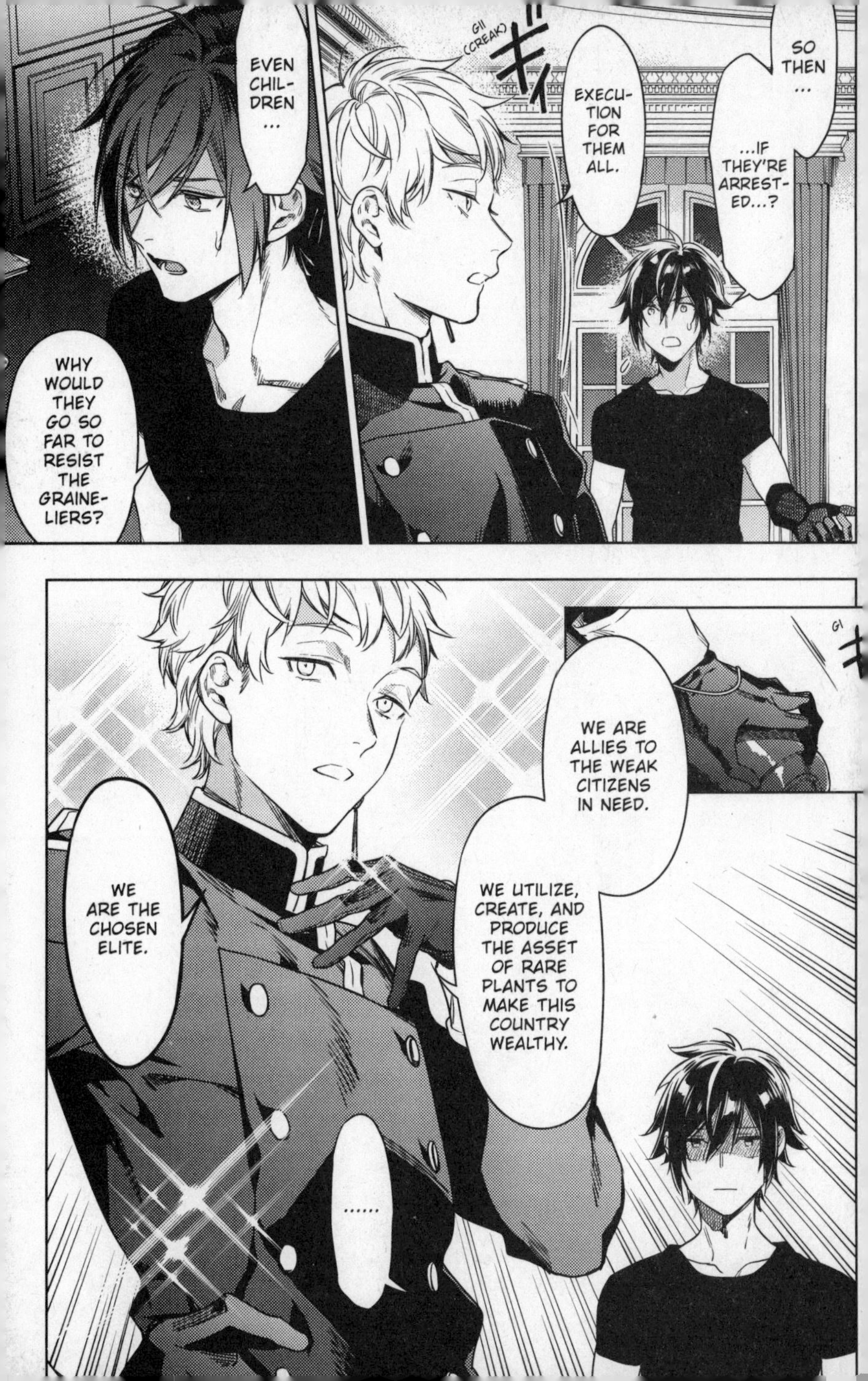
SO THEN...
...IF THEY'RE ARREST-ED...?
GII (CREAK)
EXECU-TION FOR THEM ALL.
EVEN CHIL-DREN...
WHY WOULD THEY GO SO FAR TO RESIST THE GRAINE-LIERS?
GI
WE ARE ALLIES TO THE WEAK CITIZENS IN NEED.
WE UTILIZE, CREATE, AND PRODUCE THE ASSET OF RARE PLANTS TO MAKE THIS COUNTRY WEALTHY.
WE ARE THE CHOSEN ELITE.
......

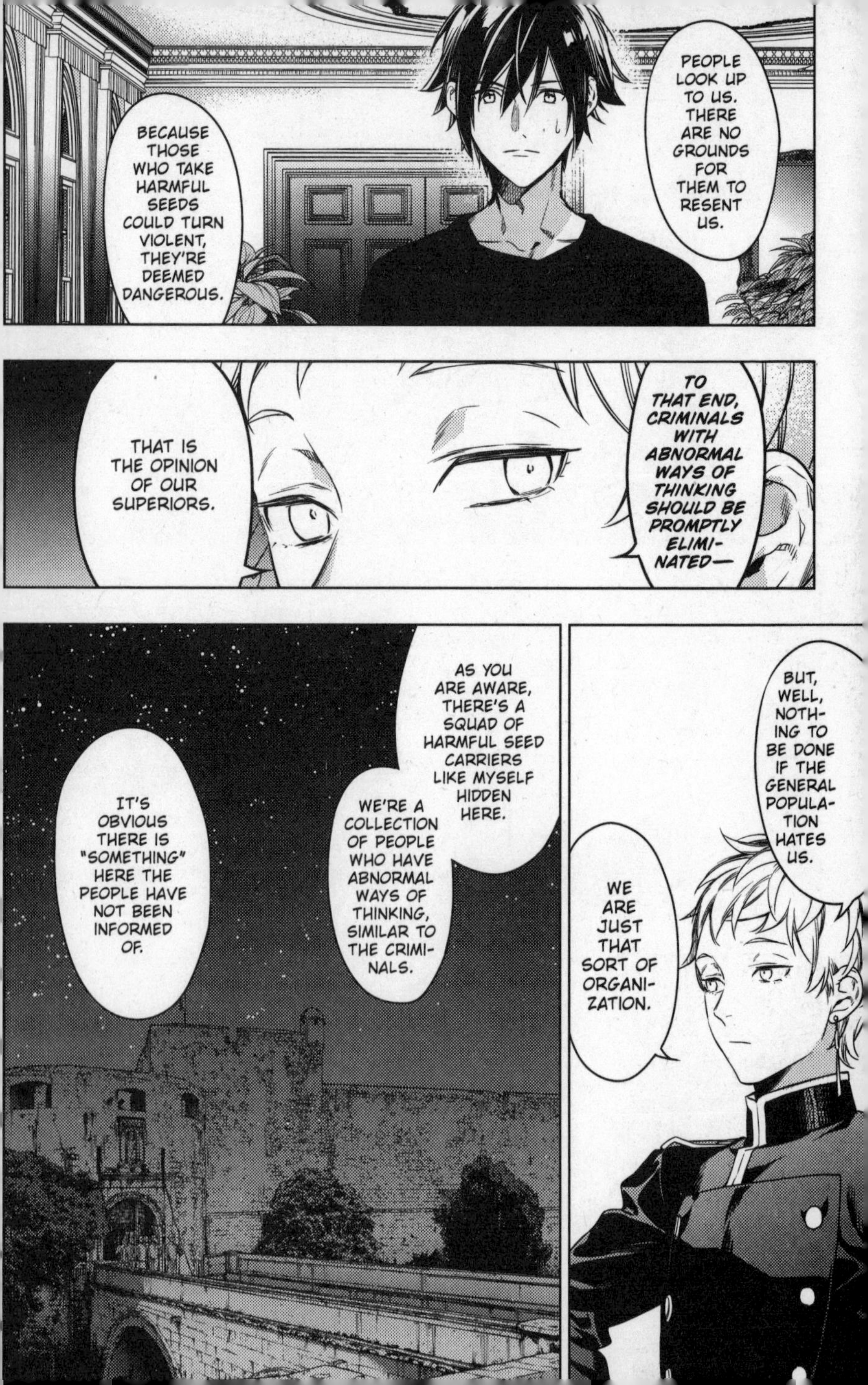
PEOPLE LOOK UP TO US. THERE ARE NO GROUNDS FOR THEM TO RESENT US.
BECAUSE THOSE WHO TAKE HARMFUL SEEDS COULD TURN VIOLENT, THEY'RE DEEMED DANGEROUS.
TO THAT END, CRIMINALS WITH ABNORMAL WAYS OF THINKING SHOULD BE PROMPTLY ELIMI-NATED—
THAT IS THE OPINION OF OUR SUPERIORS.
BUT, WELL, NOTH-ING TO BE DONE IF THE GENERAL POPULA-TION HATES US.
WE ARE JUST THAT SORT OF ORGANI-ZATION.
AS YOU ARE AWARE, THERE'S A SQUAD OF HARMFUL SEED CARRIERS LIKE MYSELF HIDDEN HERE.
WE'RE A COLLECTION OF PEOPLE WHO HAVE ABNORMAL WAYS OF THINKING, SIMILAR TO THE CRIMI-NALS.
IT'S OBVIOUS THERE IS "SOMETHING" HERE THE PEOPLE HAVE NOT BEEN INFORMED OF.

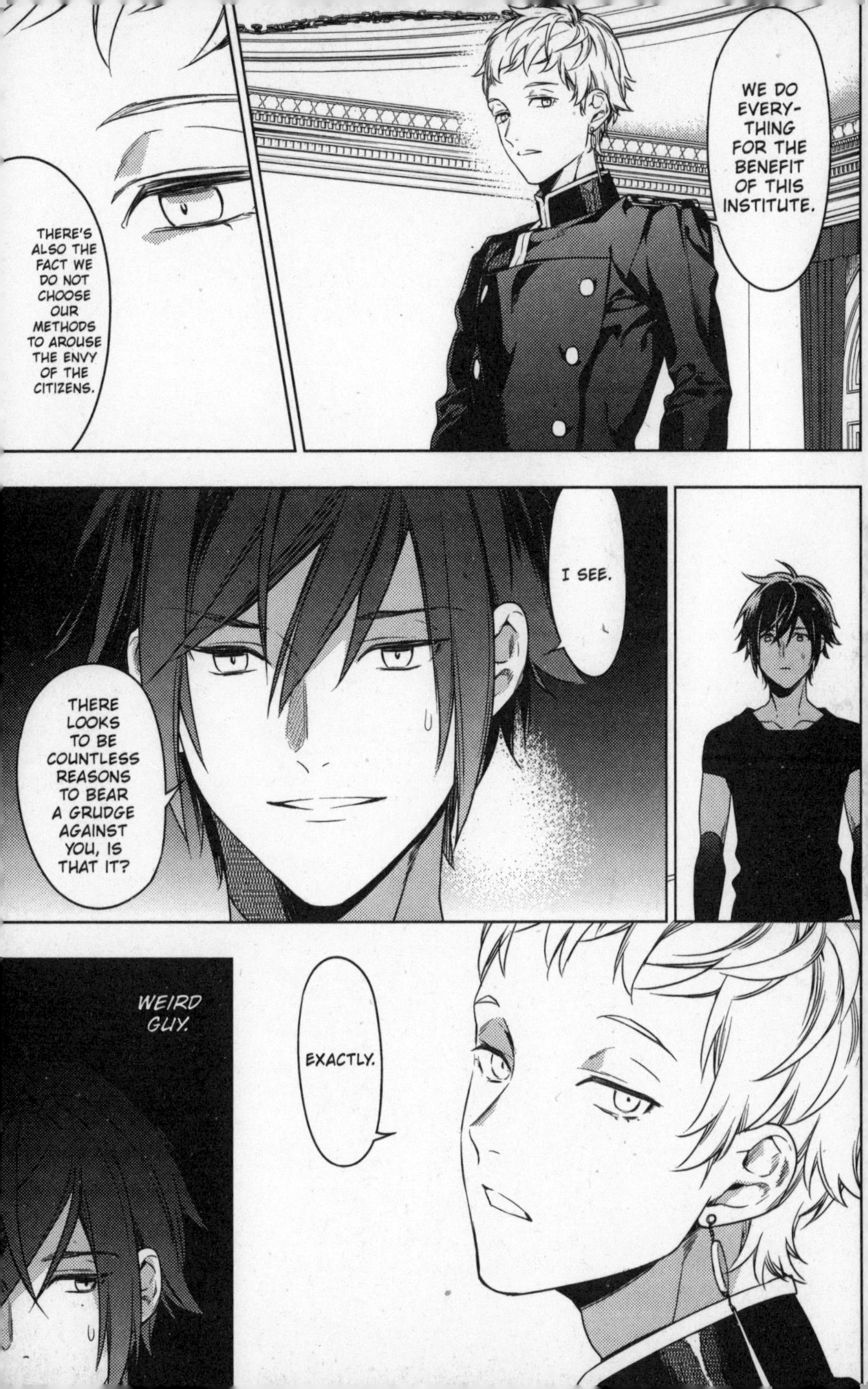
WE DO EVERYTHING FOR THE BENEFIT OF THIS INSTITUTE.
THERE'S ALSO THE FACT WE DO NOT CHOOSE OUR METHODS TO AROUSE THE ENVY OF THE CITIZENS.
I SEE.
THERE LOOKS TO BE COUNTLESS REASONS TO BEAR A GRUDGE AGAINST YOU, IS THAT IT?
EXACTLY.
WEIRD GUY.

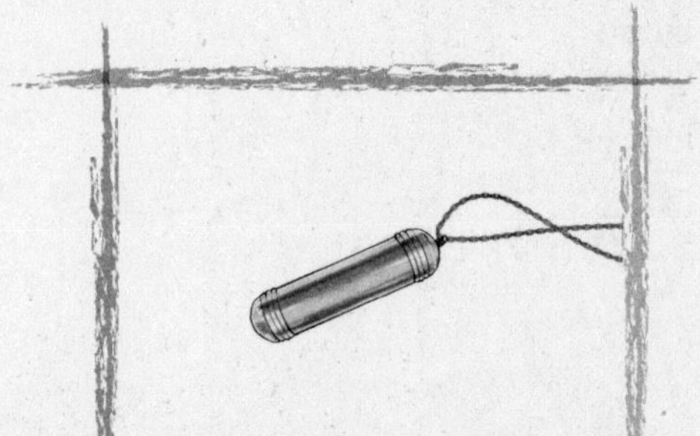

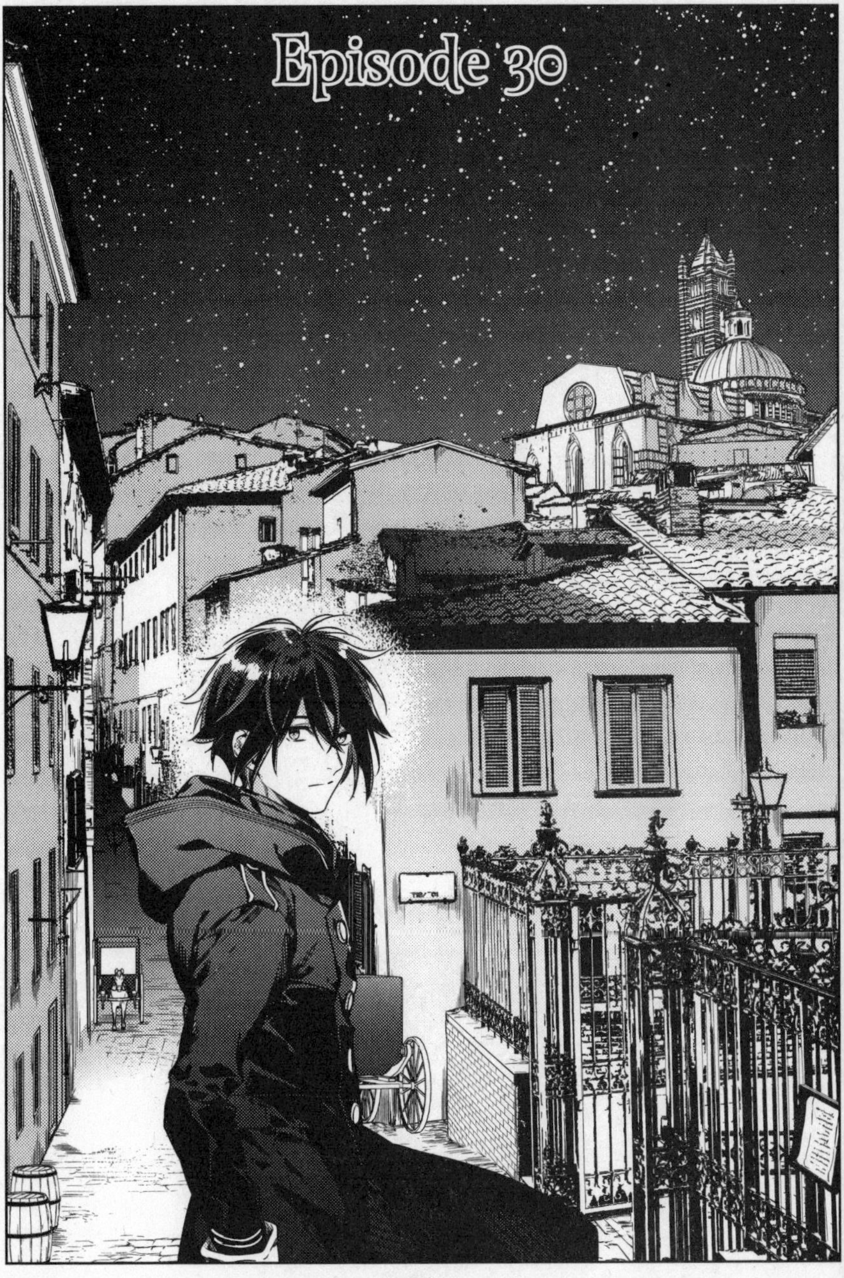
Episode 30

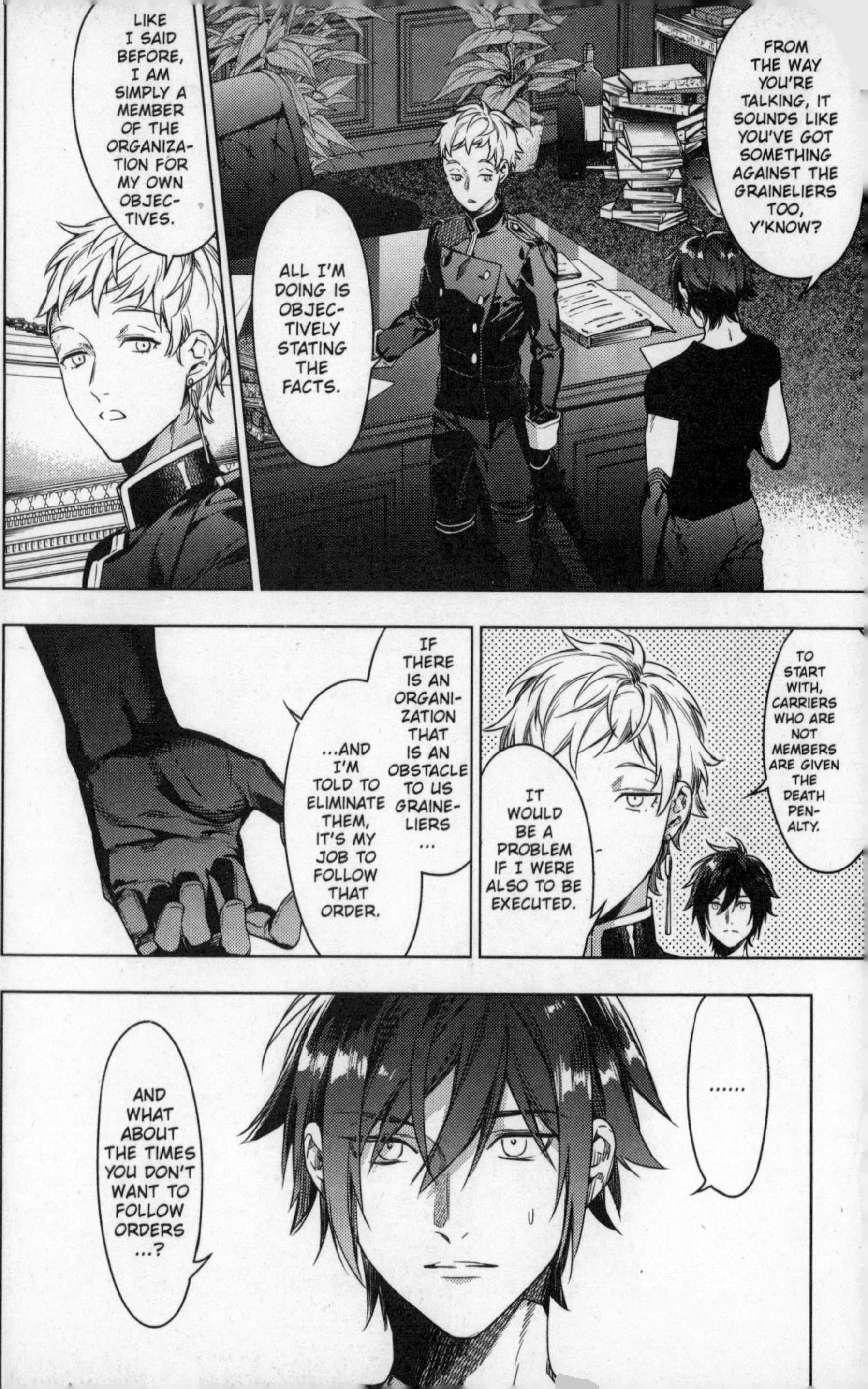
FROM THE WAY YOU'RE TALKING, IT SOUNDS LIKE YOU'VE GOT SOMETHING AGAINST THE GRAINELIERS TOO, Y'KNOW?
ALL I'M DOING IS OBJECTIVELY STATING THE FACTS.
LIKE I SAID BEFORE, I AM SIMPLY A MEMBER OF THE ORGANIZATION FOR MY OWN OBJECTIVES.
TO START WITH, CARRIERS WHO ARE NOT MEMBERS ARE GIVEN THE DEATH PENALTY.
IT WOULD BE A PROBLEM IF I WERE ALSO TO BE EXECUTED.
IF THERE IS AN ORGANIZATION THAT IS AN OBSTACLE TO US GRAINELIERS...
...AND I'M TOLD TO ELIMINATE THEM, IT'S MY JOB TO FOLLOW THAT ORDER.
......
AND WHAT ABOUT THE TIMES YOU DON'T WANT TO FOLLOW ORDERS...?

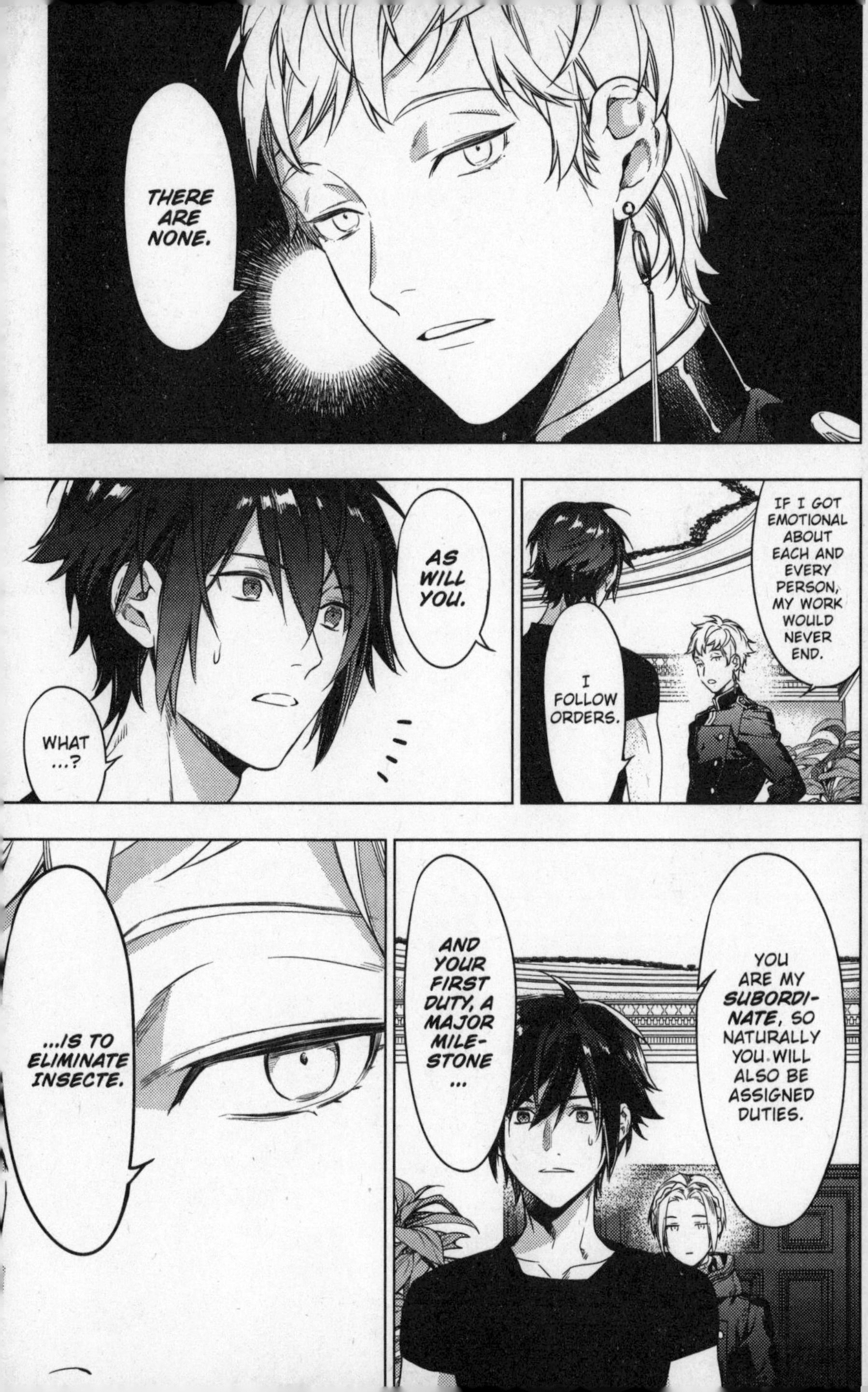
THERE ARE NONE.
IF I GOT EMOTIONAL ABOUT EACH AND EVERY PERSON, MY WORK WOULD NEVER END.
I FOLLOW ORDERS.
AS WILL YOU.
WHAT...?
YOU ARE MY SUBORDINATE, SO NATURALLY YOU WILL ALSO BE ASSIGNED DUTIES.
AND YOUR FIRST DUTY, A MAJOR MILESTONE...
...IS TO ELIMINATE INSECTE.

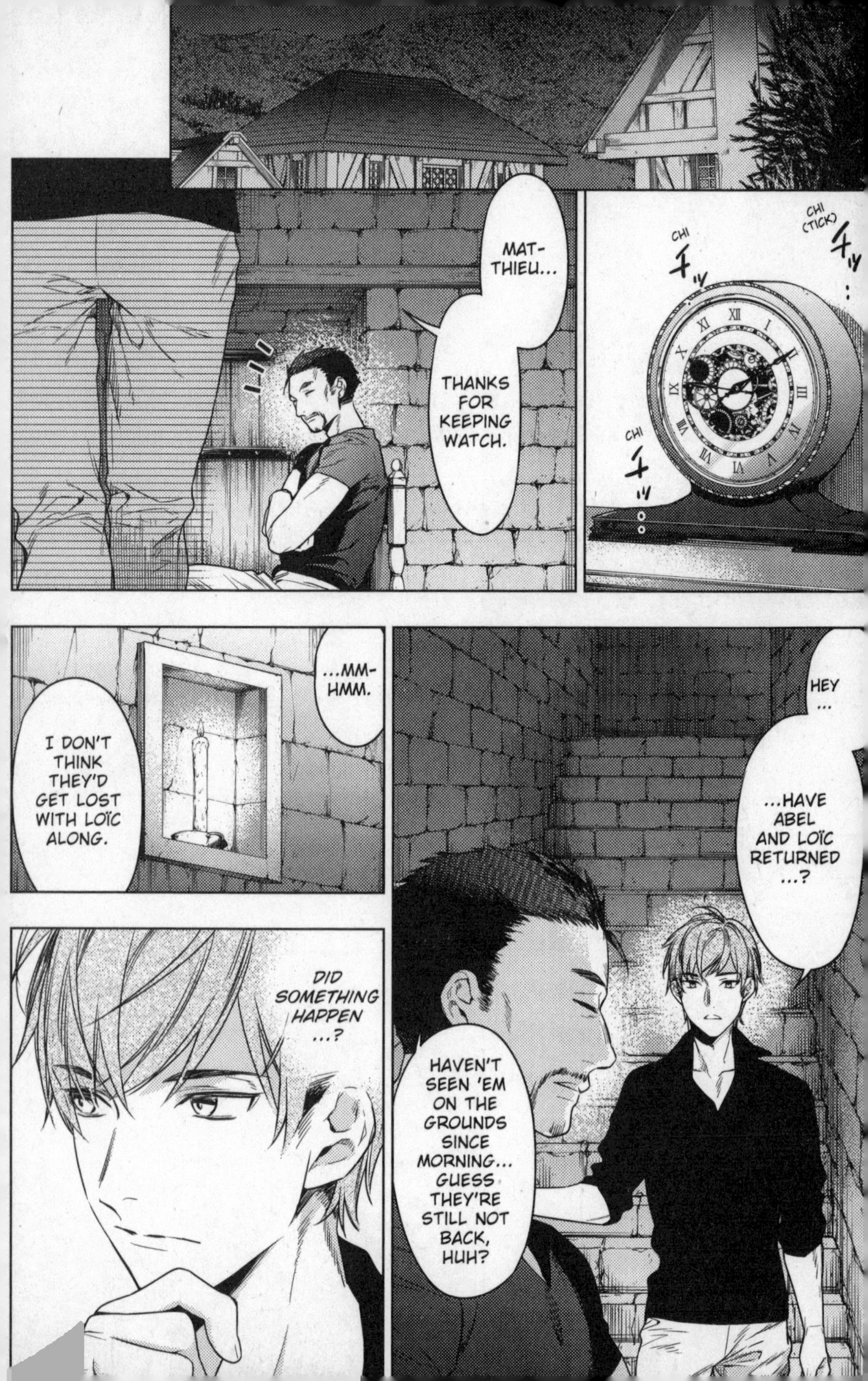
CHI (TICK)
CHI
CHI
MAT-THIEU...
THANKS FOR KEEPING WATCH.
HEY...
...HAVE ABEL AND LOÏC RETURNED...?
HAVEN'T SEEN 'EM ON THE GROUNDS SINCE MORNING... GUESS THEY'RE STILL NOT BACK, HUH?
...MM-HMM.
I DON'T THINK THEY'D GET LOST WITH LOÏC ALONG.
DID SOMETHING HAPPEN...?

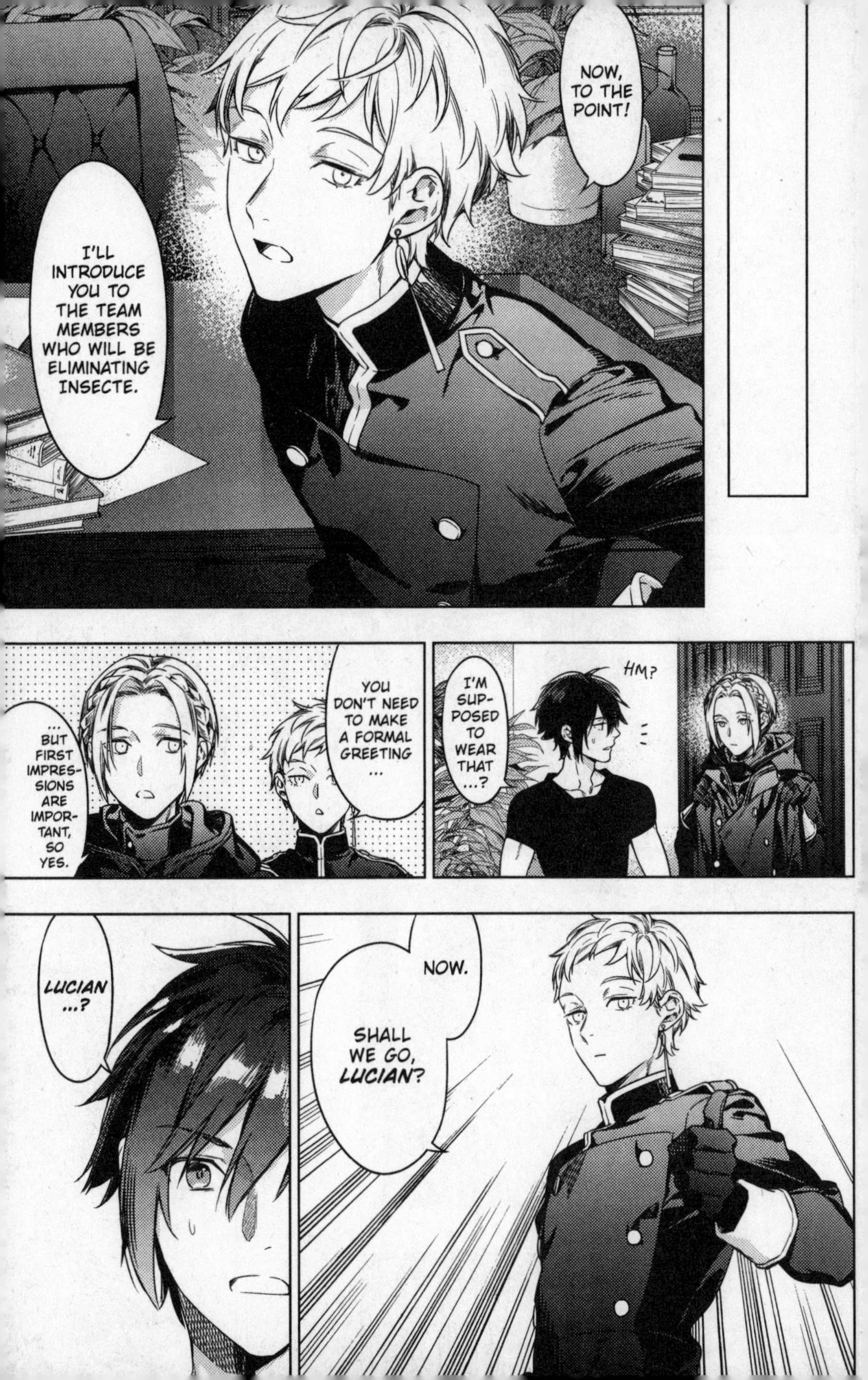
NOW, TO THE POINT!
I'LL INTRODUCE YOU TO THE TEAM MEMBERS WHO WILL BE ELIMINATING INSECTE.
HM?
I'M SUP-POSED TO WEAR THAT...?
YOU DON'T NEED TO MAKE A FORMAL GREETING...
...BUT FIRST IMPRES-SIONS ARE IMPOR-TANT, SO YES.
NOW.
SHALL WE GO, *LUCIAN*?
LUCIAN...?

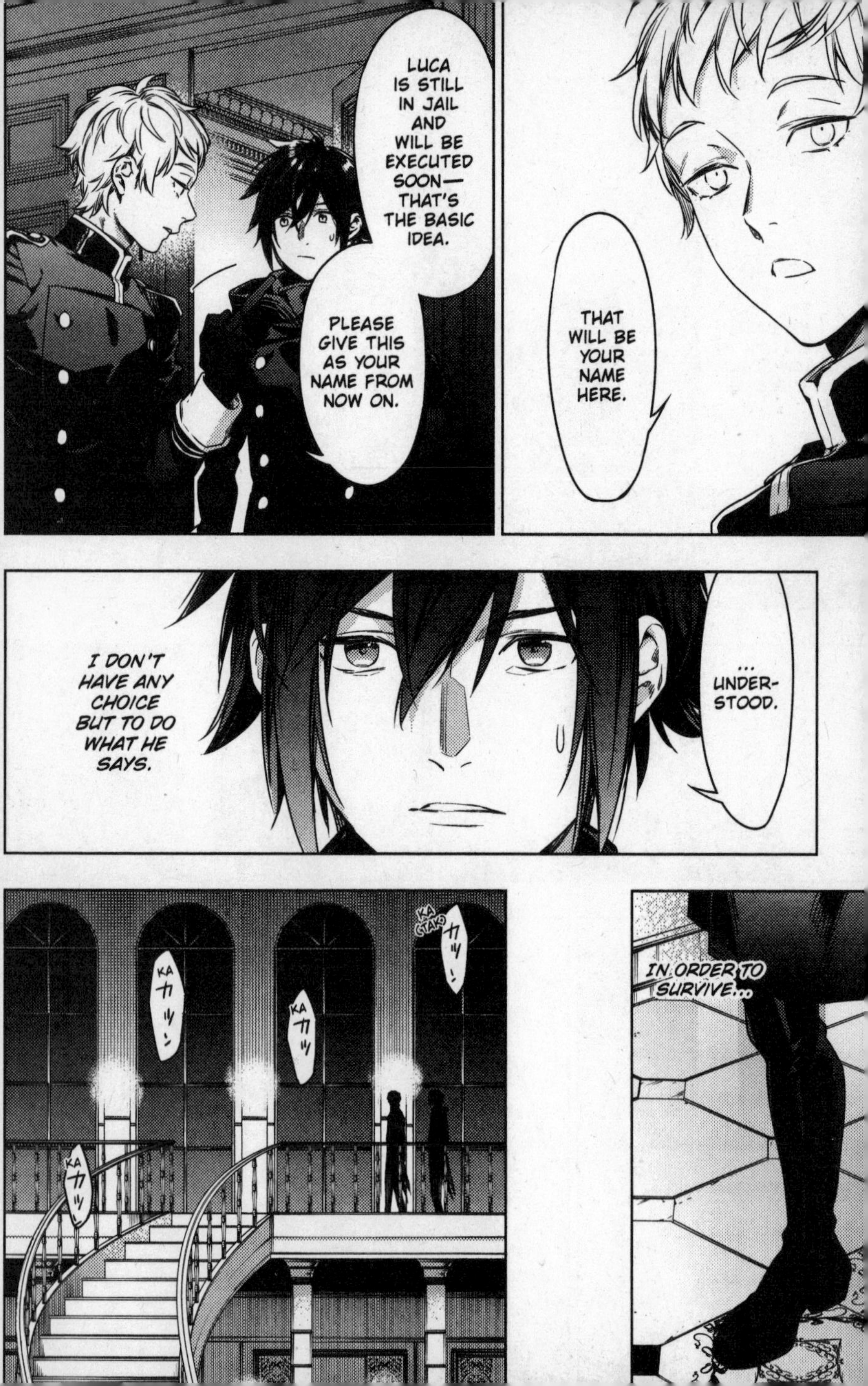
THAT WILL BE YOUR NAME HERE.
LUCA IS STILL IN JAIL AND WILL BE EXECUTED SOON—THAT'S THE BASIC IDEA.
PLEASE GIVE THIS AS YOUR NAME FROM NOW ON.
...UNDERSTOOD.
I DON'T HAVE ANY CHOICE BUT TO DO WHAT HE SAYS.
IN ORDER TO SURVIVE...
KA (TAK) カッ!
KA カッ!
KA カッ
KA カッ!

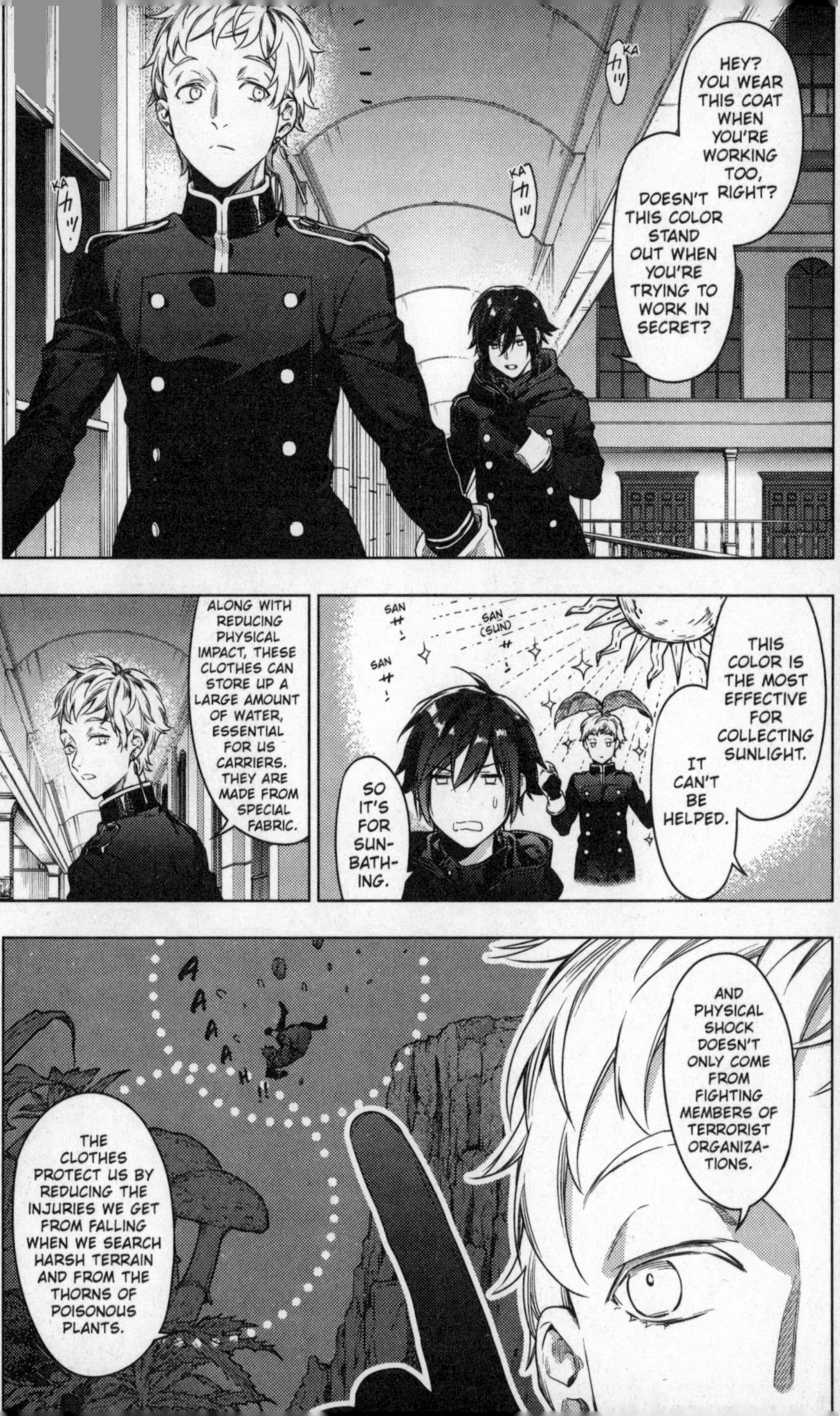
HEY? YOU WEAR THIS COAT WHEN YOU'RE WORKING TOO, RIGHT?
DOESN'T THIS COLOR STAND OUT WHEN YOU'RE TRYING TO WORK IN SECRET?
KA
KA
KA
THIS COLOR IS THE MOST EFFECTIVE FOR COLLECTING SUNLIGHT.
IT CAN'T BE HELPED.
SAN (SUN)
SAN
SAN
SO IT'S FOR SUN-BATH-ING.
ALONG WITH REDUCING PHYSICAL IMPACT, THESE CLOTHES CAN STORE UP A LARGE AMOUNT OF WATER, ESSENTIAL FOR US CARRIERS. THEY ARE MADE FROM SPECIAL FABRIC.
AND PHYSICAL SHOCK DOESN'T ONLY COME FROM FIGHTING MEMBERS OF TERRORIST ORGANIZA-TIONS.
AAAAAH!!
THE CLOTHES PROTECT US BY REDUCING THE INJURIES WE GET FROM FALLING WHEN WE SEARCH HARSH TERRAIN AND FROM THE THORNS OF POISONOUS PLANTS.

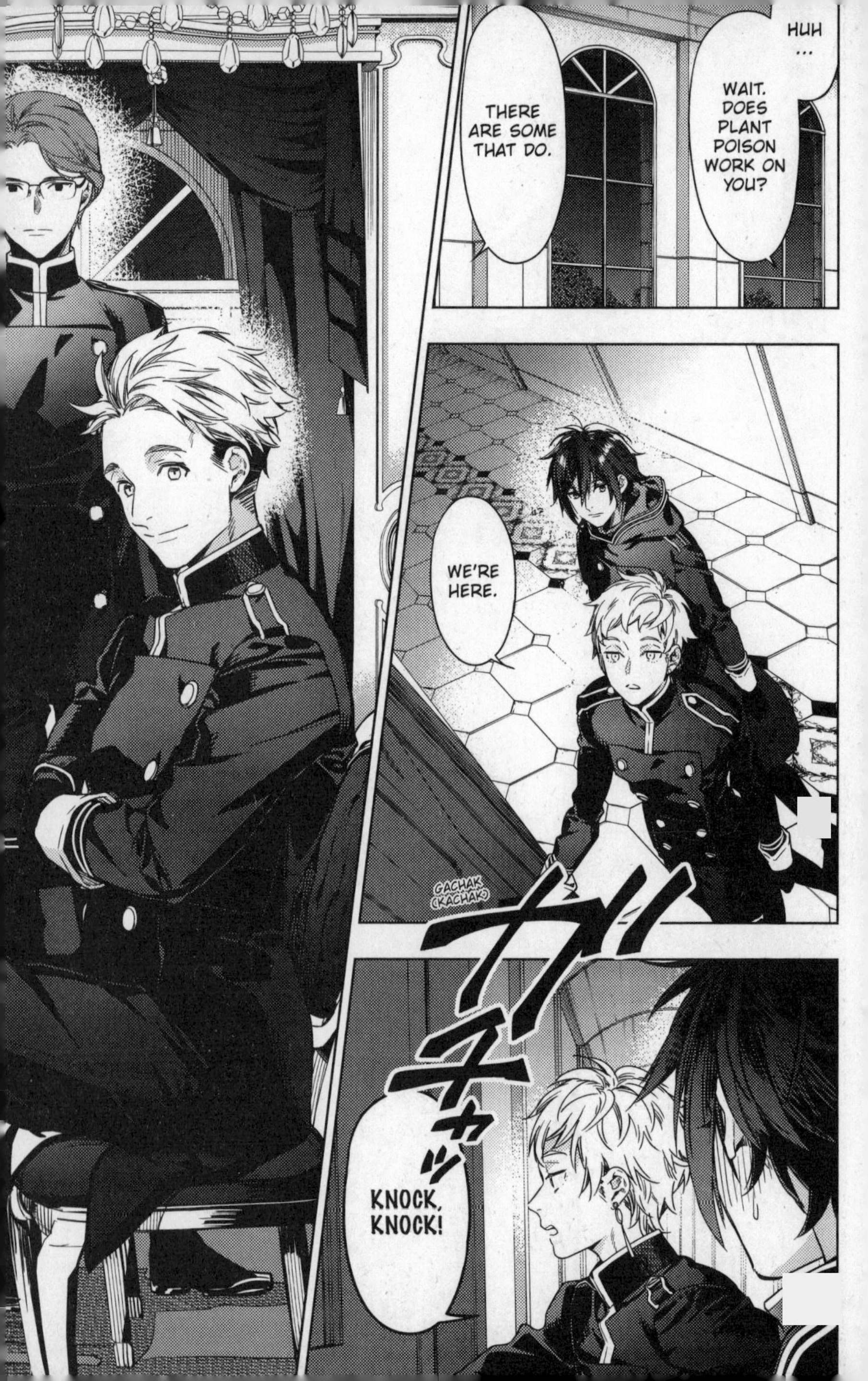
HUH ...
WAIT. DOES PLANT POISON WORK ON YOU?
THERE ARE SOME THAT DO.
WE'RE HERE.
GACHAK (KACHAK)
KNOCK, KNOCK!

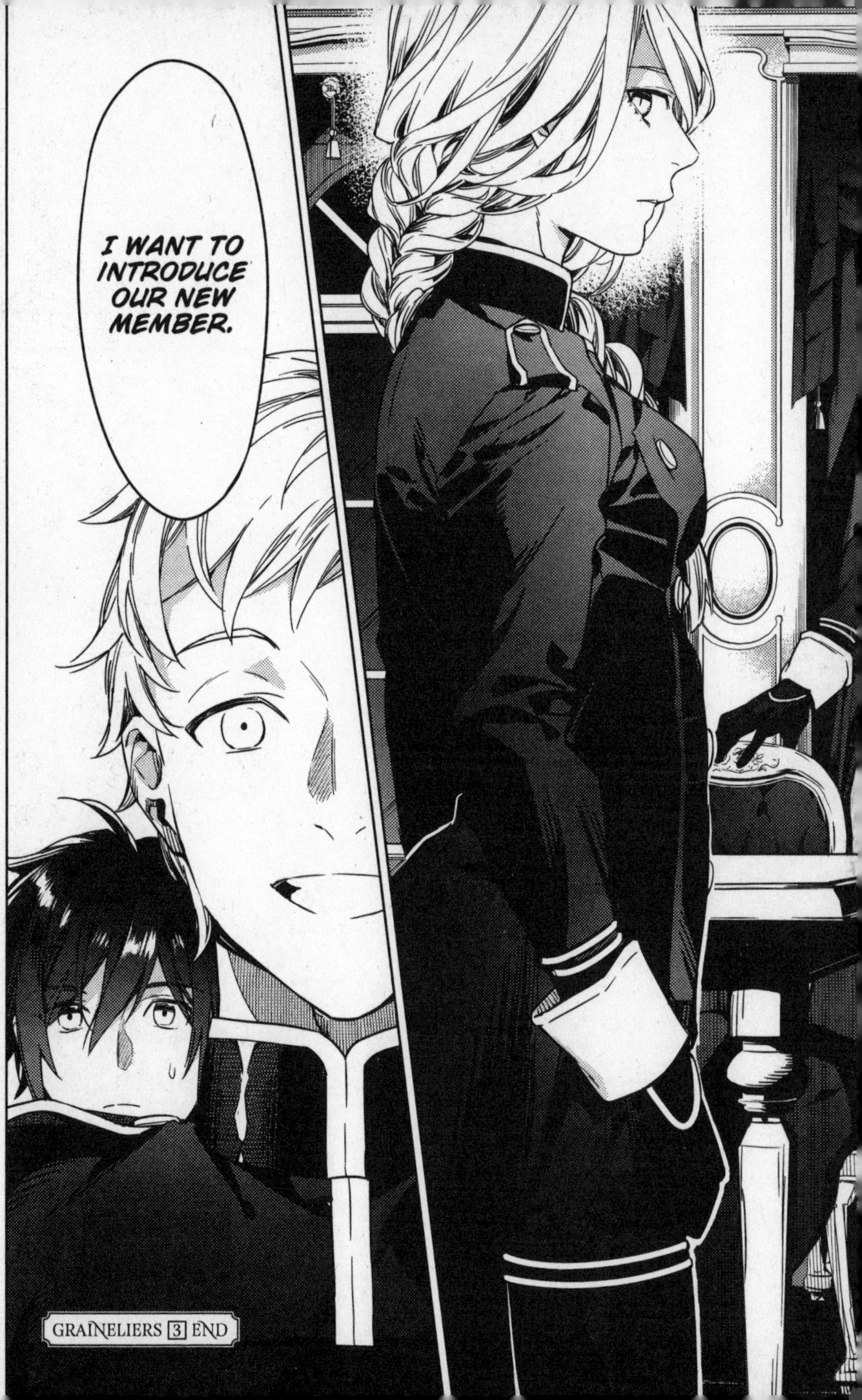
I WANT TO INTRODUCE OUR NEW MEMBER.
GRAINELIERS 3 END

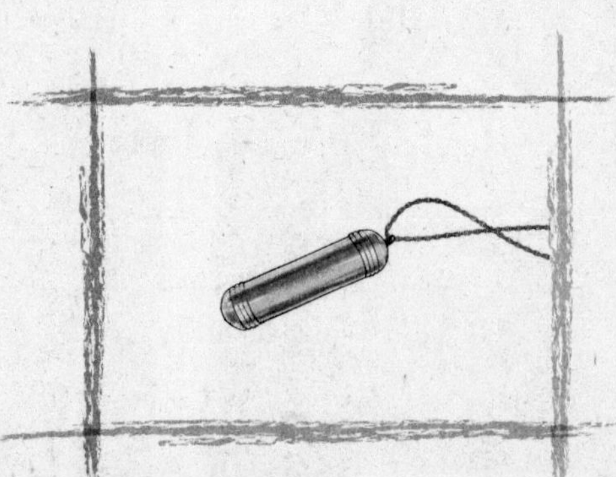

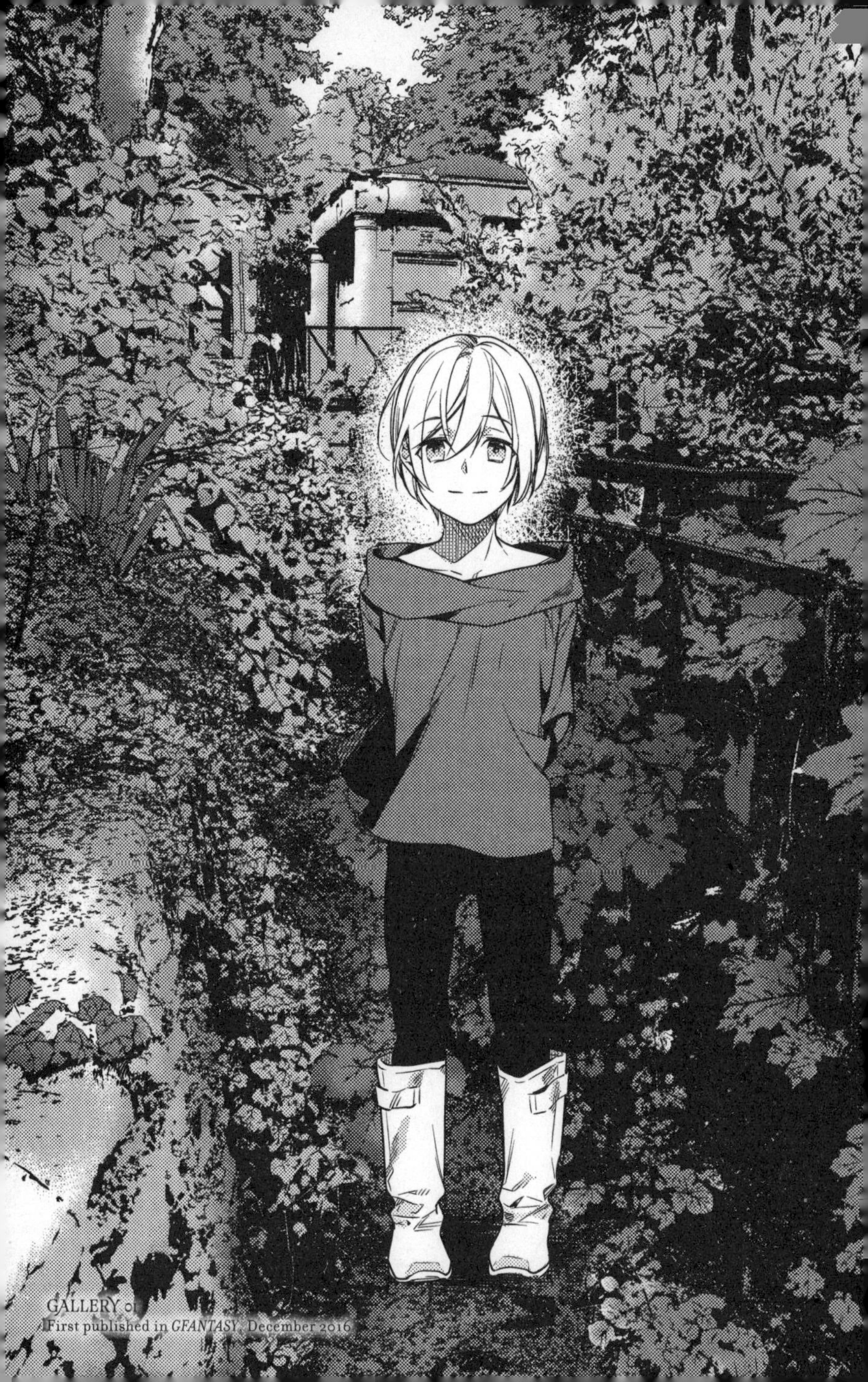

GALLERY 01
First published in *GFANTASY*, December 2016

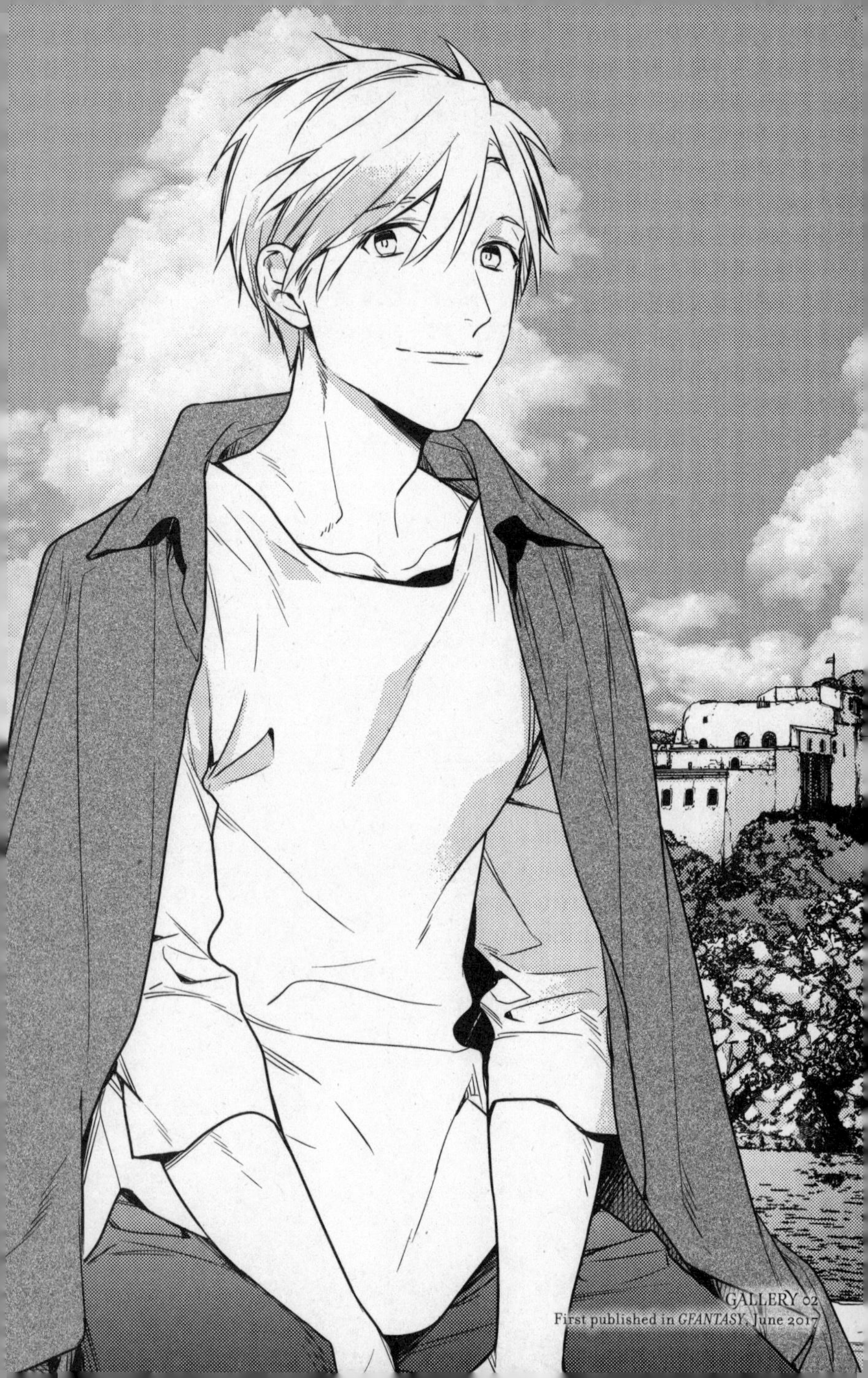

GALLERY 02
First published in *GFANTASY*, June 2017

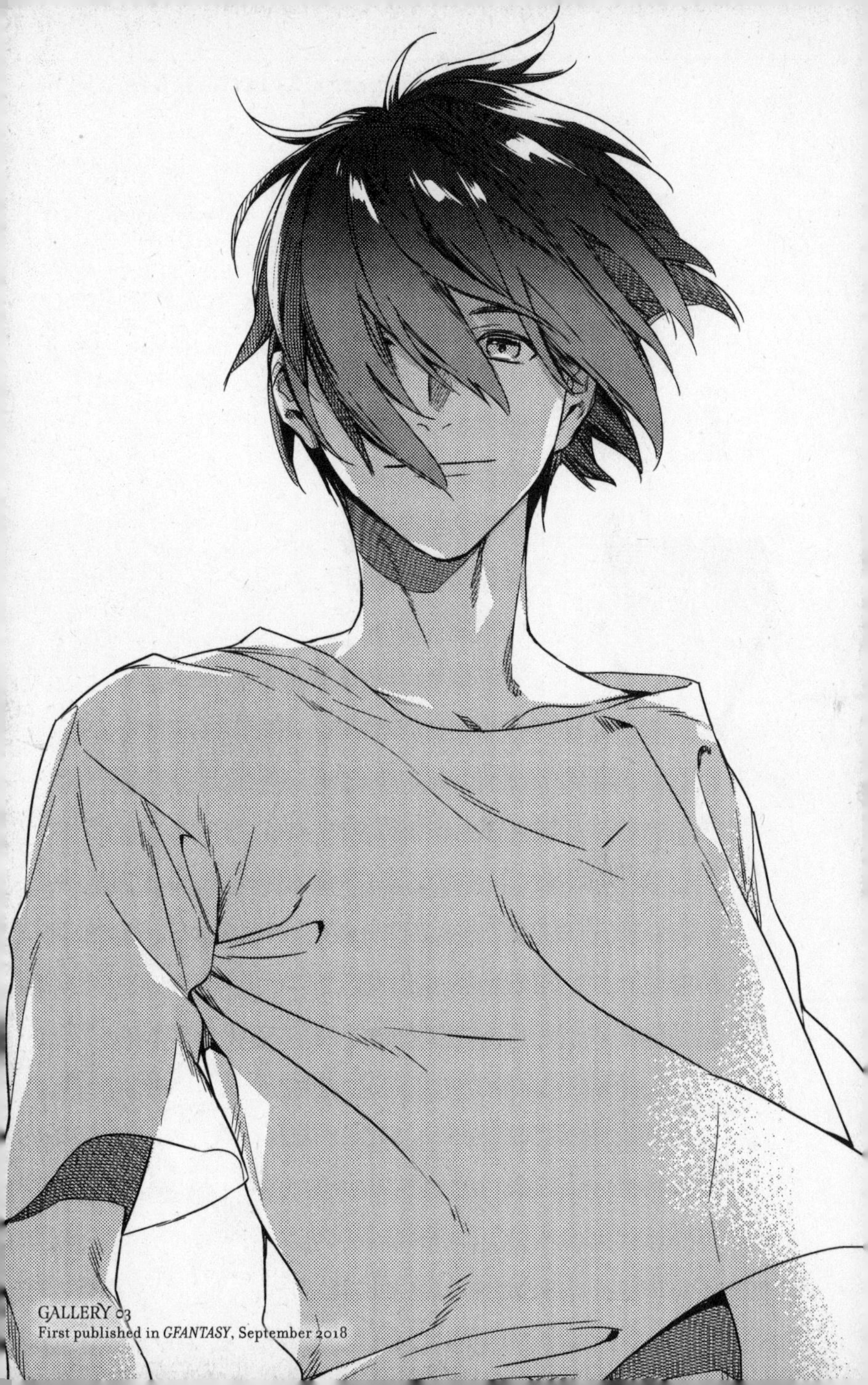

GALLERY 03
First published in *GFANTASY*, September 2018

Character Relationship Chart

Luca has been captured as a seed carrier. Abel wants to save him and so turns to the rebel group Insecte. Examine this pair toyed with by fate through the diagram of their relationships with others.

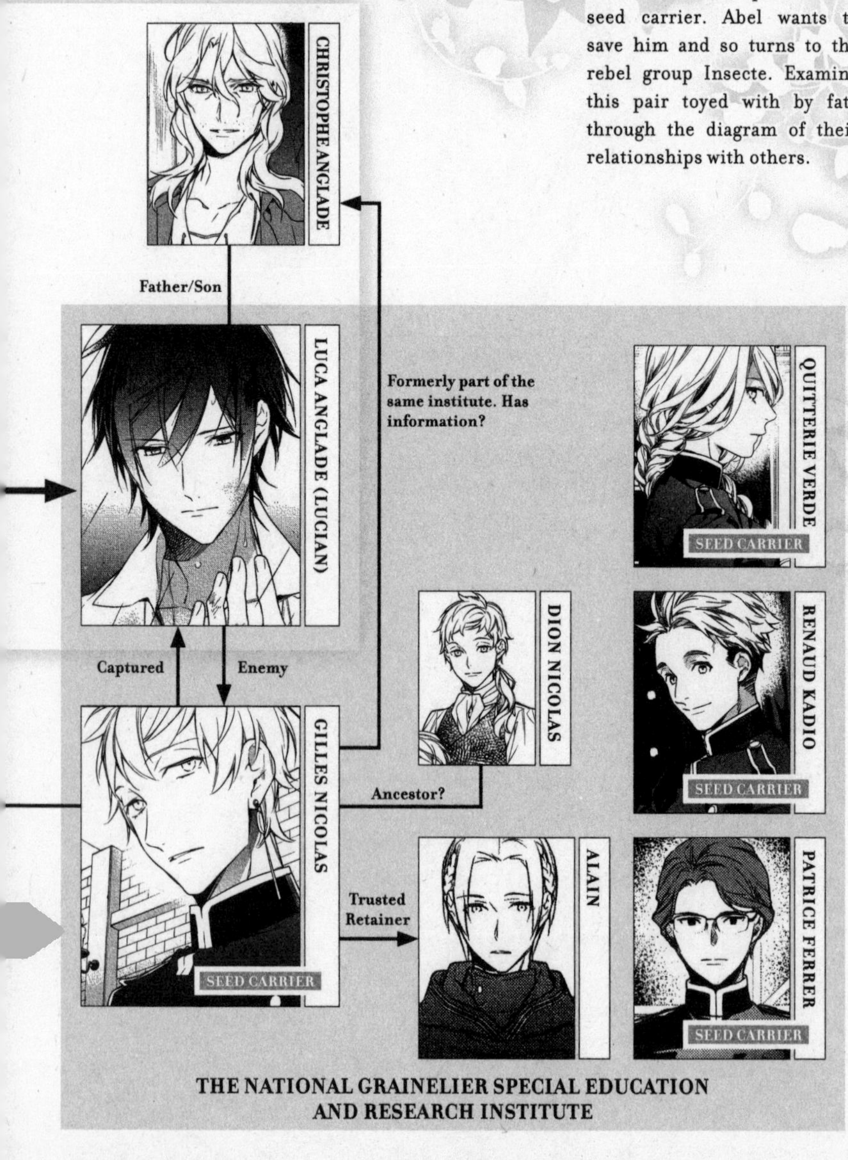

CHRISTOPHE ANGLADE
Father/Son
LUCA ANGLADE (LUCIAN)
Formerly part of the same institute. Has information?
Captured
Enemy
GILLES NICOLAS
SEED CARRIER
DION NICOLAS
Ancestor?
Trusted Retainer
ALAIN
QUITTERIE VERDE
SEED CARRIER
RENAUD KADIO
SEED CARRIER
PATRICE FERRER
SEED CARRIER
THE NATIONAL GRAINELIER SPECIAL EDUCATION AND RESEARCH INSTITUTE

Characters

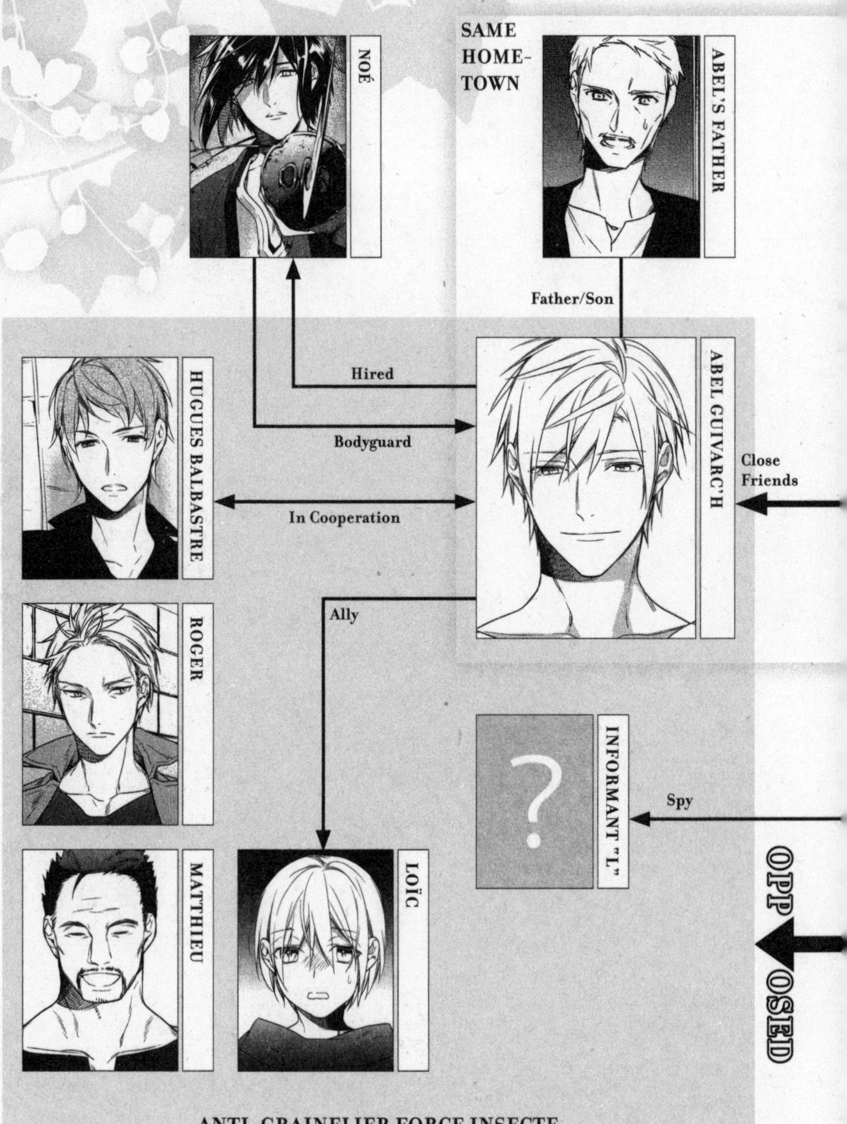
SAME HOME-TOWN
NOÉ
ABEL'S FATHER
Father/Son
Hired
Bodyguard
HUGUES BALBASTRE
In Cooperation
ABEL GUIVARC'H
Close Friends
ROGER
Ally
INFORMANT "L"
Spy
OPP
OSED
MATTHIEU
LOÏC
ANTI-GRAINELIER FORCE INSECTE

Next time...

I want to save the boy...

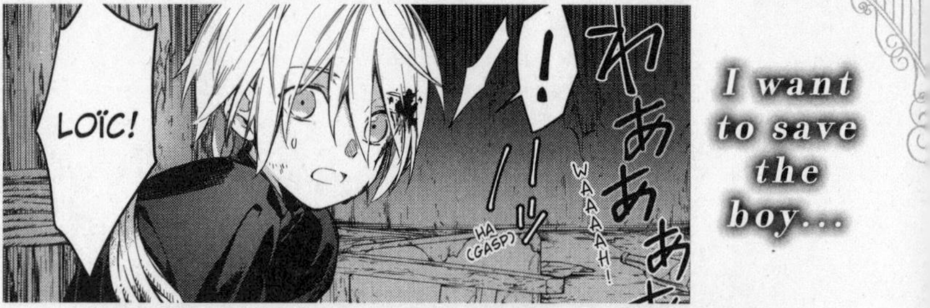
わああ
WAAAAAH!
ハッ
HA (GASP)
!
LOÏC!

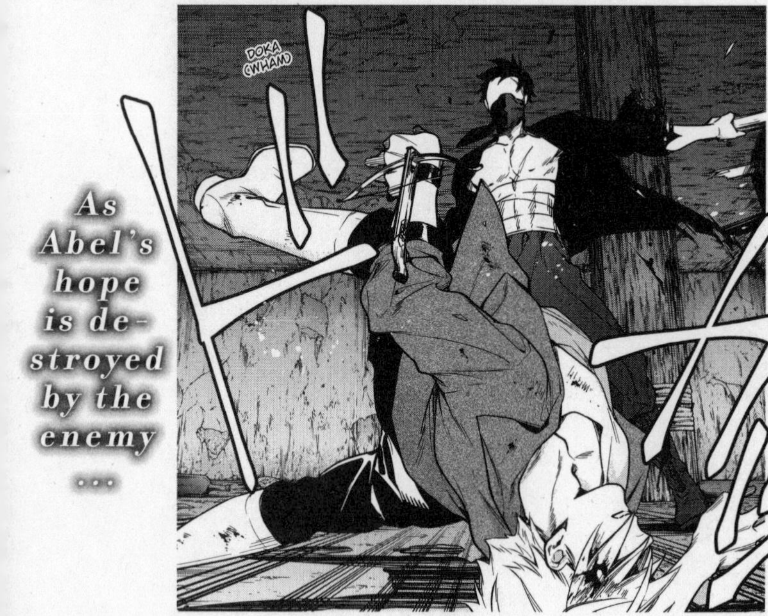
ドカッ
DOKA (WHAM)

As Abel's hope is de-stroyed by the enemy...

...a heroic ending awaits...

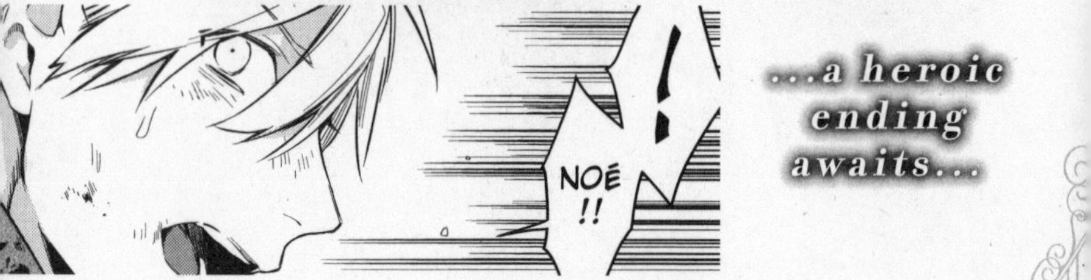
!
NOÉ !!

Graineliers Volume 4 — Coming soon!

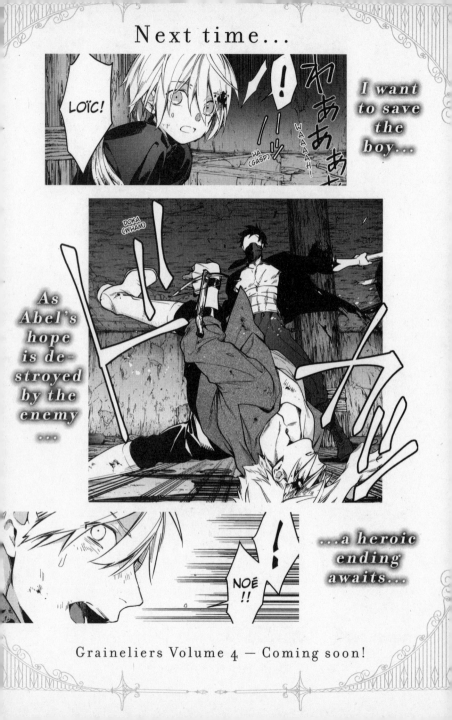

Thank you!

Thank you so much for reading volume three! This book was mostly about Abel, but I'd like to see more activity from Nicolas and Luca in the next volume. Please join me for the next book.

Rihito Takarai

GRAINELIERS

Rihito Takarai

Translation: JOCELYNE ALLEN
Lettering: BIANCA PISTILLO

This book is a work of fiction. Names, characters, places, and incidents are the product of the author's imagination or are used fictitiously. Any resemblance to actual events, locales, or persons, living or dead, is coincidental.

GRAINELIERS, Vol. 3 © 2018 Rihito Takarai / SQUARE ENIX CO., LTD. First published in Japan in 2018 by SQUARE ENIX CO., LTD. English translation rights arranged with SQUARE ENIX CO., LTD. and Yen Press, LLC through Tuttle-Mori Agency, Inc.

English translation © 2019 by SQUARE ENIX CO., LTD.

Yen Press, LLC supports the right to free expression and the value of copyright. The purpose of copyright is to encourage writers and artists to produce the creative works that enrich our culture.

The scanning, uploading, and distribution of this book without permission is a theft of the author's intellectual property. If you would like permission to use material from the book (other than for review purposes), please contact the publisher. Thank you for your support of the author's rights.

Yen Press
1290 Avenue of the Americas
New York, NY 10104

Visit us at yenpress.com
facebook.com/yenpress
twitter.com/yenpress
yenpress.tumblr.com
instagram.com/yenpress

First Yen Press Edition: May 2019

Yen Press is an imprint of Yen Press, LLC.
The Yen Press name and logo are trademarks of Yen Press, LLC.

The publisher is not responsible for websites (or their content) that are not owned by the publisher.

Library of Congress Control Number: 2017949554

ISBNs: 978-1-9753-5682-8 (paperback)
       978-1-9753-5683-5 (ebook)

10 9 8 7 6 5 4 3 2 1

WOR

Printed in the United States of America